Things that are really enormous are frightening. Just being near something like that makes me tremble, be it steel towers, ridiculously thick pillars, or the huge whale statue that hangs in that shopping mall.

I heard that the kanji that expresses such fear is 聳 (towering), but it doesn't show up in the manga...

By the way, I look calm in the photo, but I was actually really scared.

—HIROSHI SHIIBASHI,
2008

HIROSHI SHIIBASHI debuted in BUSINESS JUMP magazine with *Aratama*. NURA: RISE OF THE YOKAI CLAN is his breakout hit. He was an assistant to manga artist Hirohiko Araki, the creator of *Jojo's Bizarre Adventure*. *Steel Ball Run* by Araki is one of his favorite manga.

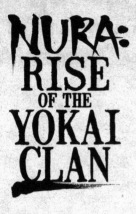

NURA: RISE OF THE YOKAI CLAN
VOLUME 2
SHONEN JUMP Manga Edition

Story and Art by HIROSHI SHIIBASHI

Translation – Nabe Watanabe, Cindy Yamauchi
Adaptation – Mark Giambruno
Touch-up Art and Lettering – Gia Cam Luc
Graphics and Cover Design – Fawn Lau
Editor – Daniel Gillespie

NURARIHYON NO MAGO © 2008 by Hiroshi Shiibashi. All rights reserved. First published in Japan in 2008 by SHUEISHA Inc., Tokyo. English translation rights arranged by SHUEISHA Inc.

Printed in the U.S.A.

Published by VIZ Media, LLC
P.O. Box 77010
San Francisco, CA 94107

10 9 8 7 6 5 4 3 2 1
First printing, April 2011

www.viz.com   www.shonenjump.com

PARENTAL ADVISORY
NURA: RISE OF THE YOKAI CLAN is rated T for Teen and is suitable for ages 13 and up. This volume contains fantasy and realistic violence, alcohol and tobacco usage, and brief nudity.
ratings.viz.com

NURA: RISE OF THE YOKAI CLAN

2

RIKUO VS. GYUKI

STORY AND ART BY
HIROSHI SHIIBASHI

CHARACTERS

NURARIHYON

Rikuo's grandfather and the Lord of Pandemonium. He intends to pass leadership of the Nura clan—leaders of the yokai world—to Rikuo.

RIKUO NURA

Though he appears to be a human boy, he's actually the grandson of Nurarihyon, a yokai. His grandfather's blood makes him one-quarter yokai, and he transforms into a yokai at times.

KIYOTSUGU

Rikuo's classmate. He has adored yokai ever since he was saved by Rikuo in his yokai form, leading him to form the "Kiyojuji Paranormal Patrol."

KANA IENAGA

Rikuo's classmate and a childhood friend. Even though she hates scary things, she's a member of the "Kiyojuji Paranormal Patrol" for some reason.

YUKI-ONNA

A yokai of the Nura clan who is in charge of looking after Rikuo. She disguises herself as a human and attends the same school as Rikuo to protect him from danger. When in human form, she goes by the name Tsurara Oikawa.

YURA KEIKAIN

Rikuo's classmate and a descendant of the Keikain family of onmyoji. She transferred into Ukiyoe Middle School to do field training in yokai exorcism. She has the power to control her shikigami and uses them to destroy yokai.

AOTABO

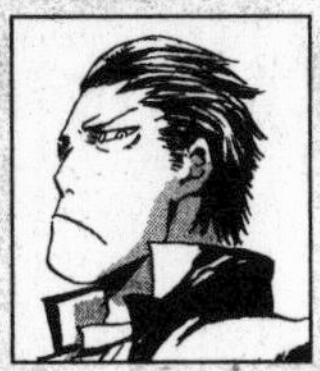

Another Nura clan yokai who, along with Yuki-Onna, looks after and protects Rikuo when he attends school. He uses the name Kurata when disguised as a human.

ZEN

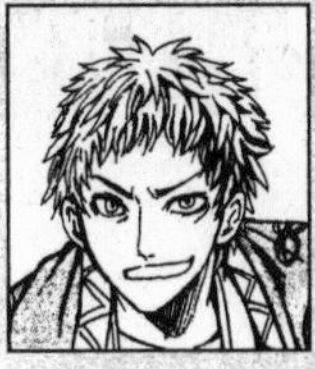

The leader of Zen Group, a branch of the Nura clan. He's a bird yokai who can produce medicine and poisons, and is physically fragile due to that special quality. He has undergone the "brotherhood" rite with Night Rikuo, in which they interlocked arms and drank sake together.

KYUSO

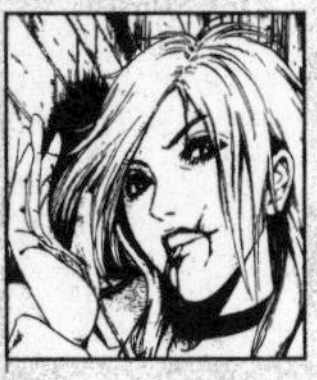

A giant, kitten-eating rat yokai, and the leader of the Kyuso clan. He abducts Yura and Kana in an attempt to destroy the Nura clan.

SHIMA

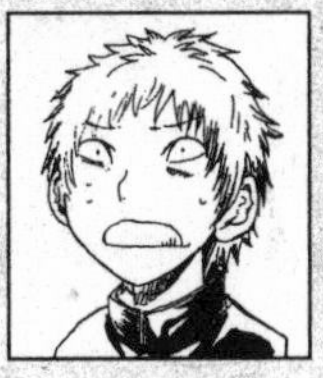

Rikuo's classmate, an acquaintance he's known since grade school. He's part of Kiyotsugu's circle and a member of the "Kiyojuji Paranormal Patrol."

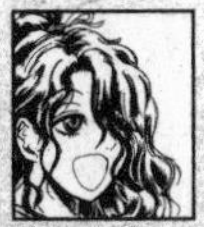

KEJORO

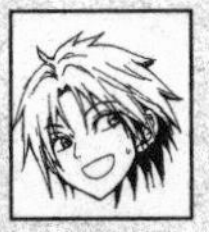

KUBINASHI

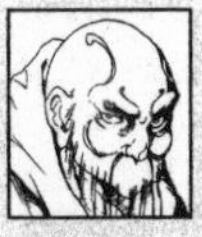

MOKUGYO-DARUMA

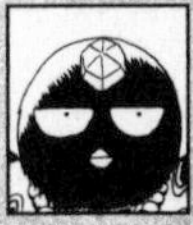

KARASU-TENGU

STORY SO FAR

Although Rikuo Nura appears to be human, he's actually the grandson of the yokai Nurarihyon. He is also the heir apparent to the position of the third Supreme Commander of the Nura clan, which rules over all the other yokai. At first, Rikuo can't wait until the day he'll succeed his grandfather. However, when he learns that yokai are despised by humans, he decides to give up his birthright. On top of that, many yokai aren't happy that a mostly human boy is about to become their leader. A yokai affiliated with the Nura clan attacks the bus that Rikuo takes to school, in hopes of taking Rikuo out. Rikuo misses the bus that day, but when he realizes that his classmates are in grave danger, the blood that Rikuo inherited from his grandfather awakens and he transforms into a yokai. He gathers the other yokai and does an impressive job of resolving the situation.

Several years pass, and Rikuo is now in middle school. He still refuses to become the Third, and he no longer mentions yokai while at school. He has never repeated his transformation into a yokai and doesn't even remember it happening, including the part where he declared that he would become the third Supreme Commander. When danger arises for his childhood friend, the yokai Zen, Rikuo transforms into a yokai once again and crushes those who are plotting against him. Later, Kyuso—a giant rat yokai and leader of the Kyuso Clan—abducts Rikuo's classmates Kana and Yura as part of a plot to destroy the Nura clan. To that end, he demands that Rikuo officially announce that he is permanently abandoning his right to become the Third.

TABLE OF CONTENTS

NURA:RISE OF THE YOKAI CLAN

ACT 8
Rikuo vs. the Fangs of Kyuso — 7

ACT 9
Rikuo Gets a Fever — 49

ACT 10
Rikuo Goes on a Mystery Tour — 69

ACT 11
Rikuo Spends the Night on Mt. Nejireme — 89

ACT 12
Rikuo Goes on a Nighttime Investigation — 109

ACT 13
Rikuo on the Night of the New Moon — 129

ACT 14
Rikuo Stands on the Summit of Mt. Nejireme — 149

ACT 15
Rikuo vs. Gyuki — 169

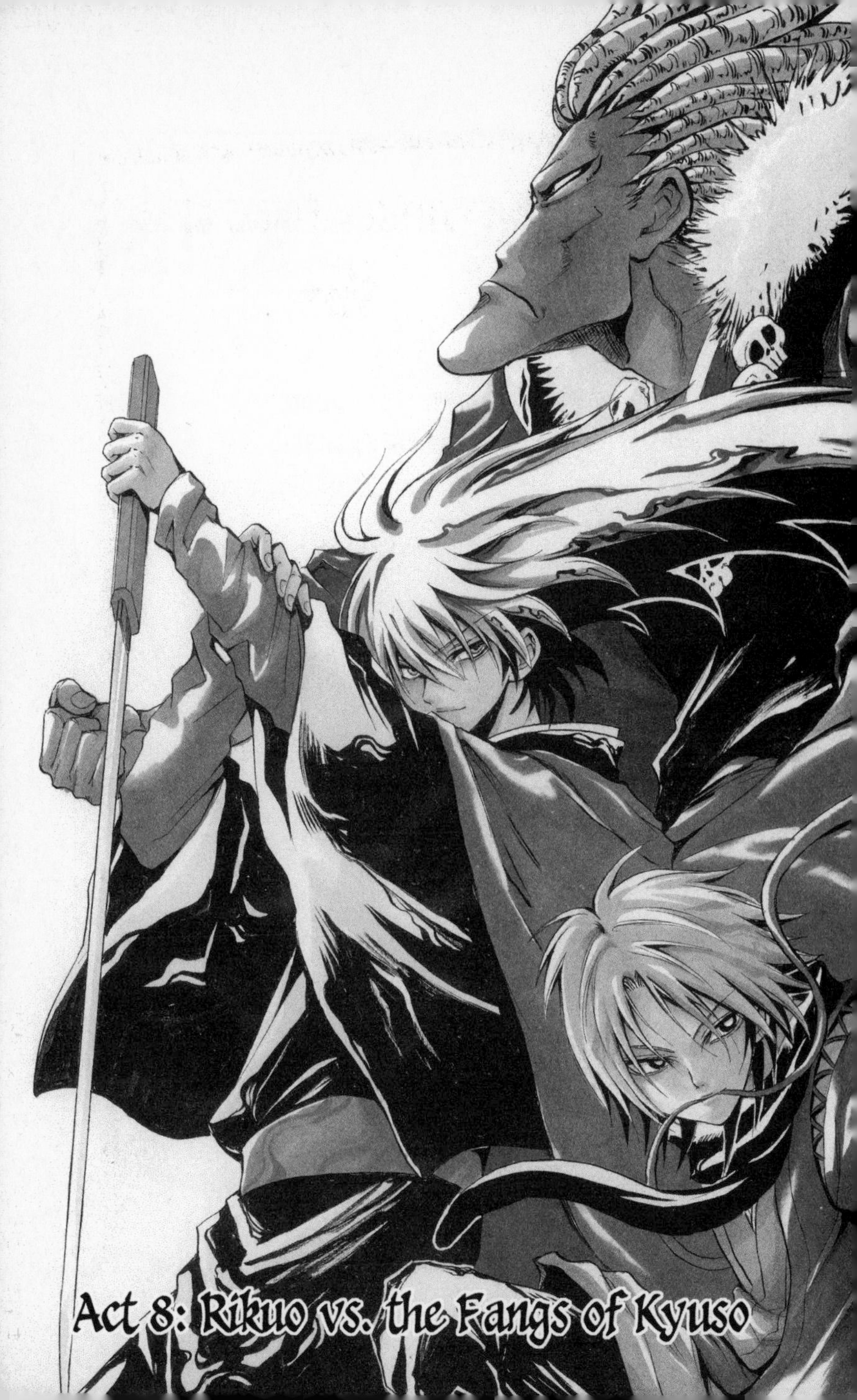

Act 8: Rikuo vs. the Fangs of Kyuso

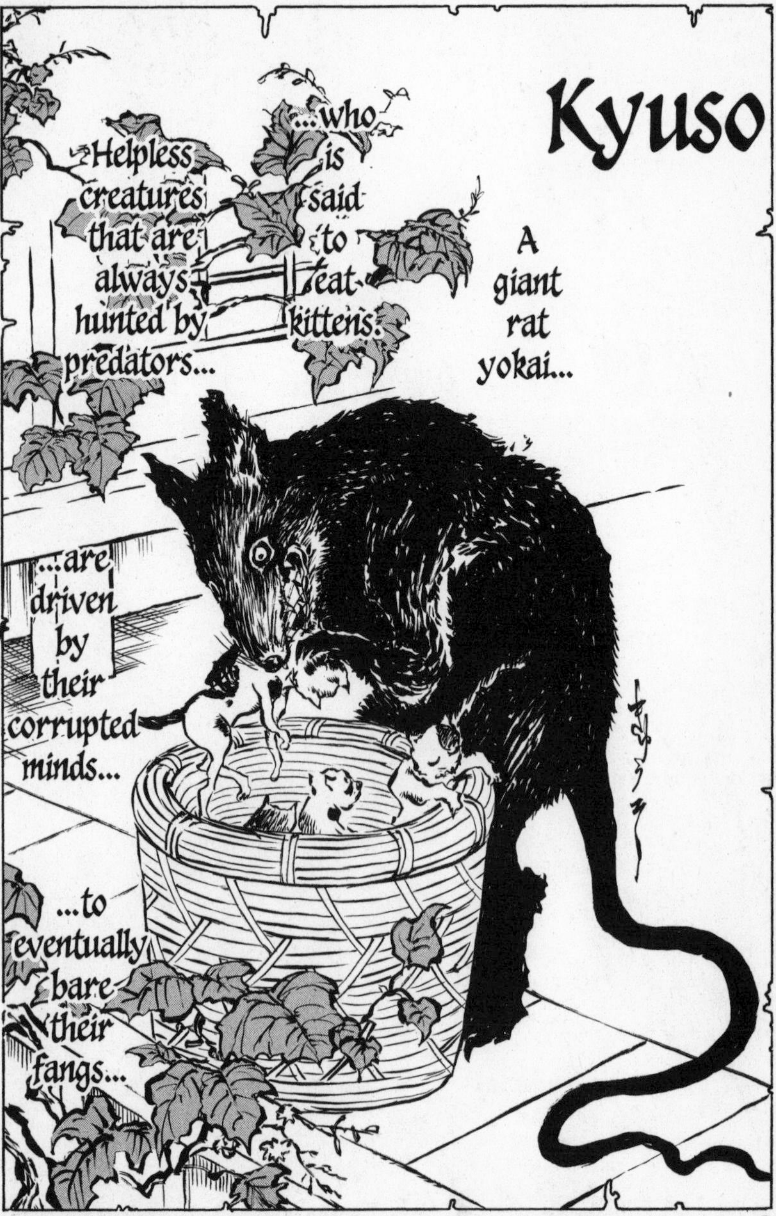
Kyuso
A giant rat yokai...
...who is said to eat kittens.
Helpless creatures that are always hunted by predators...
...are driven by their corrupted minds...
...to eventually bare their fangs...

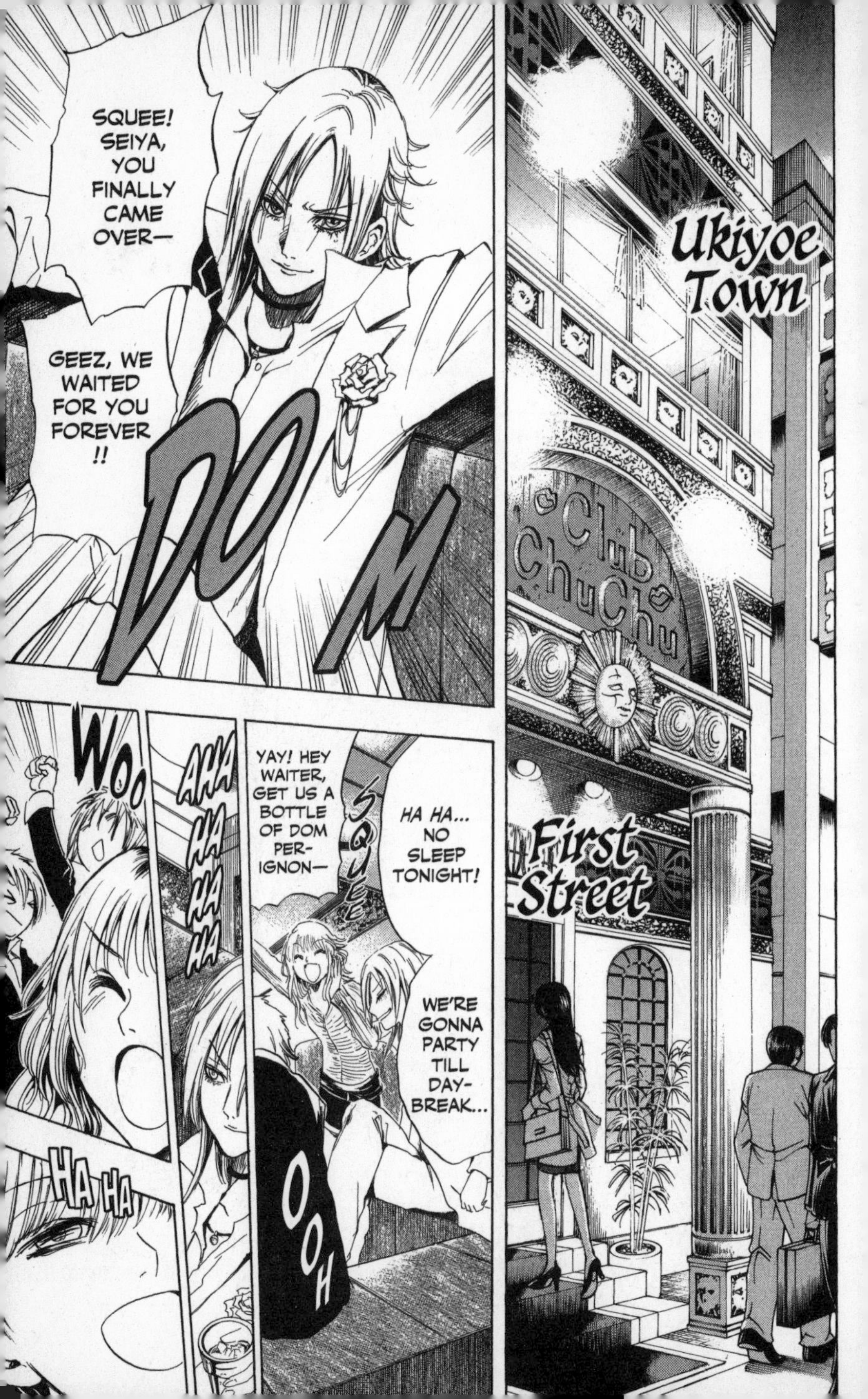
Ukiyoe Town
Club ChuChu
First Street
SQUEE! SEIYA, YOU FINALLY CAME OVER—
GEEZ, WE WAITED FOR YOU FOREVER !!
DOM
HA HA... NO SLEEP TONIGHT!
YAY! HEY WAITER, GET US A BOTTLE OF DOM PER-IGNON—
SQUEE
WE'RE GONNA PARTY TILL DAY-BREAK...
OOH
AHA HA HA HA HA
WOO
HA HA

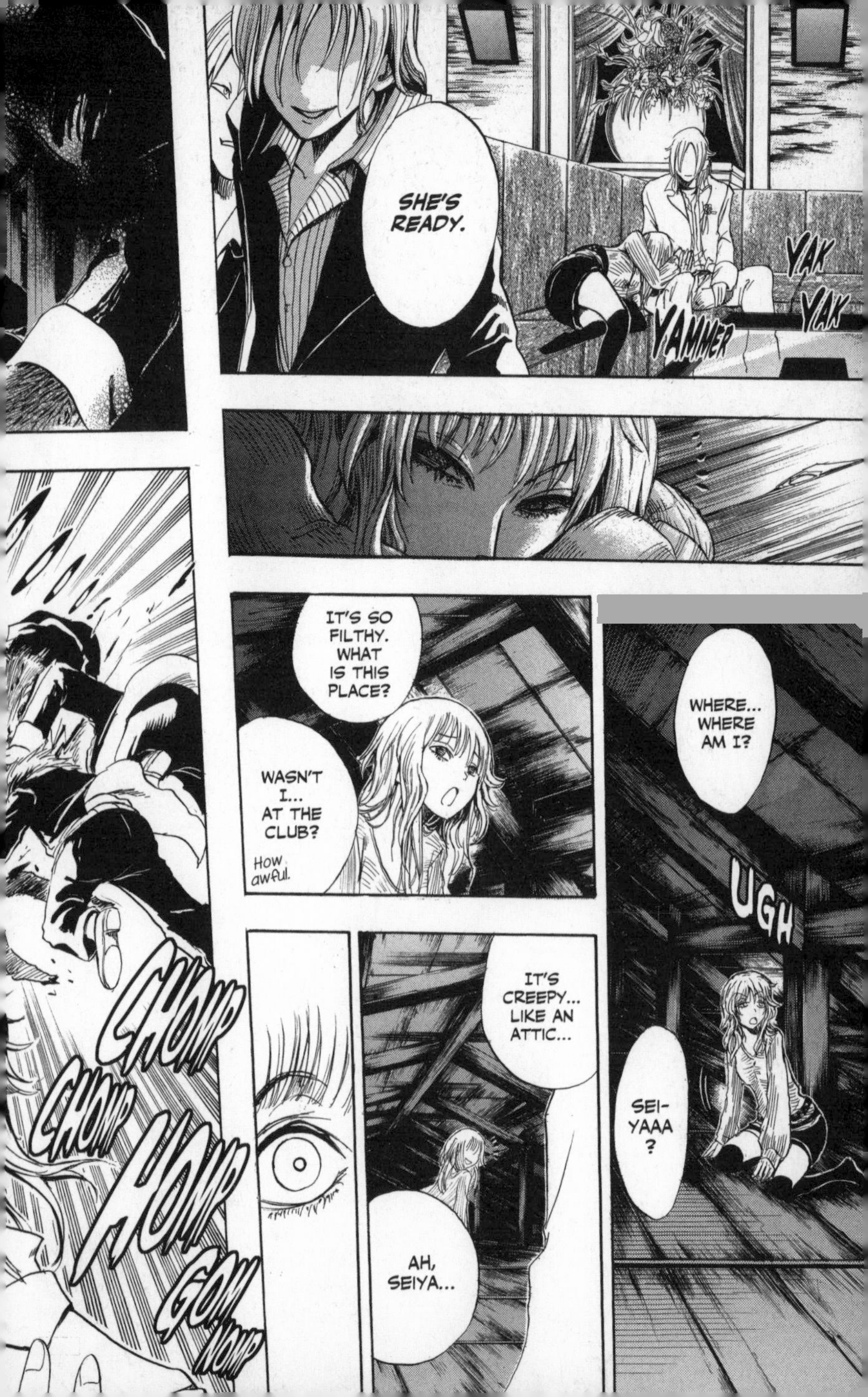
YAK
YAK
YAMMER
SHE'S READY.
WHERE... WHERE AM I?
UGH
SEI-YAAA?
IT'S SO FILTHY. WHAT IS THIS PLACE?
WASN'T I... AT THE CLUB?
How awful.
IT'S CREEPY... LIKE AN ATTIC...
AH, SEIYA...
CHOMP
CHOMP
HOMP
GOMP
NOMP

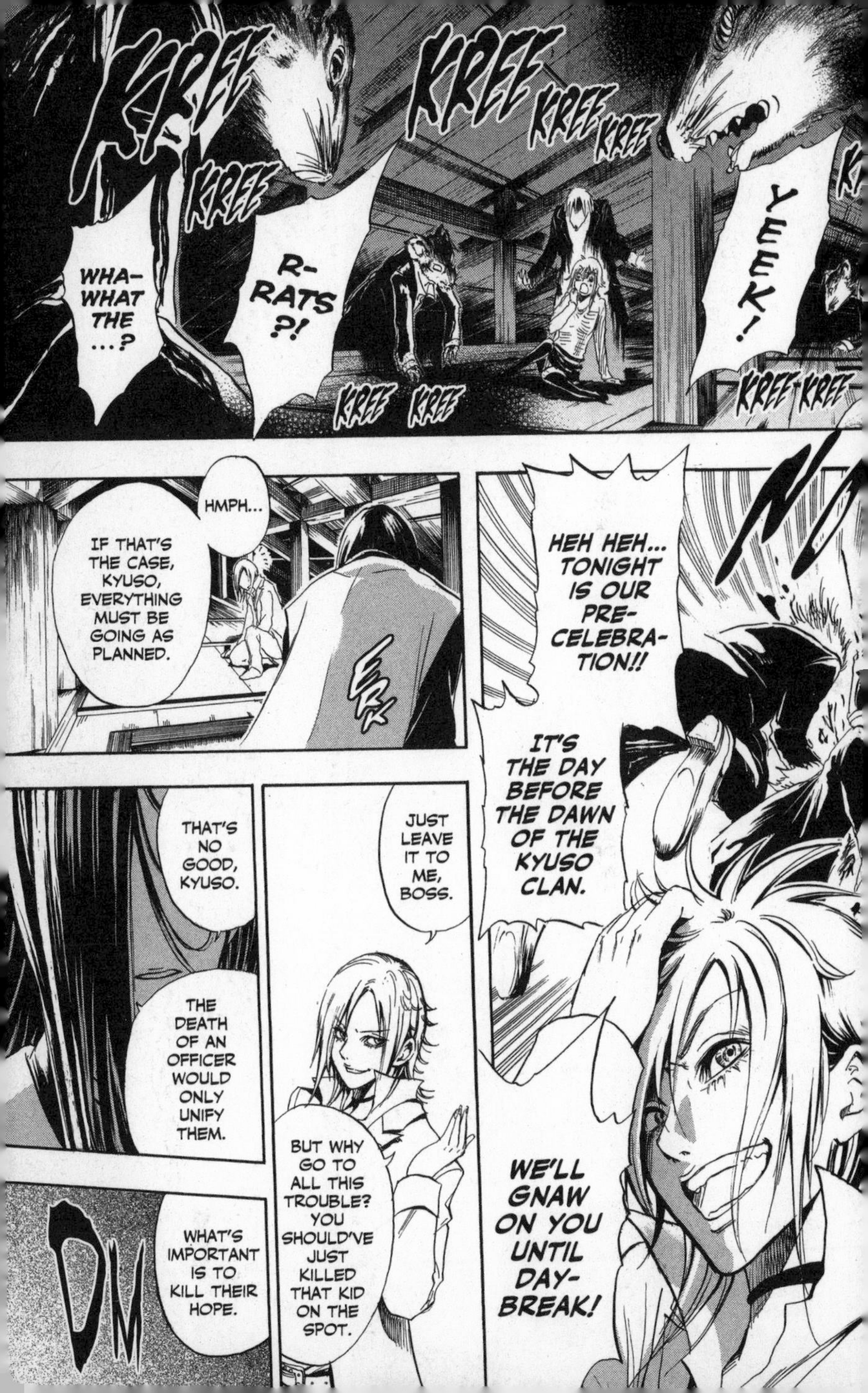

KREE KREE KREE
YEEK!
KREE KREE
R-RATS?!
WHA-WHAT THE...?
KREE KREE
KREE
KREE
HEH HEH... TONIGHT IS OUR PRE-CELEBRATION!!
IT'S THE DAY BEFORE THE DAWN OF THE KYUSO CLAN.
WE'LL GNAW ON YOU UNTIL DAY-BREAK!
HMPH...
IF THAT'S THE CASE, KYUSO, EVERYTHING MUST BE GOING AS PLANNED.
JUST LEAVE IT TO ME, BOSS.
BUT WHY GO TO ALL THIS TROUBLE? YOU SHOULD'VE JUST KILLED THAT KID ON THE SPOT.
THAT'S NO GOOD, KYUSO.
THE DEATH OF AN OFFICER WOULD ONLY UNIFY THEM.
DM
WHAT'S IMPORTANT IS TO KILL THEIR HOPE.

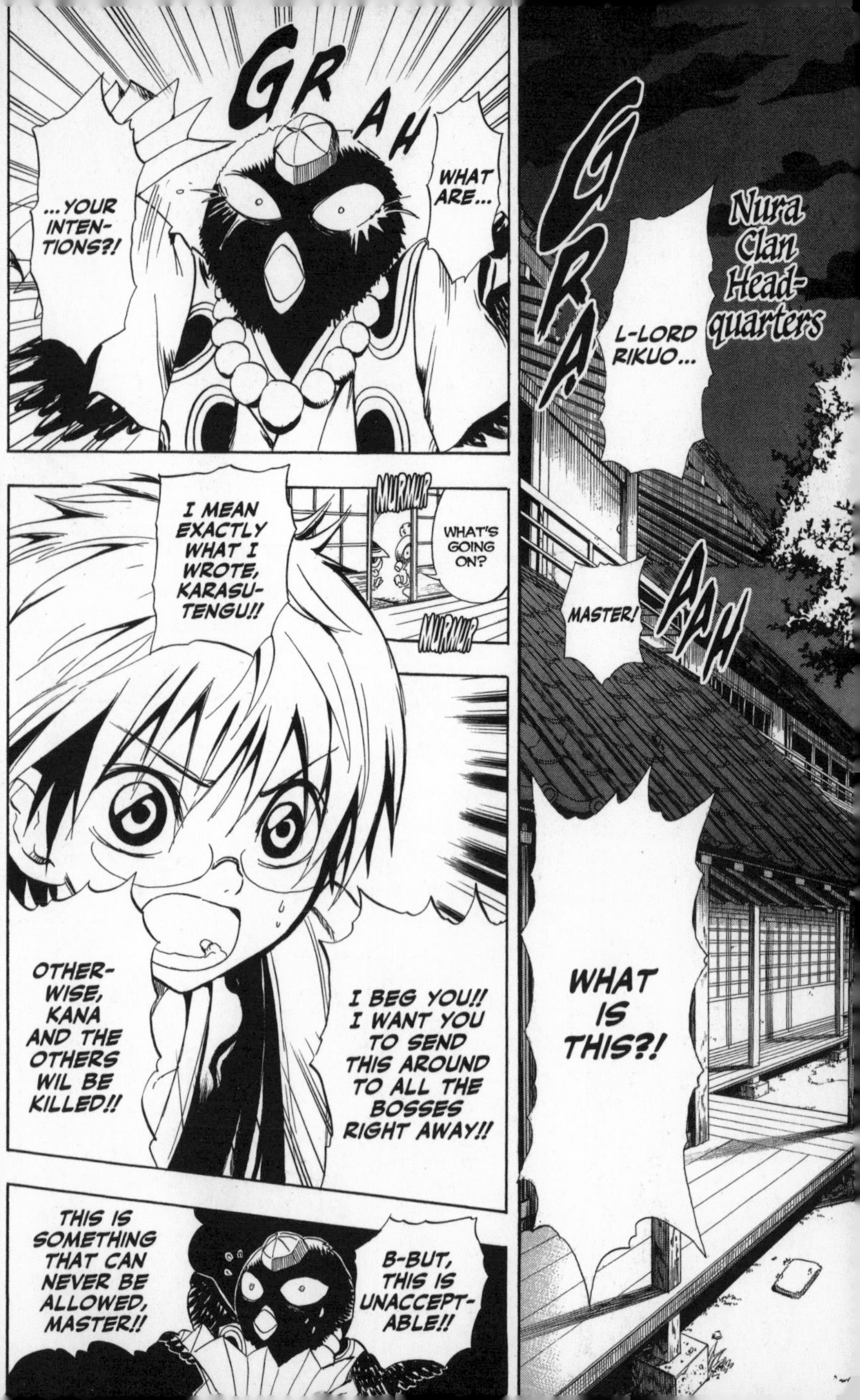

Nura Clan Head-quarters
L-LORD RIKUO...
MASTER!
WHAT IS THIS?!
GRAH
WHAT ARE...
...YOUR INTEN-TIONS?!
I MEAN EXACTLY WHAT I WROTE, KARASU-TENGU!!
MURMUR
WHAT'S GOING ON?
MURMUR
I BEG YOU!! I WANT YOU TO SEND THIS AROUND TO ALL THE BOSSES RIGHT AWAY!!
OTHER-WISE, KANA AND THE OTHERS WIL BE KILLED!!
B-BUT, THIS IS UNACCEPT-ABLE!!
THIS IS SOMETHING THAT CAN NEVER BE ALLOWED, MASTER!!

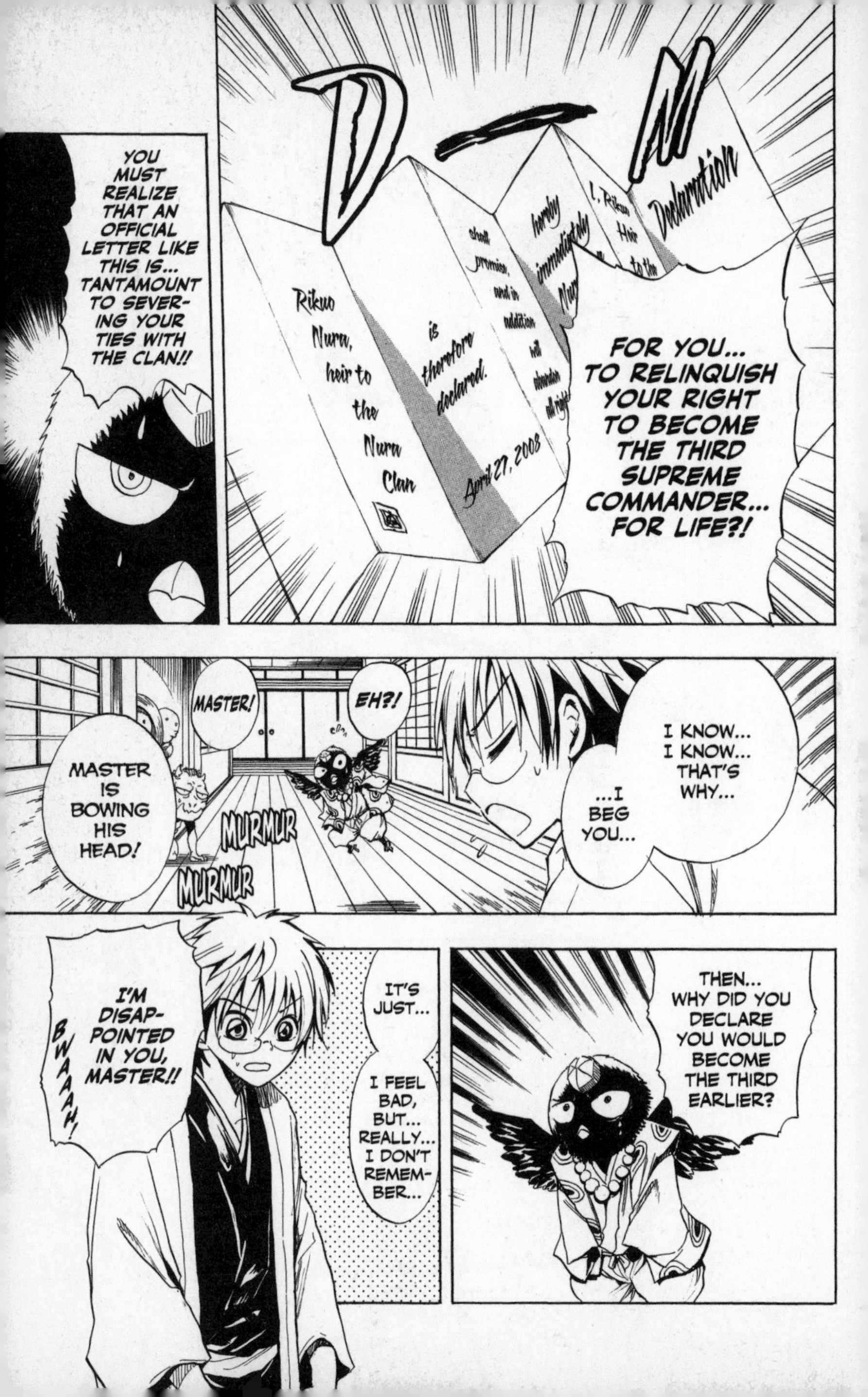
D—N
Declaration
I, Rikuo
Heir
to the
hereby
immediately
shall
promise,
and in
addition
will
abandon
is therefore declared.
Rikuo Nura, heir to the Nura Clan
April 27, 2008
FOR YOU... TO RELINQUISH YOUR RIGHT TO BECOME THE THIRD SUPREME COMMANDER... FOR LIFE?!
YOU MUST REALIZE THAT AN OFFICIAL LETTER LIKE THIS IS... TANTAMOUNT TO SEVER-ING YOUR TIES WITH THE CLAN!!
I KNOW... I KNOW... THAT'S WHY...
...I BEG YOU...
EH?!
MASTER!
MASTER IS BOWING HIS HEAD!
MURMUR
MURMUR
THEN... WHY DID YOU DECLARE YOU WOULD BECOME THE THIRD EARLIER?
IT'S JUST...
I FEEL BAD, BUT... REALLY... I DON'T REMEM-BER...
I'M DISAP-POINTED IN YOU, MASTER!!
BWAAAAH!

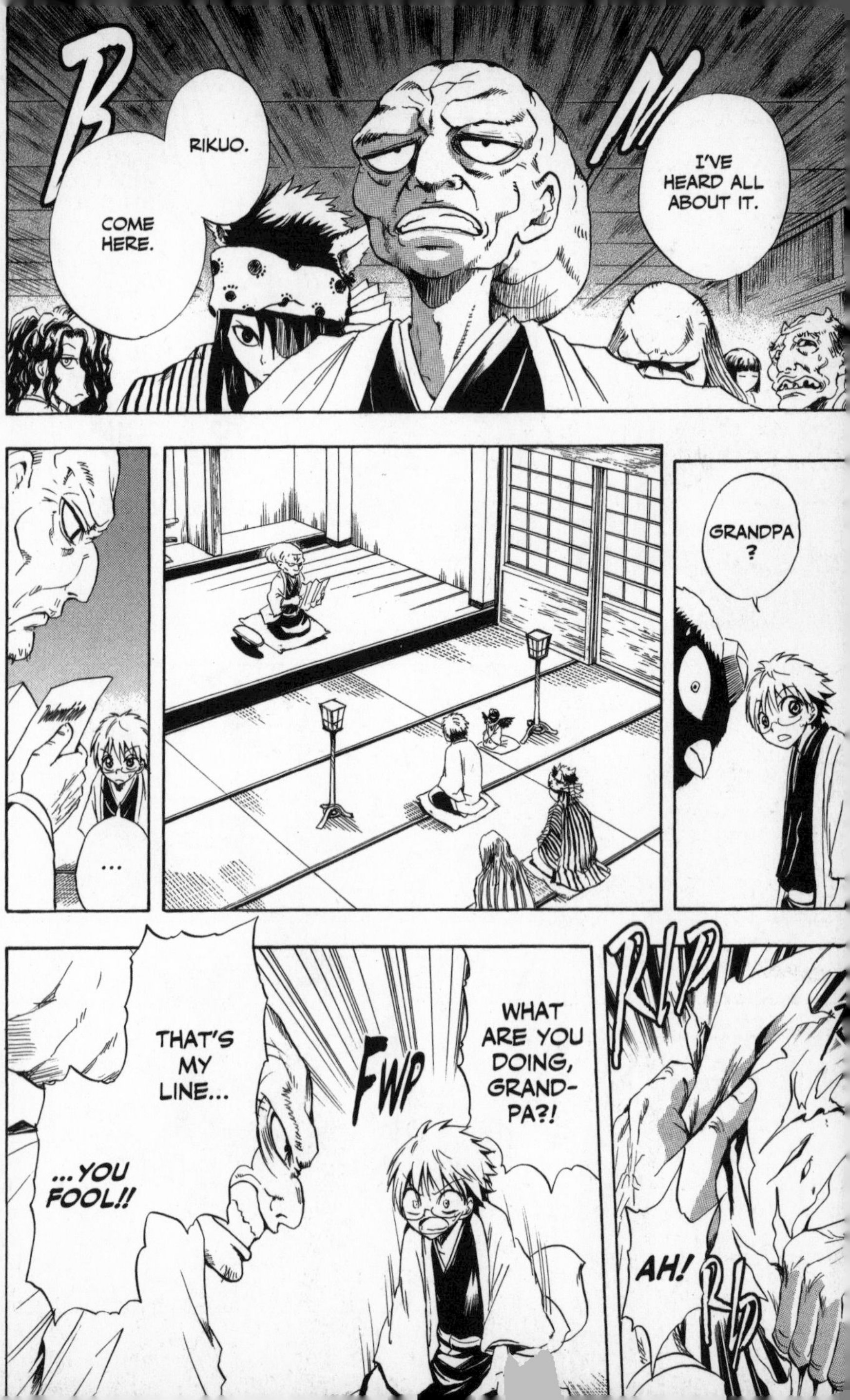
I'VE HEARD ALL ABOUT IT.
RIKUO.
COME HERE.
GRANDPA?
...
RIP
AH!
RIP
WHAT ARE YOU DOING, GRAND-PA?!
FWP
THAT'S MY LINE...
...YOU FOOL!!

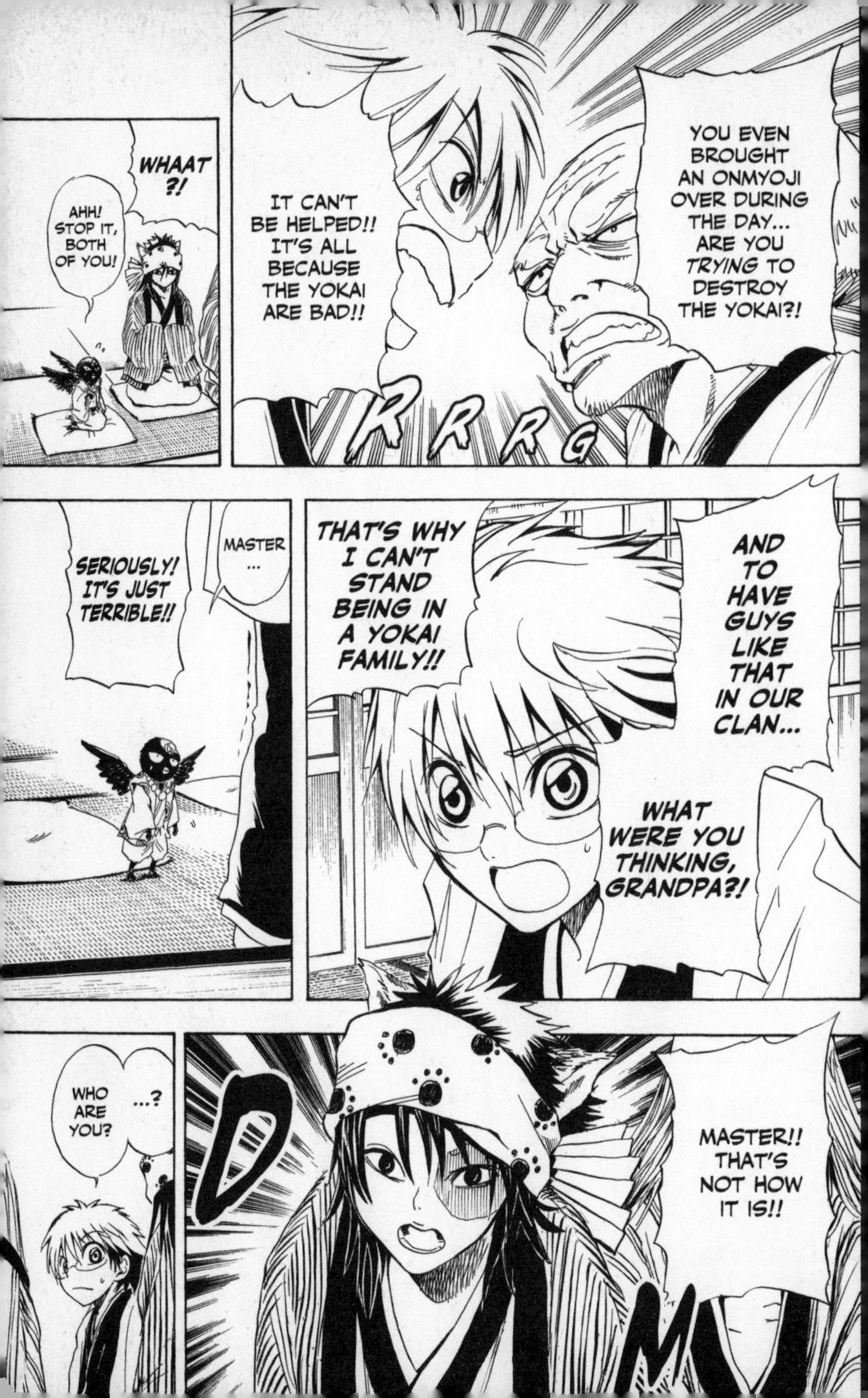
YOU EVEN BROUGHT AN ONMYOJI OVER DURING THE DAY... ARE YOU *TRYING* TO DESTROY THE YOKAI?!
IT CAN'T BE HELPED!! IT'S ALL BECAUSE THE YOKAI ARE BAD!!
RRRG
WHAAT?!
AHH! STOP IT, BOTH OF YOU!
AND TO HAVE GUYS LIKE THAT IN OUR CLAN...
WHAT WERE YOU THINKING, GRANDPA?!
THAT'S WHY I CAN'T STAND BEING IN A YOKAI FAMILY!!
MASTER...
SERIOUSLY! IT'S JUST TERRIBLE!!
MASTER!! THAT'S NOT HOW IT IS!!
...?
WHO ARE YOU?

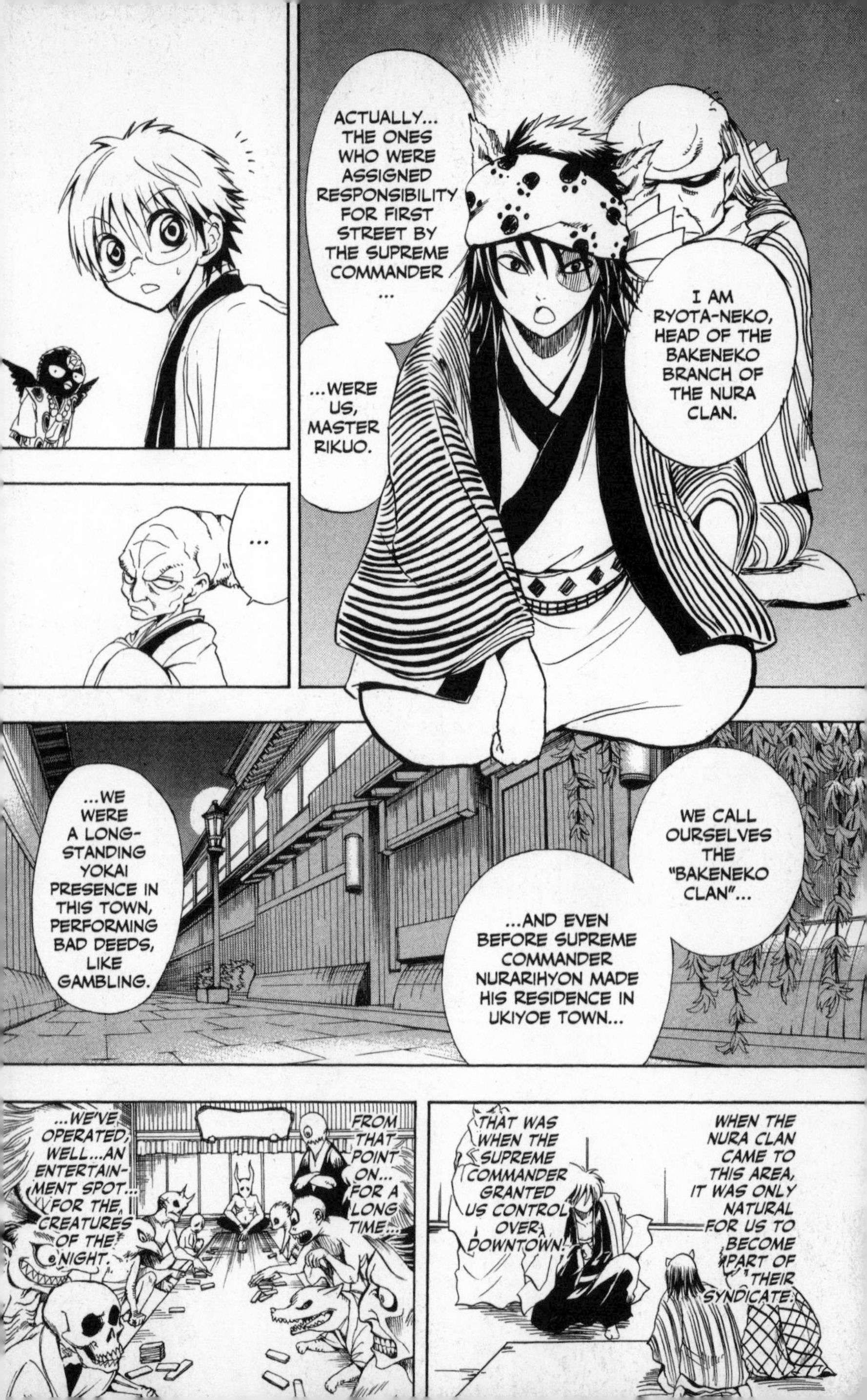
ACTUALLY... THE ONES WHO WERE ASSIGNED RESPONSIBILITY FOR FIRST STREET BY THE SUPREME COMMANDER ...
...WERE US, MASTER RIKUO.
I AM RYOTA-NEKO, HEAD OF THE BAKENEKO BRANCH OF THE NURA CLAN.
...
WE CALL OURSELVES THE "BAKENEKO CLAN"...
...AND EVEN BEFORE SUPREME COMMANDER NURARIHYON MADE HIS RESIDENCE IN UKIYOE TOWN...
...WE WERE A LONG-STANDING YOKAI PRESENCE IN THIS TOWN, PERFORMING BAD DEEDS, LIKE GAMBLING.
WHEN THE NURA CLAN CAME TO THIS AREA, IT WAS ONLY NATURAL FOR US TO BECOME PART OF THEIR SYNDICATE.
THAT WAS WHEN THE SUPREME COMMANDER GRANTED US CONTROL OVER DOWNTOWN.
FROM THAT POINT ON... FOR A LONG TIME...
...WE'VE OPERATED, WELL...AN ENTERTAINMENT SPOT... FOR THE CREATURES OF THE NIGHT.

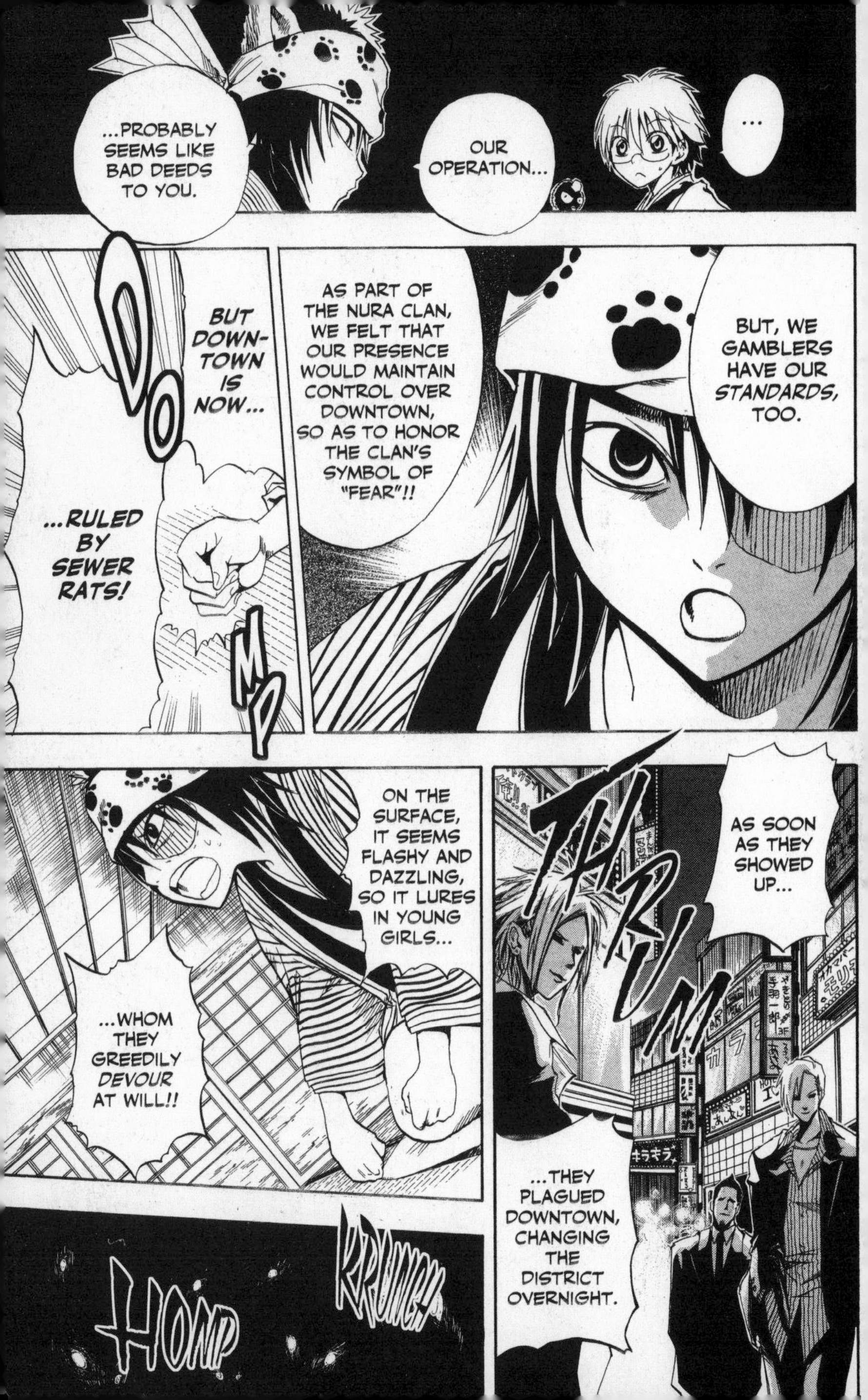
...
OUR OPERATION...
...PROBABLY SEEMS LIKE BAD DEEDS TO YOU.
BUT, WE GAMBLERS HAVE OUR *STANDARDS*, TOO.
AS PART OF THE NURA CLAN, WE FELT THAT OUR PRESENCE WOULD MAINTAIN CONTROL OVER DOWNTOWN, SO AS TO HONOR THE CLAN'S SYMBOL OF "FEAR"!!
BUT DOWNTOWN IS NOW...
DOMP
...RULED BY SEWER RATS!
THRUM
AS SOON AS THEY SHOWED UP...
キラキラ
...THEY PLAGUED DOWNTOWN, CHANGING THE DISTRICT OVERNIGHT.
ON THE SURFACE, IT SEEMS FLASHY AND DAZZLING, SO IT LURES IN YOUNG GIRLS...
...WHOM THEY GREEDILY *DEVOUR* AT WILL!!
KRUNCH!
HOMP

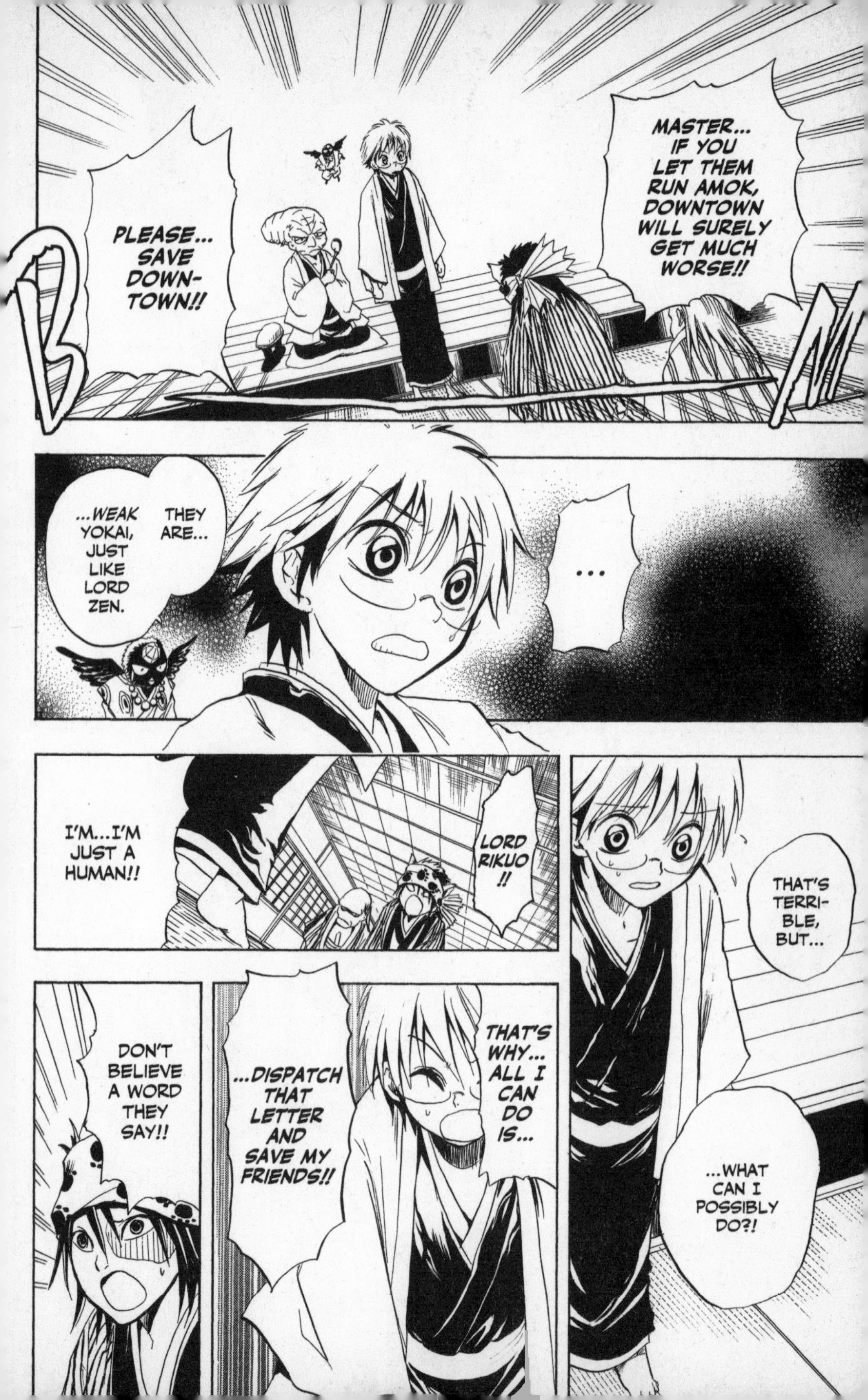
MASTER... IF YOU LET THEM RUN AMOK, DOWNTOWN WILL SURELY GET MUCH WORSE!!
PLEASE... SAVE DOWN-TOWN!!
...
THEY ARE...
...WEAK YOKAI, JUST LIKE LORD ZEN.
THAT'S TERRIBLE, BUT...
...WHAT CAN I POSSIBLY DO?!
LORD RIKUO!!
I'M...I'M JUST A HUMAN!!
THAT'S WHY... ALL I CAN DO IS...
...DISPATCH THAT LETTER AND SAVE MY FRIENDS!!
DON'T BELIEVE A WORD THEY SAY!!

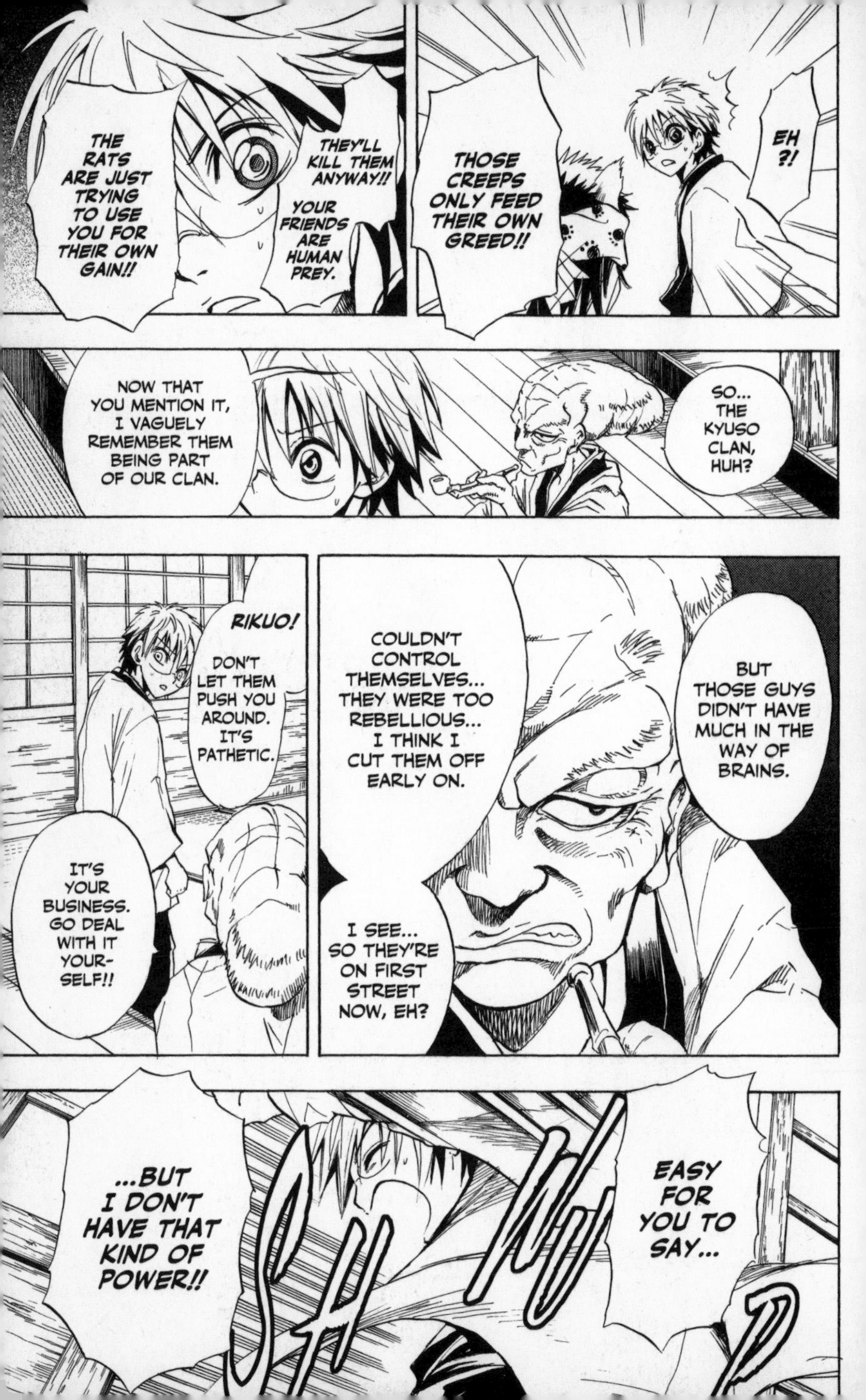
EH ?!
THOSE CREEPS ONLY FEED THEIR OWN GREED!!
THEY'LL KILL THEM ANYWAY!! YOUR FRIENDS ARE HUMAN PREY.
THE RATS ARE JUST TRYING TO USE YOU FOR THEIR OWN GAIN!!
SO... THE KYUSO CLAN, HUH?
NOW THAT YOU MENTION IT, I VAGUELY REMEMBER THEM BEING PART OF OUR CLAN.
BUT THOSE GUYS DIDN'T HAVE MUCH IN THE WAY OF BRAINS.
COULDN'T CONTROL THEMSELVES... THEY WERE TOO REBELLIOUS... I THINK I CUT THEM OFF EARLY ON.
I SEE... SO THEY'RE ON FIRST STREET NOW, EH?
RIKUO!
DON'T LET THEM PUSH YOU AROUND. IT'S PATHETIC.
IT'S YOUR BUSINESS. GO DEAL WITH IT YOURSELF!!
EASY FOR YOU TO SAY...
...BUT I DON'T HAVE THAT KIND OF POWER!!

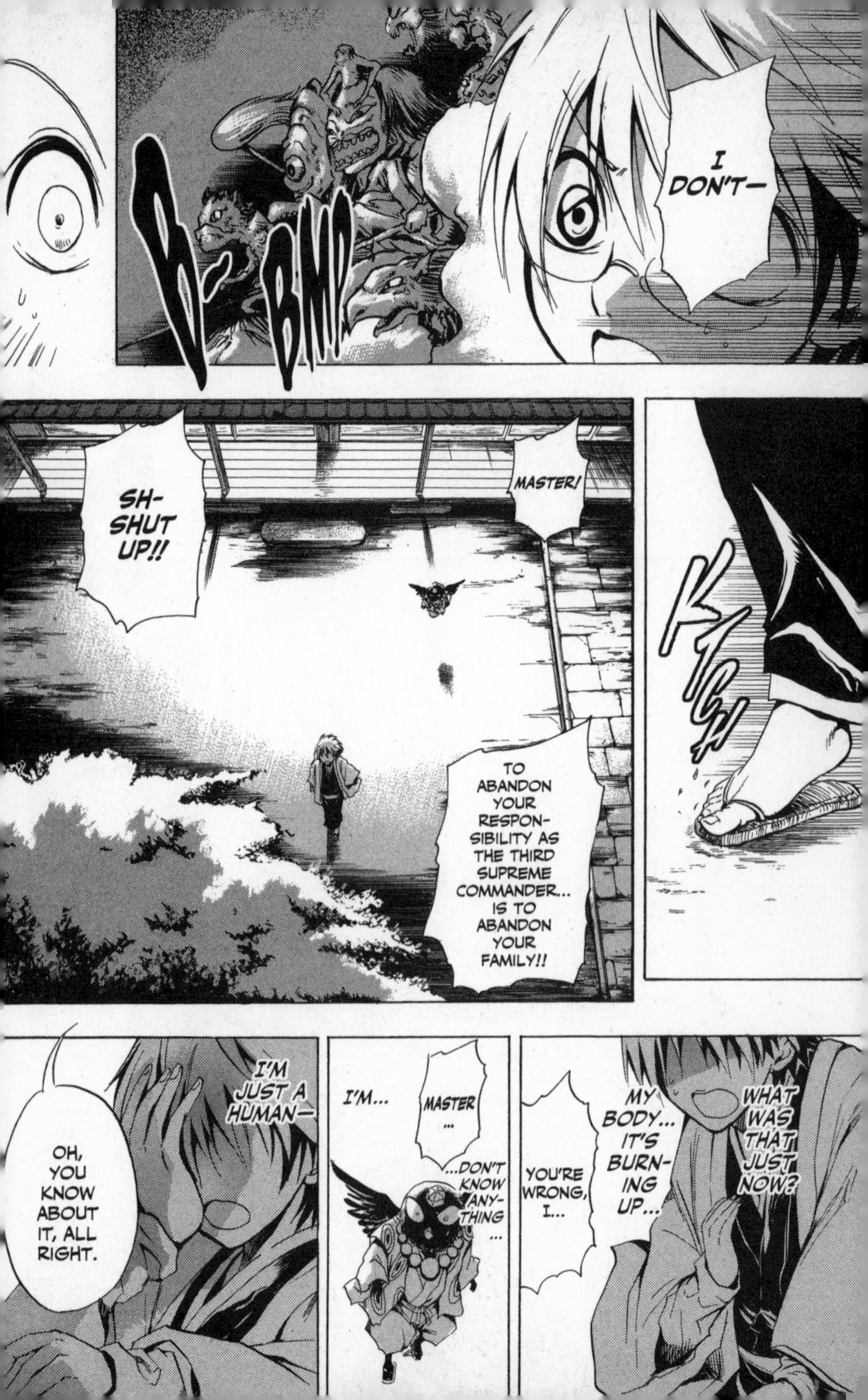
I DON'T—
B-BMP
KICK
MASTER!
TO ABANDON YOUR RESPONSIBILITY AS THE THIRD SUPREME COMMANDER... IS TO ABANDON YOUR FAMILY!!
SH-SHUT UP!!
WHAT WAS THAT JUST NOW?
MY BODY... IT'S BURNING UP...
YOU'RE WRONG, I...
MASTER...
I'M...
...DON'T KNOW ANYTHING...
I'M JUST A HUMAN—
OH, YOU KNOW ABOUT IT, ALL RIGHT.

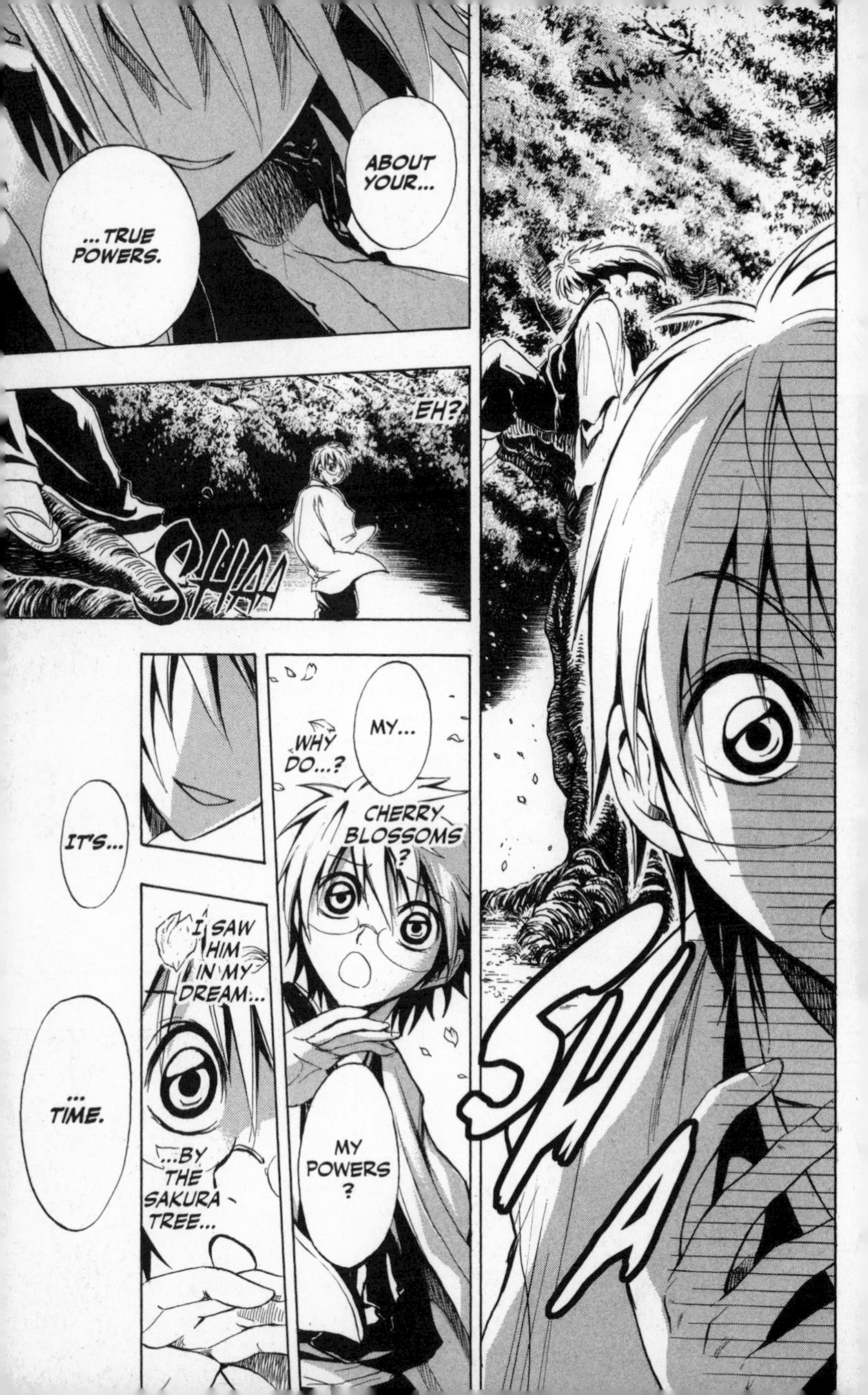
SHAA
ABOUT YOUR...
...TRUE POWERS.
EH?
SHAA
MY...
WHY DO...?
CHERRY BLOSSOMS?
MY POWERS?
IT'S...
I SAW HIM IN MY DREAM...
...BY THE SAKURA TREE...
... TIME.

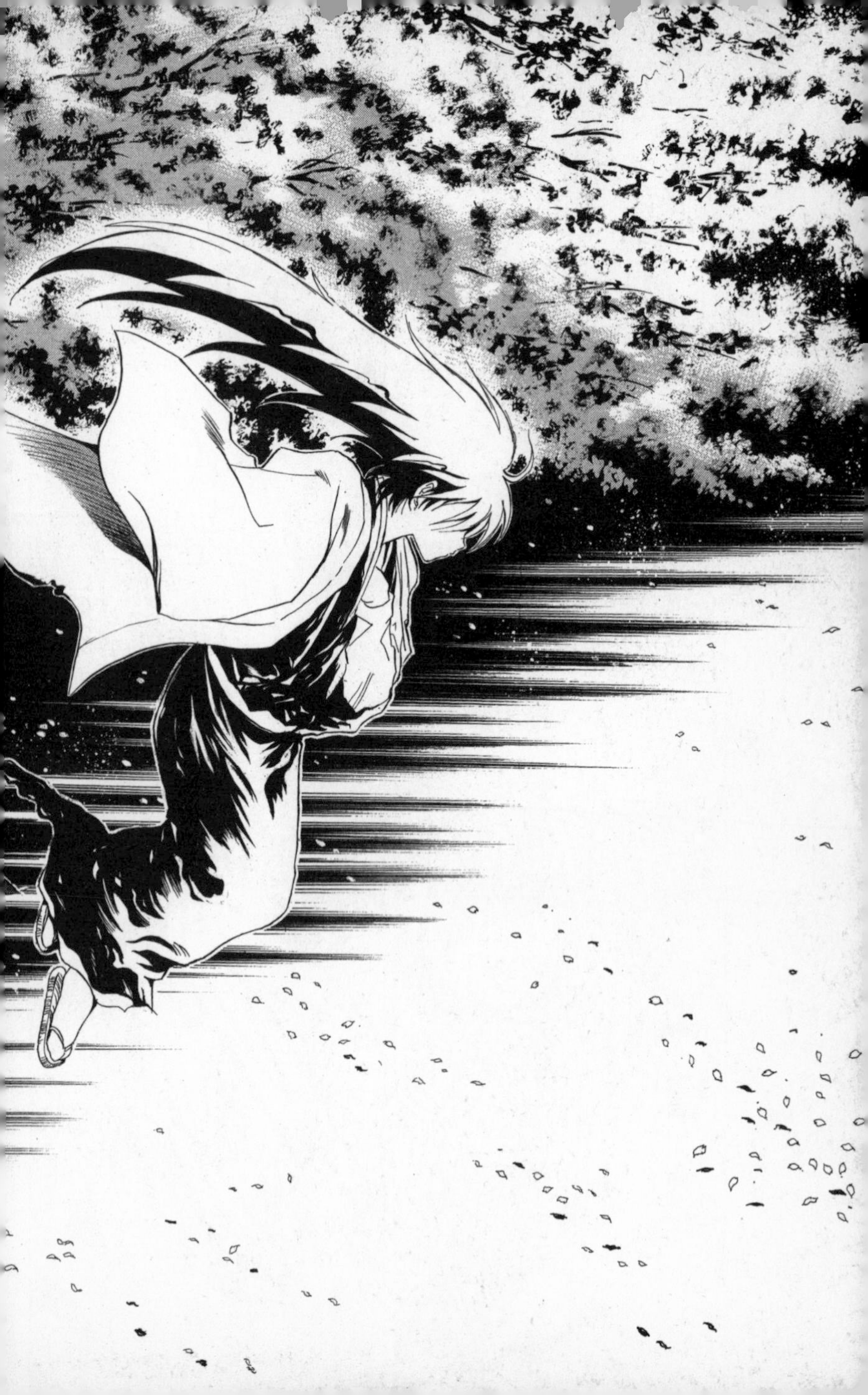

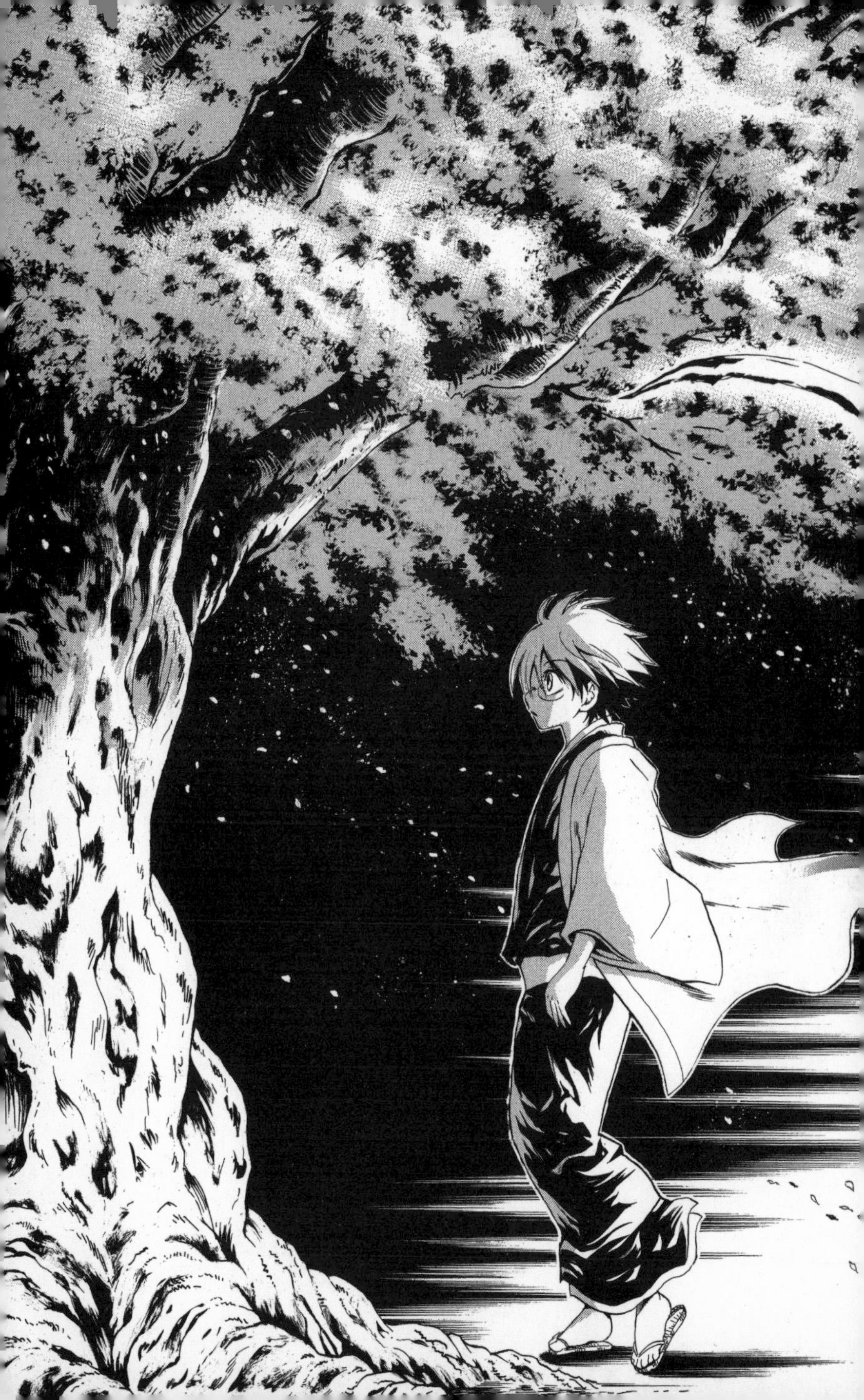

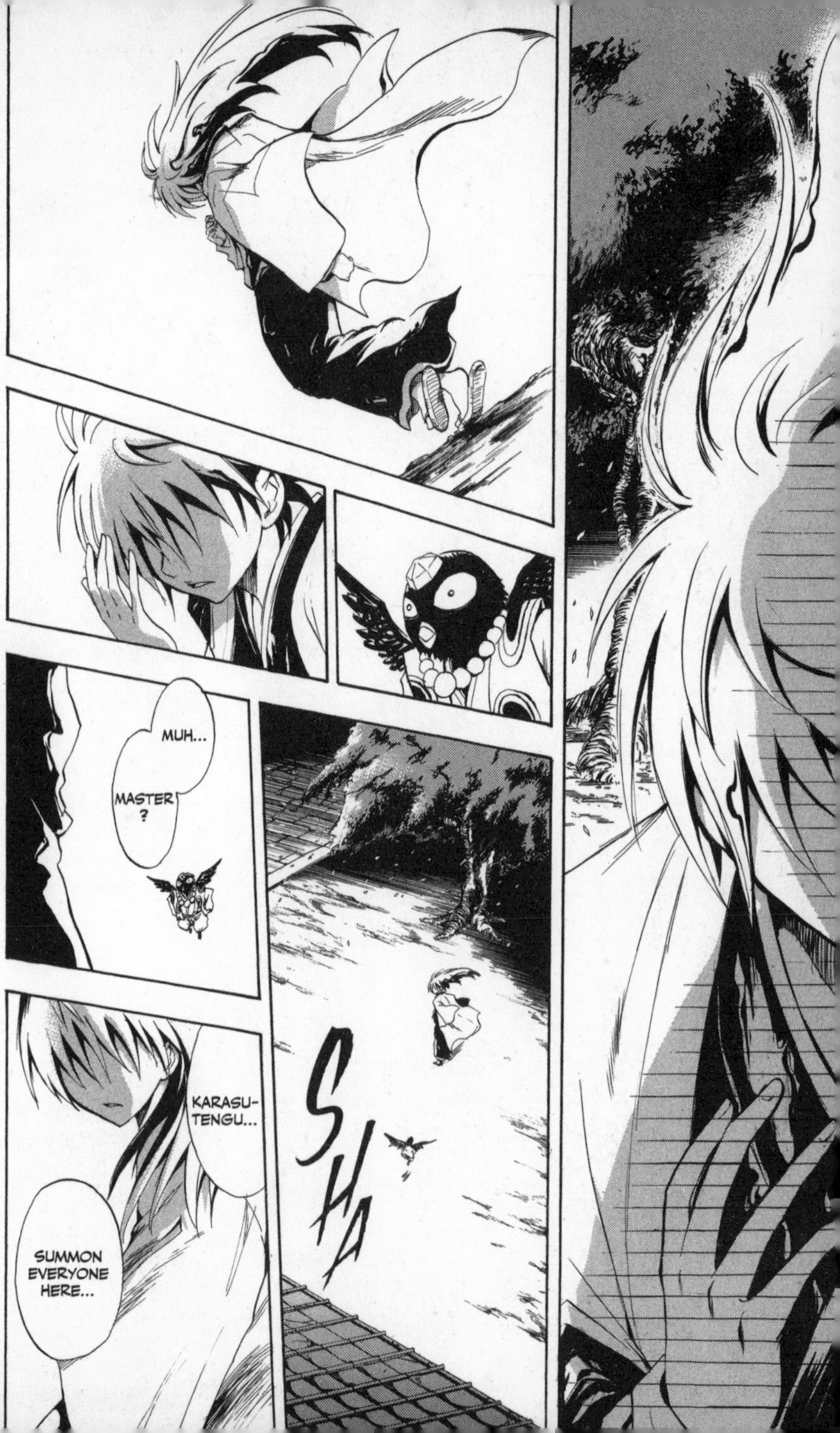
SHA
MUH...
MASTER?
KARASU-TENGU...
SUMMON EVERYONE HERE...

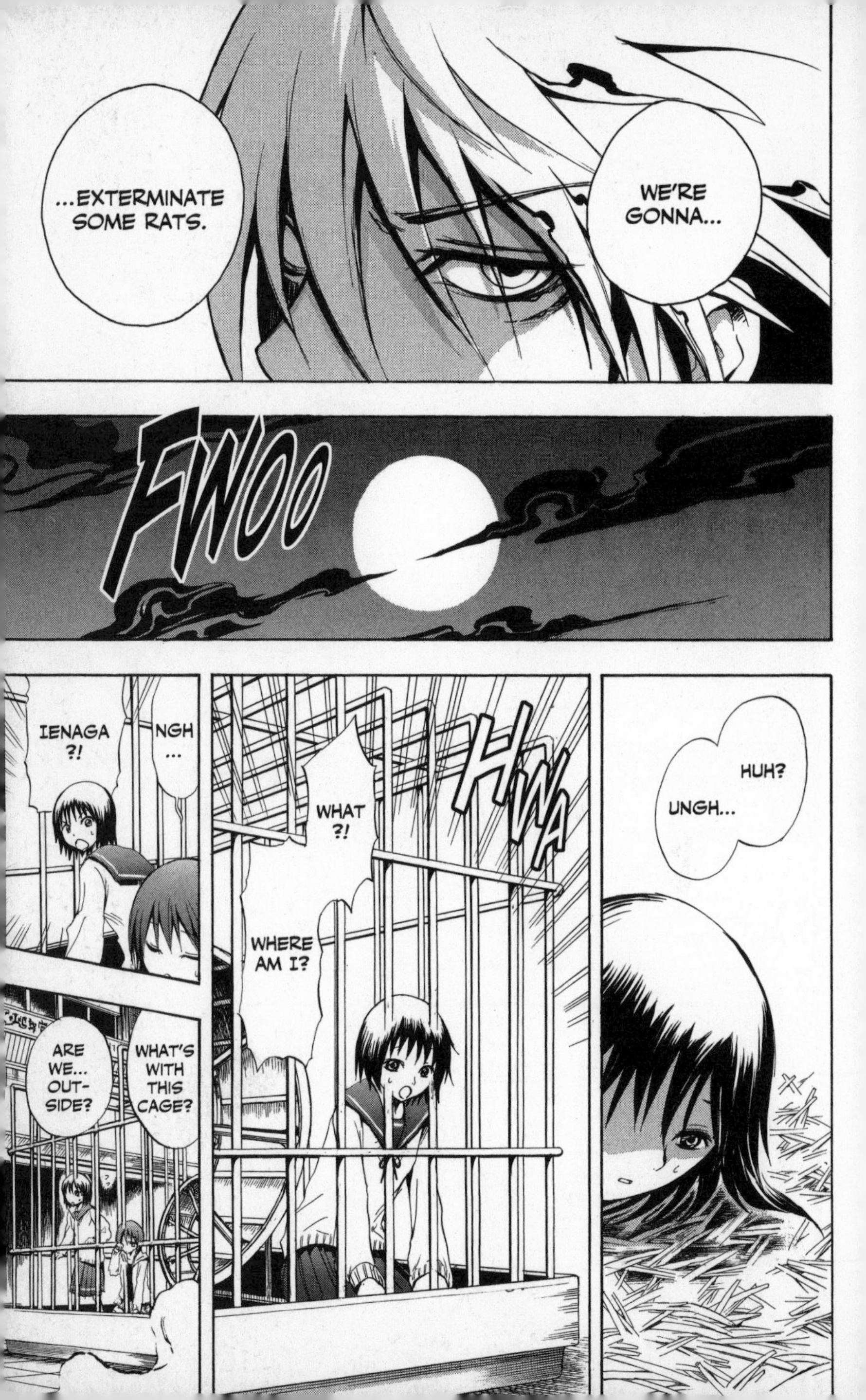
WE'RE GONNA...
...EXTERMINATE SOME RATS.
FWOO
HUH?
UNGH...
HWA
WHAT ?!
WHERE AM I?
NGH ...
IENAGA ?!
WHAT'S WITH THIS CAGE?
ARE WE... OUT-SIDE?

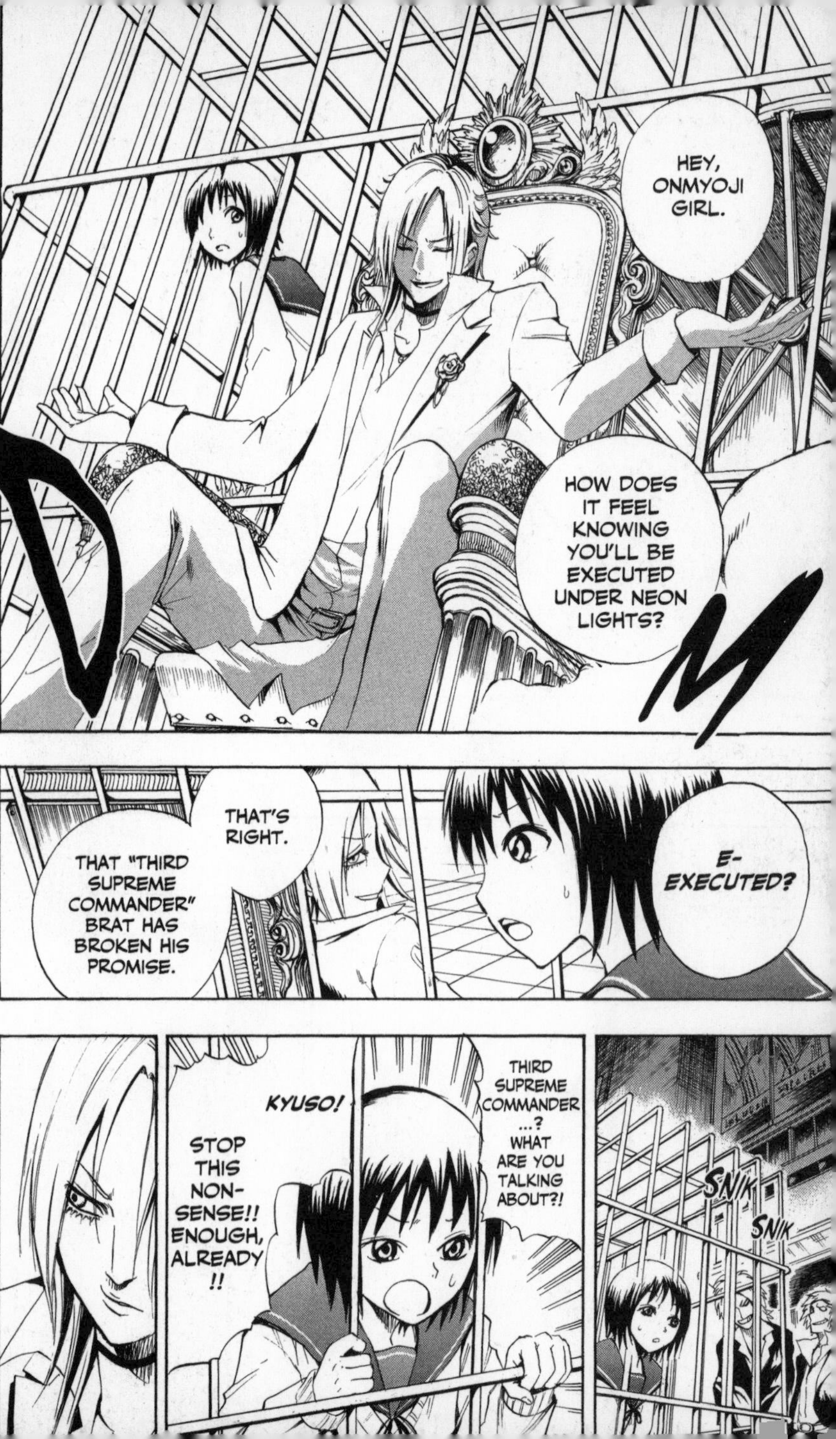
HEY, ONMYOJI GIRL.
HOW DOES IT FEEL KNOWING YOU'LL BE EXECUTED UNDER NEON LIGHTS?
D M
E-EXECUTED?
THAT'S RIGHT.
THAT "THIRD SUPREME COMMANDER" BRAT HAS BROKEN HIS PROMISE.
SNIK
SNIK
THIRD SUPREME COMMANDER ...? WHAT ARE YOU TALKING ABOUT?!
KYUSO!
STOP THIS NON-SENSE!! ENOUGH, ALREADY !!

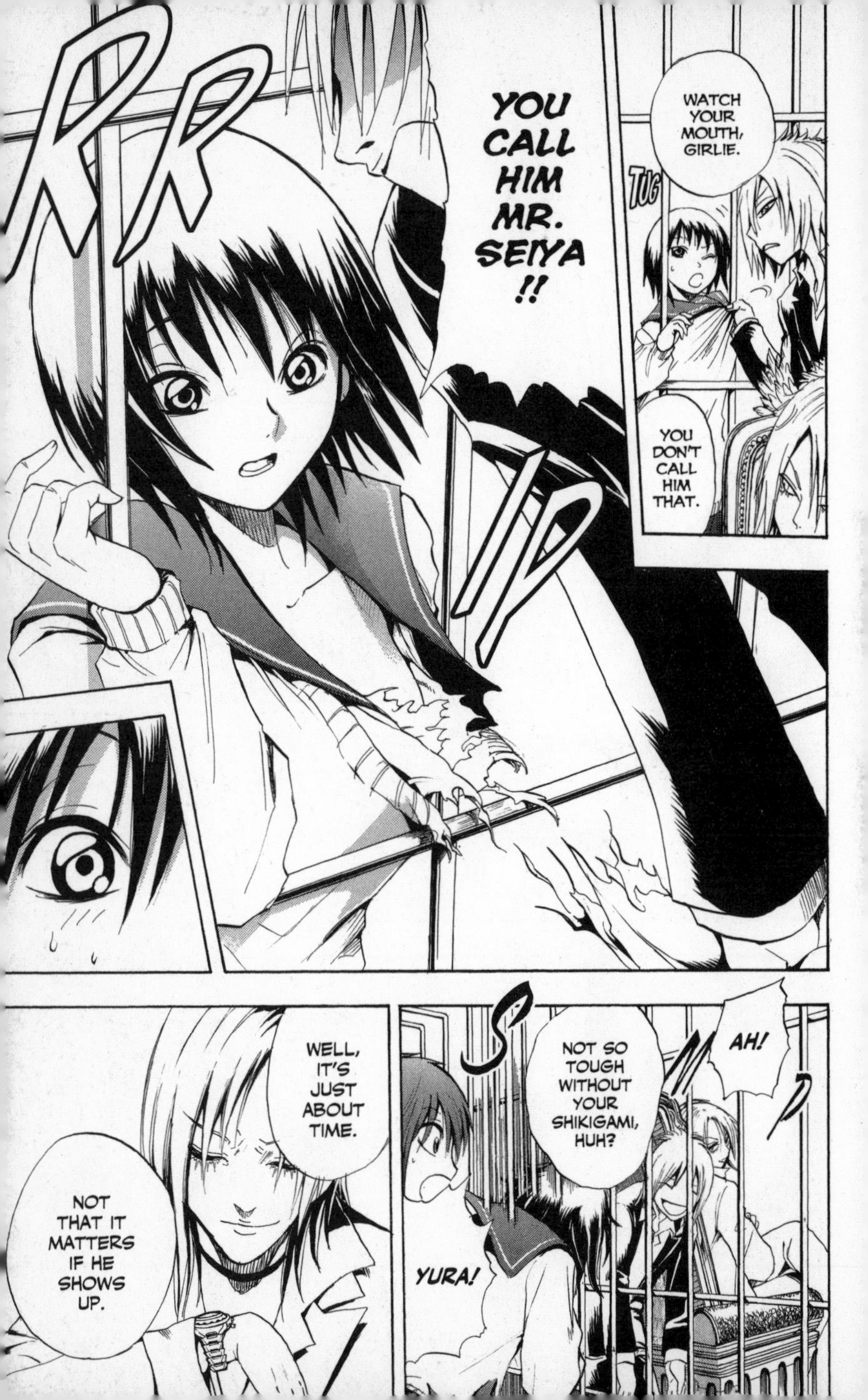
WATCH YOUR MOUTH, GIRLIE.
TUG
YOU DON'T CALL HIM THAT.
YOU CALL HIM MR. SEIYA!!
RR
AH!
NOT SO TOUGH WITHOUT YOUR SHIKIGAMI, HUH?
YURA!
WELL, IT'S JUST ABOUT TIME.
NOT THAT IT MATTERS IF HE SHOWS UP.

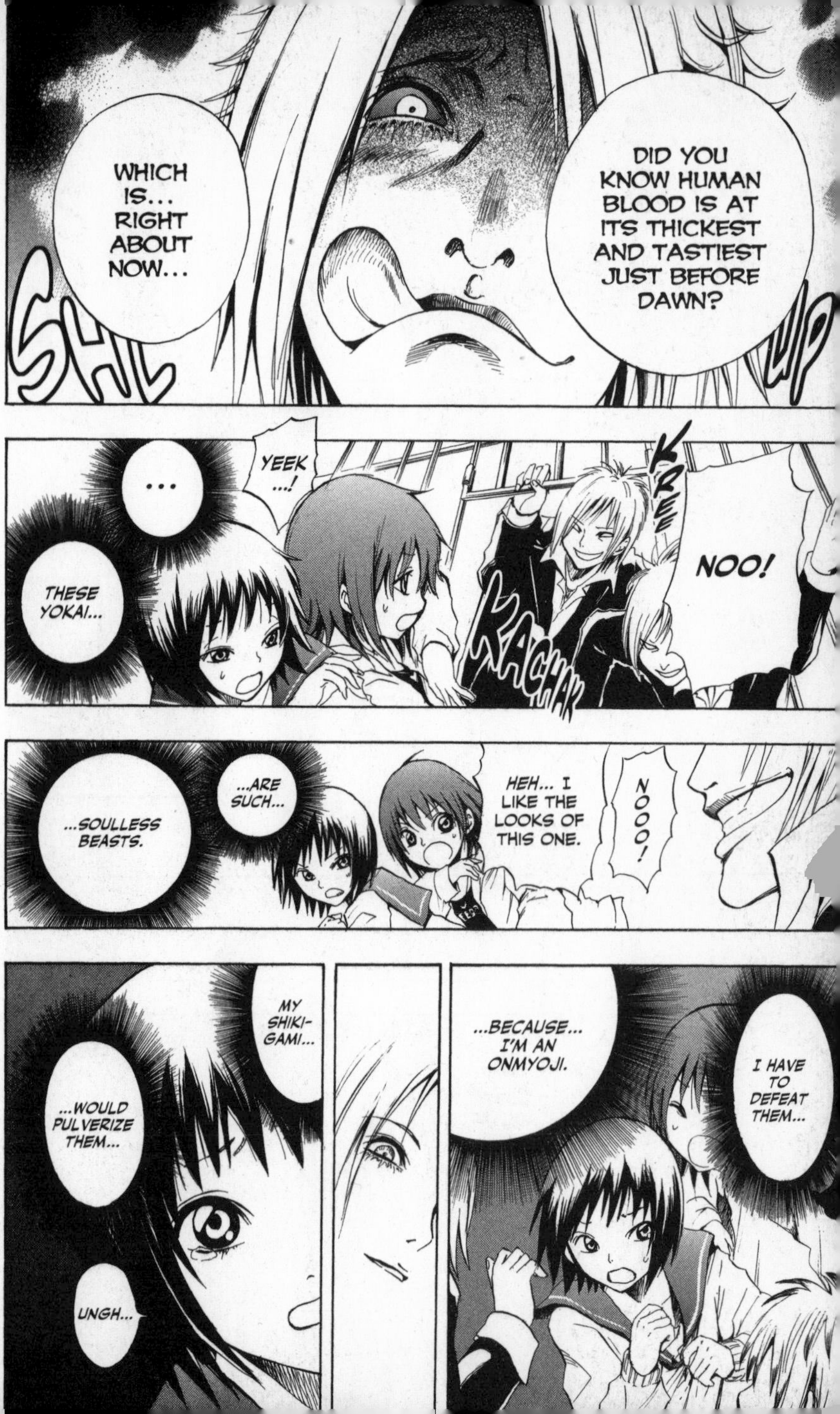

DID YOU KNOW HUMAN BLOOD IS AT ITS THICKEST AND TASTIEST JUST BEFORE DAWN?
WHICH IS... RIGHT ABOUT NOW...
SHLUP
NOO!
KREE
KACHAK
YEEK ...!
...
THESE YOKAI...
NOOOO!
HEH... I LIKE THE LOOKS OF THIS ONE.
...ARE SUCH...
...SOULLESS BEASTS.
I HAVE TO DEFEAT THEM...
...BECAUSE... I'M AN ONMYOJI.
MY SHIKI-GAMI...
...WOULD PULVERIZE THEM...
UNGH...

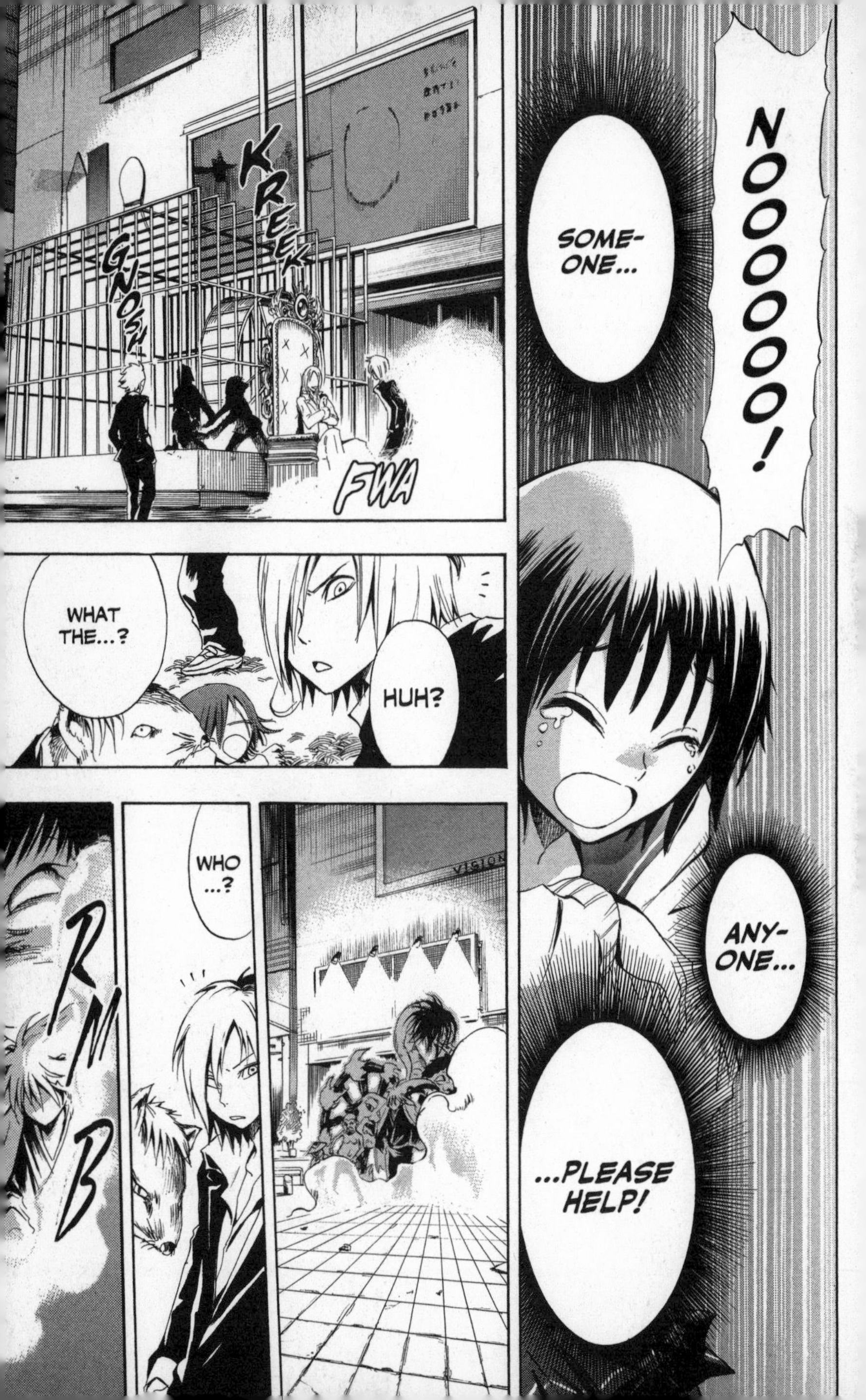
NOOOOOOO!
SOME-ONE...
ANY-ONE...
...PLEASE HELP!
KREEK
GNOSH
FWA
HUH?
WHAT THE...?
VISION
WHO ...?
RMB

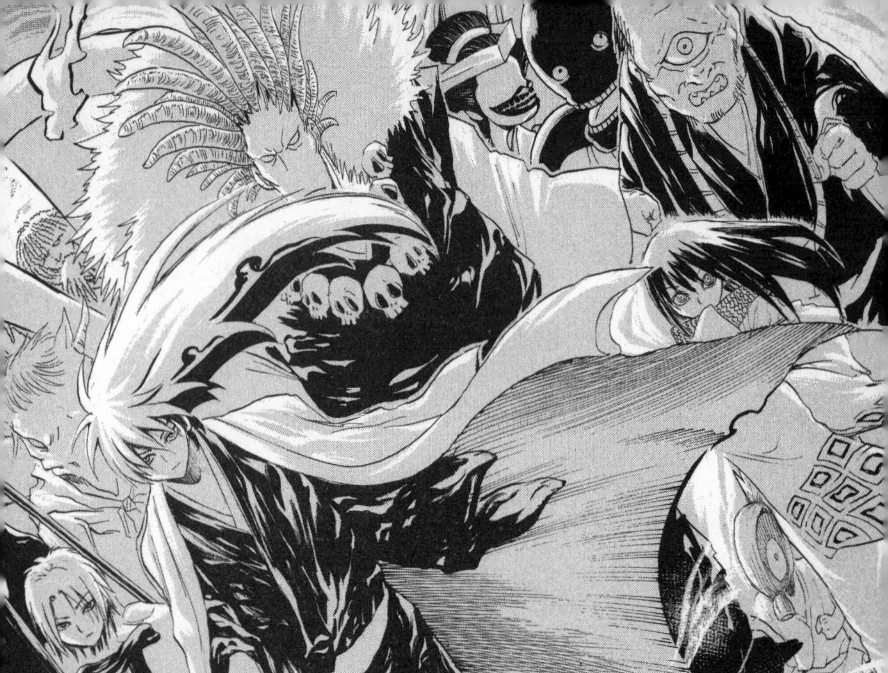

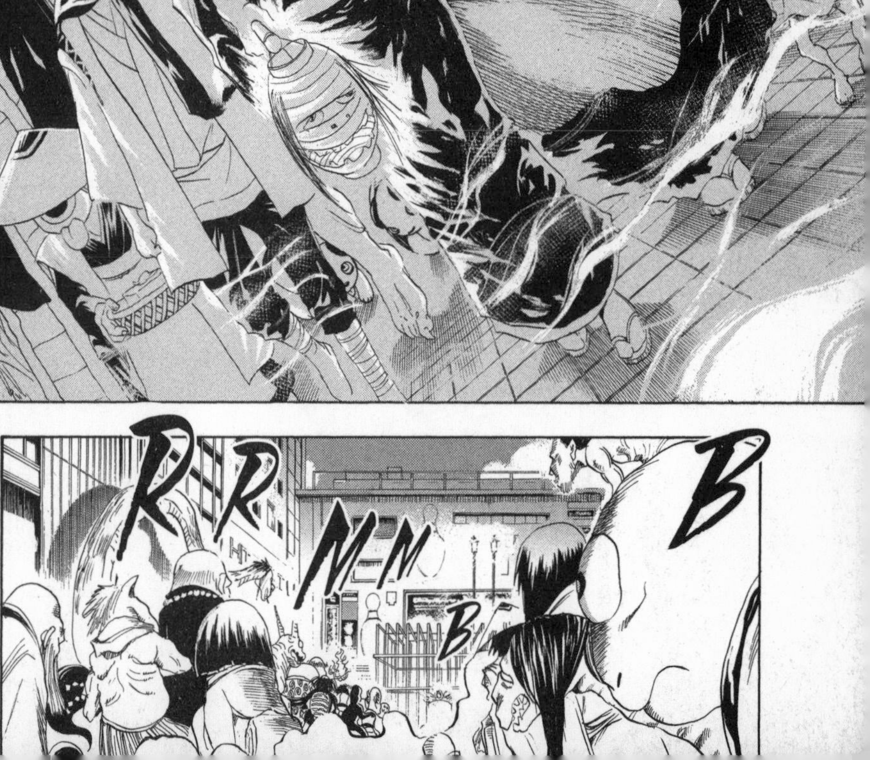
RRMMBB

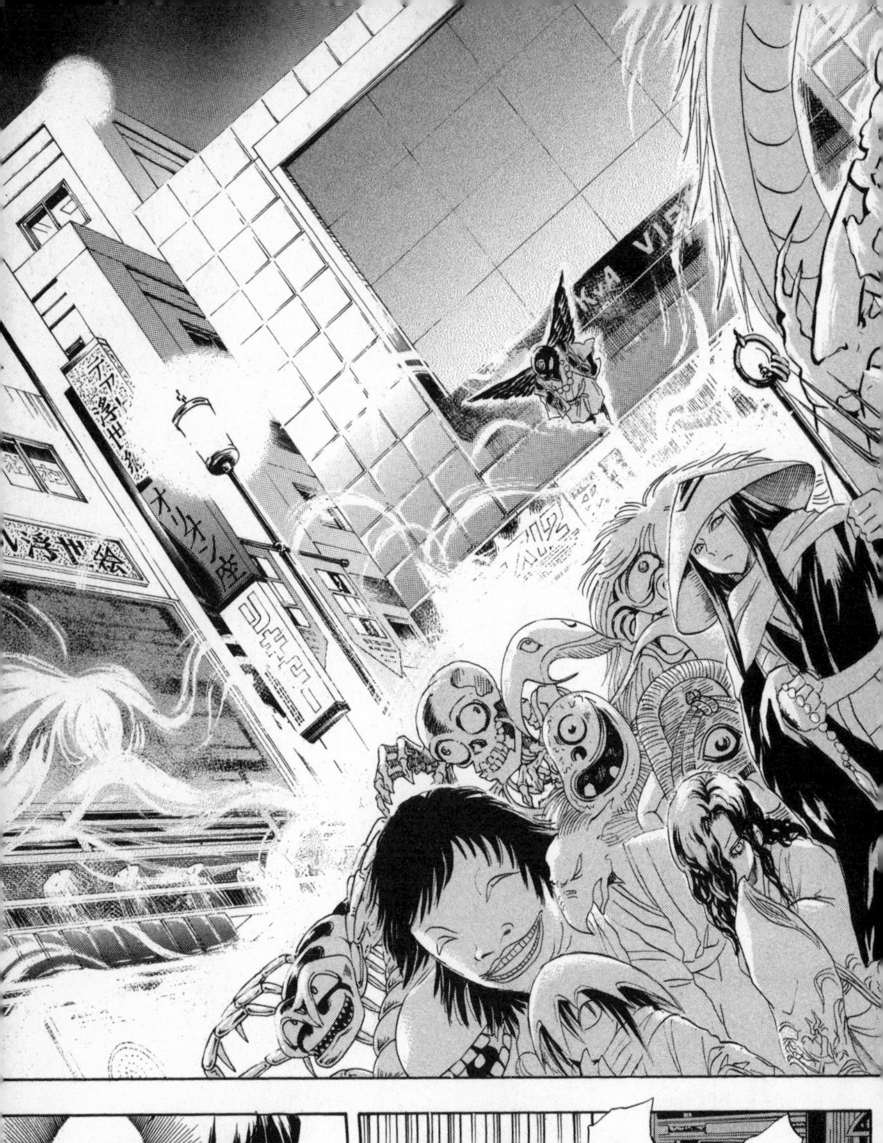

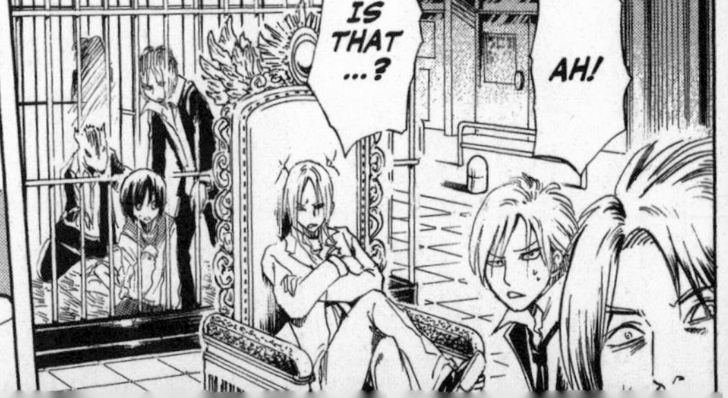
AH!
IS THAT ...?

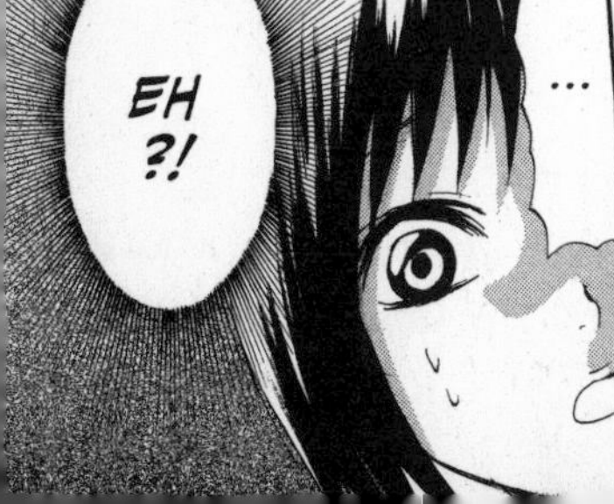
...
EH ?!

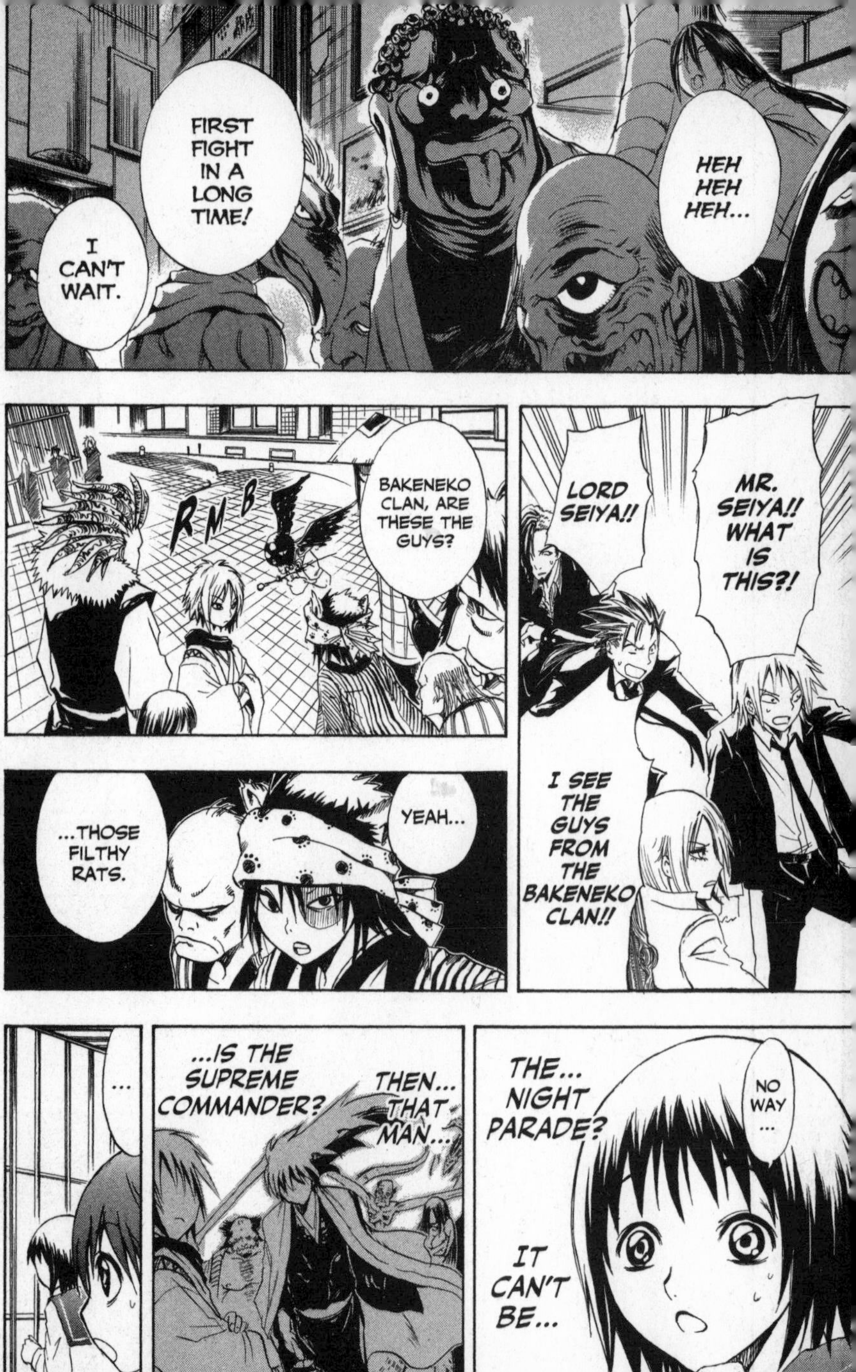
HEH HEH HEH...
FIRST FIGHT IN A LONG TIME!
I CAN'T WAIT.
MR. SEIYA!! WHAT IS THIS?!
LORD SEIYA!!
I SEE THE GUYS FROM THE BAKENEKO CLAN!!
BAKENEKO CLAN, ARE THESE THE GUYS?
RMB
YEAH...
...THOSE FILTHY RATS.
NO WAY...
THE... NIGHT PARADE?
IT CAN'T BE...
THEN... THAT MAN...
...IS THE SUPREME COMMANDER?
...

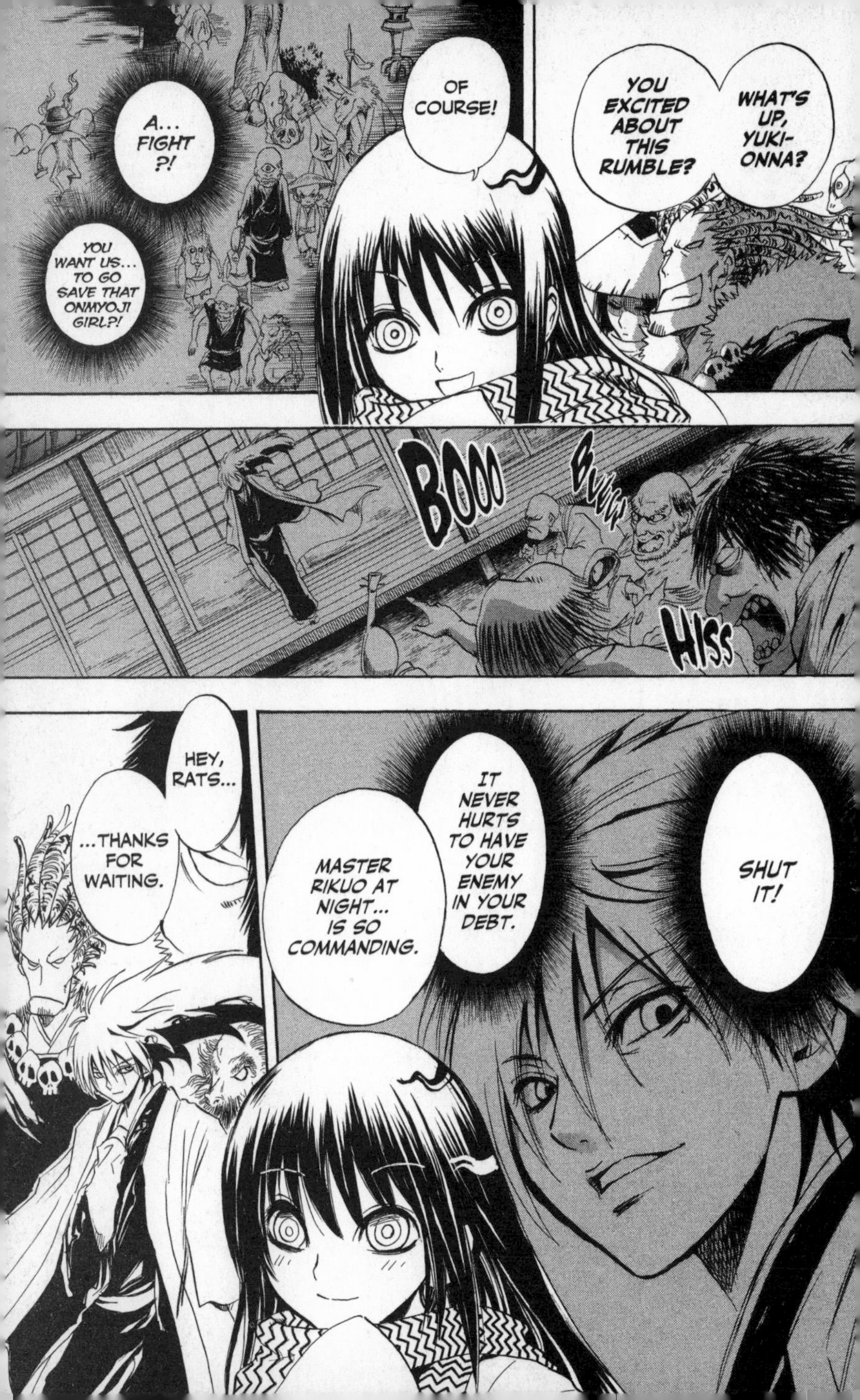
WHAT'S UP, YUKI-ONNA?
YOU EXCITED ABOUT THIS RUMBLE?
OF COURSE!
A... FIGHT?!
YOU WANT US... TO GO SAVE THAT ONMYOJI GIRL?!
BOOO
HISS
SHUT IT!
IT NEVER HURTS TO HAVE YOUR ENEMY IN YOUR DEBT.
MASTER RIKUO AT NIGHT... IS SO COMMANDING.
HEY, RATS...
...THANKS FOR WAITING.

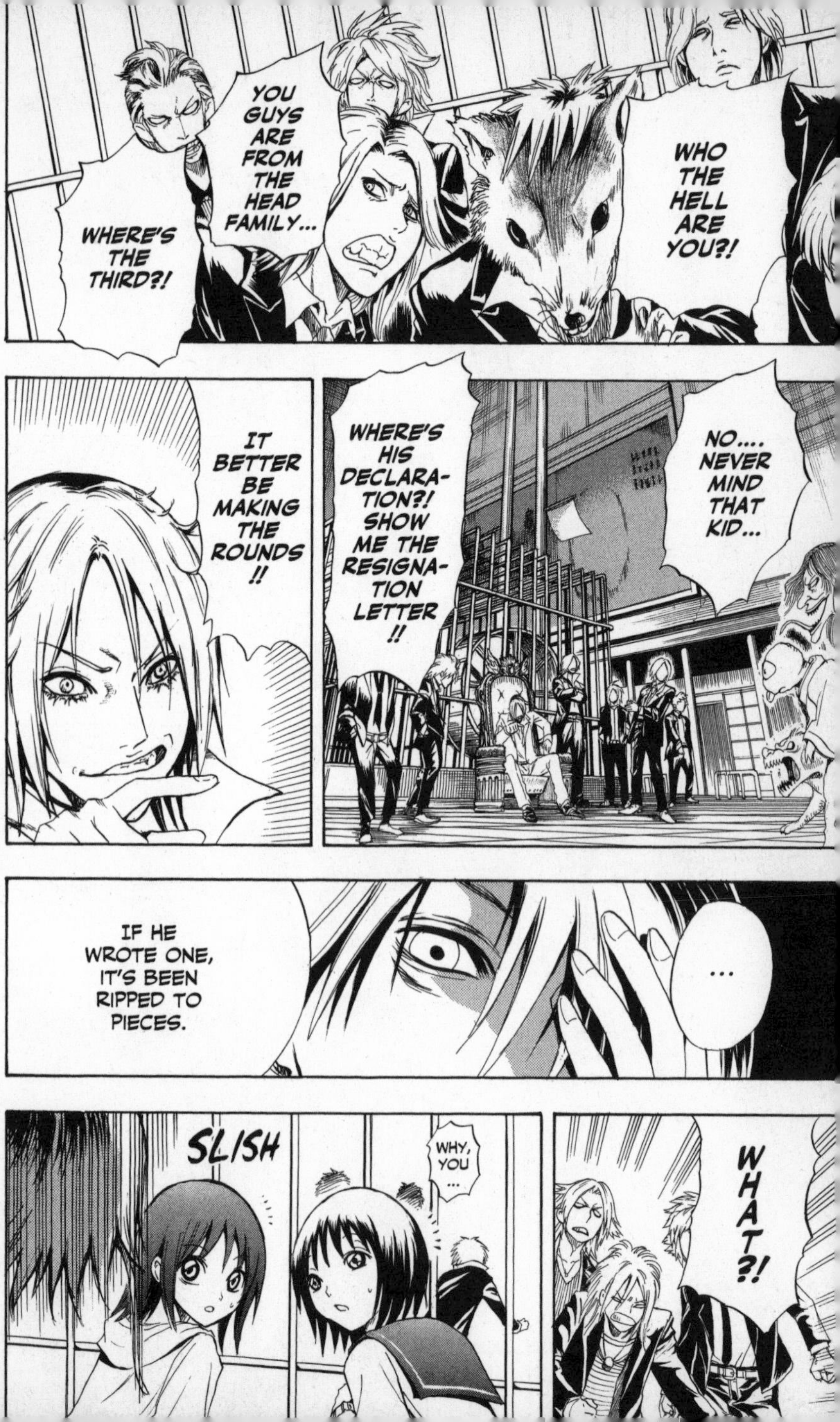
WHO THE HELL ARE YOU?!
YOU GUYS ARE FROM THE HEAD FAMILY...
WHERE'S THE THIRD?!
NO.... NEVER MIND THAT KID...
WHERE'S HIS DECLARATION?! SHOW ME THE RESIGNATION LETTER!!
IT BETTER BE MAKING THE ROUNDS!!
...
IF HE WROTE ONE, IT'S BEEN RIPPED TO PIECES.
WHAT?!
WHY, YOU ...
SLISH

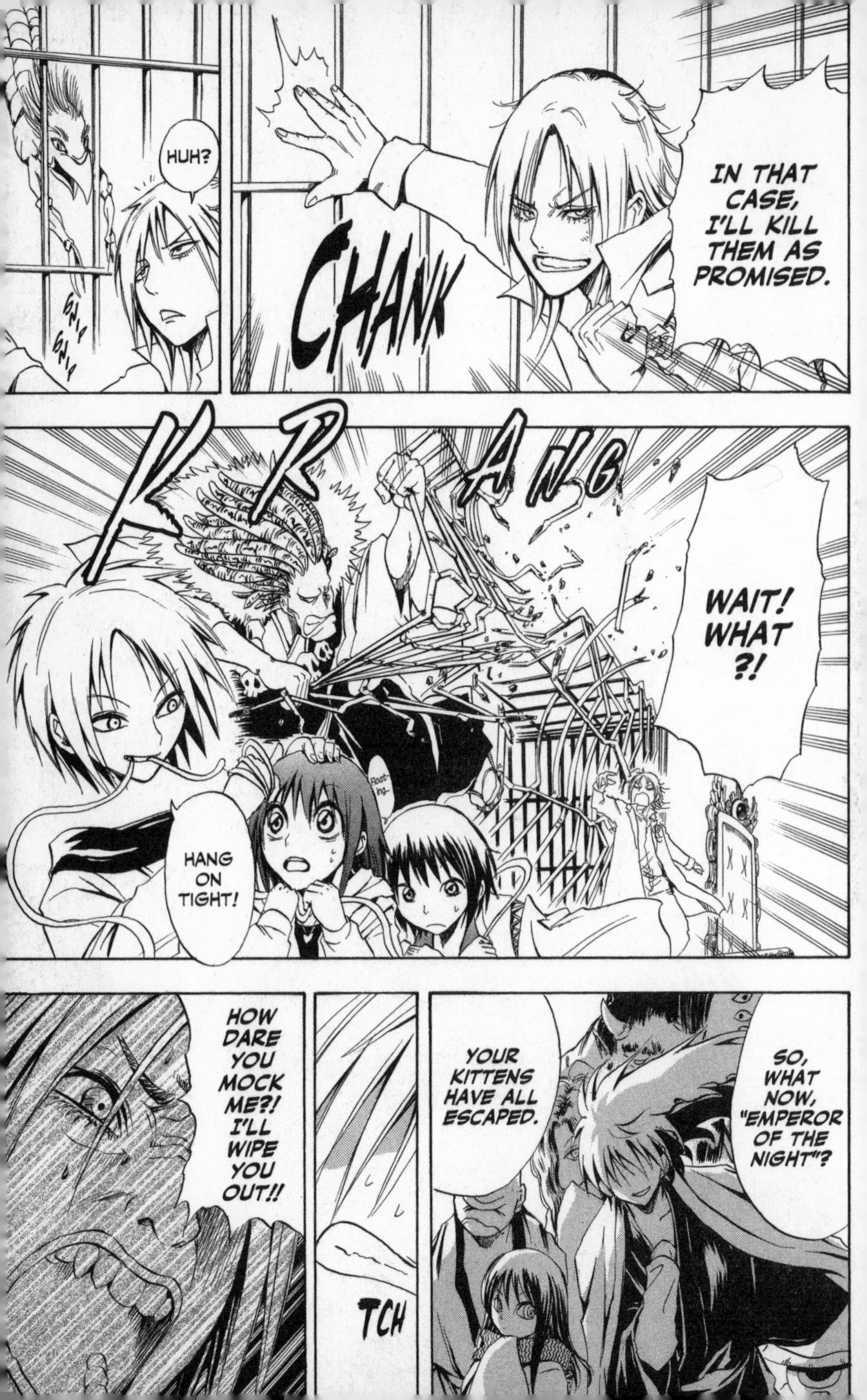
IN THAT CASE, I'LL KILL THEM AS PROMISED.
CHANK
HUH?
KRANG
WAIT! WHAT ?!
Float-ing...
HANG ON TIGHT!
SO, WHAT NOW, "EMPEROR OF THE NIGHT"?
YOUR KITTENS HAVE ALL ESCAPED.
TCH
HOW DARE YOU MOCK ME?! I'LL WIPE YOU OUT!!

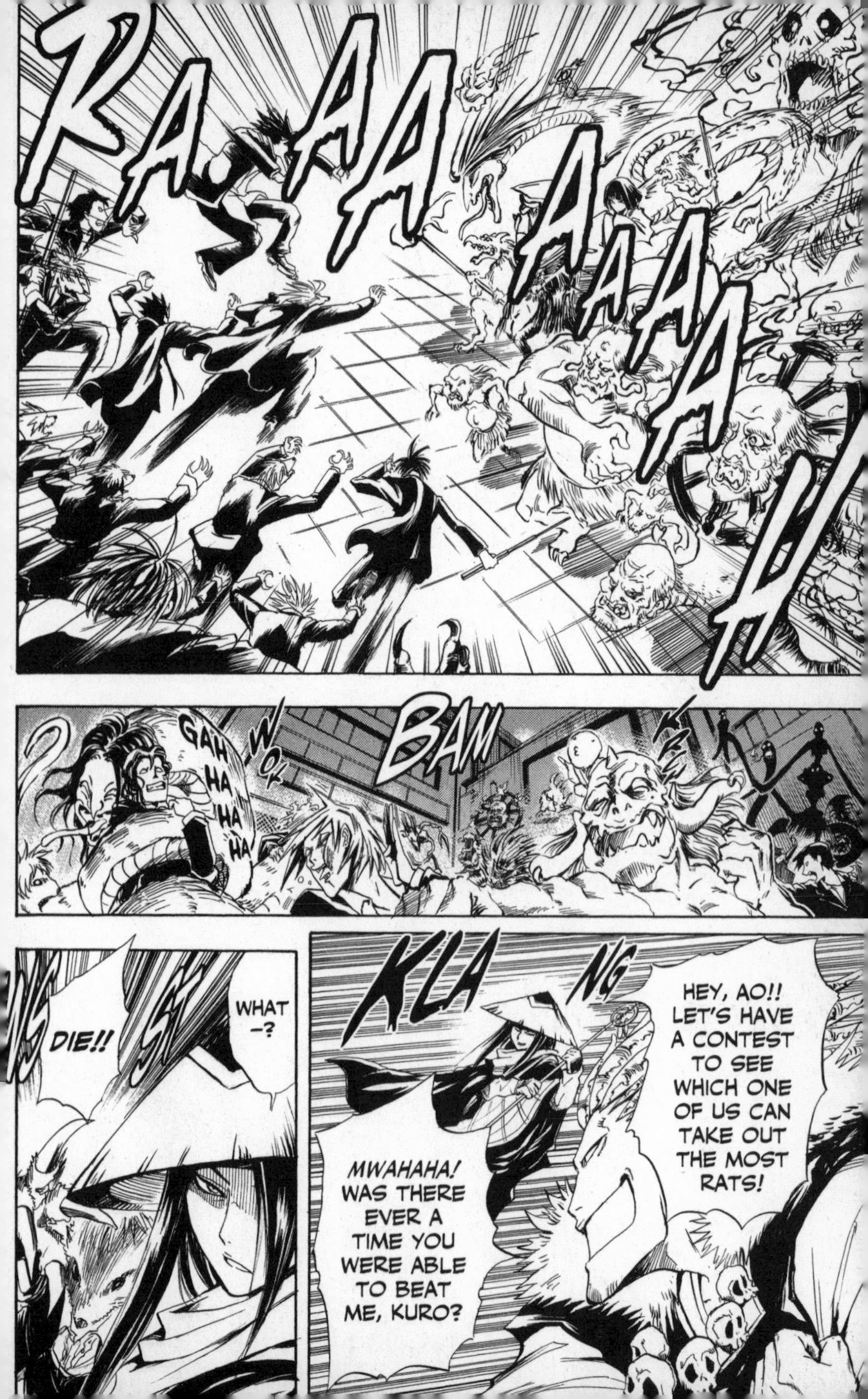
KA-AAAAAAH
BAM
GAH HA HA HA HA
KLANG
HEY, AO!! LET'S HAVE A CONTEST TO SEE WHICH ONE OF US CAN TAKE OUT THE MOST RATS!
MWAHAHA! WAS THERE EVER A TIME YOU WERE ABLE TO BEAT ME, KURO?
WHAT –?
DIE!!

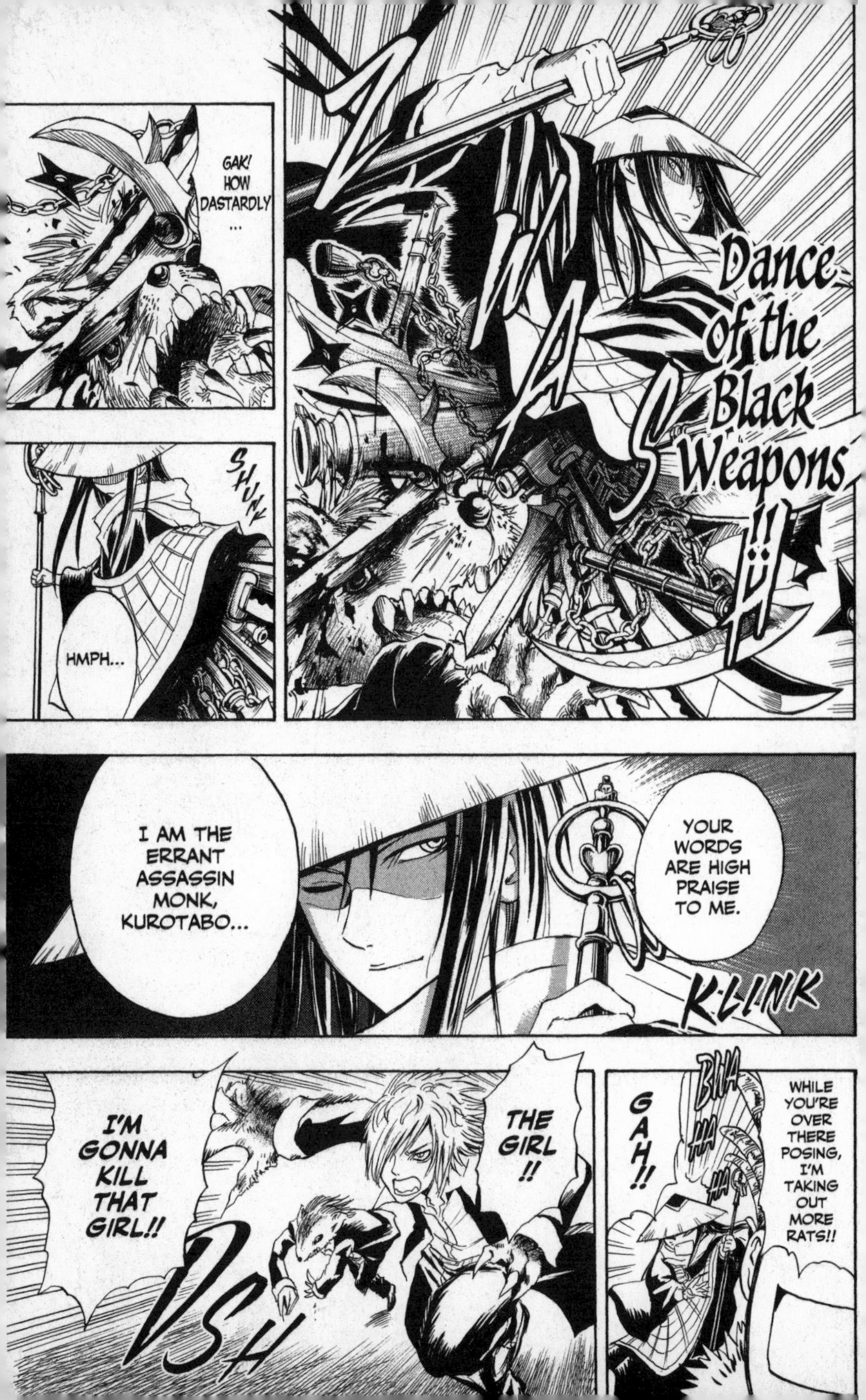
Dance of the Black Weapons!!!
GAK! HOW DASTARDLY ...
SHUNK
HMPH...
YOUR WORDS ARE HIGH PRAISE TO ME.
K-L-I-N-K
I AM THE ERRANT ASSASSIN MONK, KUROTABO...
WHILE YOU'RE OVER THERE POSING, I'M TAKING OUT MORE RATS!!
BWA HA HA
GAH!!
THE GIRL !!
I'M GONNA KILL THAT GIRL!!
VSH

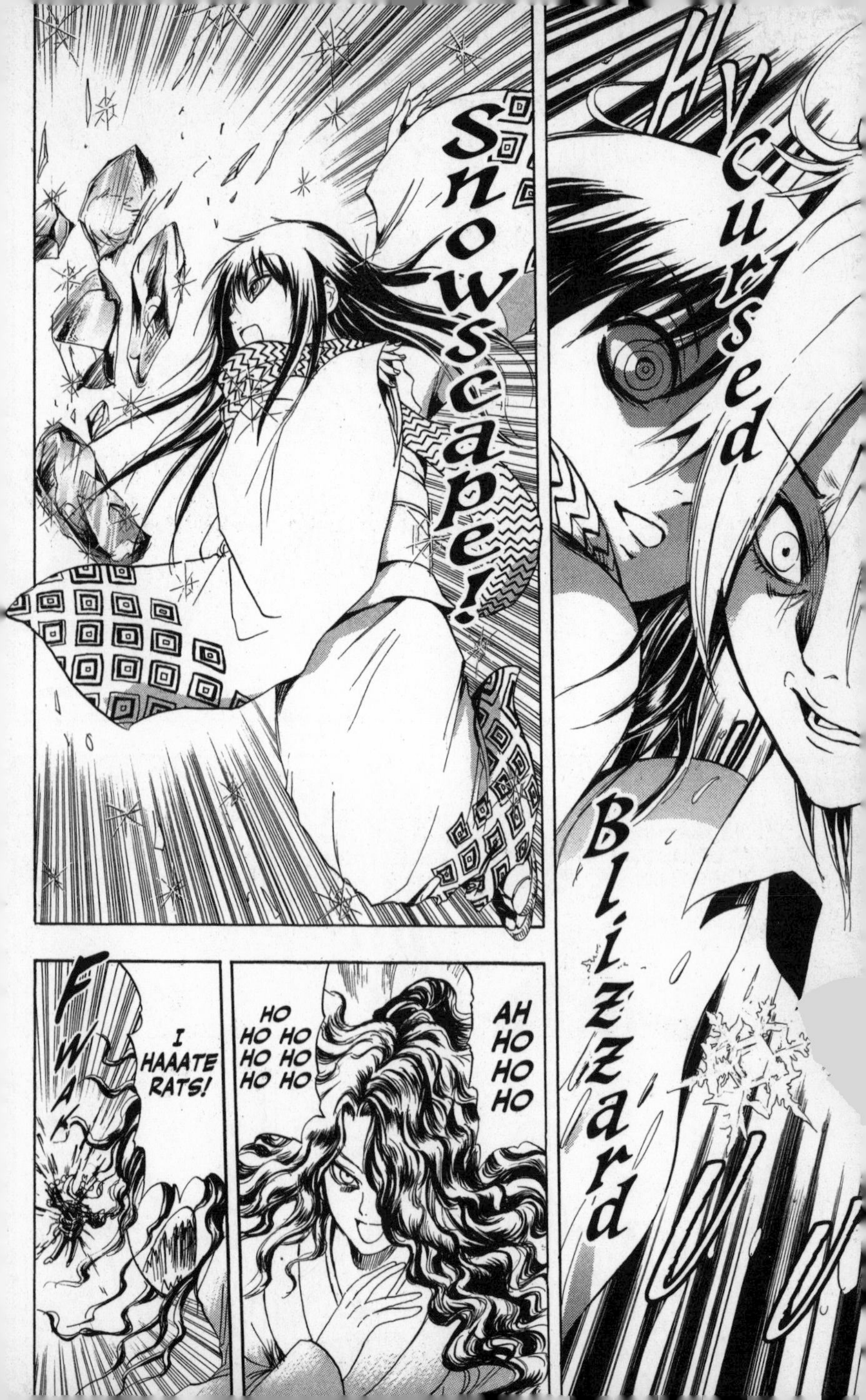
Accursed Blizzard
Snowscape!
AH HO HO HO HO
HO HO HO HO HO HO HO
I HAAATE RATS!
FWAK

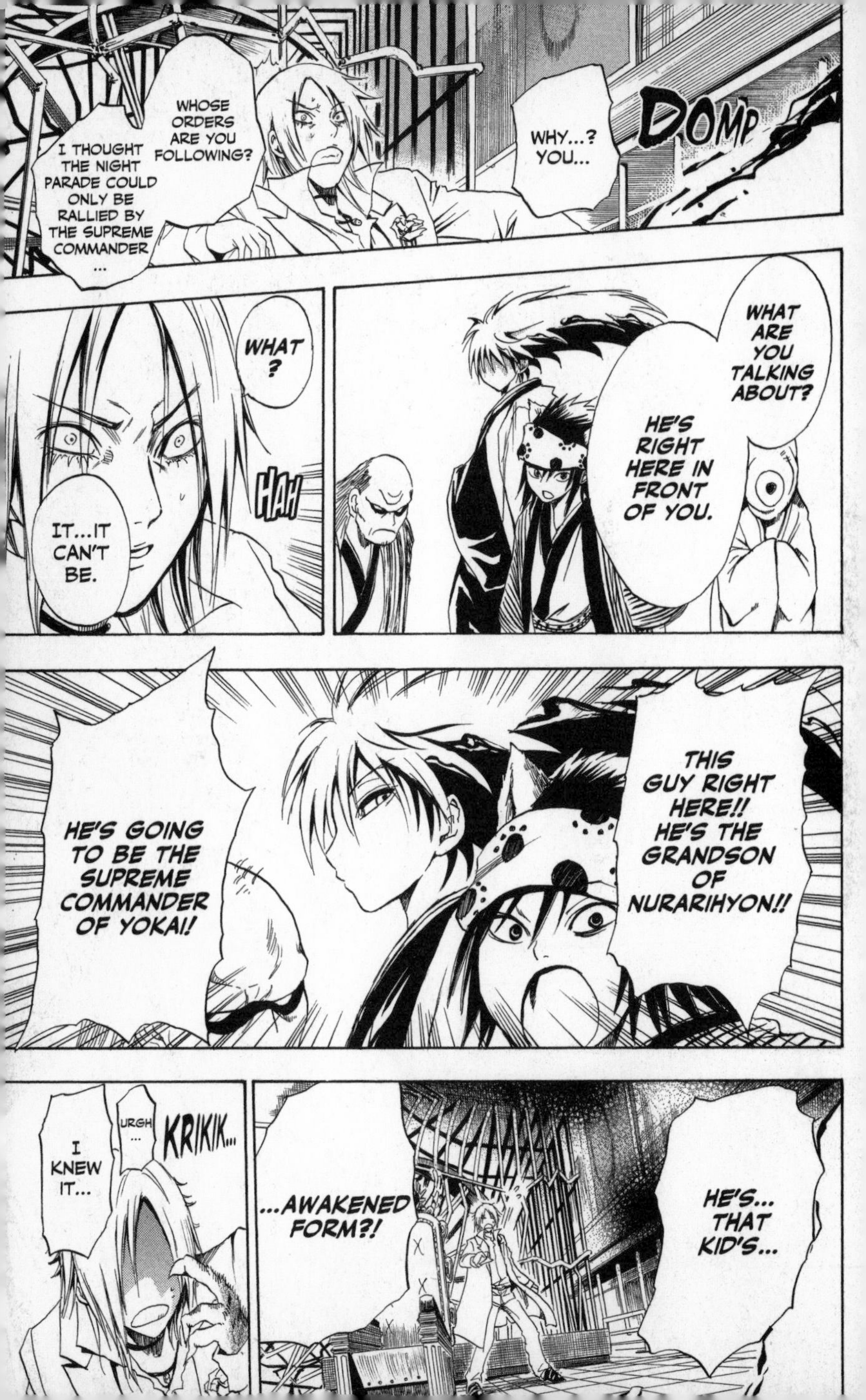
DOMP
WHY...? YOU...
WHOSE ORDERS ARE YOU FOLLOWING?
I THOUGHT THE NIGHT PARADE COULD ONLY BE RALLIED BY THE SUPREME COMMANDER ...
WHAT ARE YOU TALKING ABOUT?
HE'S RIGHT HERE IN FRONT OF YOU.
HAH
WHAT?
IT...IT CAN'T BE.
THIS GUY RIGHT HERE!! HE'S THE GRANDSON OF NURARIHYON!!
HE'S GOING TO BE THE SUPREME COMMANDER OF YOKAI!
HE'S... THAT KID'S...
...AWAKENED FORM?!
KRIKIK...
URGH ...
I KNEW IT...

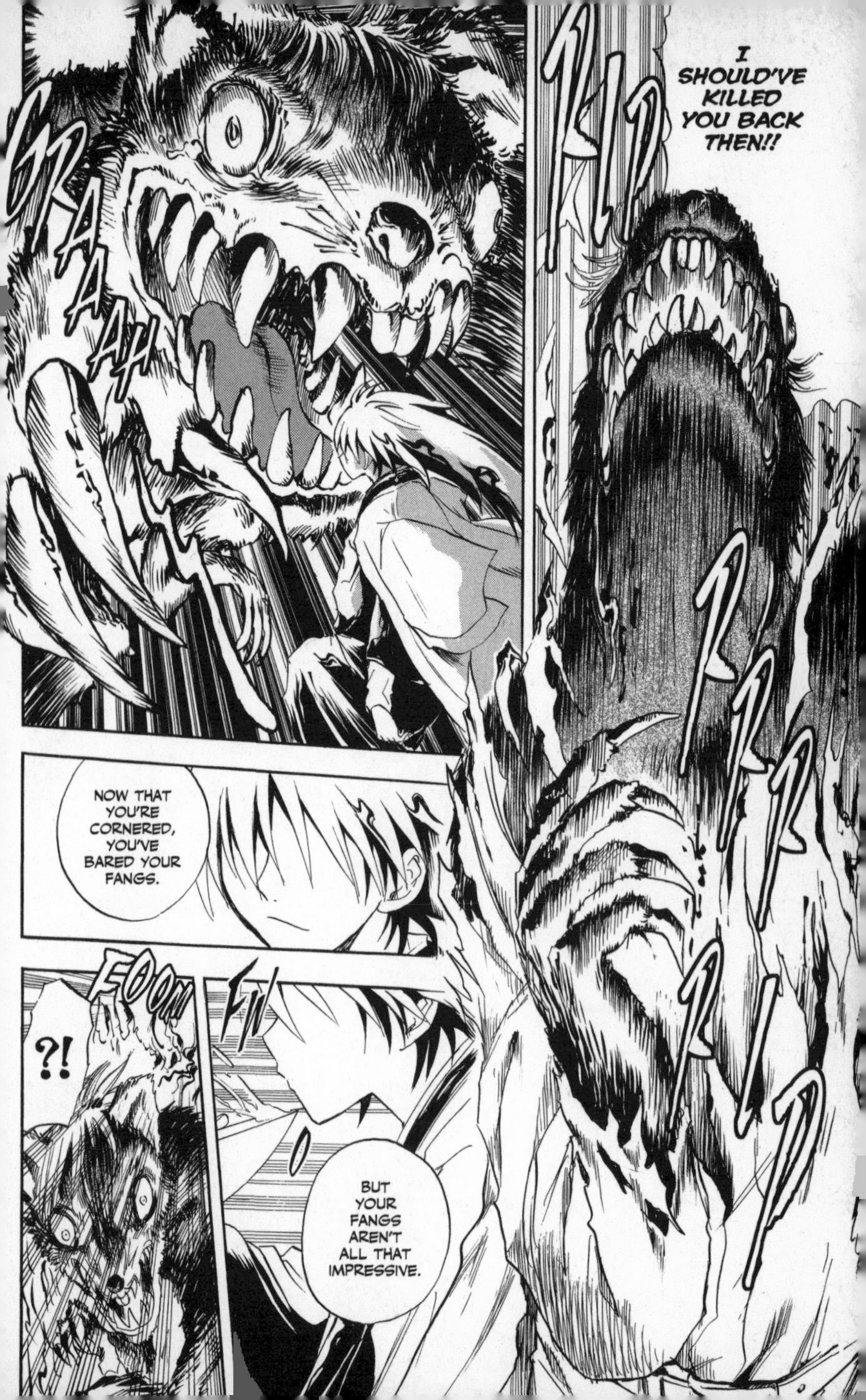
I SHOULD'VE KILLED YOU BACK THEN!!
GRAAAAH
NOW THAT YOU'RE CORNERED, YOU'VE BARED YOUR FANGS.
BUT YOUR FANGS AREN'T ALL THAT IMPRESSIVE.
FOOM
?!

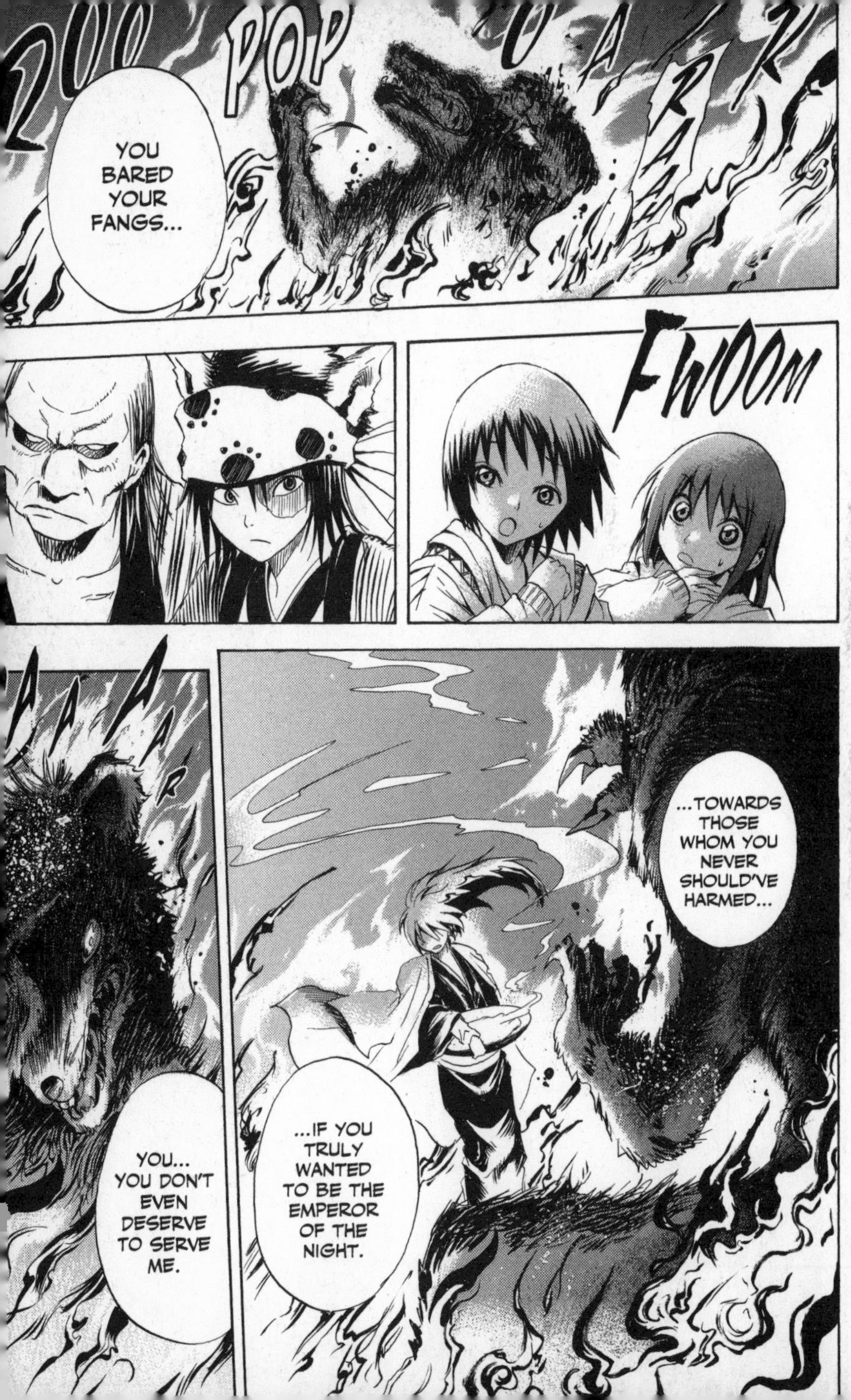
POP
YOU BARED YOUR FANGS...
FWOOM
...TOWARDS THOSE WHOM YOU NEVER SHOULD'VE HARMED...
...IF YOU TRULY WANTED TO BE THE EMPEROR OF THE NIGHT.
YOU... YOU DON'T EVEN DESERVE TO SERVE ME.

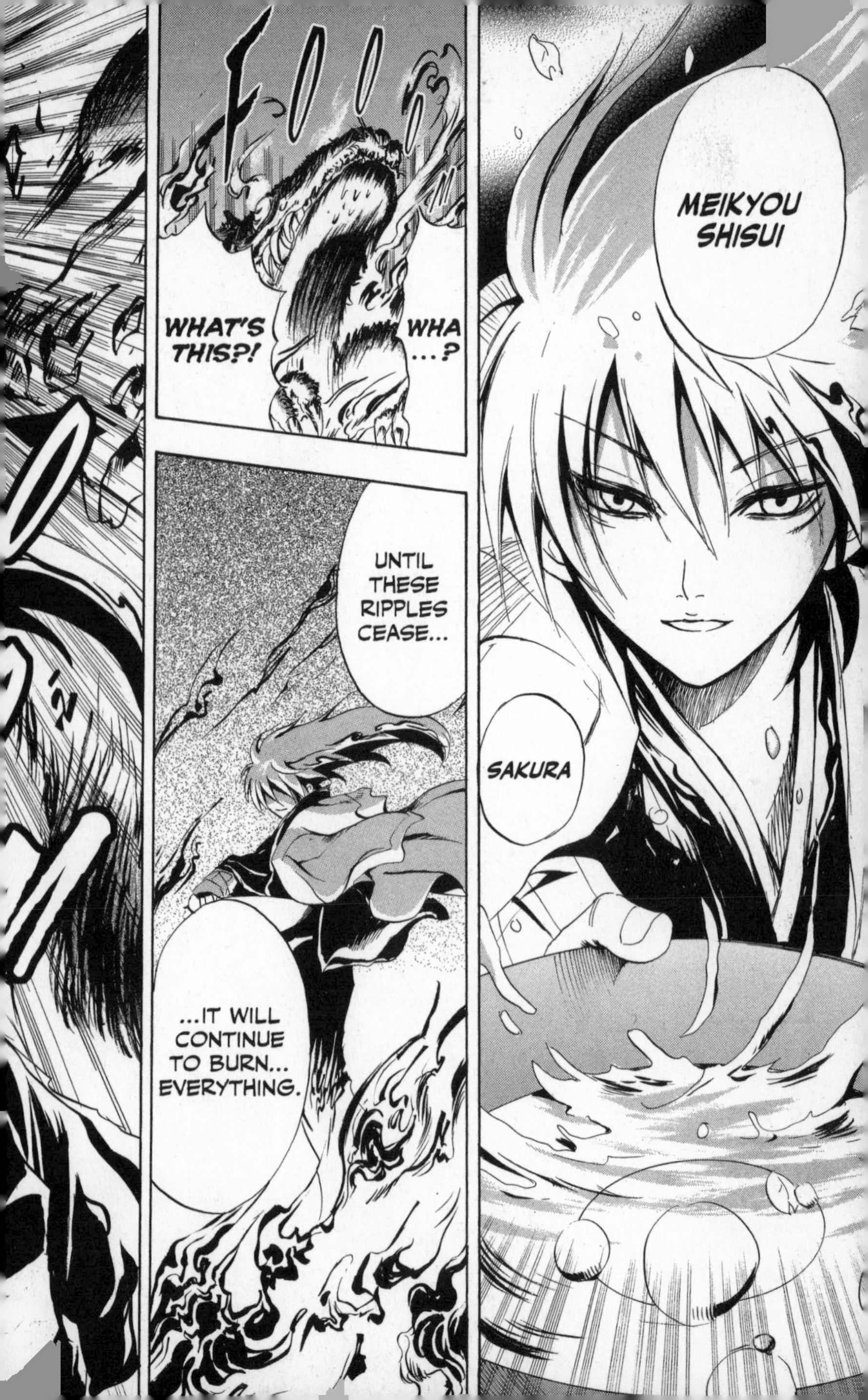
MEIKYOU SHISUI
SAKURA
FOOO
WHA...?
WHAT'S THIS?!
UNTIL THESE RIPPLES CEASE...
...IT WILL CONTINUE TO BURN... EVERYTHING.

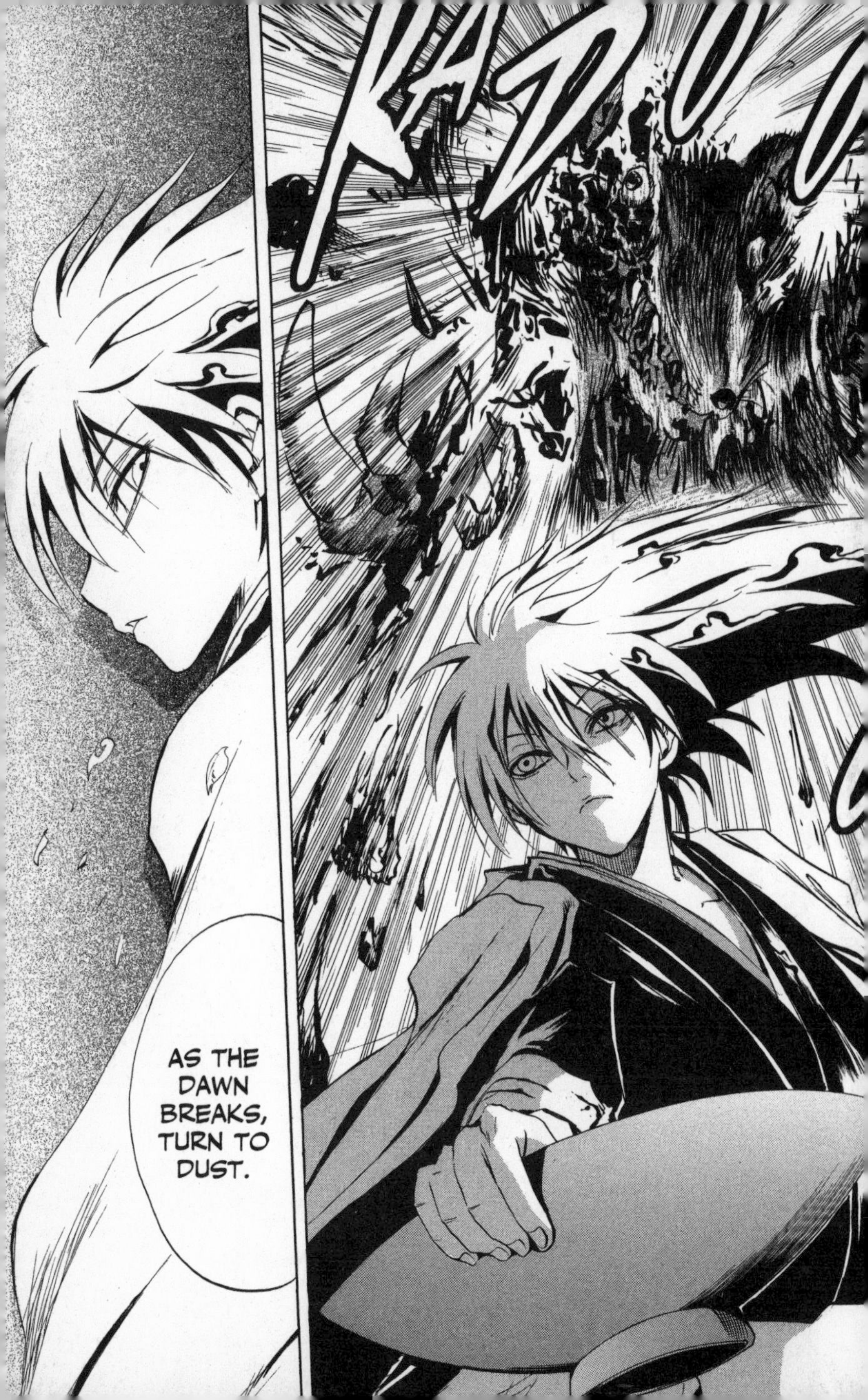
AS THE DAWN BREAKS, TURN TO DUST.

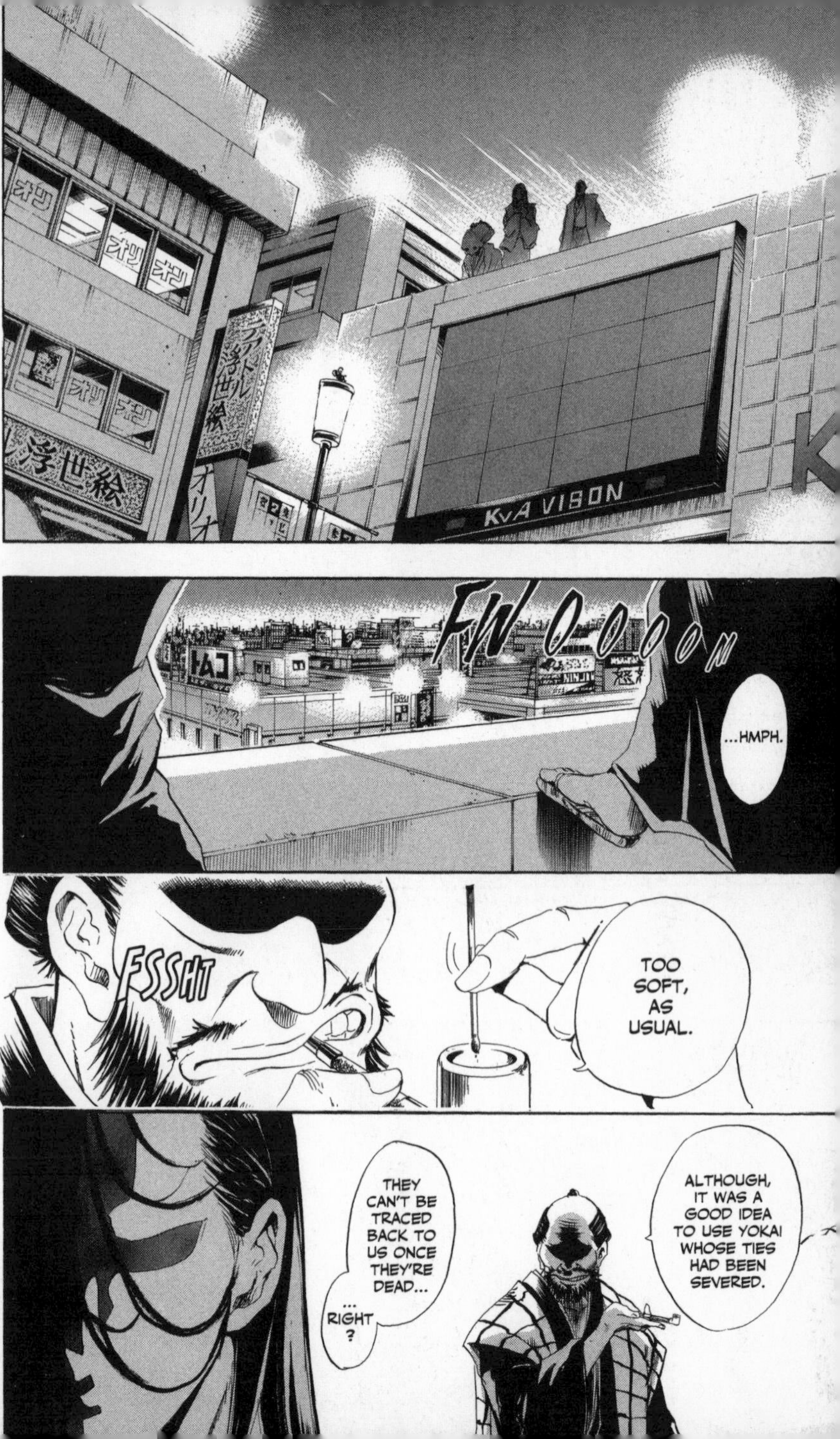

浮世絵
KvA VISON
FWOOOOOM
...HMPH.
TOO SOFT, AS USUAL.
FSSHT
ALTHOUGH, IT WAS A GOOD IDEA TO USE YOKAI WHOSE TIES HAD BEEN SEVERED.
THEY CAN'T BE TRACED BACK TO US ONCE THEY'RE DEAD...
...RIGHT?

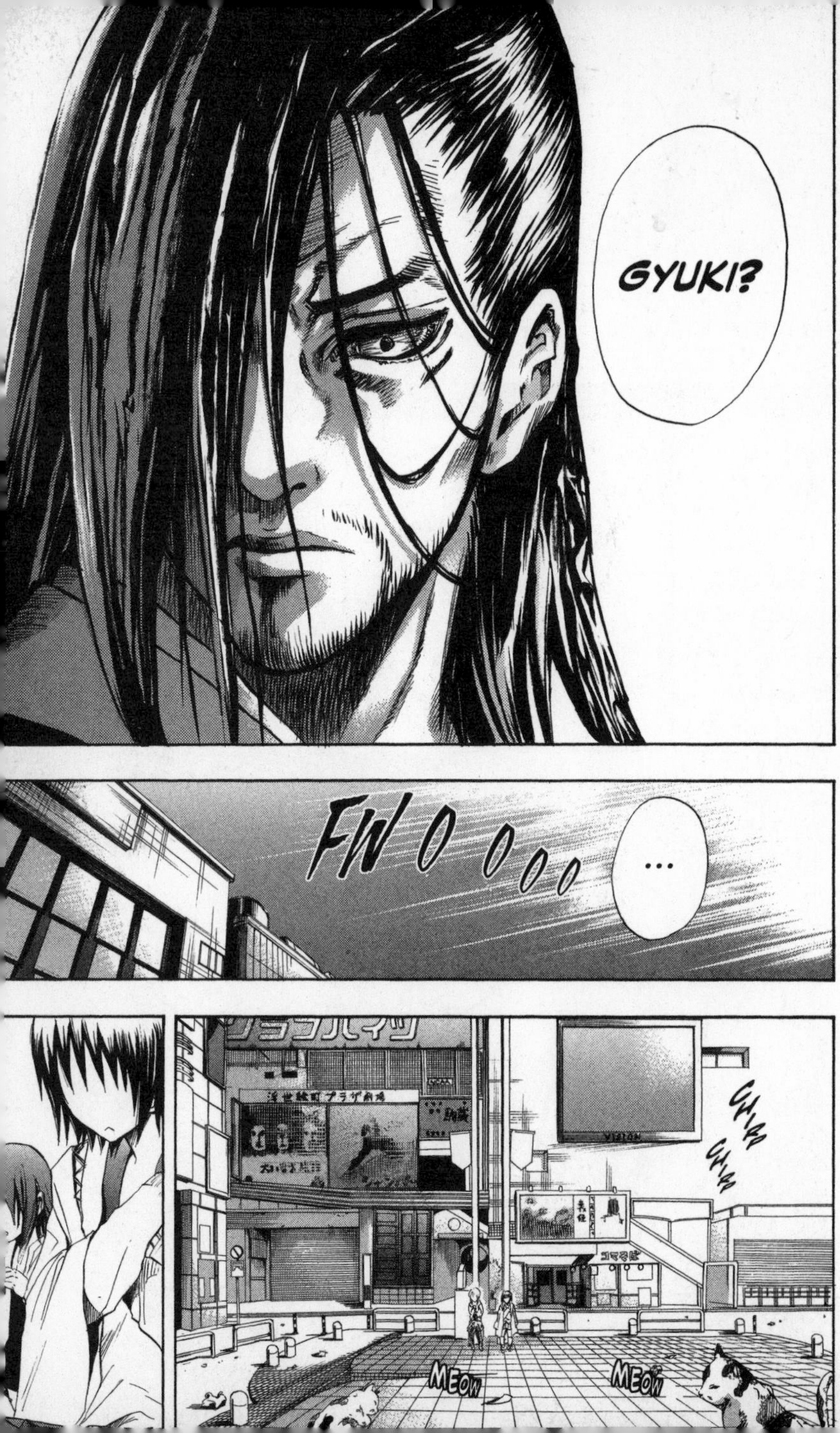
GYUKI?
FWOOOO
...
CHIRP
CHIRP
MEOW
MEOW

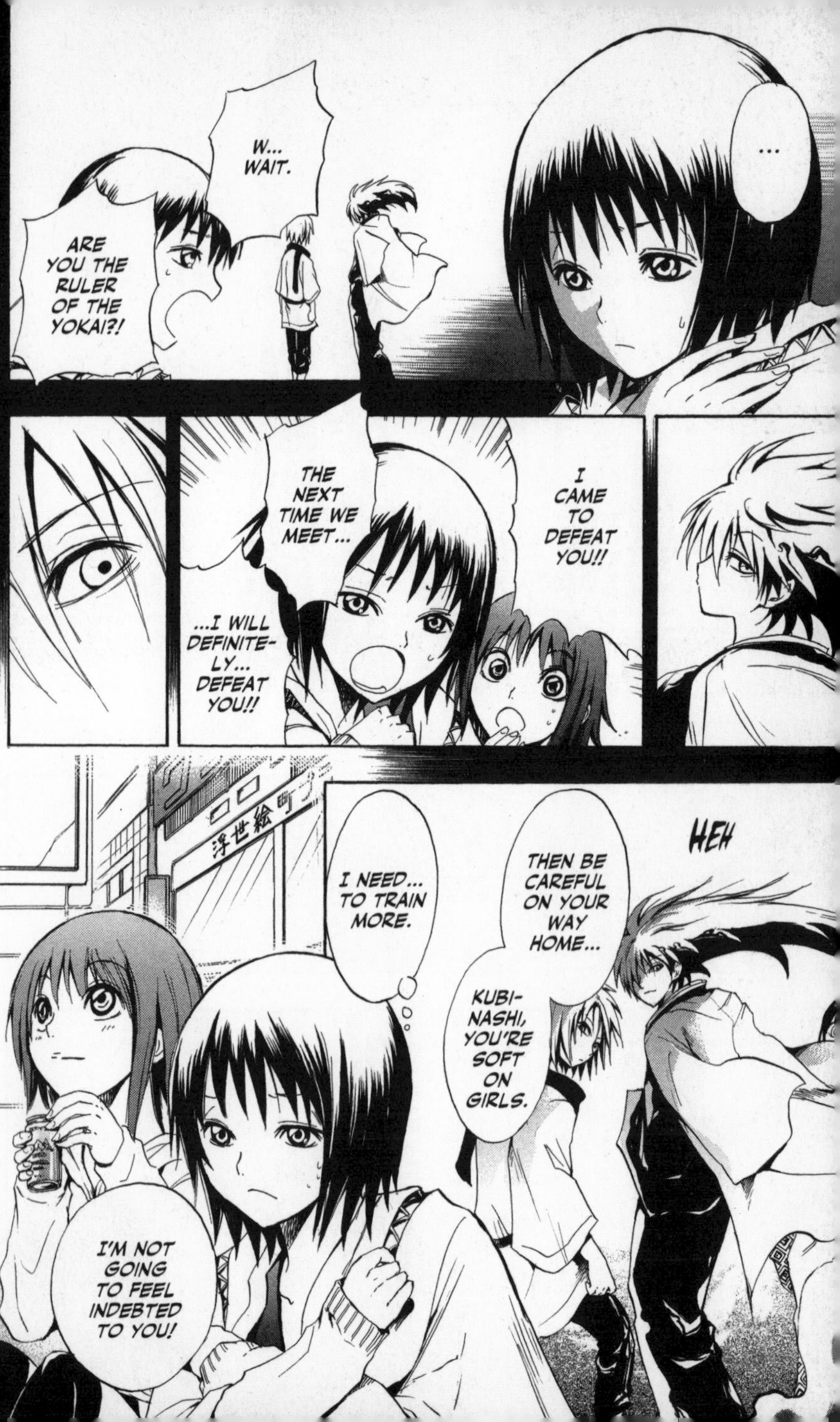
...
W... WAIT.
ARE YOU THE RULER OF THE YOKAI?!
I CAME TO DEFEAT YOU!!
THE NEXT TIME WE MEET...
...I WILL DEFINITE-LY... DEFEAT YOU!!
HEH
THEN BE CAREFUL ON YOUR WAY HOME...
KUBI-NASHI, YOU'RE SOFT ON GIRLS.
I NEED... TO TRAIN MORE.
浮世絵町
I'M NOT GOING TO FEEL INDEBTED TO YOU!

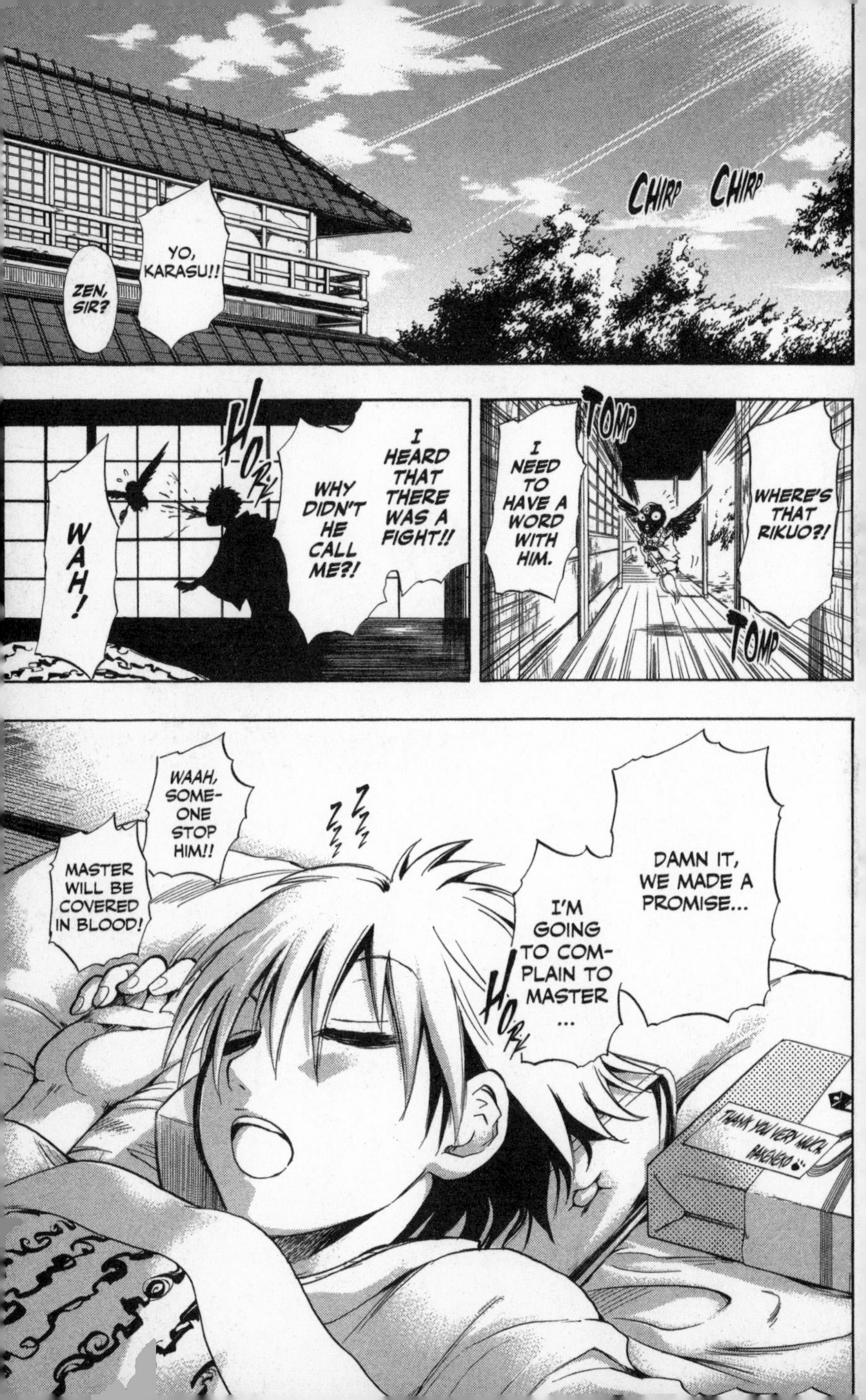
CHIRP CHIRP
YO, KARASU!!
ZEN, SIR?
WHERE'S THAT RIKUO?!
TOMP
I NEED TO HAVE A WORD WITH HIM.
TOMP
I HEARD THAT THERE WAS A FIGHT!!
WHY DIDN'T HE CALL ME?!
HORK
WAH!
DAMN IT, WE MADE A PROMISE...
I'M GOING TO COMPLAIN TO MASTER...
HORK
WAAH, SOMEONE STOP HIM!!
MASTER WILL BE COVERED IN BLOOD!
THANK YOU VERY MUCH, BAKENEKO

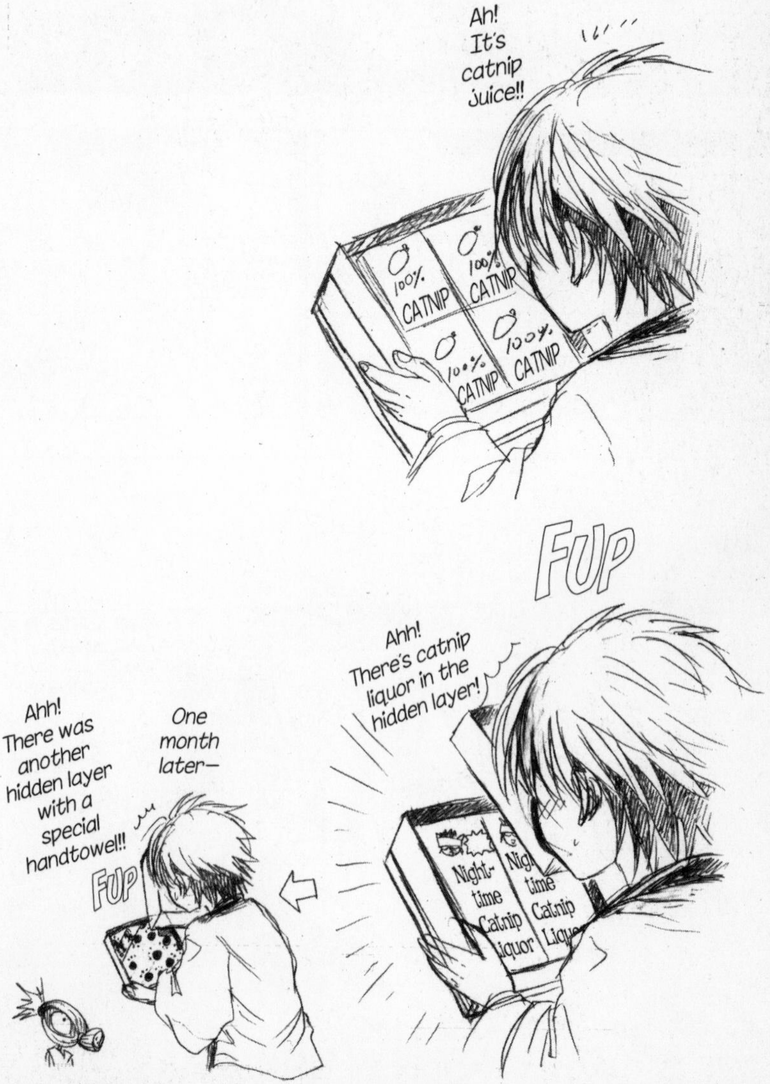
Ah! It's catnip juice!!
100% CATNIP
100% CATNIP
100% CATNIP
100% CATNIP
FUP
Ahh! There's catnip liquor in the hidden layer!
Night-time Catnip Liquor
One month later—
Ahh! There was another hidden layer with a special handtowel!!
FUP

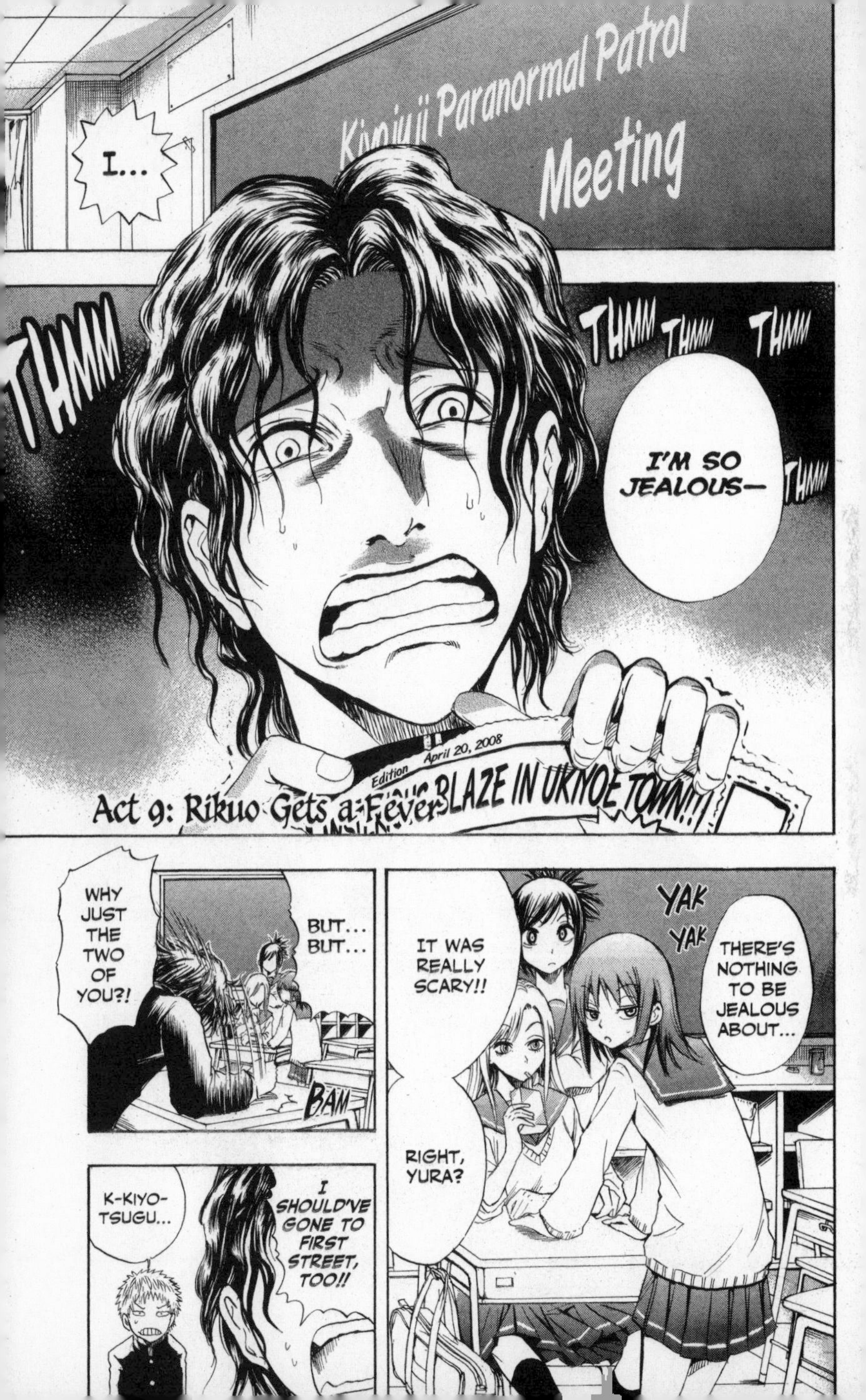
Kiyojuji Paranormal Patrol
Meeting
I...
THMM THMM THMM
I'M SO JEALOUS—
THMM
THMM
April 20, 2008
Edition
BLAZE IN UKIYOE TOWN!!
Act 9: Rikuo Gets a Fever
YAK YAK
THERE'S NOTHING TO BE JEALOUS ABOUT...
IT WAS REALLY SCARY!!
RIGHT, YURA?
BUT... BUT...
WHY JUST THE TWO OF YOU?!
BAM
I SHOULD'VE GONE TO FIRST STREET, TOO!!
K-KIYOTSUGU...

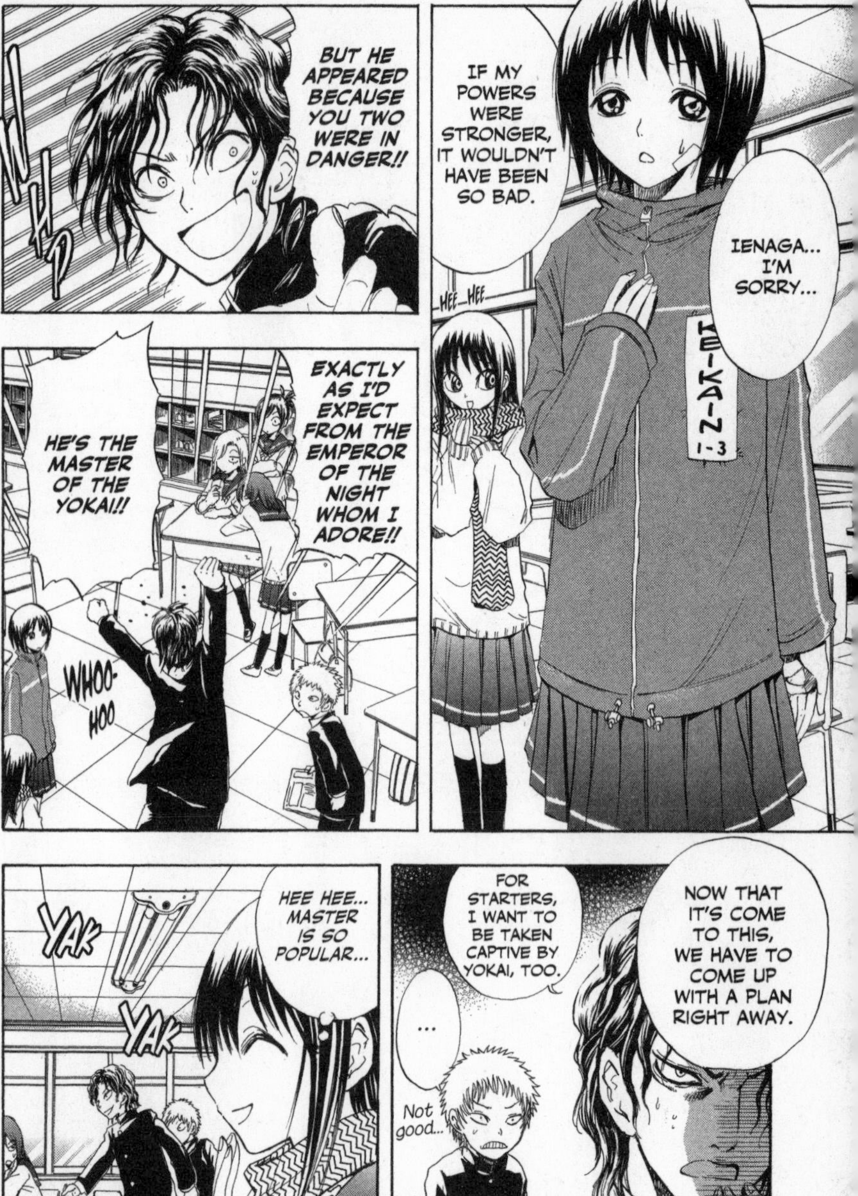
IENAGA... I'M SORRY...
IF MY POWERS WERE STRONGER, IT WOULDN'T HAVE BEEN SO BAD.
HEE HEE
KEIKAIN 1-3
BUT HE APPEARED BECAUSE YOU TWO WERE IN DANGER!!
WHIP
EXACTLY AS I'D EXPECT FROM THE EMPEROR OF THE NIGHT WHOM I ADORE!!
HE'S THE MASTER OF THE YOKAI!!
WHOO-HOO
NOW THAT IT'S COME TO THIS, WE HAVE TO COME UP WITH A PLAN RIGHT AWAY.
FOR STARTERS, I WANT TO BE TAKEN CAPTIVE BY YOKAI, TOO.
...
Not good...
HEE HEE... MASTER IS SO POPULAR...
YAK
YAK

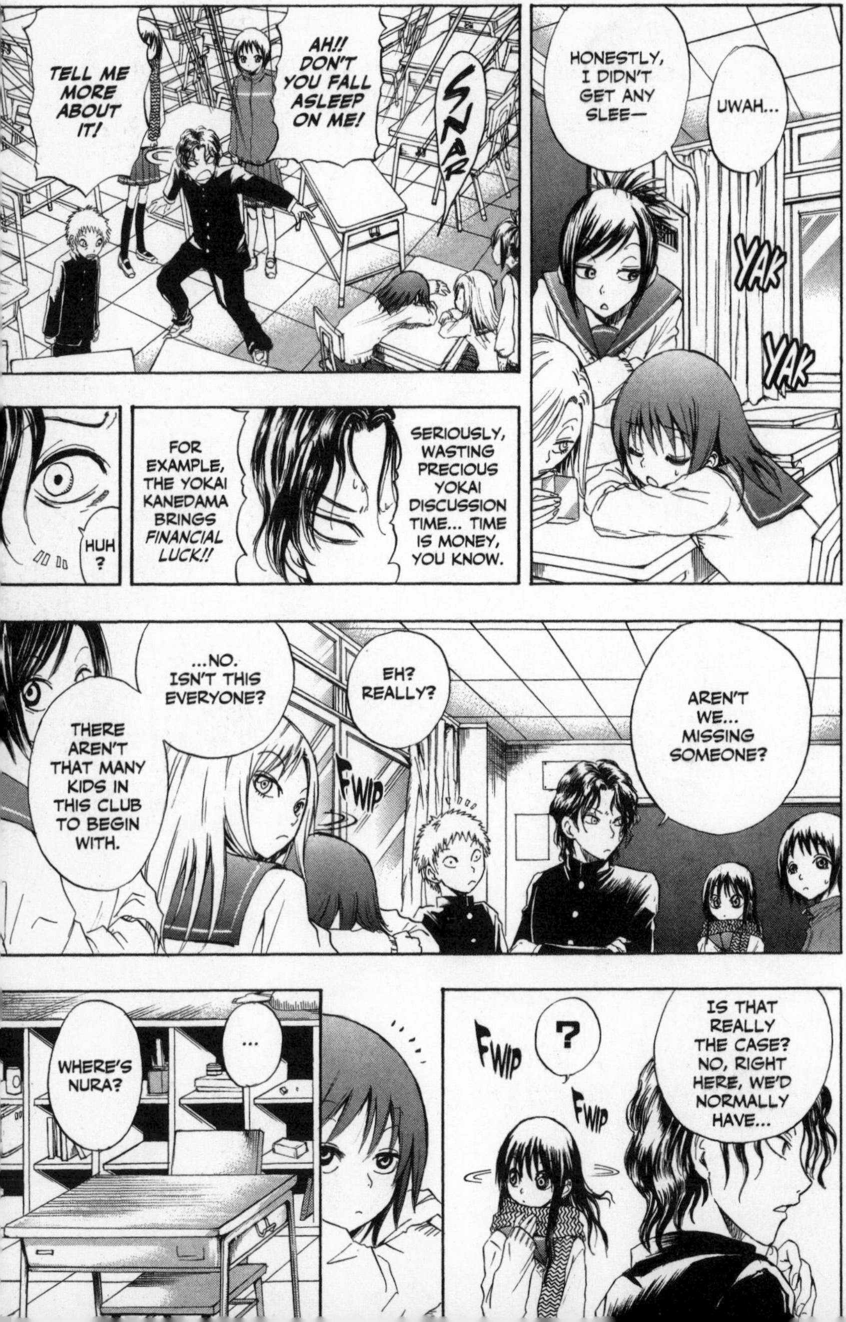

HONESTLY, I DIDN'T GET ANY SLEE—
UWAH...
YAK
YAK
SNAR
AH!! DON'T YOU FALL ASLEEP ON ME!
TELL ME MORE ABOUT IT!
SERIOUSLY, WASTING PRECIOUS YOKAI DISCUSSION TIME... TIME IS MONEY, YOU KNOW.
FOR EXAMPLE, THE YOKAI KANEDAMA BRINGS FINANCIAL LUCK!!
HUH ?
AREN'T WE... MISSING SOMEONE?
EH? REALLY?
FWIP
...NO. ISN'T THIS EVERYONE?
THERE AREN'T THAT MANY KIDS IN THIS CLUB TO BEGIN WITH.
IS THAT REALLY THE CASE? NO, RIGHT HERE, WE'D NORMALLY HAVE...
?
FWIP
FWIP
...
WHERE'S NURA?

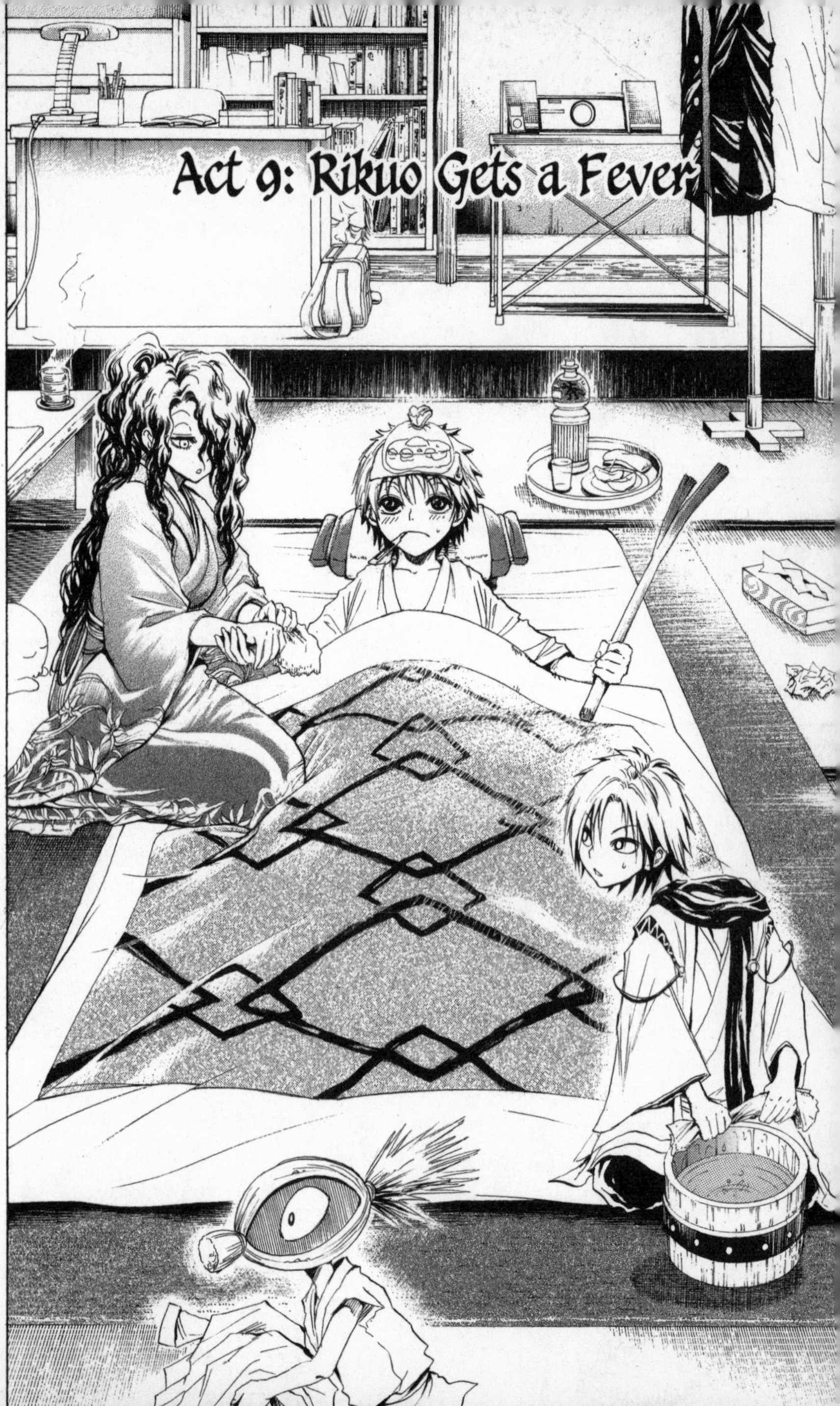
Act 9: Rikuo Gets a Fever

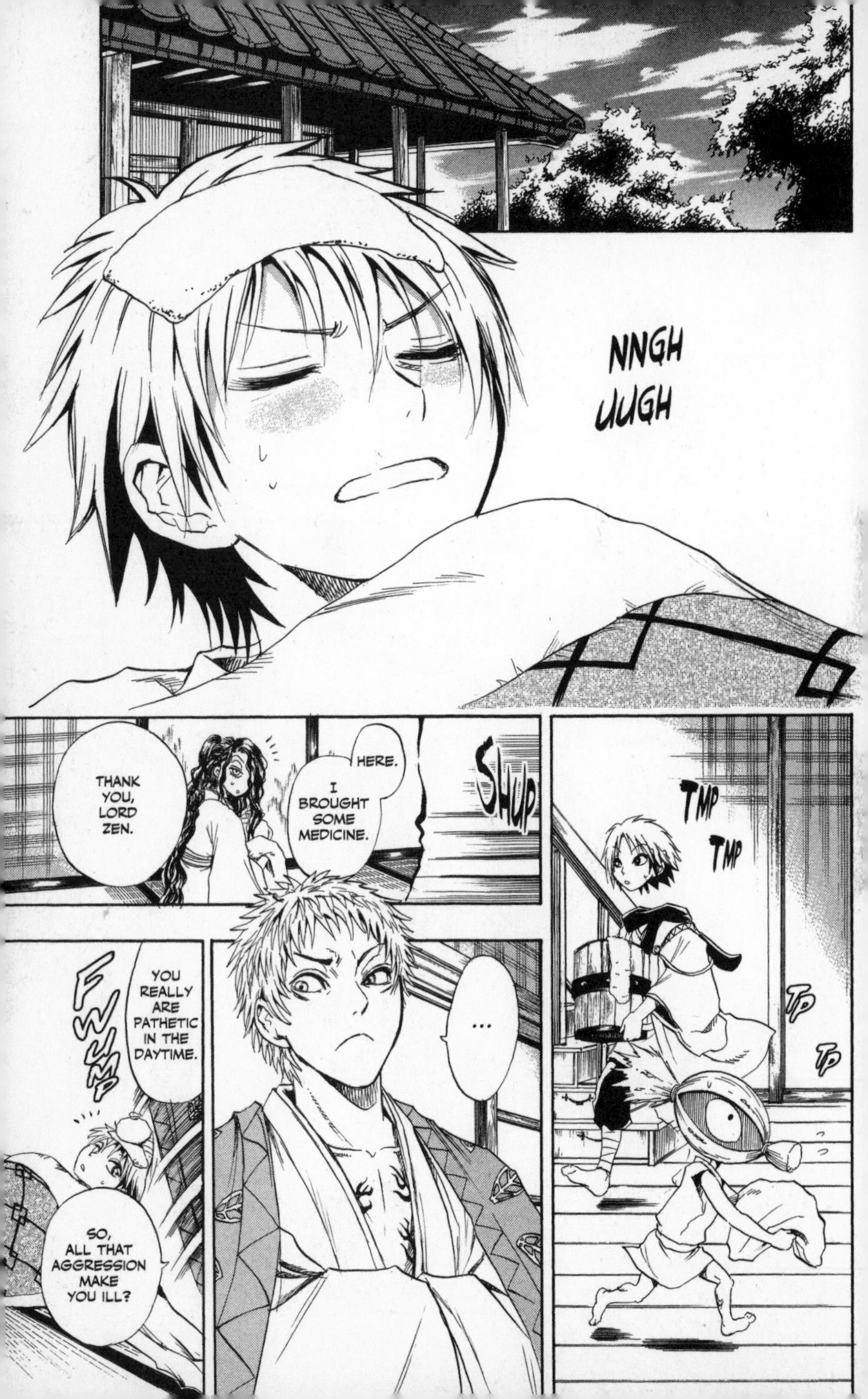
NNGH
UUGH
TMP
TMP
TP
TP
SHUP
HERE.
I BROUGHT SOME MEDICINE.
THANK YOU, LORD ZEN.
...
YOU REALLY ARE PATHETIC IN THE DAYTIME.
FWUMP
SO, ALL THAT AGGRESSION MAKE YOU ILL?

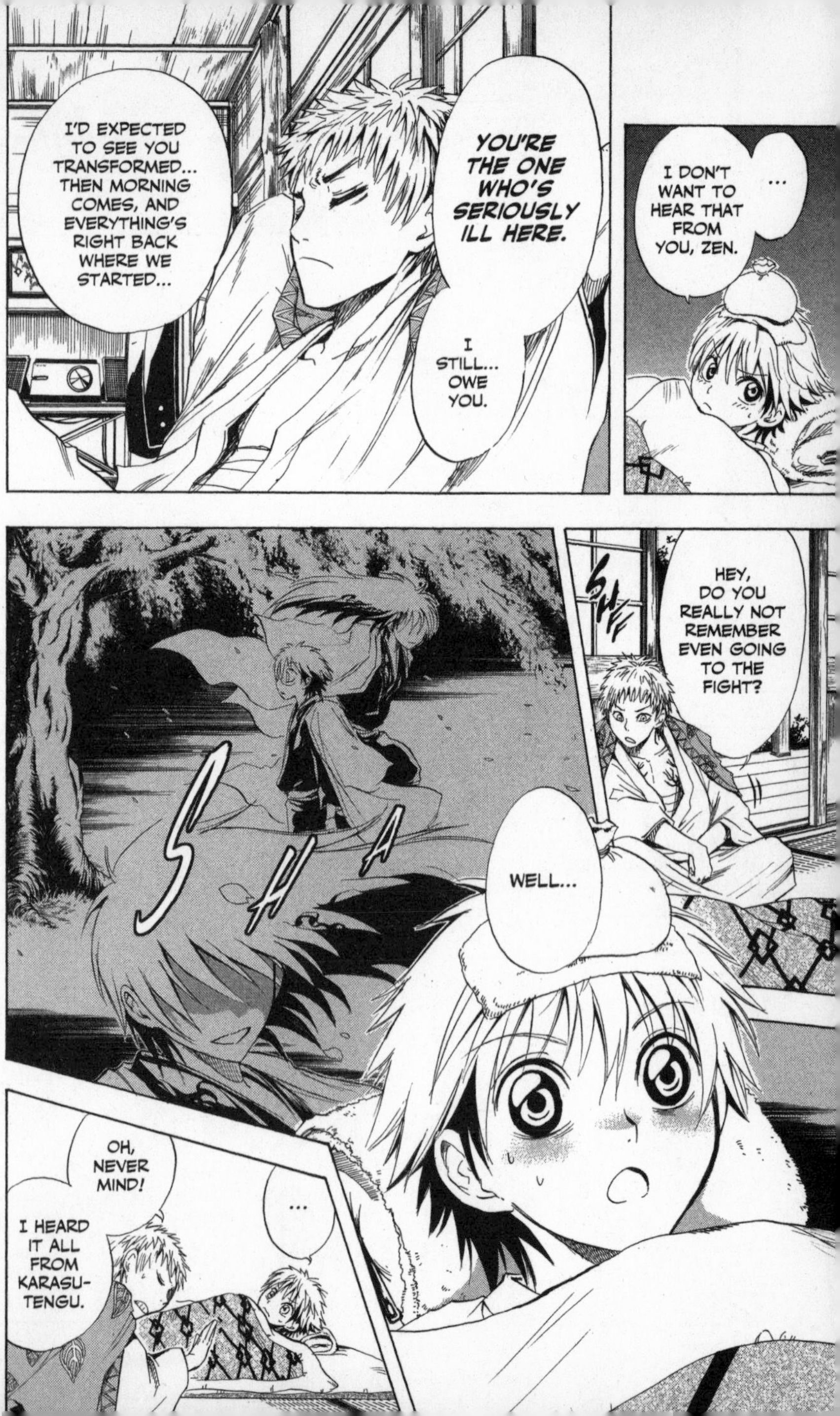
...
I DON'T WANT TO HEAR THAT FROM YOU, ZEN.
YOU'RE THE ONE WHO'S SERIOUSLY ILL HERE.
I'D EXPECTED TO SEE YOU TRANSFORMED... THEN MORNING COMES, AND EVERYTHING'S RIGHT BACK WHERE WE STARTED...
I STILL... OWE YOU.
SHF
HEY, DO YOU REALLY NOT REMEMBER EVEN GOING TO THE FIGHT?
WELL...
SHA
OH, NEVER MIND!
...
I HEARD IT ALL FROM KARASU-TENGU.

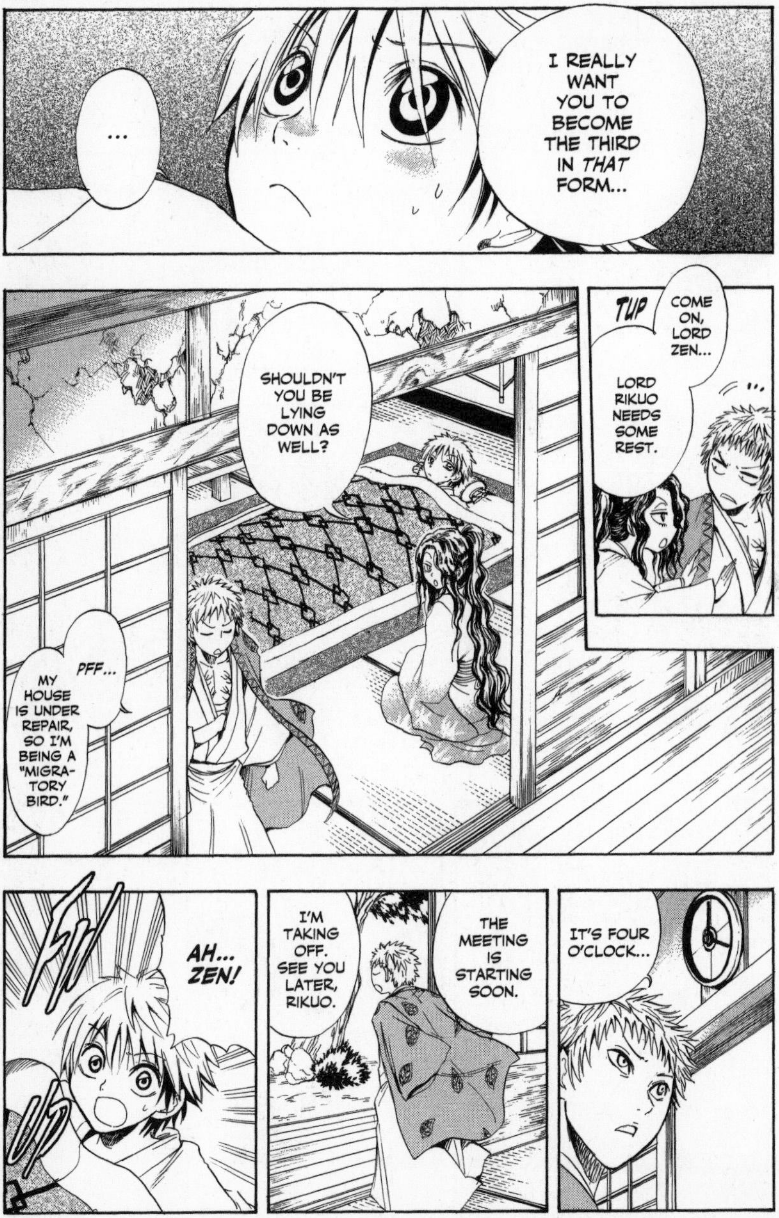
I REALLY WANT YOU TO BECOME THE THIRD IN *THAT* FORM...
...
TUP
COME ON, LORD ZEN...
LORD RIKUO NEEDS SOME REST.
...
SHOULDN'T YOU BE LYING DOWN AS WELL?
PFF...
MY HOUSE IS UNDER REPAIR, SO I'M BEING A "MIGRATORY BIRD."
IT'S FOUR O'CLOCK...
THE MEETING IS STARTING SOON.
I'M TAKING OFF. SEE YOU LATER, RIKUO.
AH... ZEN!

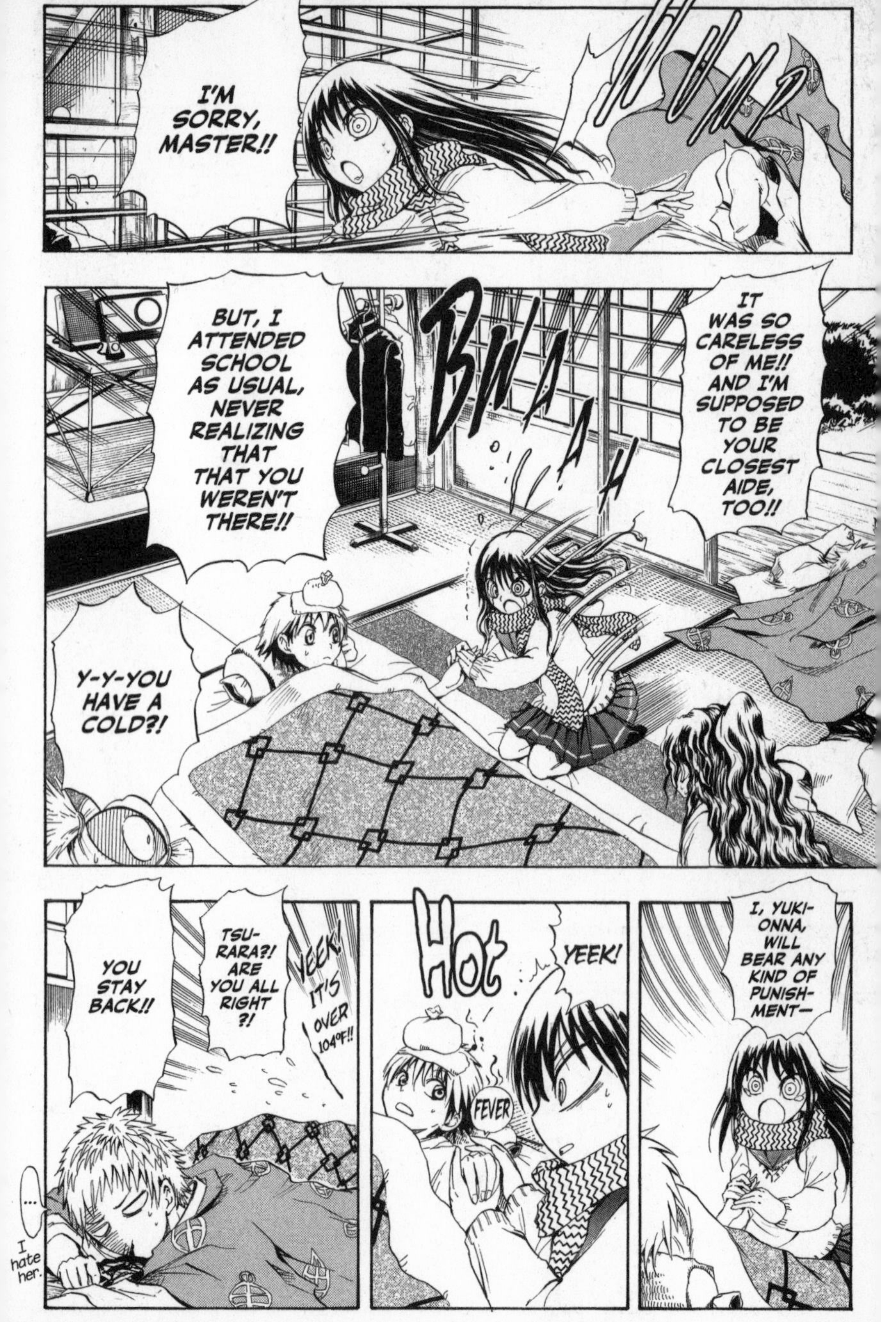
WHUMP
I'M SORRY, MASTER!!
IT WAS SO CARELESS OF ME!! AND I'M SUPPOSED TO BE YOUR CLOSEST AIDE, TOO!!
BWAAAH
BUT, I ATTENDED SCHOOL AS USUAL, NEVER REALIZING THAT THAT YOU WEREN'T THERE!!
Y-Y-YOU HAVE A COLD?!
I, YUKI-ONNA, WILL BEAR ANY KIND OF PUNISHMENT—
Hot
YEEK!
FEVER
YEEK! IT'S OVER 104°F!!
TSURARA?! ARE YOU ALL RIGHT ?!
YOU STAY BACK!!
...
I hate her.

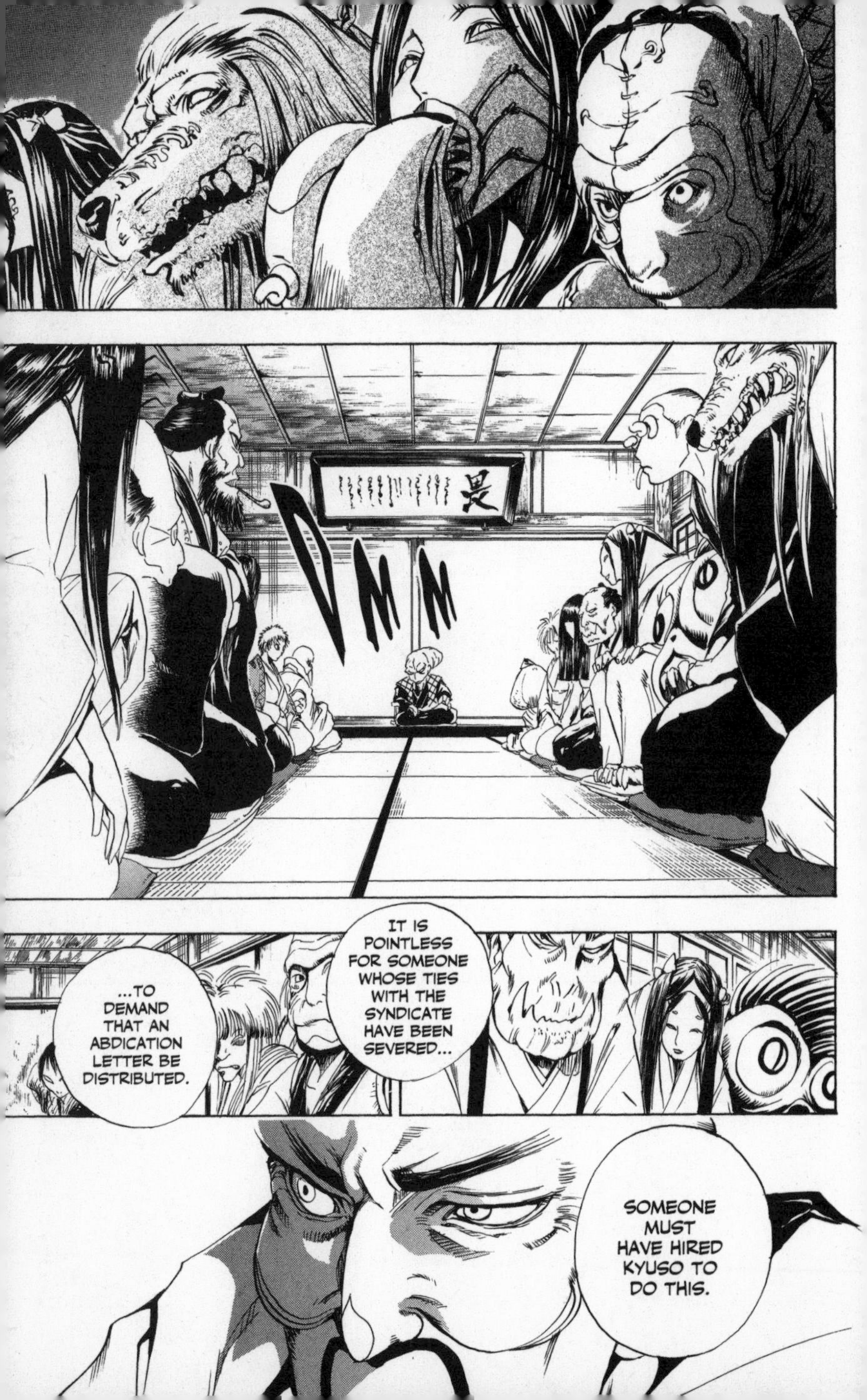
DMM
IT IS POINTLESS FOR SOMEONE WHOSE TIES WITH THE SYNDICATE HAVE BEEN SEVERED...
...TO DEMAND THAT AN ABDICATION LETTER BE DISTRIBUTED.
SOMEONE MUST HAVE HIRED KYUSO TO DO THIS.

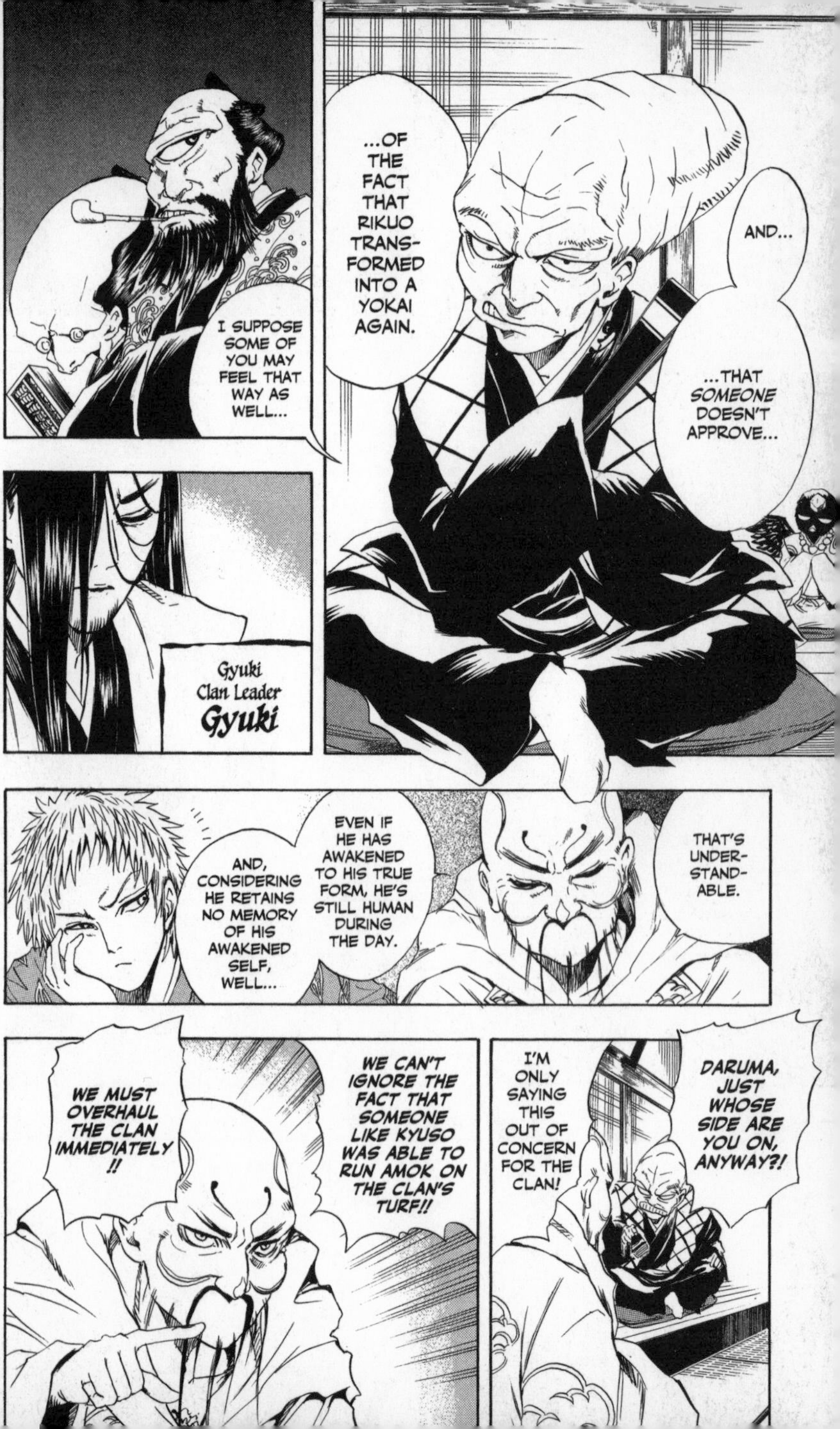
AND...
...THAT SOMEONE DOESN'T APPROVE...
...OF THE FACT THAT RIKUO TRANSFORMED INTO A YOKAI AGAIN.
I SUPPOSE SOME OF YOU MAY FEEL THAT WAY AS WELL...
Gyuki Clan Leader Gyuki
THAT'S UNDERSTANDABLE.
EVEN IF HE HAS AWAKENED TO HIS TRUE FORM, HE'S STILL HUMAN DURING THE DAY.
AND, CONSIDERING HE RETAINS NO MEMORY OF HIS AWAKENED SELF, WELL...
DARUMA, JUST WHOSE SIDE ARE YOU ON, ANYWAY?!
I'M ONLY SAYING THIS OUT OF CONCERN FOR THE CLAN!
WE CAN'T IGNORE THE FACT THAT SOMEONE LIKE KYUSO WAS ABLE TO RUN AMOK ON THE CLAN'S TURF!!
WE MUST OVERHAUL THE CLAN IMMEDIATELY!!

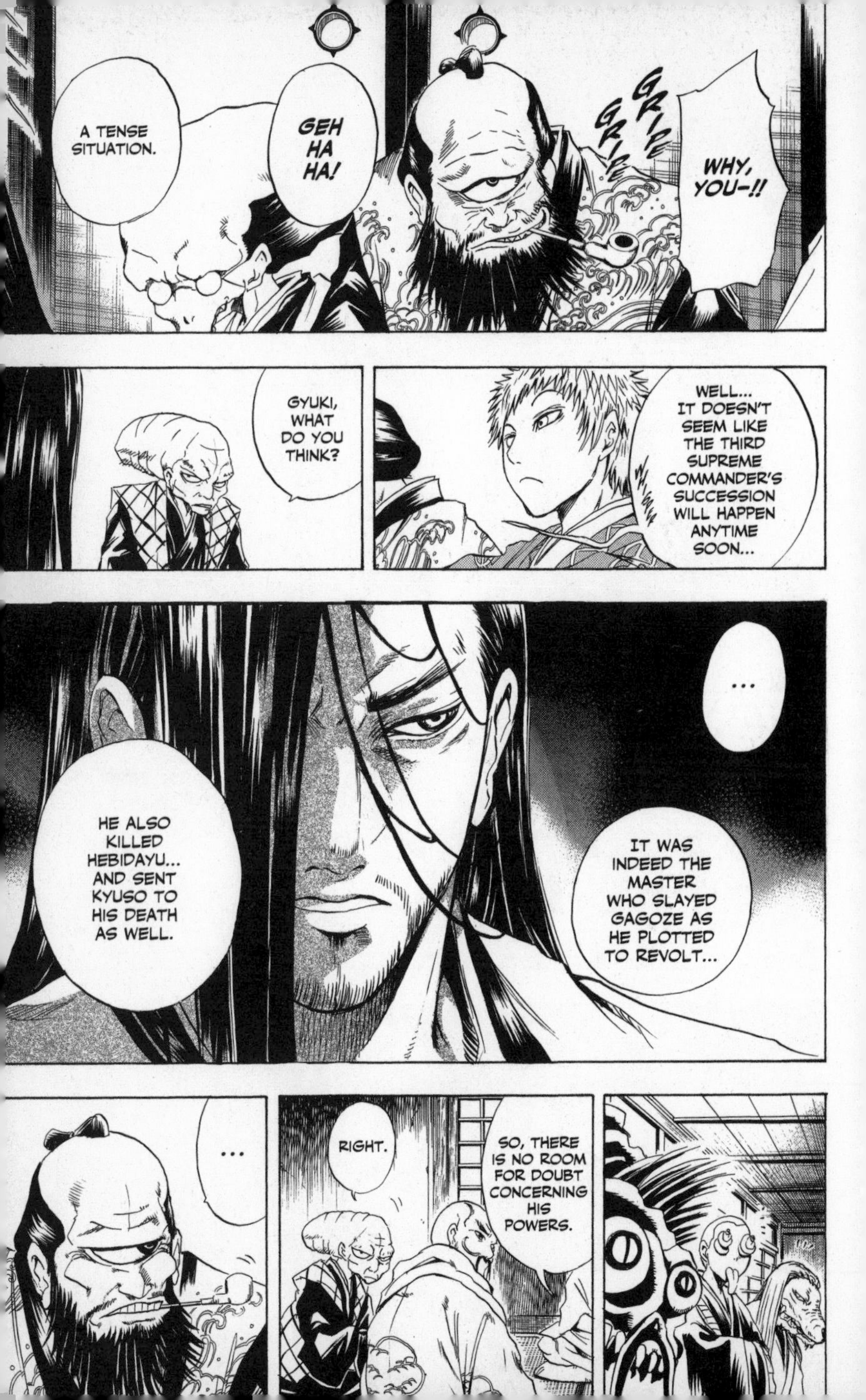

WHY, YOU-!!
GRIP GRIP
GEH HA HA!
A TENSE SITUATION.
WELL... IT DOESN'T SEEM LIKE THE THIRD SUPREME COMMANDER'S SUCCESSION WILL HAPPEN ANYTIME SOON...
GYUKI, WHAT DO YOU THINK?
...
IT WAS INDEED THE MASTER WHO SLAYED GAGOZE AS HE PLOTTED TO REVOLT...
HE ALSO KILLED HEBIDAYU... AND SENT KYUSO TO HIS DEATH AS WELL.
SO, THERE IS NO ROOM FOR DOUBT CONCERNING HIS POWERS.
RIGHT.
...

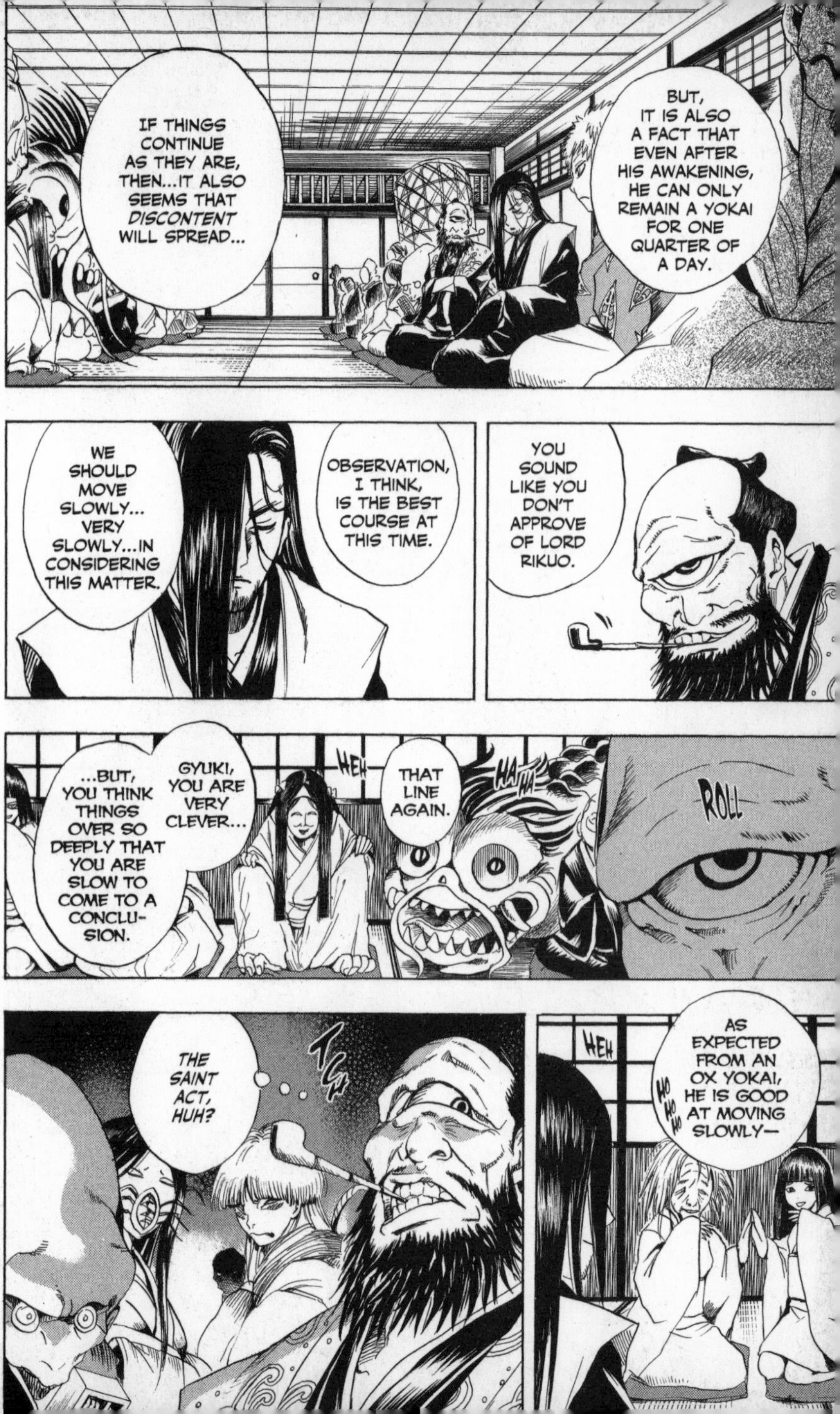
BUT, IT IS ALSO A FACT THAT EVEN AFTER HIS AWAKENING, HE CAN ONLY REMAIN A YOKAI FOR ONE QUARTER OF A DAY.
IF THINGS CONTINUE AS THEY ARE, THEN...IT ALSO SEEMS THAT *DISCONTENT* WILL SPREAD...
YOU SOUND LIKE YOU DON'T APPROVE OF LORD RIKUO.
OBSERVATION, I THINK, IS THE BEST COURSE AT THIS TIME.
WE SHOULD MOVE SLOWLY... VERY SLOWLY...IN CONSIDERING THIS MATTER.
ROLL
HA HA
THAT LINE AGAIN.
HEH
GYUKI, YOU ARE VERY CLEVER...
...BUT, YOU THINK THINGS OVER SO DEEPLY THAT YOU ARE SLOW TO COME TO A CONCLUSION.
AS EXPECTED FROM AN OX YOKAI, HE IS GOOD AT MOVING SLOWLY—
HO HO HO
HEH
TCH
THE SAINT ACT, HUH?

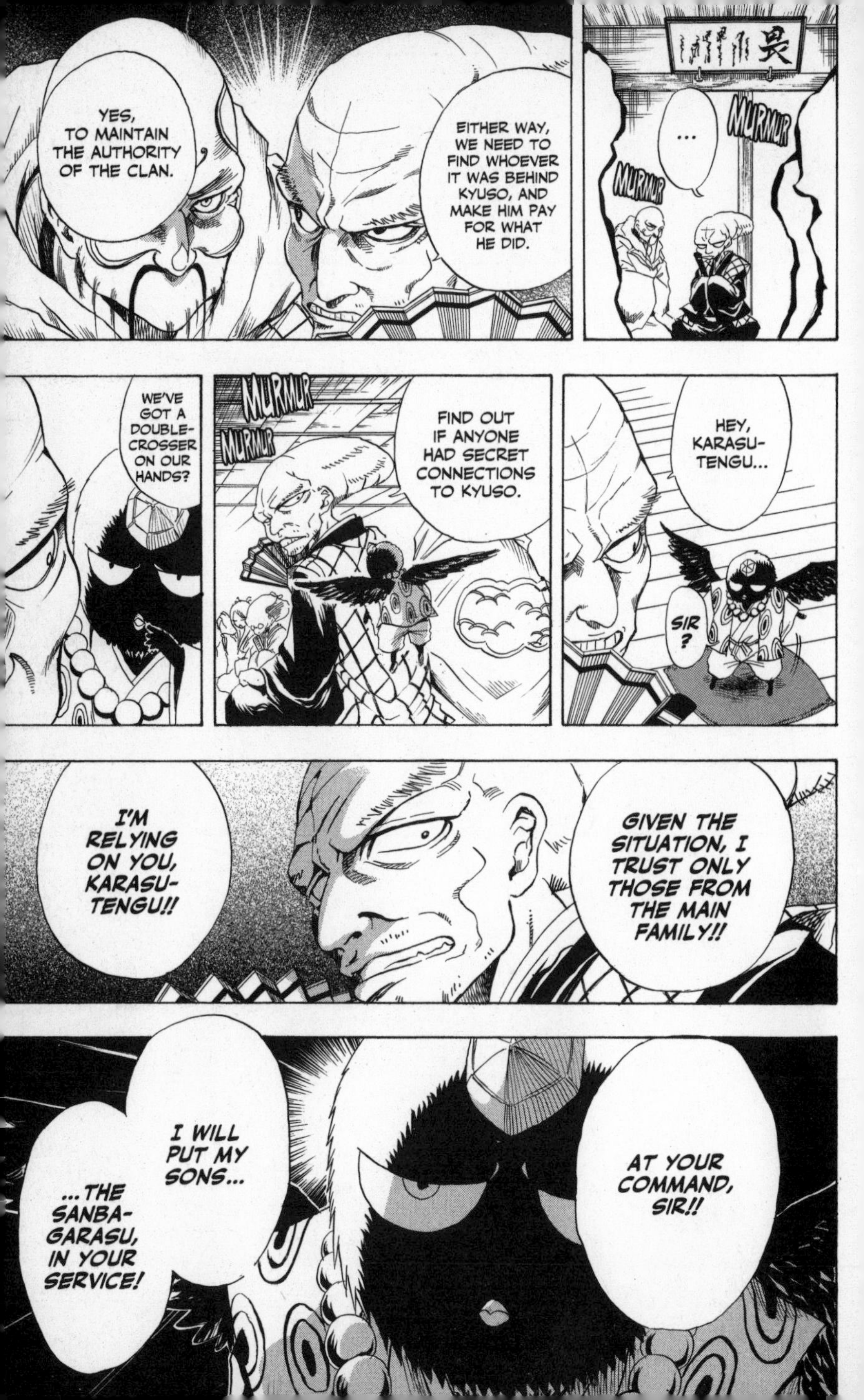
...
MURMUR
MURMUR
EITHER WAY, WE NEED TO FIND WHOEVER IT WAS BEHIND KYUSO, AND MAKE HIM PAY FOR WHAT HE DID.
YES, TO MAINTAIN THE AUTHORITY OF THE CLAN.
HEY, KARASU-TENGU...
SIR?
FIND OUT IF ANYONE HAD SECRET CONNECTIONS TO KYUSO.
MURMUR
MURMUR
WE'VE GOT A DOUBLE-CROSSER ON OUR HANDS?
GIVEN THE SITUATION, I TRUST ONLY THOSE FROM THE MAIN FAMILY!!
I'M RELYING ON YOU, KARASU-TENGU!!
AT YOUR COMMAND, SIR!!
I WILL PUT MY SONS...
...THE SANBA-GARASU, IN YOUR SERVICE!

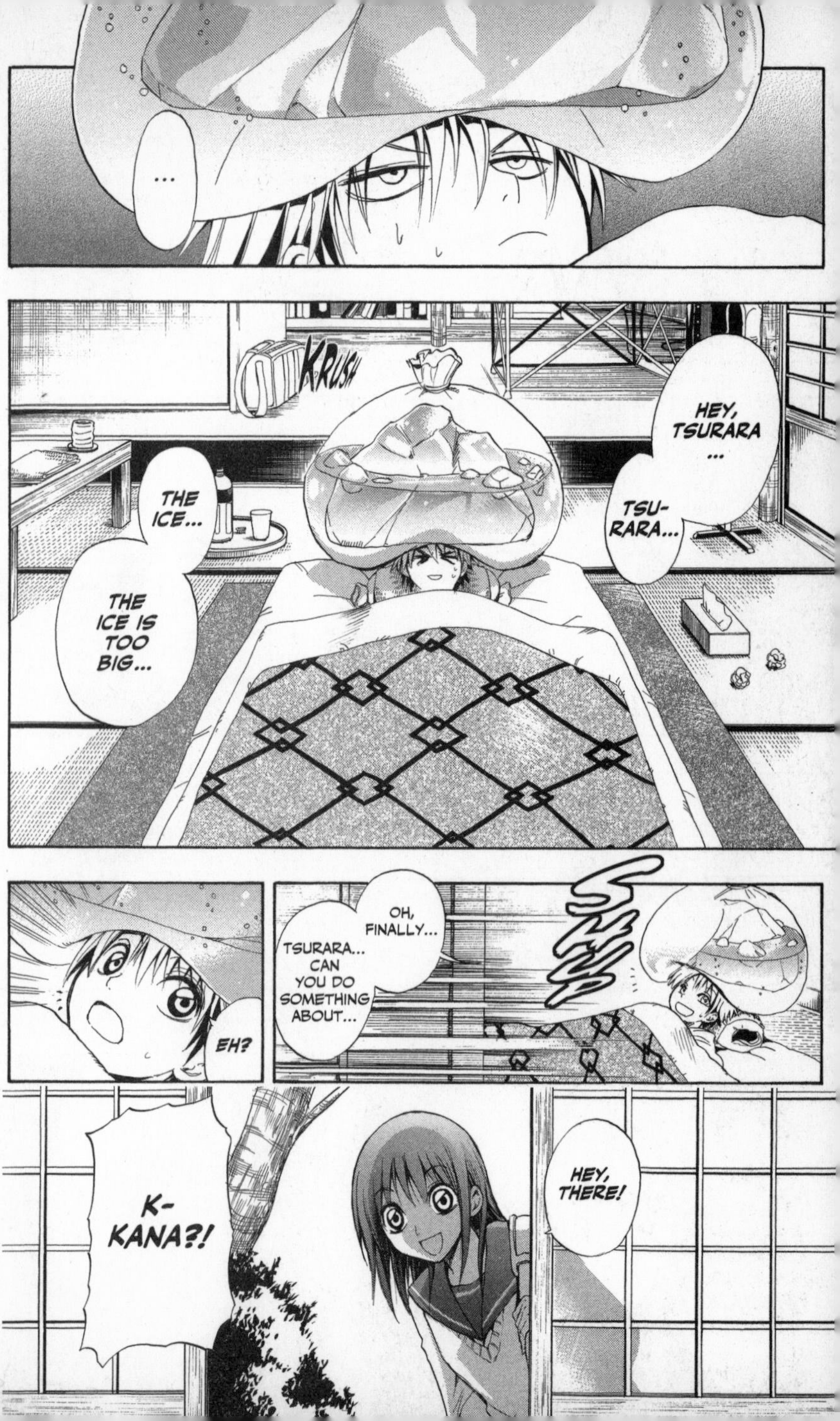
...
HEY, TSURARA ...
TSU-RARA...
KRUSH
THE ICE...
THE ICE IS TOO BIG...
OH, FINALLY...
TSURARA... CAN YOU DO SOMETHING ABOUT...
EH?
HEY, THERE!
K-KANA?!

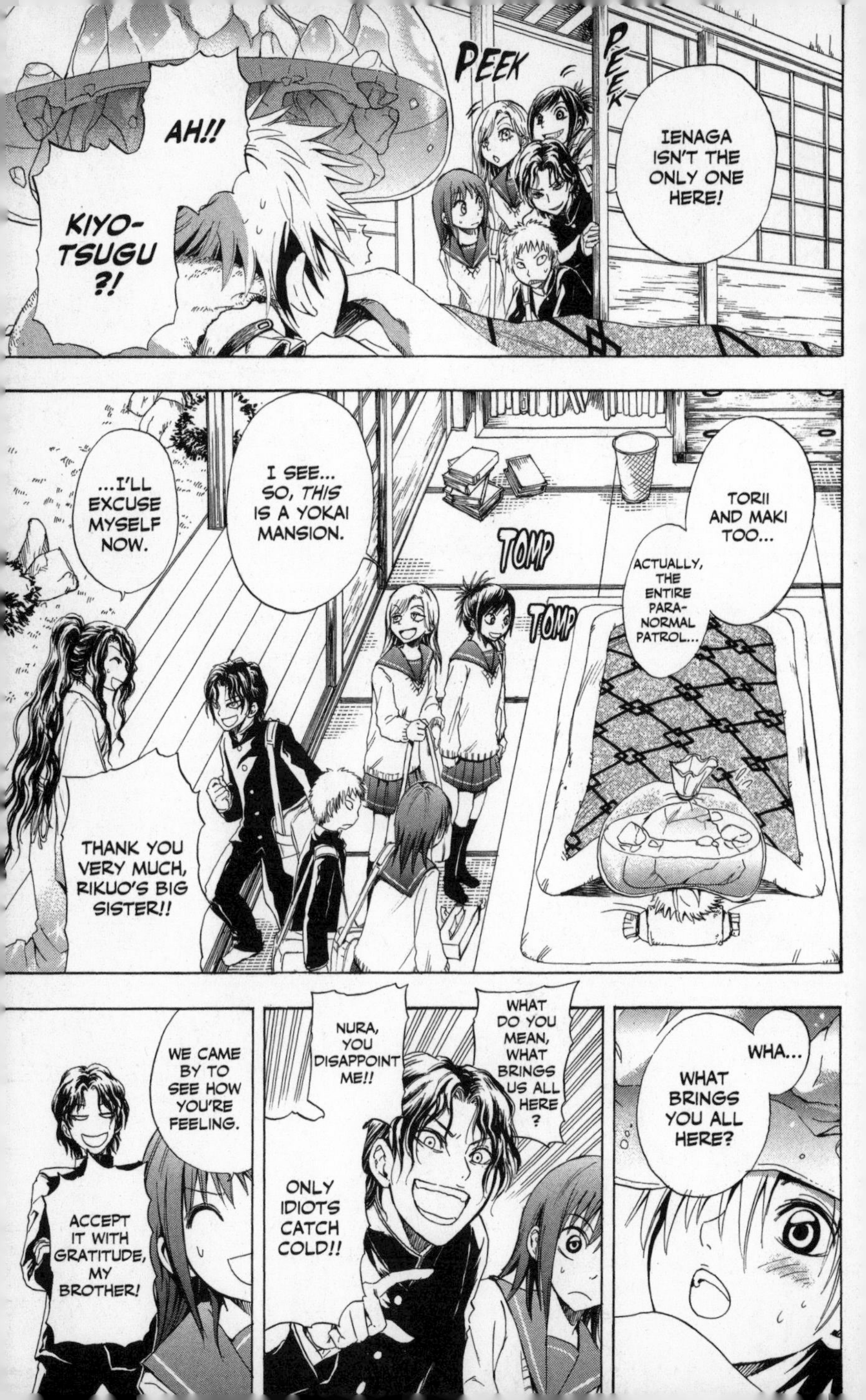
PEEK
PEEK
IENAGA ISN'T THE ONLY ONE HERE!
AH!!
KIYO-TSUGU?!
TORII AND MAKI TOO...
ACTUALLY, THE ENTIRE PARA-NORMAL PATROL...
TOMP
TOMP
I SEE... SO, *THIS* IS A YOKAI MANSION.
...I'LL EXCUSE MYSELF NOW.
THANK YOU VERY MUCH, RIKUO'S BIG SISTER!!
WHA...
WHAT BRINGS YOU ALL HERE?
WHAT DO YOU MEAN, WHAT BRINGS US ALL HERE?
NURA, YOU DISAPPOINT ME!!
ONLY IDIOTS CATCH COLD!!
WE CAME BY TO SEE HOW YOU'RE FEELING.
ACCEPT IT WITH GRATITUDE, MY BROTHER!

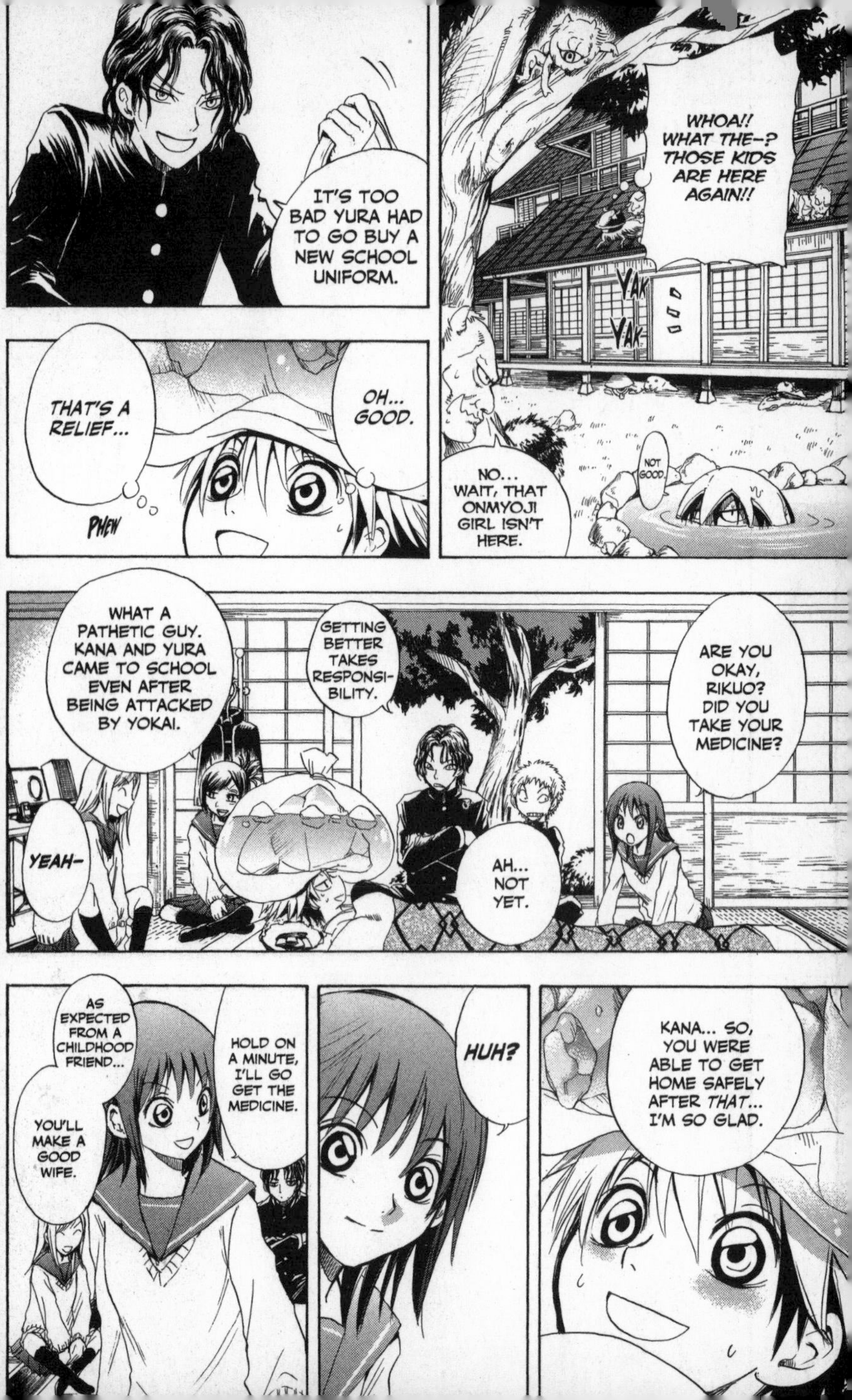
WHOA!! WHAT THE-? THOSE KIDS ARE HERE AGAIN!!
YAK YAK
NO... WAIT, THAT ONMYOJI GIRL ISN'T HERE.
NOT GOOD.
IT'S TOO BAD YURA HAD TO GO BUY A NEW SCHOOL UNIFORM.
OH... GOOD.
THAT'S A RELIEF...
PHEW
ARE YOU OKAY, RIKUO? DID YOU TAKE YOUR MEDICINE?
AH... NOT YET.
GETTING BETTER TAKES RESPONSIBILITY.
WHAT A PATHETIC GUY. KANA AND YURA CAME TO SCHOOL EVEN AFTER BEING ATTACKED BY YOKAI.
YEAH-
KANA... SO, YOU WERE ABLE TO GET HOME SAFELY AFTER THAT... I'M SO GLAD.
HUH?
HOLD ON A MINUTE, I'LL GO GET THE MEDICINE.
AS EXPECTED FROM A CHILDHOOD FRIEND...
YOU'LL MAKE A GOOD WIFE.

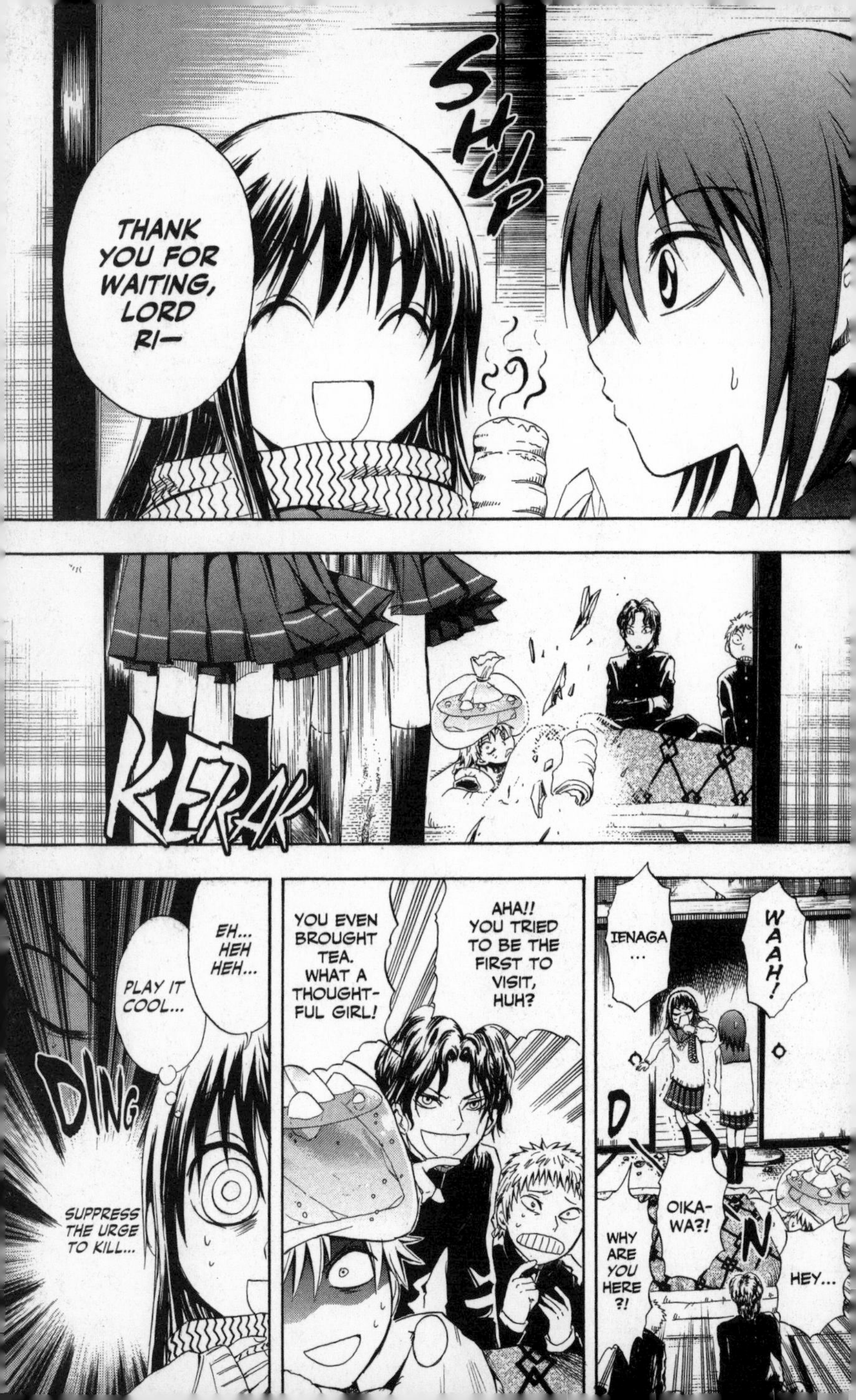
SHUP
THANK YOU FOR WAITING, LORD RI—
KERAK
WAAAH!
IENAGA...
DON
OIKAWA?!
WHY ARE YOU HERE?!
HEY...
AHA!! YOU TRIED TO BE THE FIRST TO VISIT, HUH?
YOU EVEN BROUGHT TEA. WHAT A THOUGHTFUL GIRL!
EH... HEH HEH...
PLAY IT COOL...
DING
SUPPRESS THE URGE TO KILL...

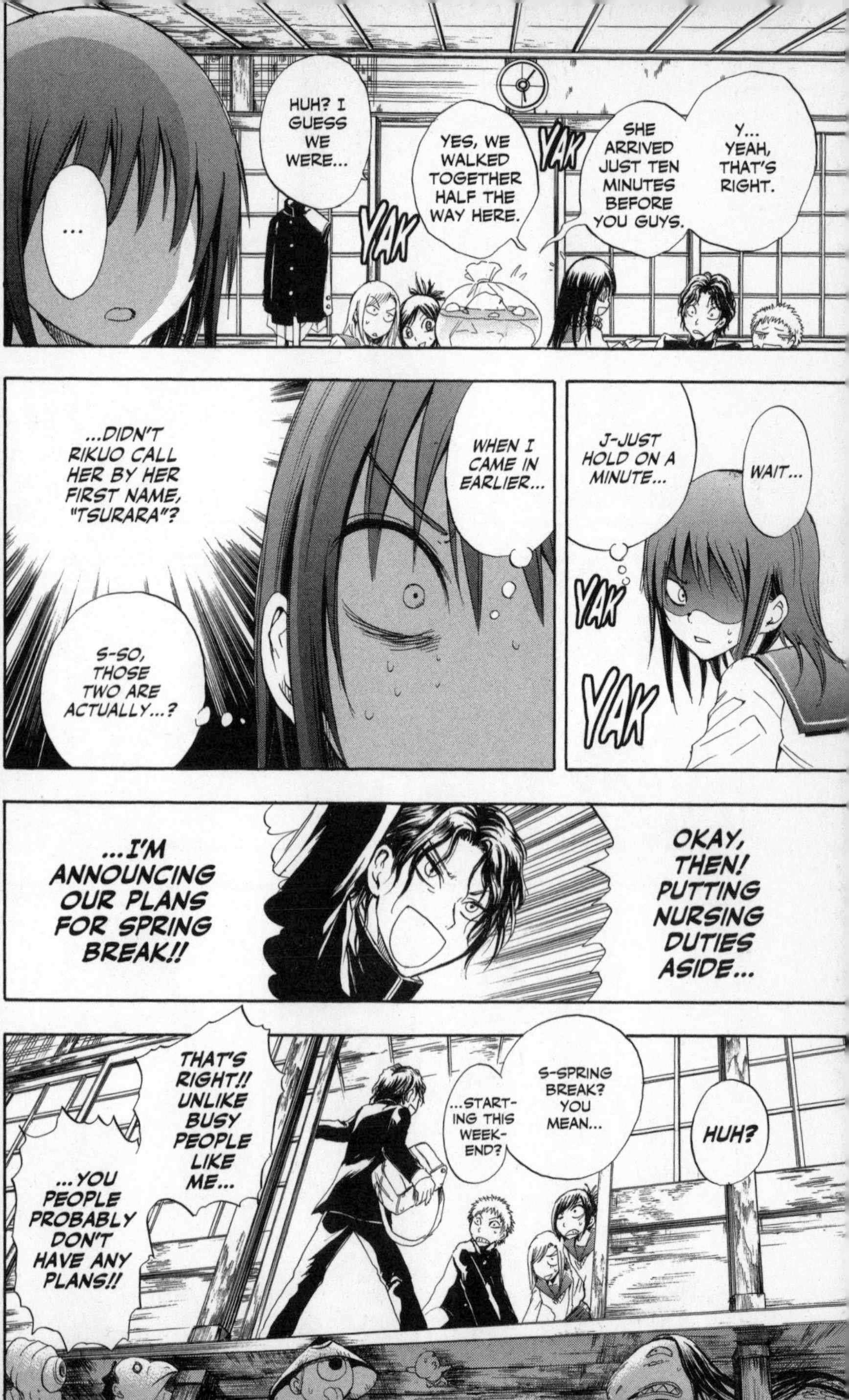
Y... YEAH, THAT'S RIGHT.
SHE ARRIVED JUST TEN MINUTES BEFORE YOU GUYS.
YAK
YES, WE WALKED TOGETHER HALF THE WAY HERE.
YAK
HUH? I GUESS WE WERE...
...
WAIT...
J-JUST HOLD ON A MINUTE...
YAK
YAK
WHEN I CAME IN EARLIER...
...DIDN'T RIKUO CALL HER BY HER FIRST NAME, "TSURARA"?
S-SO, THOSE TWO ARE ACTUALLY...?
OKAY, THEN! PUTTING NURSING DUTIES ASIDE...
...I'M ANNOUNCING OUR PLANS FOR SPRING BREAK!!
HUH?
S-SPRING BREAK? YOU MEAN...
...START-ING THIS WEEK-END?
THAT'S RIGHT!! UNLIKE BUSY PEOPLE LIKE ME...
...YOU PEOPLE PROBABLY DON'T HAVE ANY PLANS!!

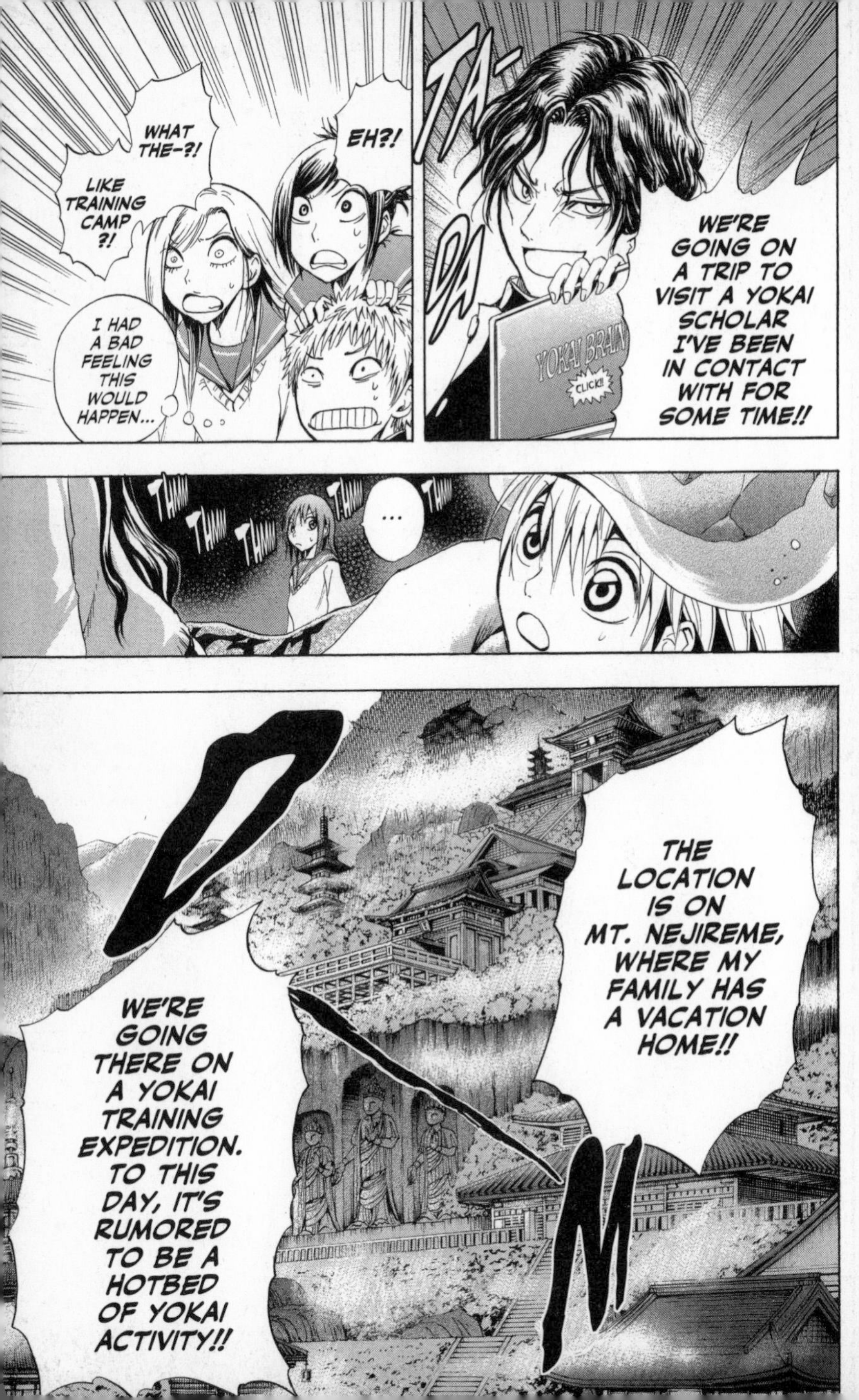
TA-DA
WE'RE GOING ON A TRIP TO VISIT A YOKAI SCHOLAR I'VE BEEN IN CONTACT WITH FOR SOME TIME!!
YOKAI BRAIN
CLICK!!
EH?!
WHAT THE-?!
LIKE TRAINING CAMP ?!
I HAD A BAD FEELING THIS WOULD HAPPEN...
THMM THMM THMM THMM THMM
...
THE LOCATION IS ON MT. NEJIREME, WHERE MY FAMILY HAS A VACATION HOME!!
WE'RE GOING THERE ON A YOKAI TRAINING EXPEDITION. TO THIS DAY, IT'S RUMORED TO BE A HOTBED OF YOKAI ACTIVITY!!

Eh? "What would a normal girl bring on a trip?"

... Rikuo, why are you asking?

Well, uh...

YATTO FUTA HASSIE YOJIN

ICE

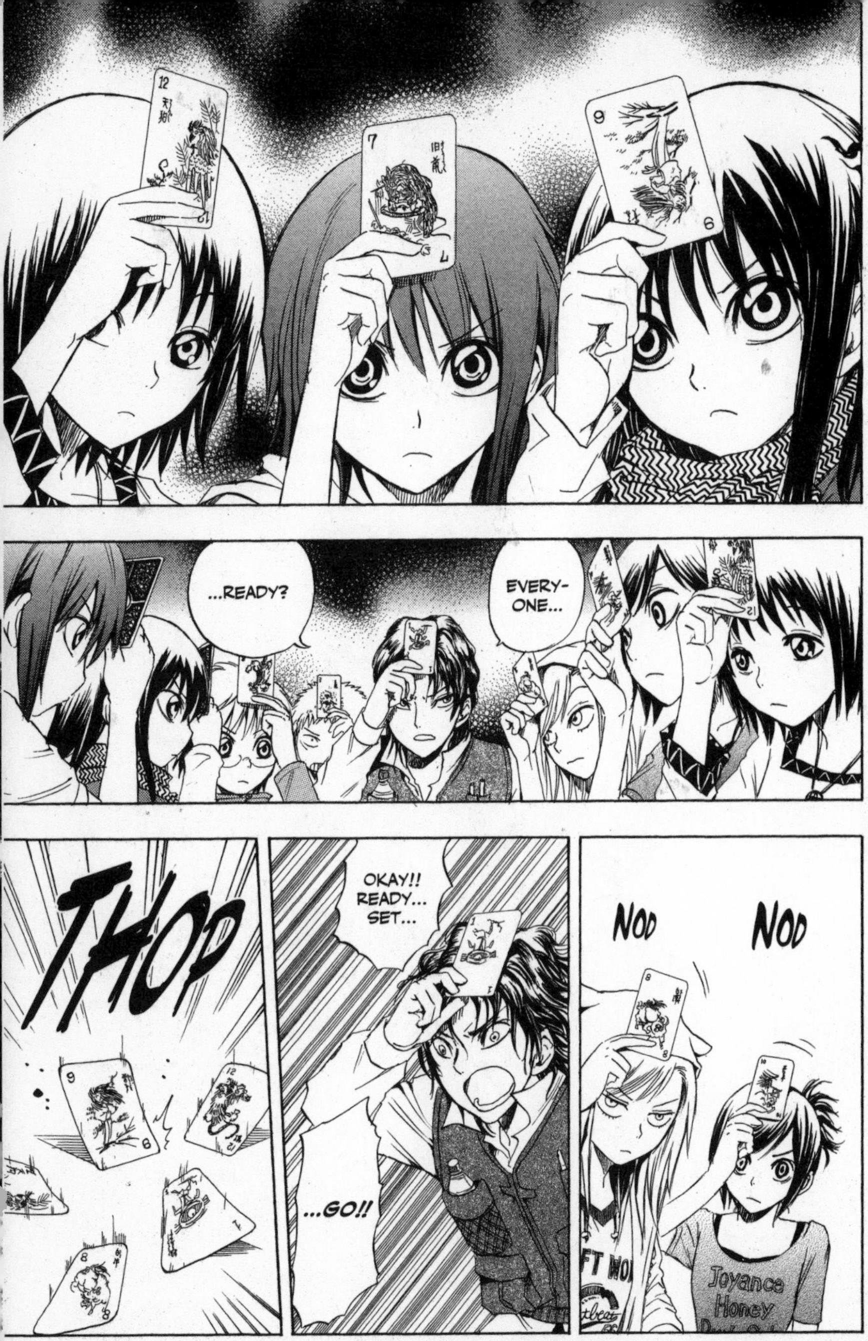
EVERY-ONE...
...READY?
NOD
NOD
Joyance Honey
OKAY!! READY... SET...
...GO!!
THOP

Act 10: Rikuo Goes on a Mystery Tour

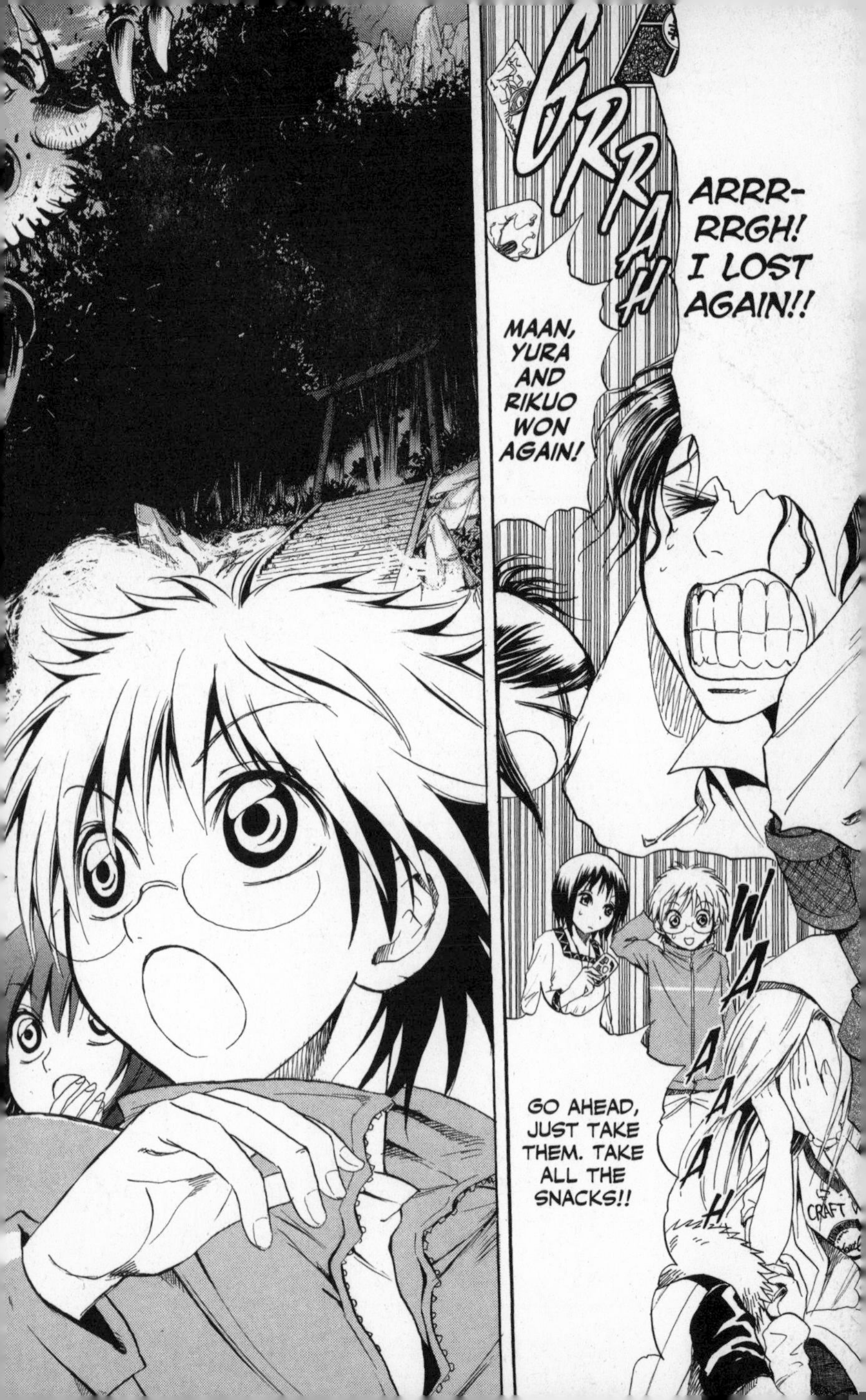
GRRAH
ARRR-RRGH! I LOST AGAIN!!
MAAN, YURA AND RIKUO WON AGAIN!
WAAAAAAH
GO AHEAD, JUST TAKE THEM. TAKE ALL THE SNACKS!!
CRAFT

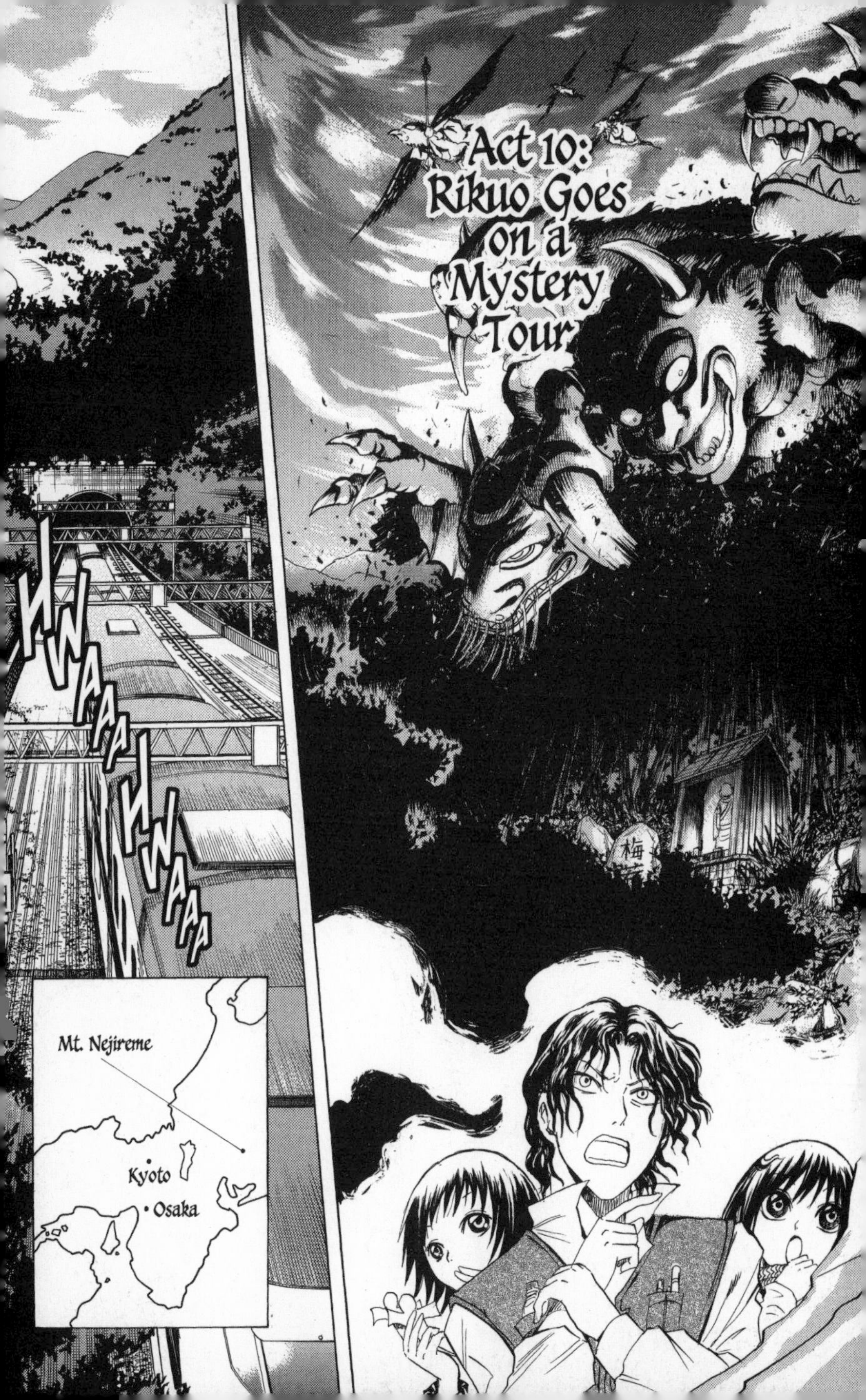
Act 10:
Rikuo Goes on a Mystery Tour
梅
HWAAAA HWAAAA
Mt. Nejireme
Kyoto
Osaka

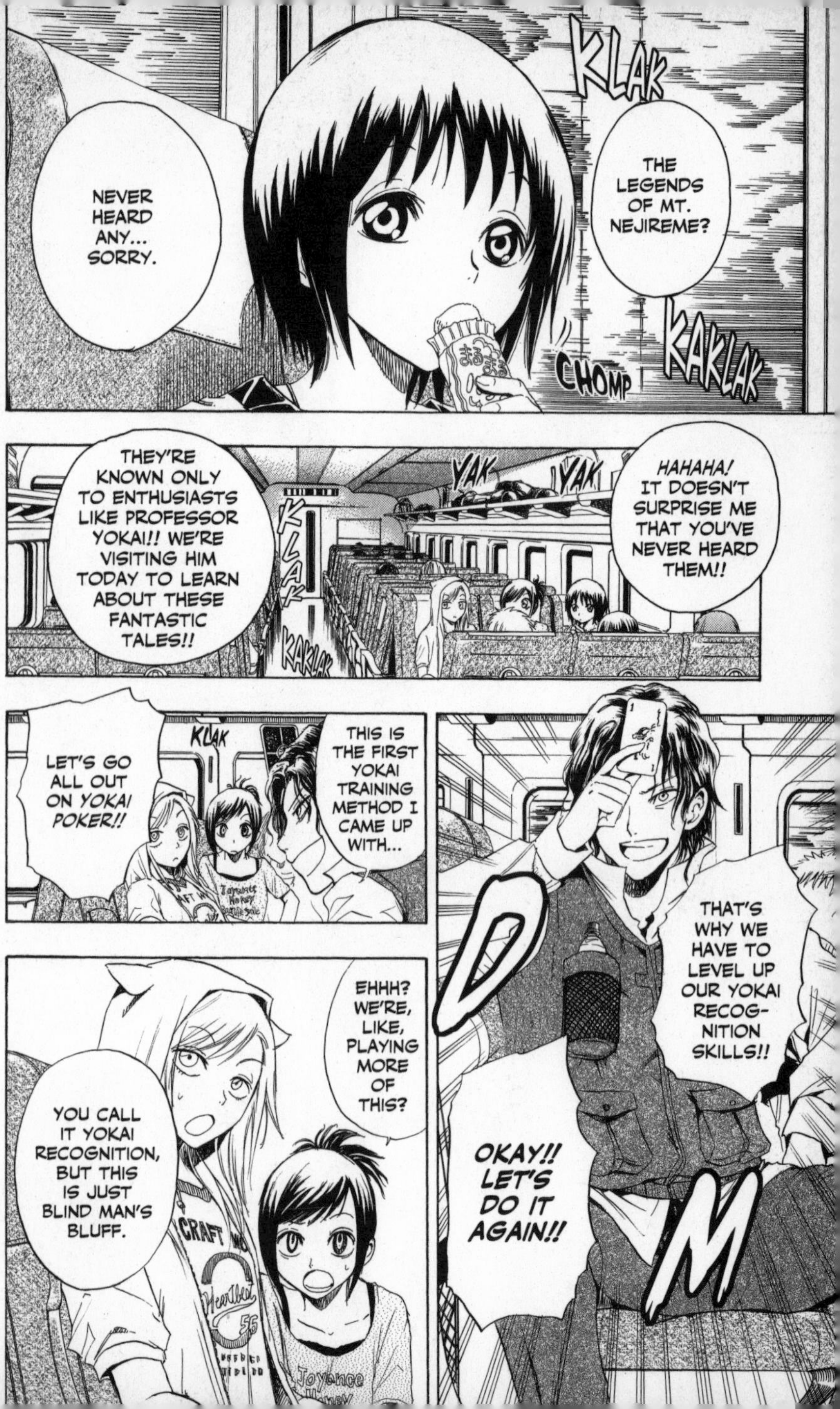
KLAK
THE LEGENDS OF MT. NEJIREME?
KAKLAK
CHOMP
NEVER HEARD ANY... SORRY.
HAHAHA! IT DOESN'T SURPRISE ME THAT YOU'VE NEVER HEARD THEM!!
YAK YAK
THEY'RE KNOWN ONLY TO ENTHUSIASTS LIKE PROFESSOR YOKAI!! WE'RE VISITING HIM TODAY TO LEARN ABOUT THESE FANTASTIC TALES!!
KLAK
KAKLAK
THAT'S WHY WE HAVE TO LEVEL UP OUR YOKAI RECOG-NITION SKILLS!!
OKAY!! LET'S DO IT AGAIN!!
KLAK
THIS IS THE FIRST YOKAI TRAINING METHOD I CAME UP WITH...
LET'S GO ALL OUT ON *YOKAI POKER!!*
EHHH? WE'RE, LIKE, PLAYING MORE OF THIS?
YOU CALL IT YOKAI RECOGNITION, BUT THIS IS JUST BLIND MAN'S BLUFF.

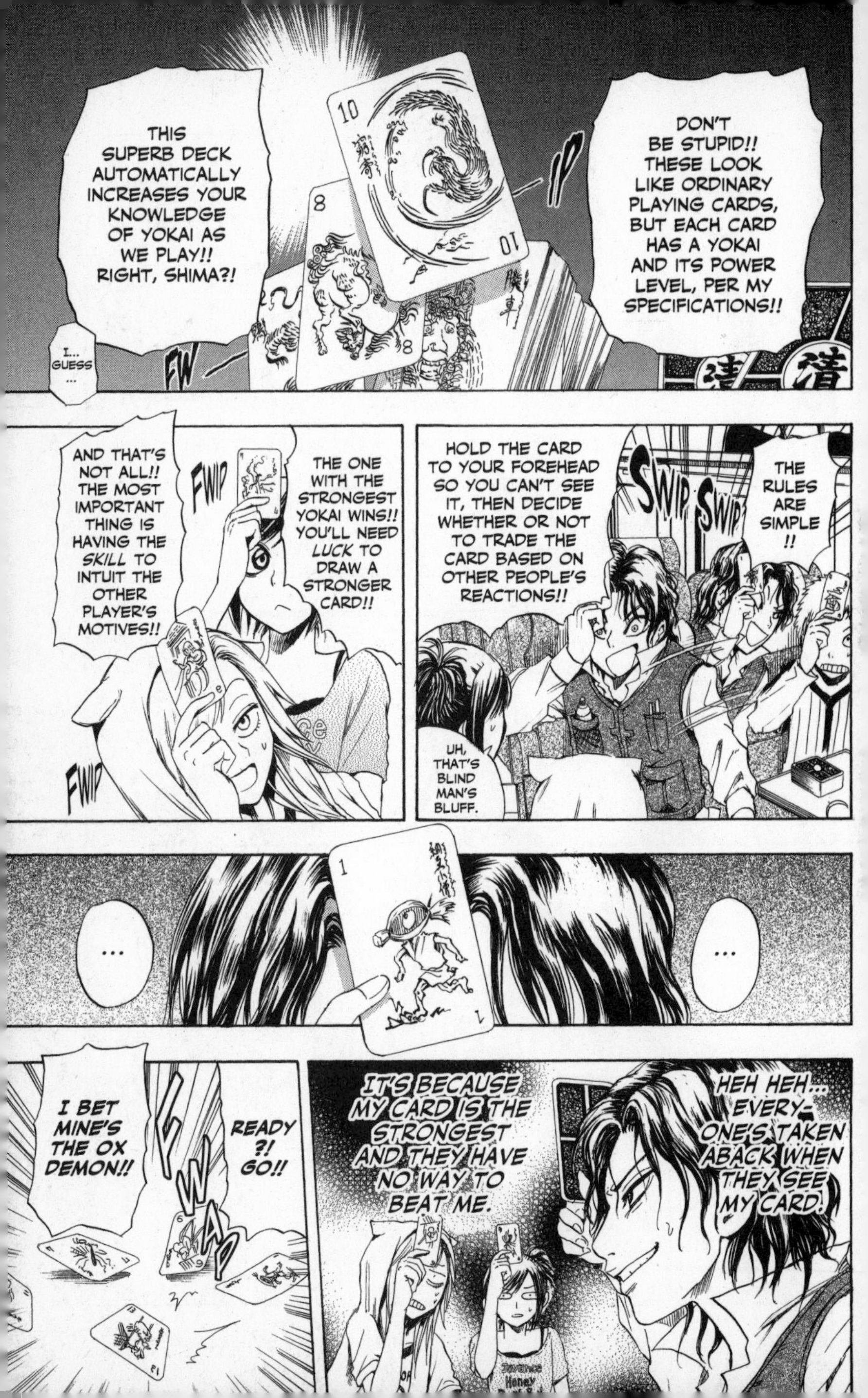
DON'T BE STUPID!! THESE LOOK LIKE ORDINARY PLAYING CARDS, BUT EACH CARD HAS A YOKAI AND ITS POWER LEVEL, PER MY SPECIFICATIONS!!
THIS SUPERB DECK AUTOMATICALLY INCREASES YOUR KNOWLEDGE OF YOKAI AS WE PLAY!! RIGHT, SHIMA?!
FW
I... GUESS...
THE RULES ARE SIMPLE!!
SWIP SWIP
HOLD THE CARD TO YOUR FOREHEAD SO YOU CAN'T SEE IT, THEN DECIDE WHETHER OR NOT TO TRADE THE CARD BASED ON OTHER PEOPLE'S REACTIONS!!
UH, THAT'S BLIND MAN'S BLUFF.
THE ONE WITH THE STRONGEST YOKAI WINS!! YOU'LL NEED *LUCK* TO DRAW A STRONGER CARD!!
FWIP
AND THAT'S NOT ALL!! THE MOST IMPORTANT THING IS HAVING THE *SKILL* TO INTUIT THE OTHER PLAYER'S MOTIVES!!
FWIP
...
...
HEH HEH... EVERY-ONE'S TAKEN ABACK WHEN THEY SEE MY CARD.
IT'S BECAUSE MY CARD IS THE STRONGEST AND THEY HAVE NO WAY TO BEAT ME.
READY?! GO!!
I BET MINE'S THE OX DEMON!!

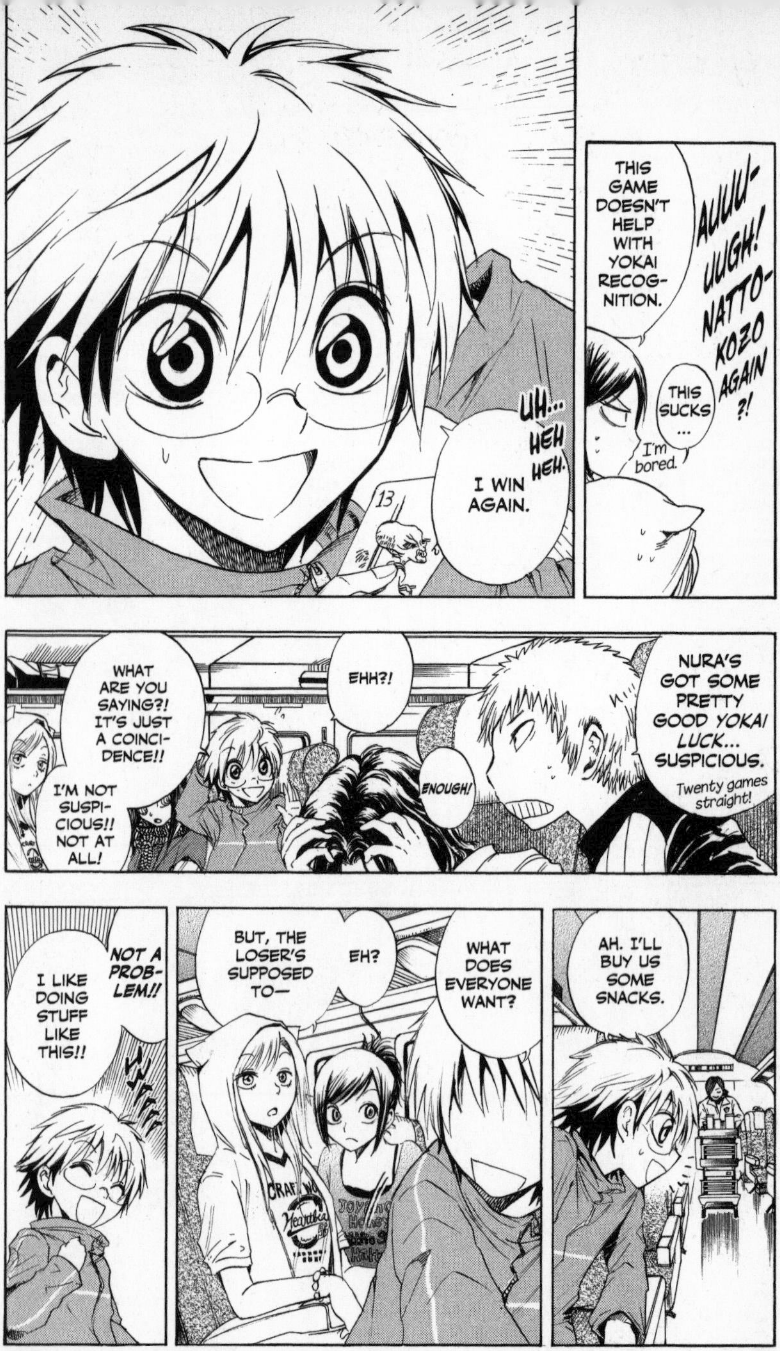
AUUU-UUGH! NATTO-KOZO AGAIN?!
THIS GAME DOESN'T HELP WITH YOKAI RECOGNITION.
THIS SUCKS...
I'm bored.
UH... HEH HEH.
I WIN AGAIN.
NURA'S GOT SOME PRETTY GOOD YOKAI LUCK... SUSPICIOUS.
Twenty games straight!
EHH?!
ENOUGH!
WHAT ARE YOU SAYING?! IT'S JUST A COINCIDENCE!!
I'M NOT SUSPICIOUS!! NOT AT ALL!
AH. I'LL BUY US SOME SNACKS.
WHAT DOES EVERYONE WANT?
EH?
BUT, THE LOSER'S SUPPOSED TO—
NOT A PROBLEM!!
I LIKE DOING STUFF LIKE THIS!!

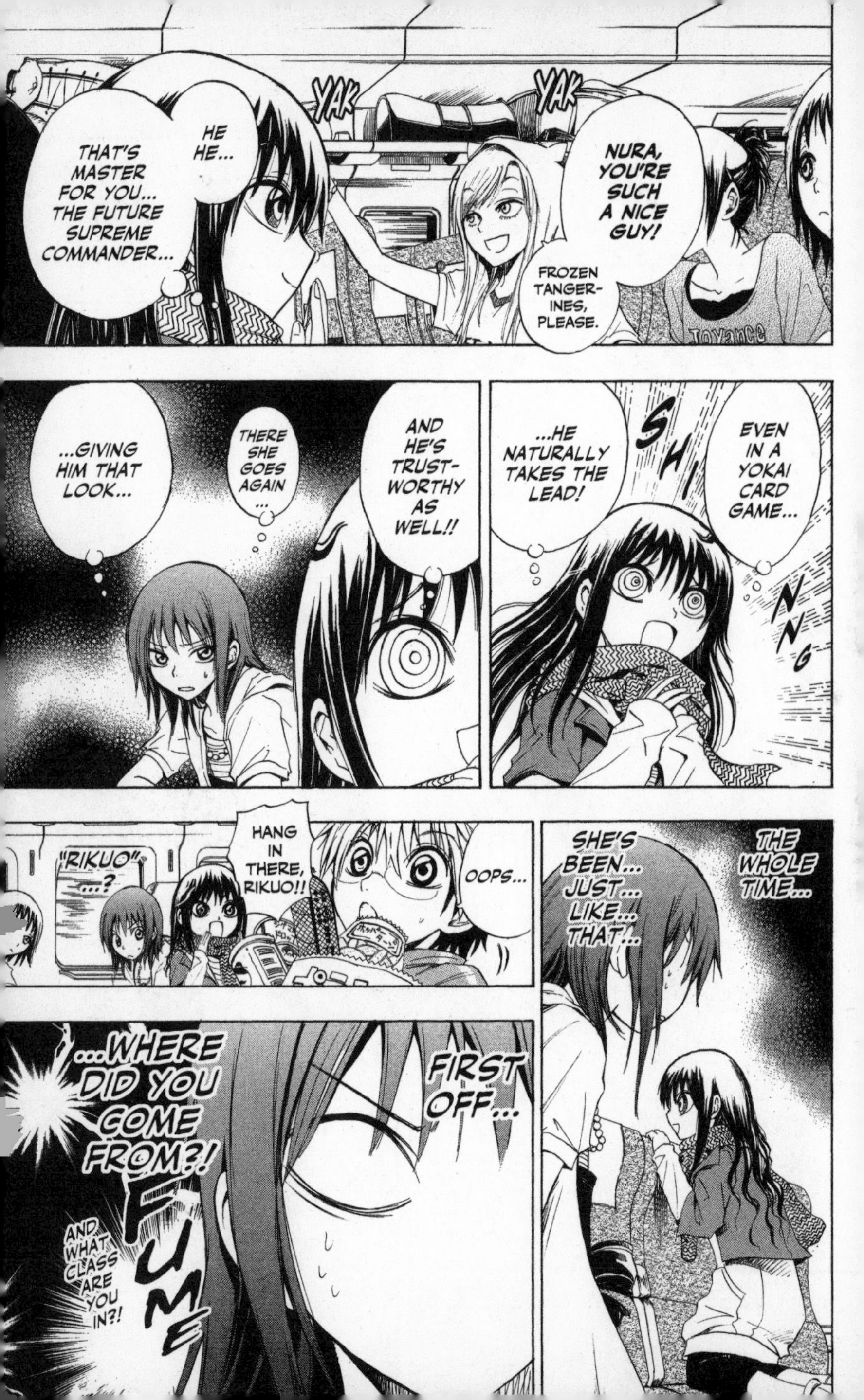
NURA, YOU'RE SUCH A NICE GUY!
FROZEN TANGER-INES, PLEASE.
YAK
YAK
HE HE...
THAT'S MASTER FOR YOU... THE FUTURE SUPREME COMMANDER...
EVEN IN A YOKAI CARD GAME...
SHINNG
...HE NATURALLY TAKES THE LEAD!
AND HE'S TRUST-WORTHY AS WELL!!
THERE SHE GOES AGAIN...
...GIVING HIM THAT LOOK...
THE WHOLE TIME...
SHE'S BEEN... JUST... LIKE... THAT...
OOPS...
HANG IN THERE, RIKUO!!
"RIKUO"...?
FIRST OFF...
...WHERE DID YOU COME FROM?!
FUME
AND WHAT CLASS ARE YOU IN?!

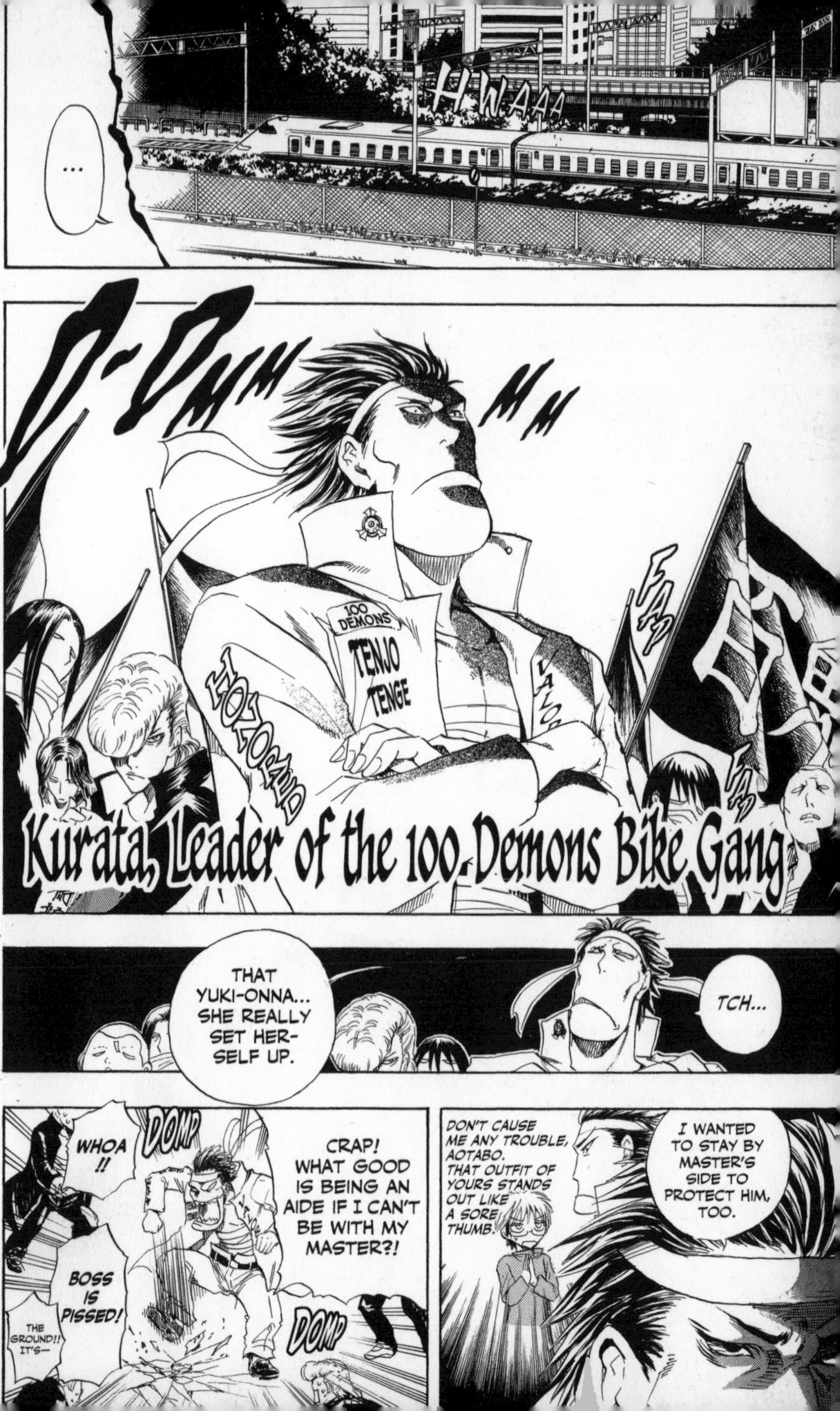
HWAAA
...
FAP
100 DEMONS
TENJO TENGE
Kurata, Leader of the 100-Demons Bike Gang
TCH...
THAT YUKI-ONNA... SHE REALLY SET HERSELF UP.
I WANTED TO STAY BY MASTER'S SIDE TO PROTECT HIM, TOO.
DON'T CAUSE ME ANY TROUBLE, AOTABO. THAT OUTFIT OF YOURS STANDS OUT LIKE A SORE THUMB.
CRAP! WHAT GOOD IS BEING AN AIDE IF I CAN'T BE WITH MY MASTER?!
DOMP
WHOA !!
BOSS IS PISSED!
THE GROUND!! IT'S—
DOMP

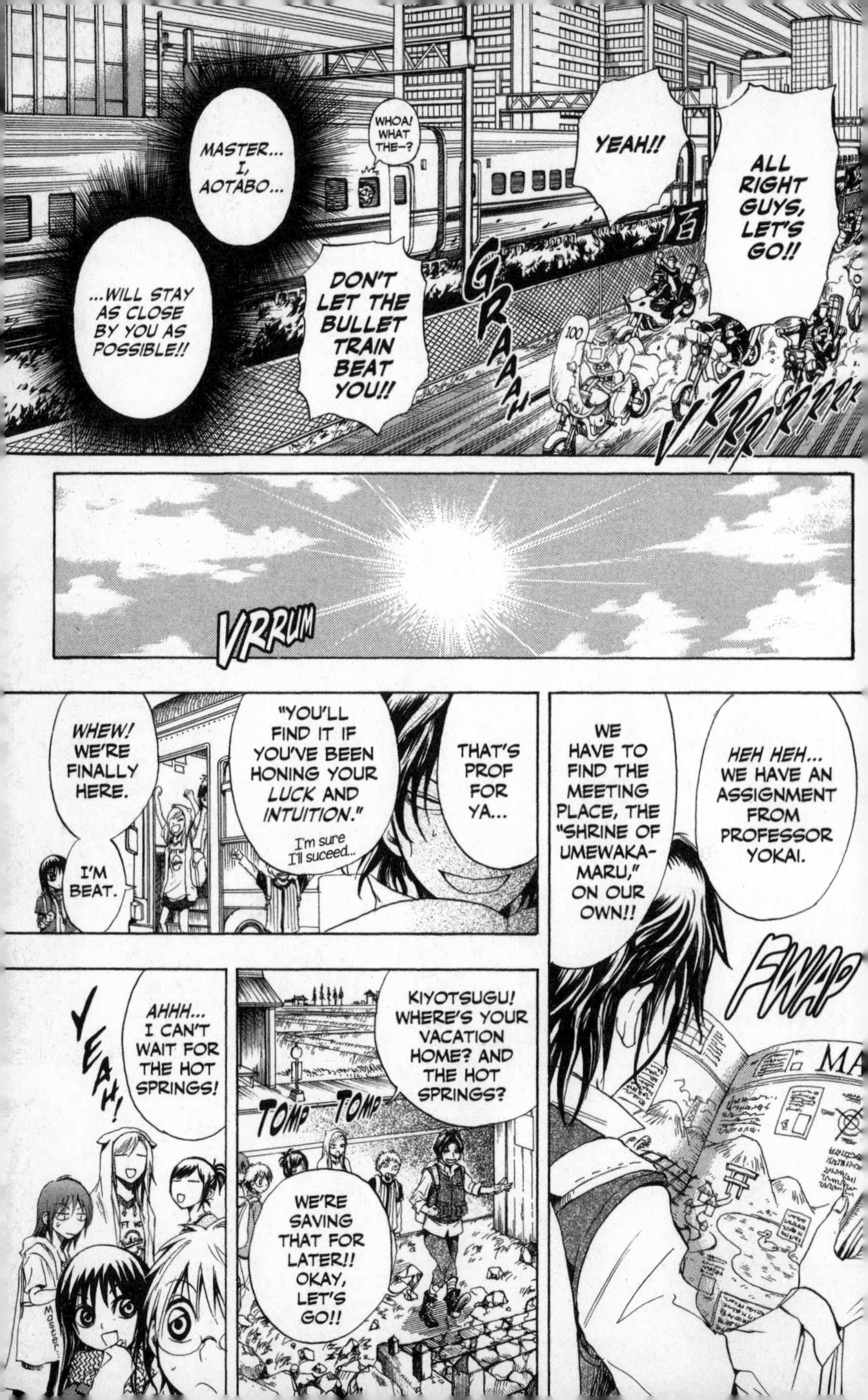
ALL RIGHT GUYS, LET'S GO!!
YEAH!!
VRRRRRRRR
GRAAAH
DON'T LET THE BULLET TRAIN BEAT YOU!!
WHOA! WHAT THE–?
MASTER... I, AOTABO...
...WILL STAY AS CLOSE BY YOU AS POSSIBLE!!
VRRUM
HEH HEH... WE HAVE AN ASSIGNMENT FROM PROFESSOR YOKAI.
WE HAVE TO FIND THE MEETING PLACE, THE "SHRINE OF UMEWAKA-MARU," ON OUR OWN!!
FWAP
THAT'S PROF FOR YA...
"YOU'LL FIND IT IF YOU'VE BEEN HONING YOUR LUCK AND INTUITION."
I'm sure I'll suceed...
WHEW! WE'RE FINALLY HERE.
I'M BEAT.
KIYOTSUGU! WHERE'S YOUR VACATION HOME? AND THE HOT SPRINGS?
TOMP TOMP
WE'RE SAVING THAT FOR LATER!! OKAY, LET'S GO!!
AHHH... I CAN'T WAIT FOR THE HOT SPRINGS!
YEAH!
Master...

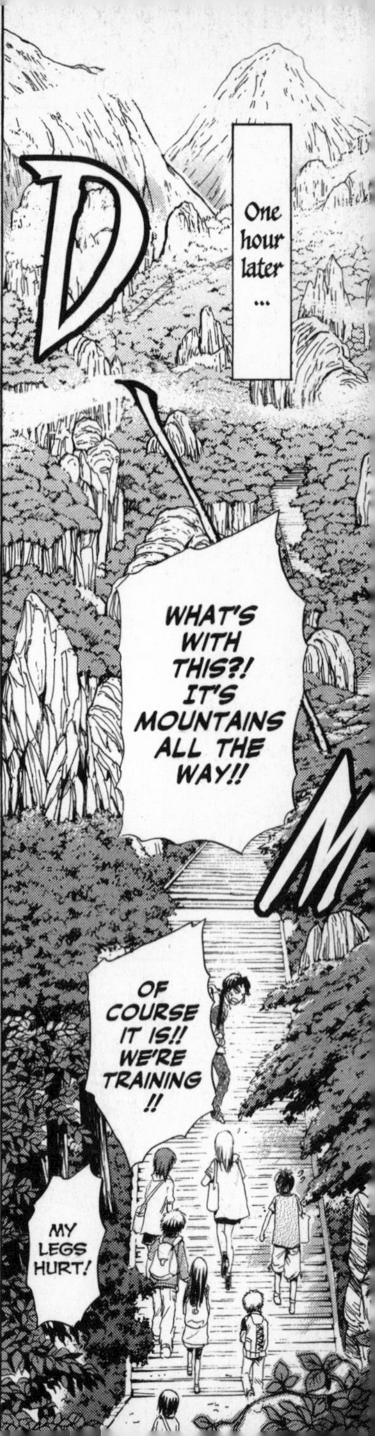
One hour later...
WHAT'S WITH THIS?! IT'S MOUNTAINS ALL THE WAY!!
OF COURSE IT IS!! WE'RE TRAINING!!
MY LEGS HURT!

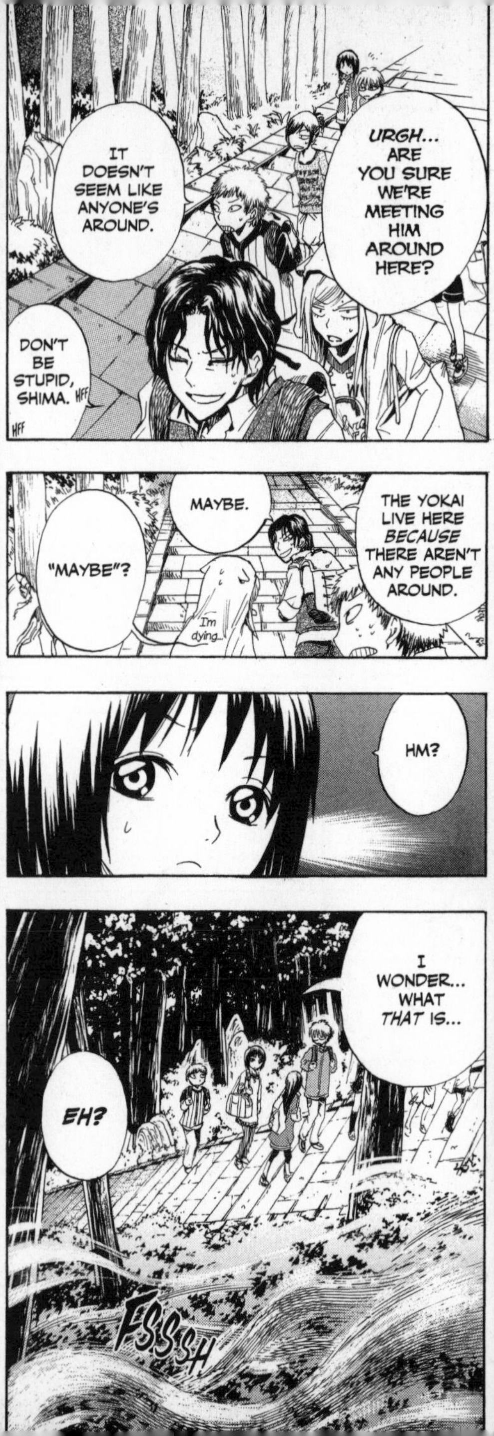
URGH... ARE YOU SURE WE'RE MEETING HIM AROUND HERE?
IT DOESN'T SEEM LIKE ANYONE'S AROUND.
DON'T BE STUPID, SHIMA.
HFF
HFF
THE YOKAI LIVE HERE BECAUSE THERE AREN'T ANY PEOPLE AROUND.
MAYBE.
"MAYBE"?
I'm dying...
HM?
I WONDER... WHAT THAT IS...
EH?
FSSSH

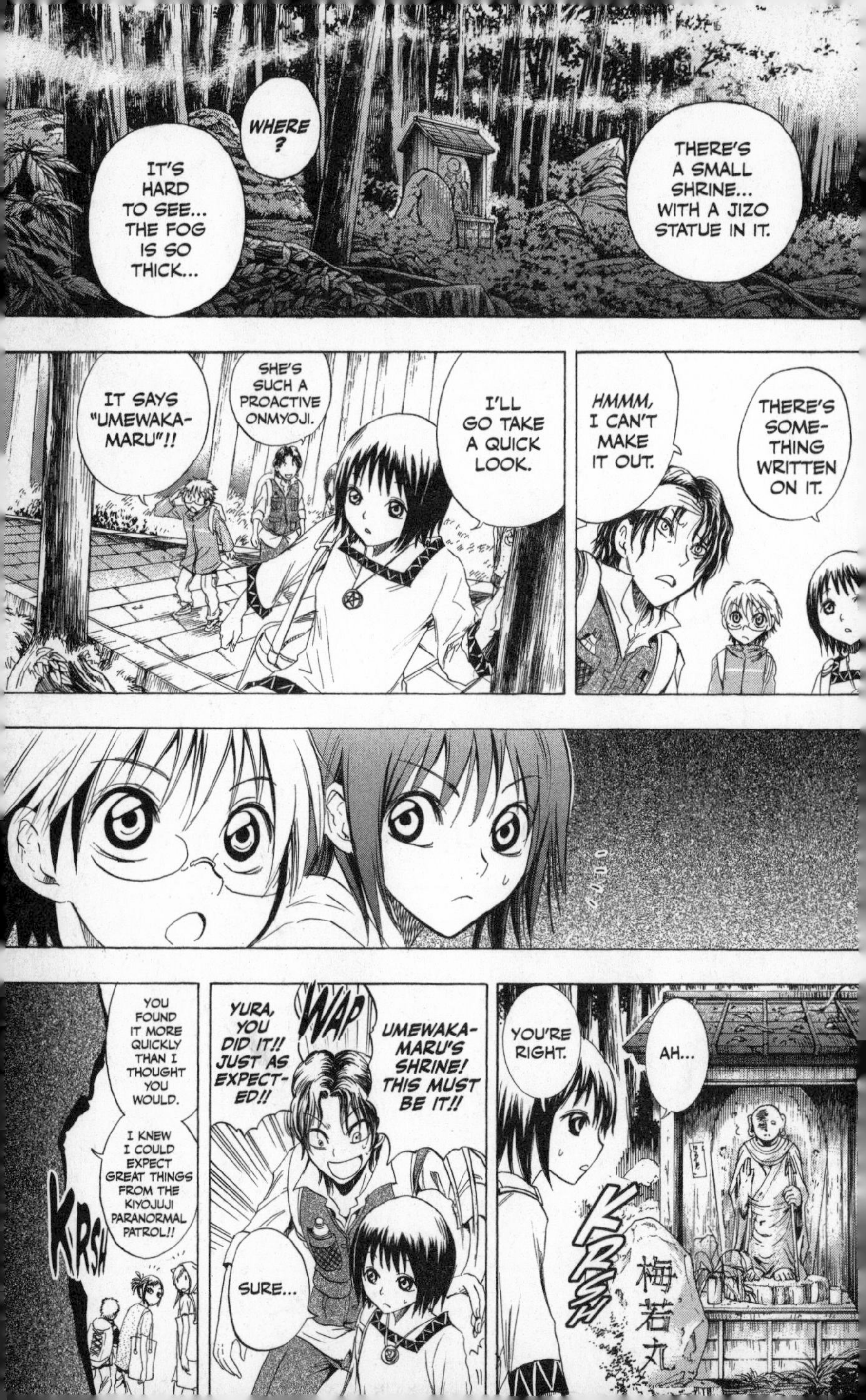
THERE'S A SMALL SHRINE... WITH A JIZO STATUE IN IT.
WHERE?
IT'S HARD TO SEE... THE FOG IS SO THICK...
THERE'S SOMETHING WRITTEN ON IT.
HMMM, I CAN'T MAKE IT OUT.
I'LL GO TAKE A QUICK LOOK.
SHE'S SUCH A PROACTIVE ONMYOJI.
IT SAYS "UMEWAKA-MARU"!!
AH...
梅若丸
YOU'RE RIGHT.
WAP
UMEWAKA-MARU'S SHRINE! THIS MUST BE IT!!
YURA, YOU DID IT!! JUST AS EXPECTED!!
SURE...
YOU FOUND IT MORE QUICKLY THAN I THOUGHT YOU WOULD.
I KNEW I COULD EXPECT GREAT THINGS FROM THE KIYOJUJI PARANORMAL PATROL!!
KRSH

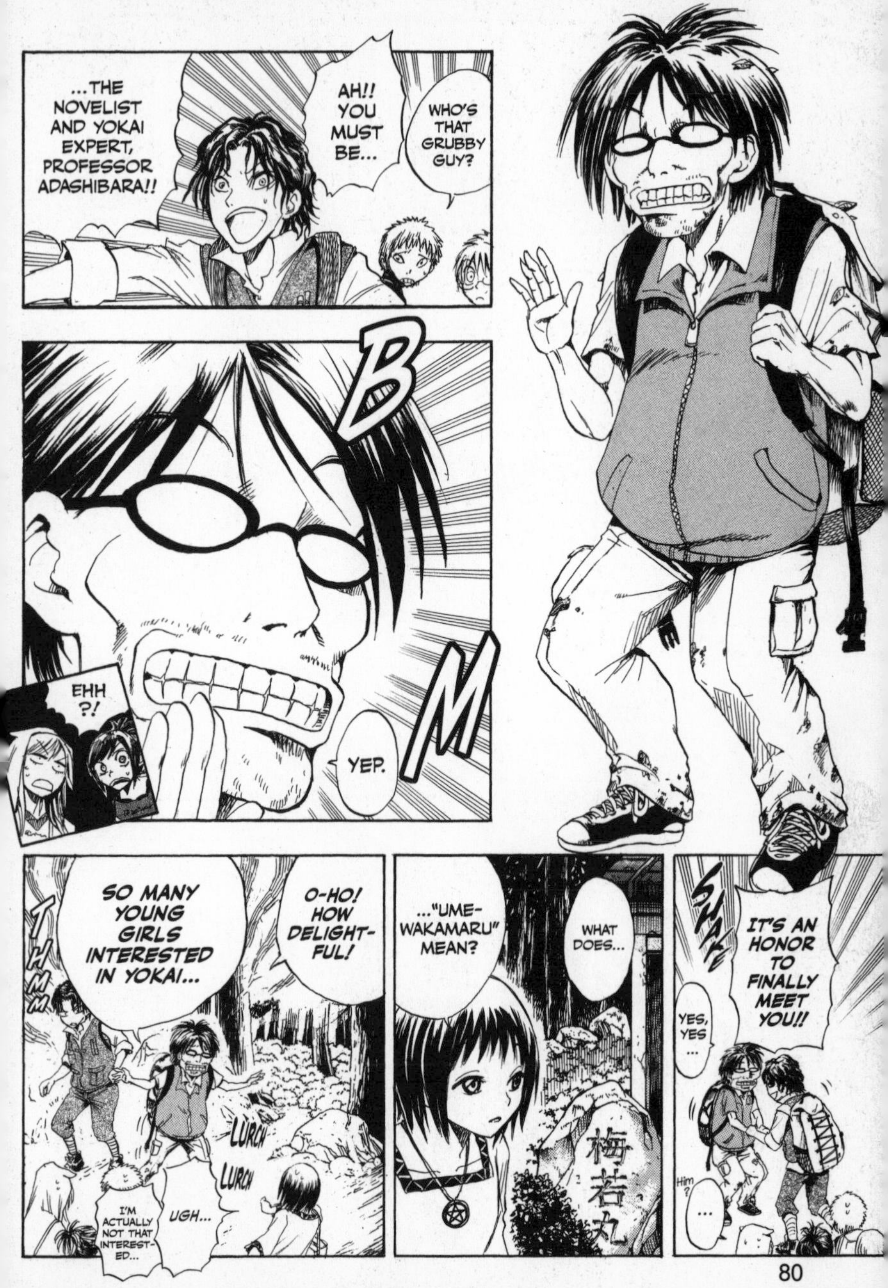
WHO'S THAT GRUBBY GUY?
AH!! YOU MUST BE...
...THE NOVELIST AND YOKAI EXPERT, PROFESSOR ADASHIBARA!!
BM
YEP.
EHH ?!
SHAKE
IT'S AN HONOR TO FINALLY MEET YOU!!
YES, YES ...
Him ?
...
WHAT DOES...
..."UME-WAKAMARU" MEAN?
梅若丸
O-HO! HOW DELIGHTFUL!
SO MANY YOUNG GIRLS INTERESTED IN YOKAI...
THMM
LURCH
LURCH
UGH...
I'M ACTUALLY NOT THAT INTERESTED...

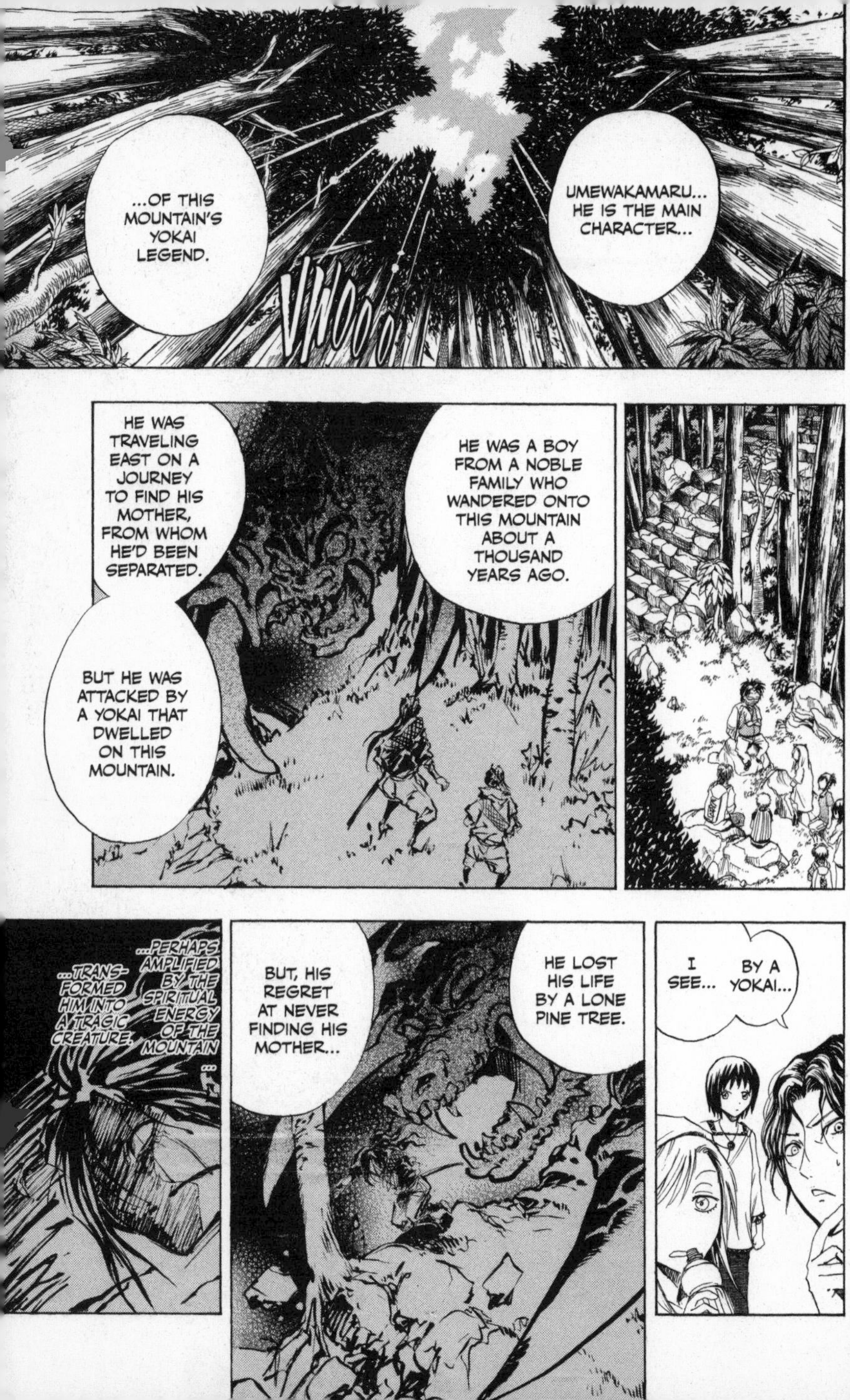
UMEWAKAMARU... HE IS THE MAIN CHARACTER...
...OF THIS MOUNTAIN'S YOKAI LEGEND.
VHOOOO
HE WAS A BOY FROM A NOBLE FAMILY WHO WANDERED ONTO THIS MOUNTAIN ABOUT A THOUSAND YEARS AGO.
HE WAS TRAVELING EAST ON A JOURNEY TO FIND HIS MOTHER, FROM WHOM HE'D BEEN SEPARATED.
BUT HE WAS ATTACKED BY A YOKAI THAT DWELLED ON THIS MOUNTAIN.
I SEE... BY A YOKAI...
HE LOST HIS LIFE BY A LONE PINE TREE.
BUT, HIS REGRET AT NEVER FINDING HIS MOTHER...
...PERHAPS AMPLIFIED BY THE SPIRITUAL ENERGY OF THE MOUNTAIN...
...TRANS-FORMED HIM INTO A TRAGIC CREATURE.

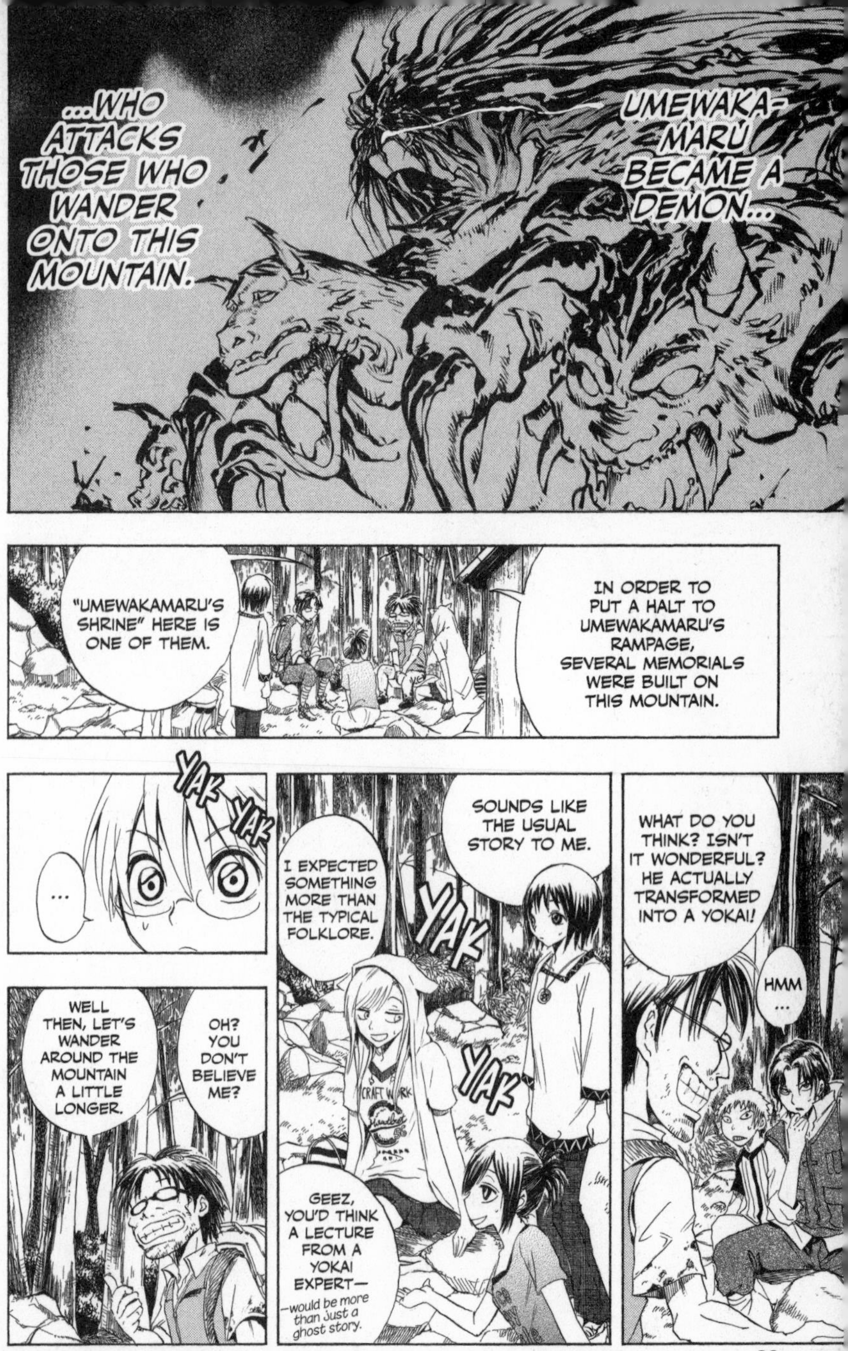
UMEWAKA-MARU BECAME A DEMON...
...WHO ATTACKS THOSE WHO WANDER ONTO THIS MOUNTAIN.
IN ORDER TO PUT A HALT TO UMEWAKAMARU'S RAMPAGE, SEVERAL MEMORIALS WERE BUILT ON THIS MOUNTAIN.
"UMEWAKAMARU'S SHRINE" HERE IS ONE OF THEM.
WHAT DO YOU THINK? ISN'T IT WONDERFUL? HE ACTUALLY TRANSFORMED INTO A YOKAI!
HMM ...
SOUNDS LIKE THE USUAL STORY TO ME.
I EXPECTED SOMETHING MORE THAN THE TYPICAL FOLKLORE.
YAK
YAK
GEEZ, YOU'D THINK A LECTURE FROM A YOKAI EXPERT—
—would be more than just a ghost story.
YAK YAK
...
OH? YOU DON'T BELIEVE ME?
WELL THEN, LET'S WANDER AROUND THE MOUNTAIN A LITTLE LONGER.

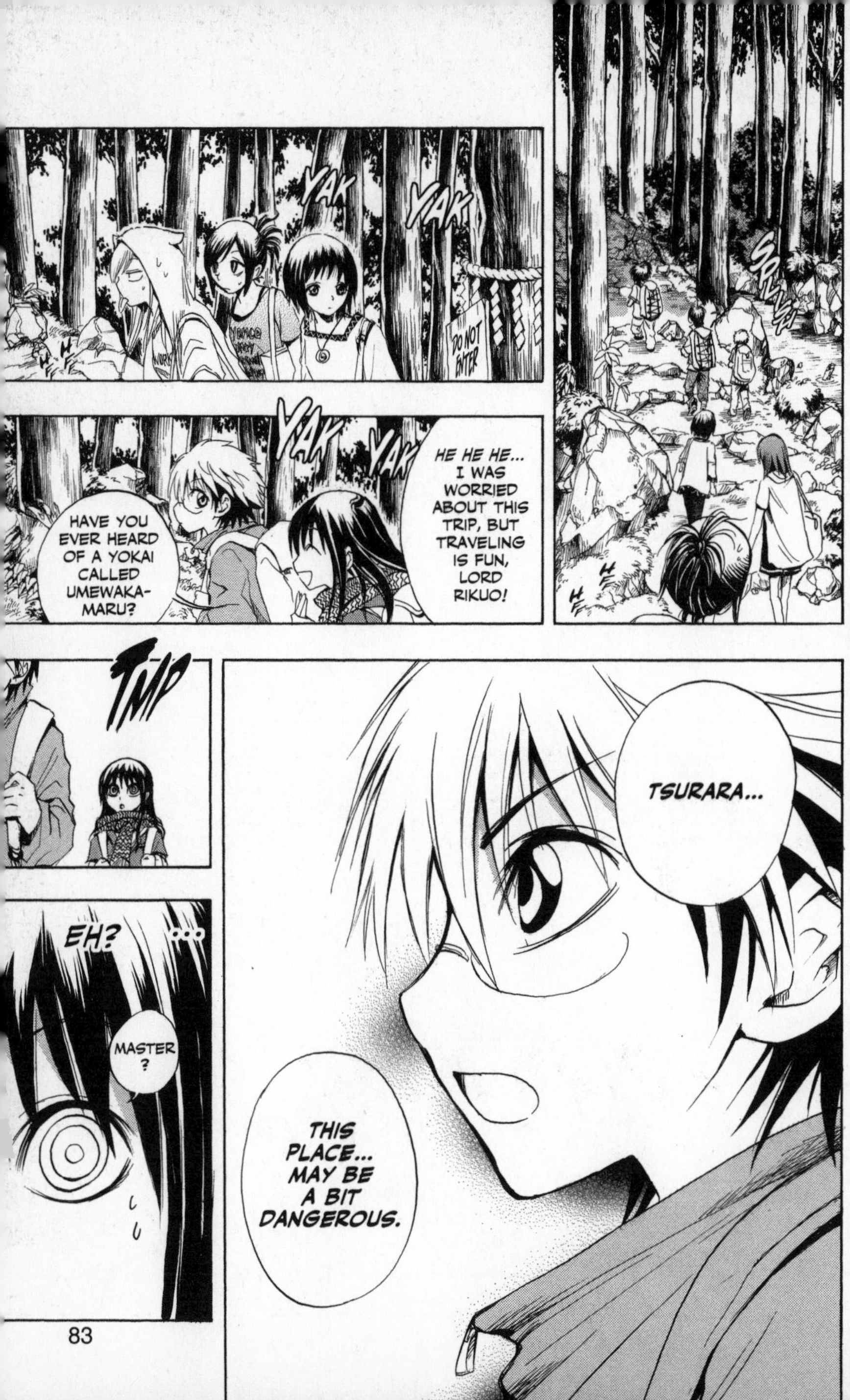
SPLVSH
HF HF
YAK YAK
DO NOT ENTER
HF HF
HE HE HE... I WAS WORRIED ABOUT THIS TRIP, BUT TRAVELING IS FUN, LORD RIKUO!
YAK YAK
HAVE YOU EVER HEARD OF A YOKAI CALLED UMEWAKA-MARU?
TSURARA...
THIS PLACE... MAY BE A BIT DANGEROUS.
TMP
... EH?
MASTER?

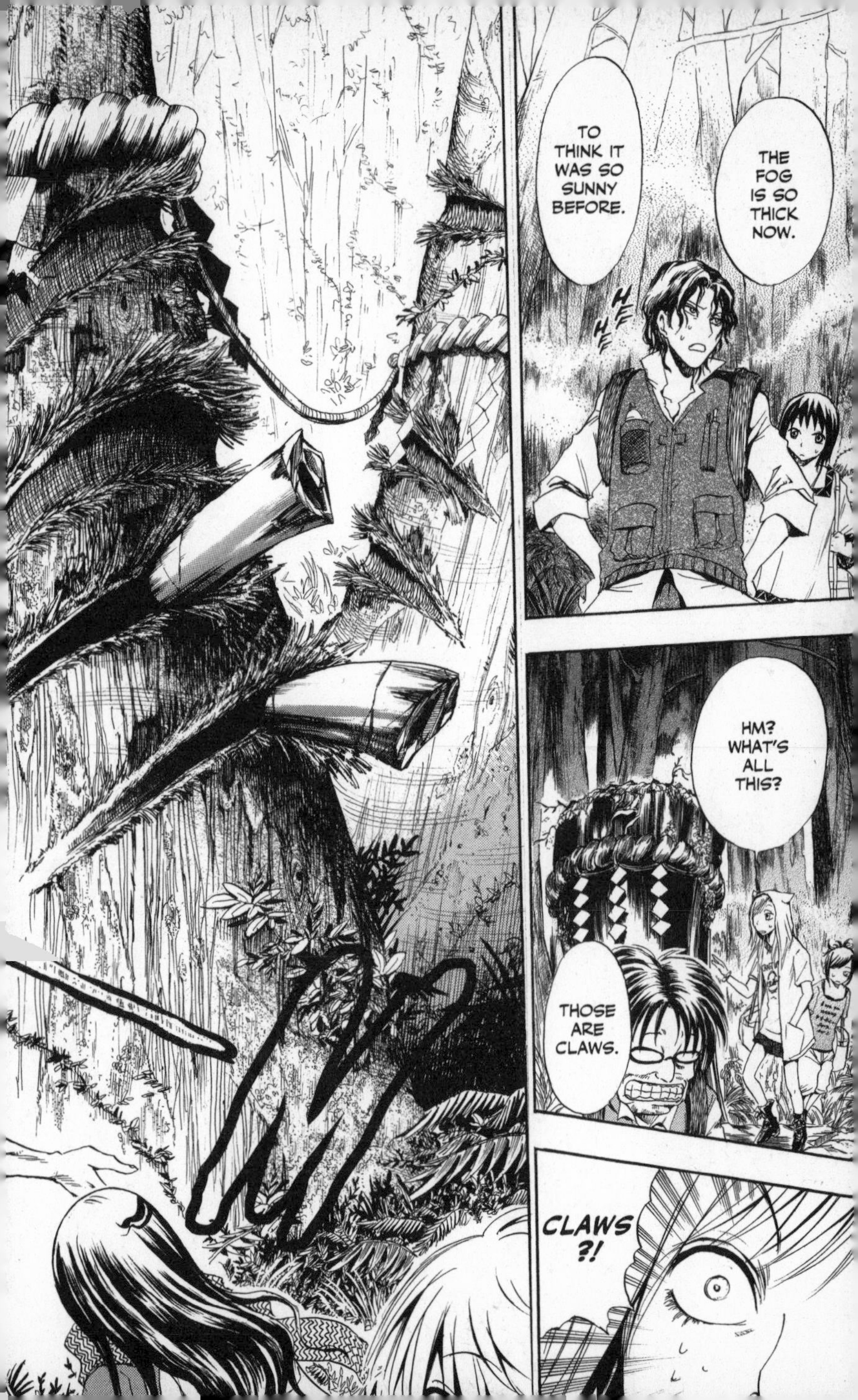
THE FOG IS SO THICK NOW.
TO THINK IT WAS SO SUNNY BEFORE.
HM? WHAT'S ALL THIS?
THOSE ARE CLAWS.
CLAWS ?!

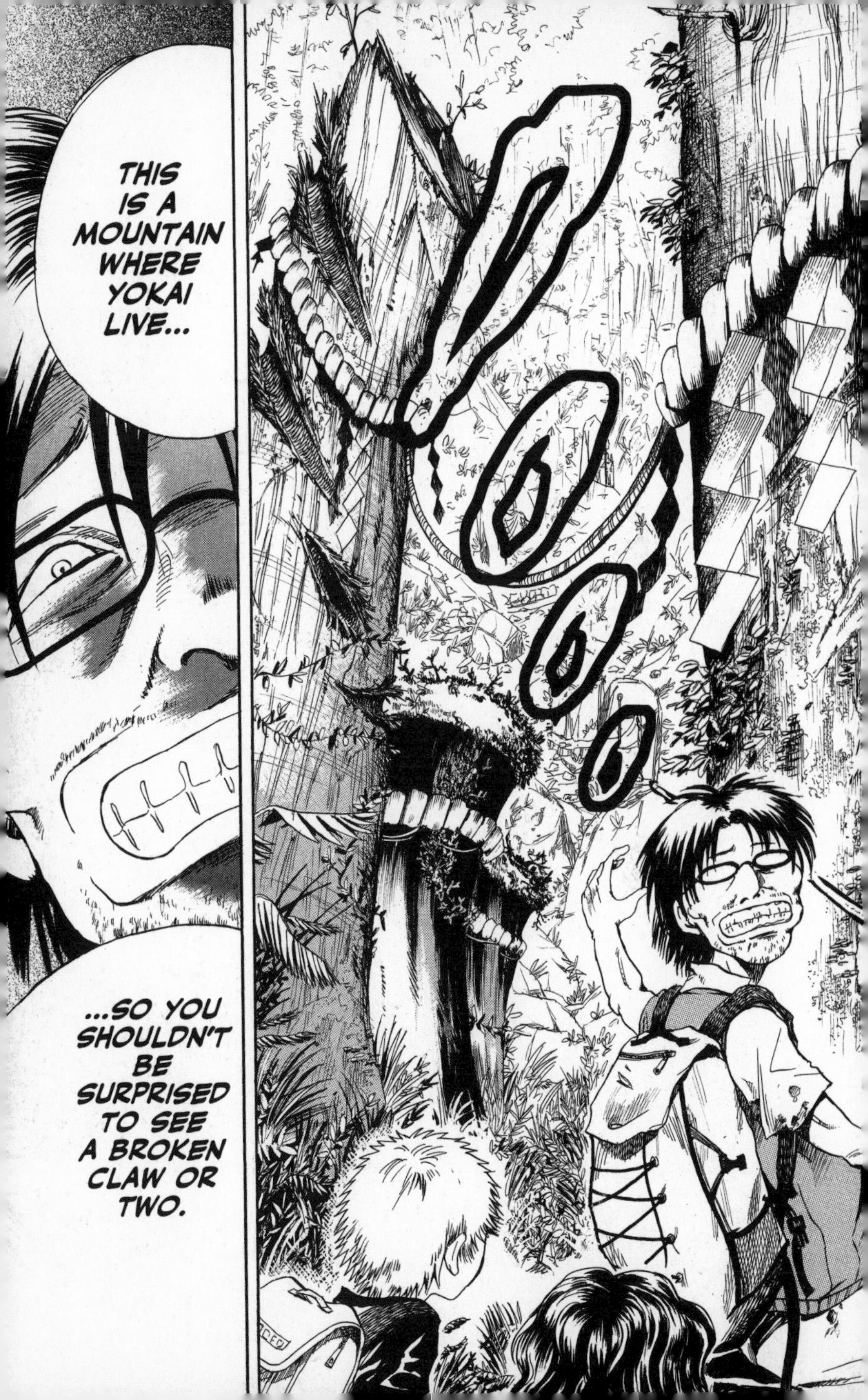
THIS IS A MOUNTAIN WHERE YOKAI LIVE...
...SO YOU SHOULDN'T BE SURPRISED TO SEE A BROKEN CLAW OR TWO.

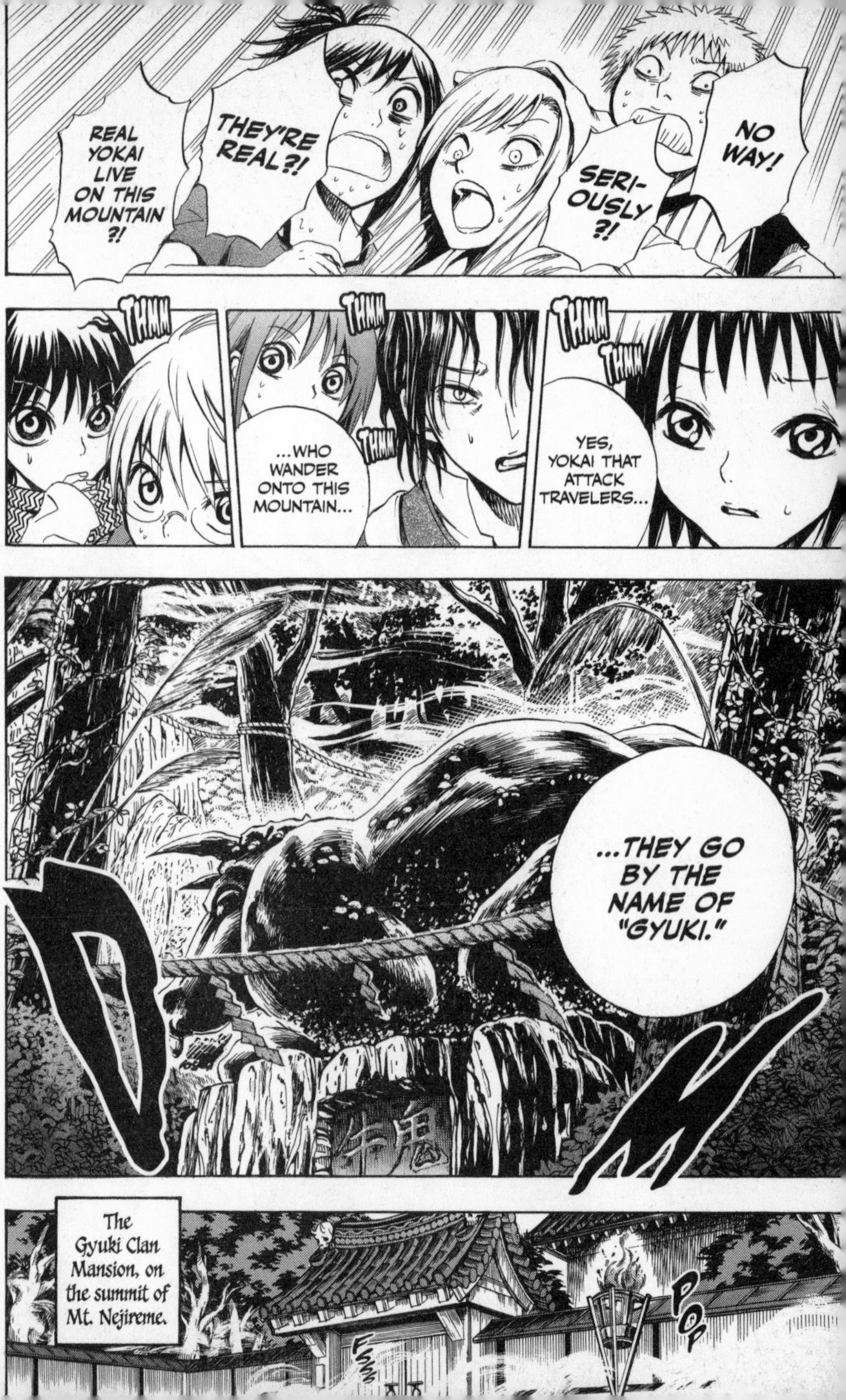
NO WAY!
SERI-OUSLY?!
THEY'RE REAL?!
REAL YOKAI LIVE ON THIS MOUNTAIN?!
THMM
THMM
YES, YOKAI THAT ATTACK TRAVELERS...
THMM
...WHO WANDER ONTO THIS MOUNTAIN...
THMM
THMM
...THEY GO BY THE NAME OF "GYUKI."
DM
牛鬼
The Gyuki Clan Mansion, on the summit of Mt. Nejireme.
POP
FSSS

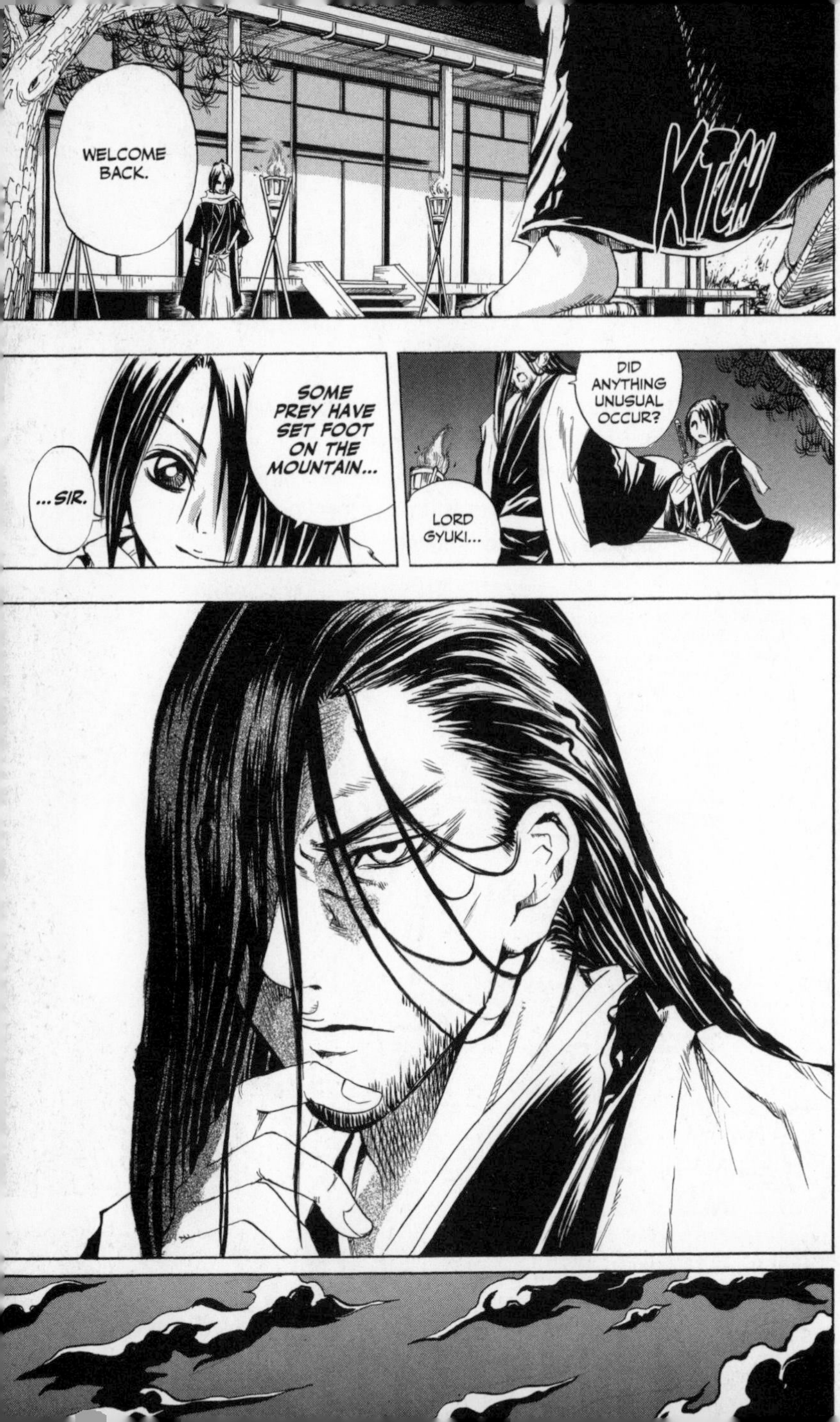
KTCH
WELCOME BACK.
DID ANYTHING UNUSUAL OCCUR?
LORD GYUKI...
SOME PREY HAVE SET FOOT ON THE MOUNTAIN...
...SIR.

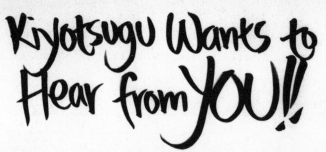

Kiyotsugu Wants to Hear from YOU!!

Introducing a website for yokai enthusiasts worldwide: **Yokai Brain**. Kiyotsugu, the webmaster of the site, is spending a huge amount from the advertising budget trying to set up a web adaptation of the Fan Art page!! Everyone, please do send letters!!

*Please include your name, age, address and phone number in the letter. If you do not want to include your name, please use a handle or nickname. Letters and illustrations mailed to us will be stored for a certain period, but then later discarded. If you wish to keep a copy, please make one yourself before mailing it in. If you'd like to have your name and address remain anonymous, please indicate that in your letter.

DIG DEEP!

MAILING ADDRESS:
Nura Editor
VIZ Media
P.O. Box 77010
San Francisco, CA 94107

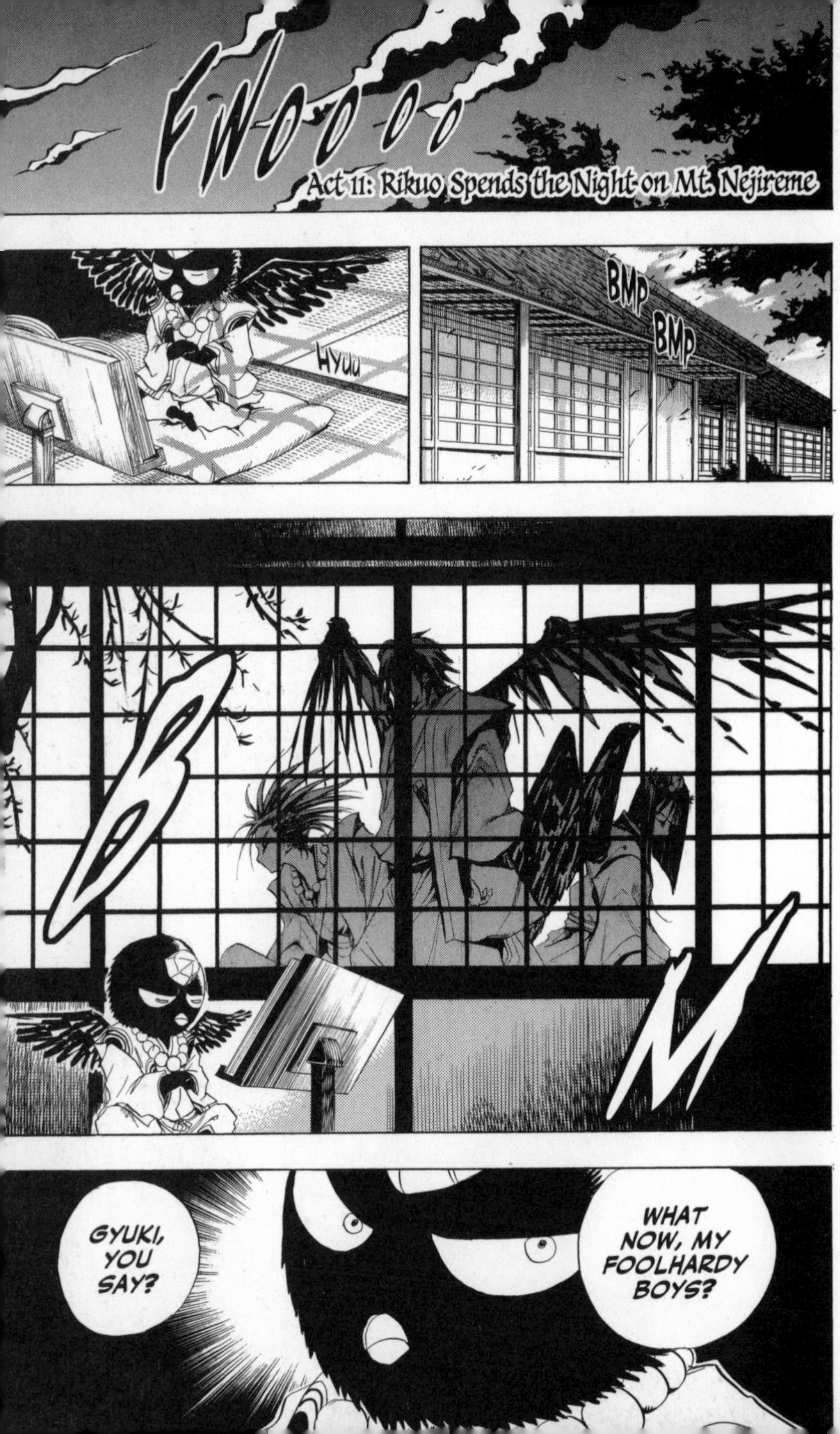
FWOOOO
Act 11: Rikuo Spends the Night on Mt. Nejireme
BMP
BMP
HYUU
WHAT NOW, MY FOOLHARDY BOYS?
GYUKI, YOU SAY?

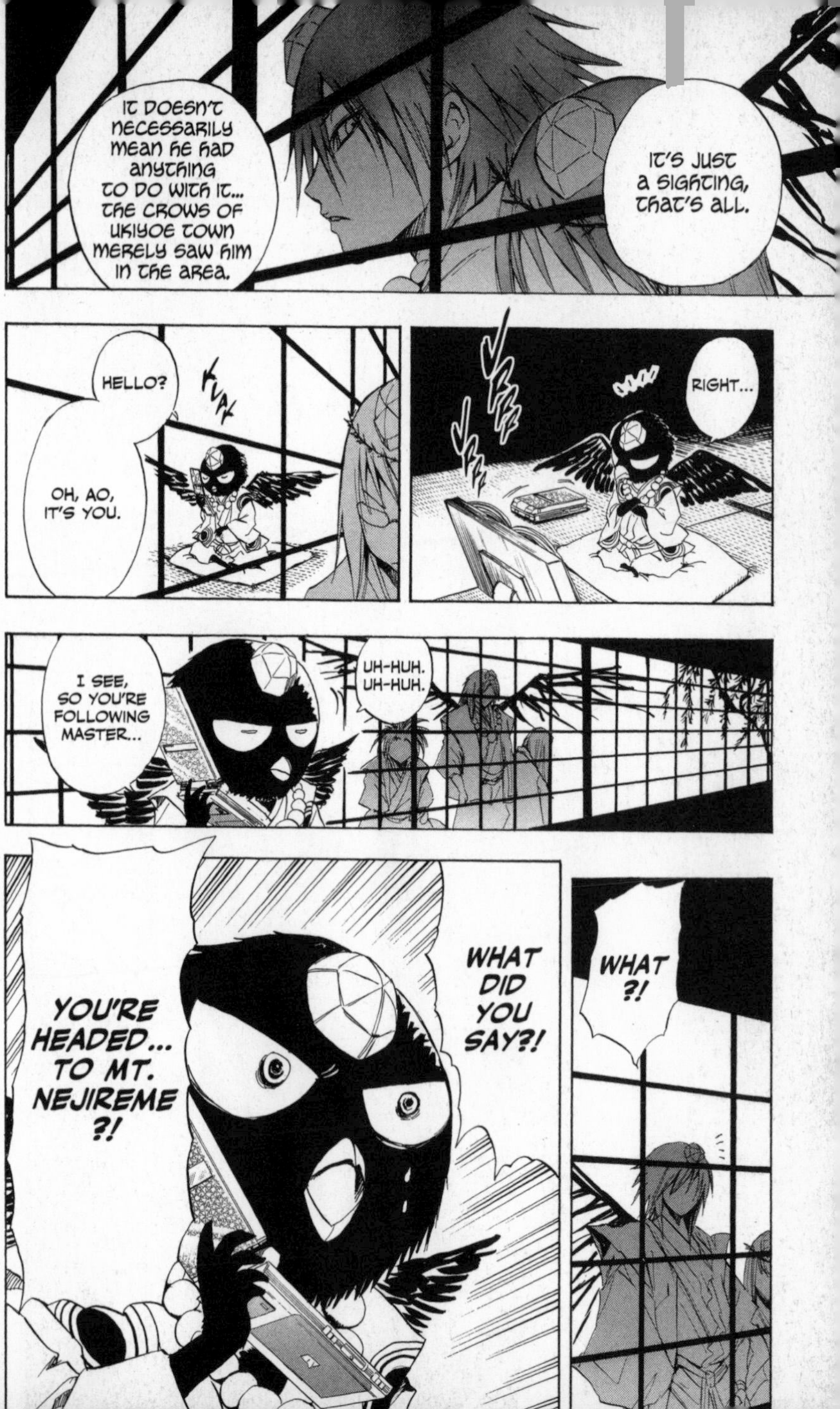
IT'S JUST A SIGHTING, THAT'S ALL.
IT DOESN'T NECESSARILY MEAN HE HAD ANYTHING TO DO WITH IT... THE CROWS OF UKIYOE TOWN MERELY SAW HIM IN THE AREA.
RIGHT...
HELLO?
OH, AO, IT'S YOU.
UH-HUH. UH-HUH.
I SEE, SO YOU'RE FOLLOWING MASTER...
WHAT ?!
WHAT DID YOU SAY?!
YOU'RE HEADED... TO MT. NEJIREME ?!

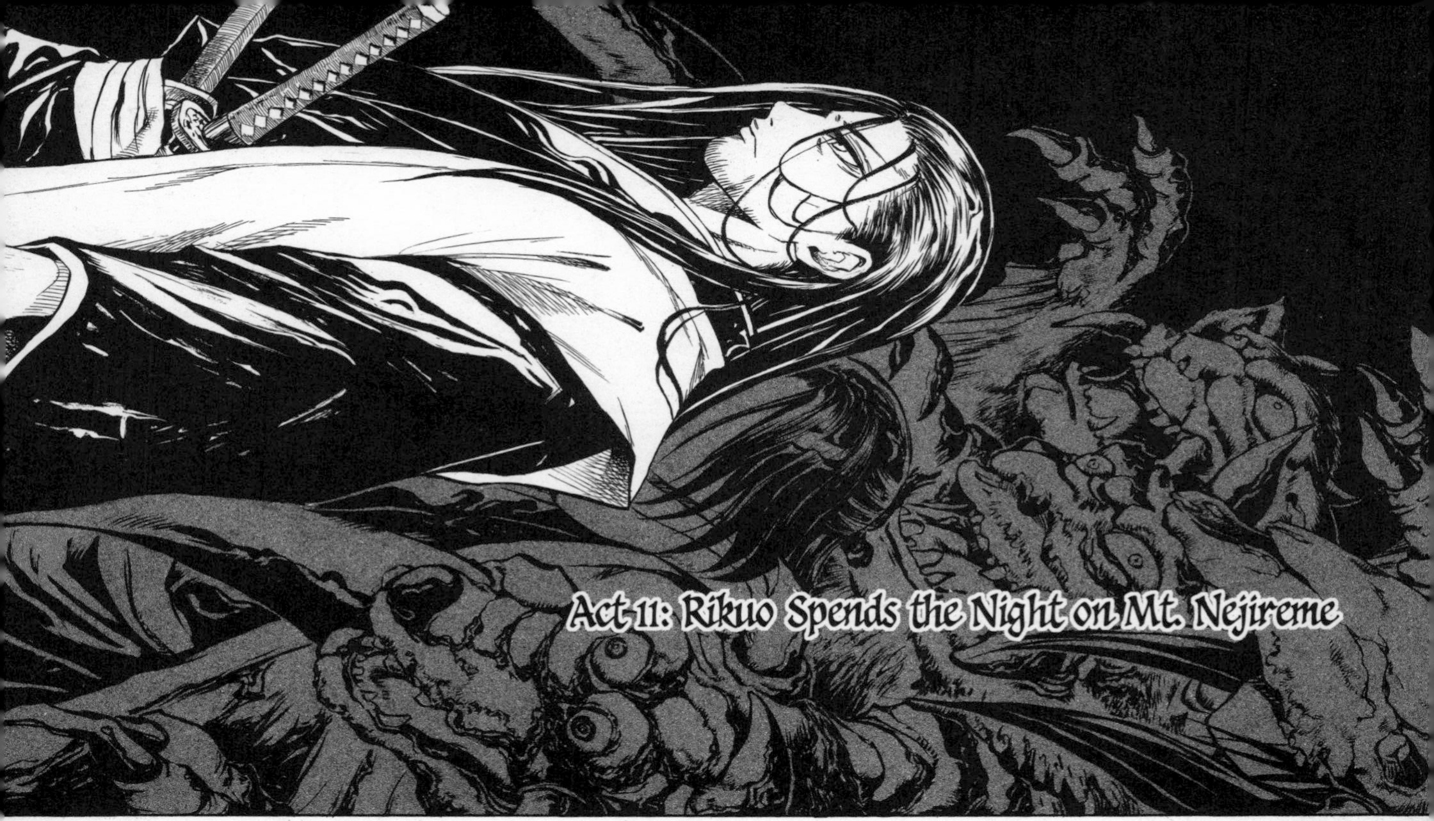
Act 11: Rikuo Spends the Night on Mt. Nejireme

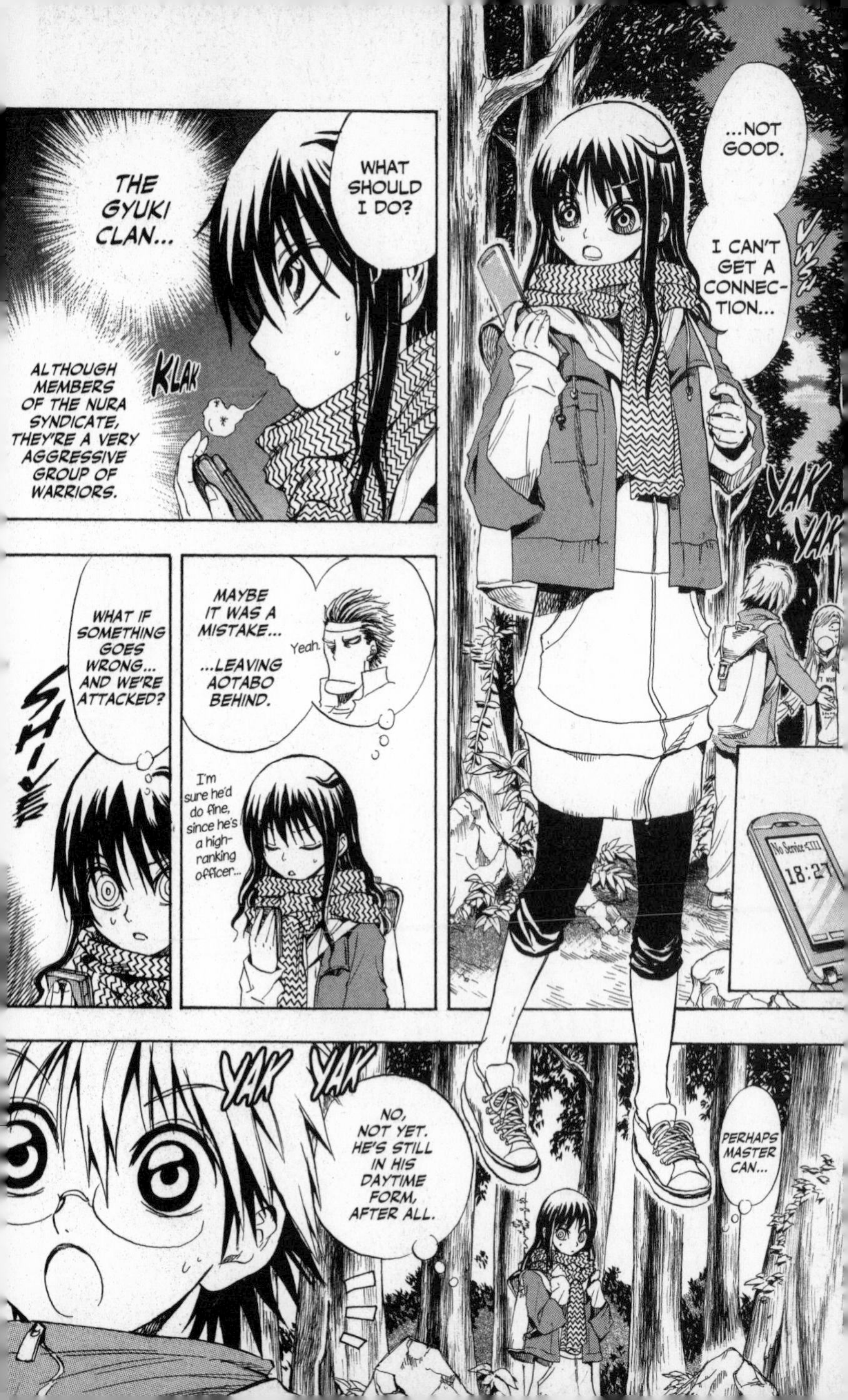
...NOT GOOD.
I CAN'T GET A CONNEC-TION...
YAK YAK
18:27
WHAT SHOULD I DO?
THE GYUKI CLAN...
KLAK
ALTHOUGH MEMBERS OF THE NURA SYNDICATE, THEY'RE A VERY AGGRESSIVE GROUP OF WARRIORS.
MAYBE IT WAS A MISTAKE... ...LEAVING AOTABO BEHIND.
Yeah.
I'm sure he'd do fine, since he's a high-ranking officer...
WHAT IF SOMETHING GOES WRONG... AND WE'RE ATTACKED?
SHIVER
PERHAPS MASTER CAN...
NO, NOT YET. HE'S STILL IN HIS DAYTIME FORM, AFTER ALL.
YAK YAK

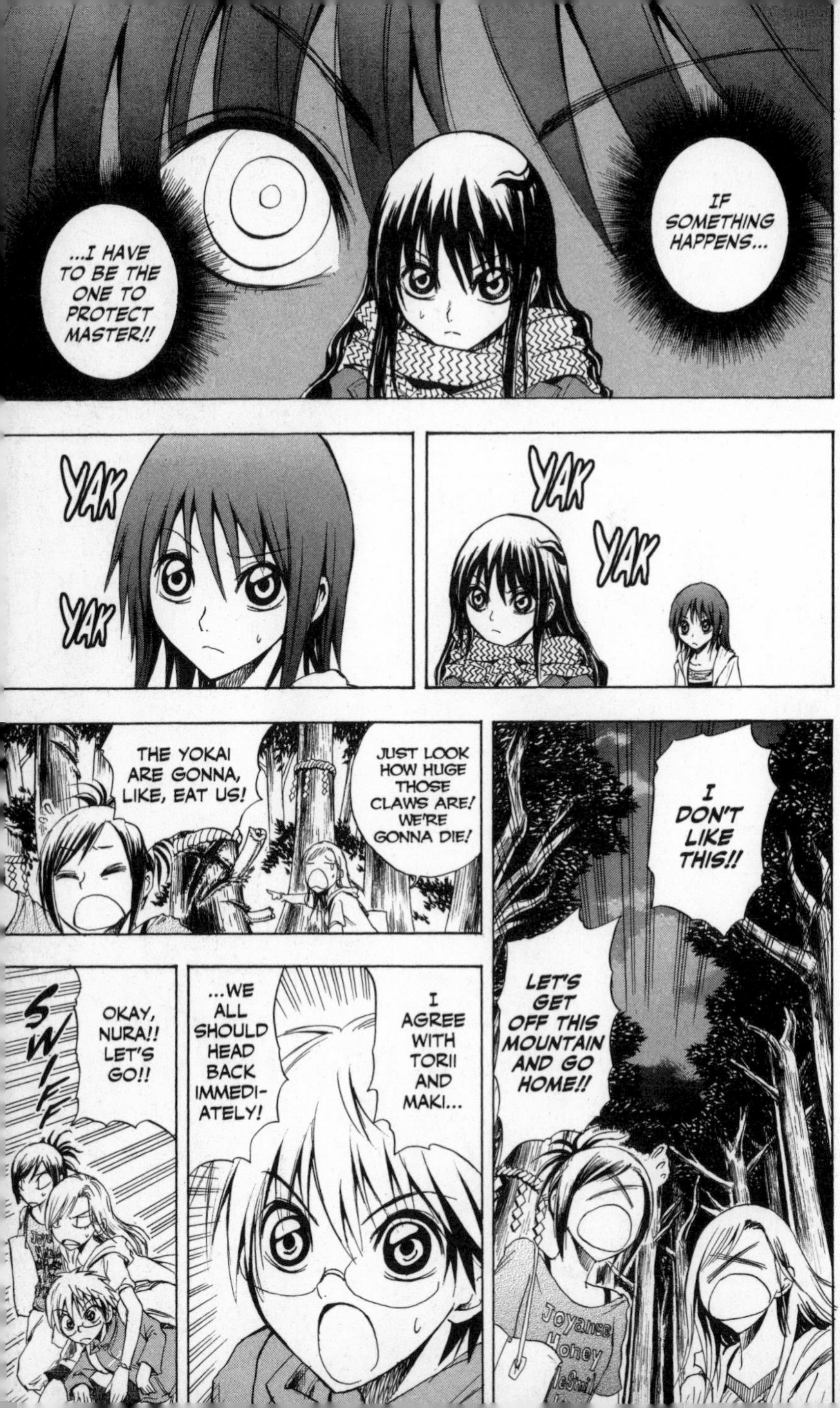
IF SOMETHING HAPPENS...
...I HAVE TO BE THE ONE TO PROTECT MASTER!!
YAK
YAK
YAK
YAK
I DON'T LIKE THIS!!
LET'S GET OFF THIS MOUNTAIN AND GO HOME!!
JUST LOOK HOW HUGE THOSE CLAWS ARE! WE'RE GONNA DIE!
THE YOKAI ARE GONNA, LIKE, EAT US!
I AGREE WITH TORII AND MAKI...
...WE ALL SHOULD HEAD BACK IMMEDI-ATELY!
SWIFF
OKAY, NURA!! LET'S GO!!

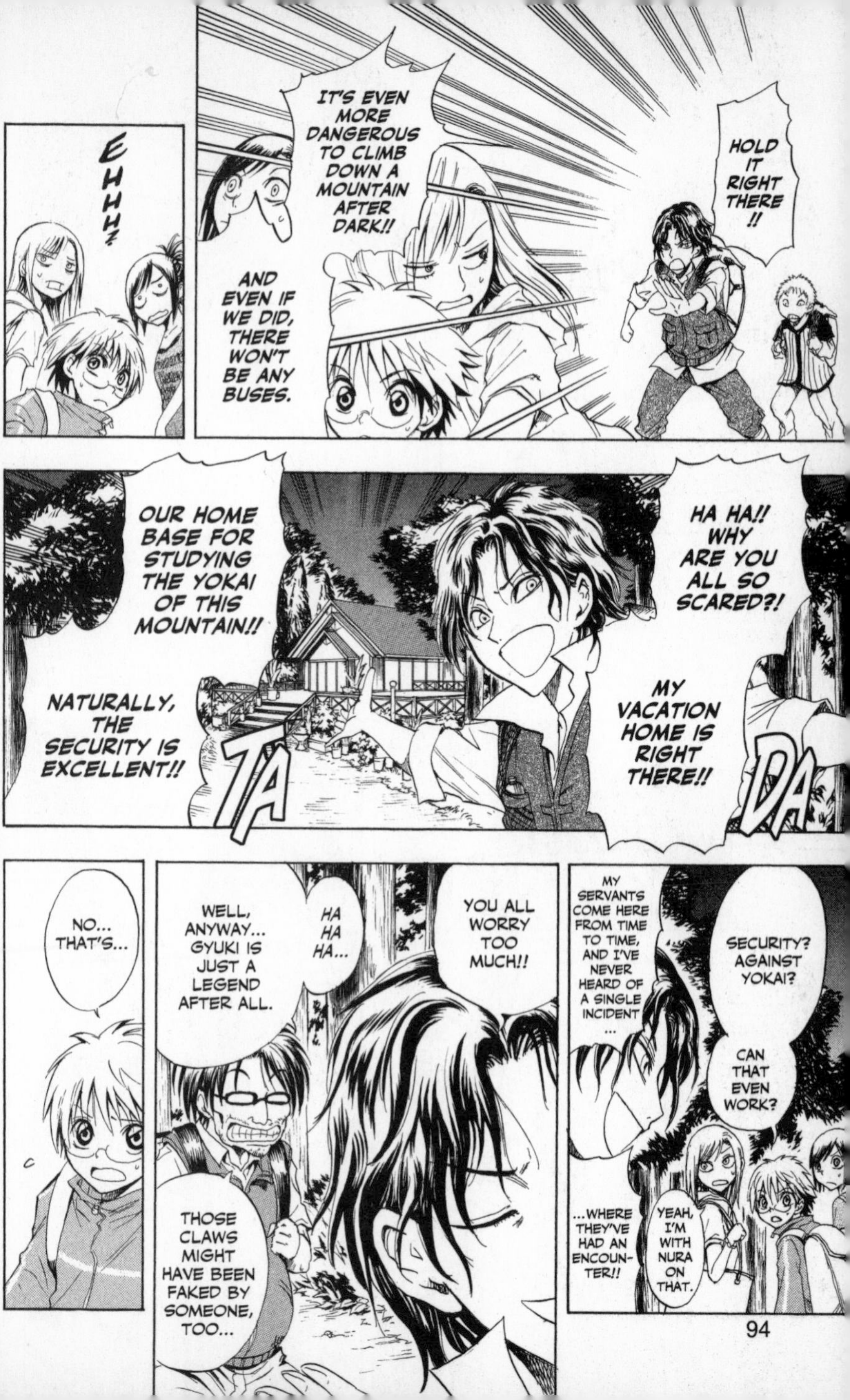
HOLD IT RIGHT THERE!!
IT'S EVEN MORE DANGEROUS TO CLIMB DOWN A MOUNTAIN AFTER DARK!!
AND EVEN IF WE DID, THERE WON'T BE ANY BUSES.
EHHHH?
HA HA!! WHY ARE YOU ALL SO SCARED?!
MY VACATION HOME IS RIGHT THERE!!
DA
OUR HOME BASE FOR STUDYING THE YOKAI OF THIS MOUNTAIN!!
NATURALLY, THE SECURITY IS EXCELLENT!!
TA
SECURITY? AGAINST YOKAI?
MY SERVANTS COME HERE FROM TIME TO TIME, AND I'VE NEVER HEARD OF A SINGLE INCIDENT ...
CAN THAT EVEN WORK?
YEAH, I'M WITH NURA ON THAT.
...WHERE THEY'VE HAD AN ENCOUNTER!!
YOU ALL WORRY TOO MUCH!!
HA HA HA...
WELL, ANYWAY... GYUKI IS JUST A LEGEND AFTER ALL.
THOSE CLAWS MIGHT HAVE BEEN FAKED BY SOMEONE, TOO...
NO... THAT'S...

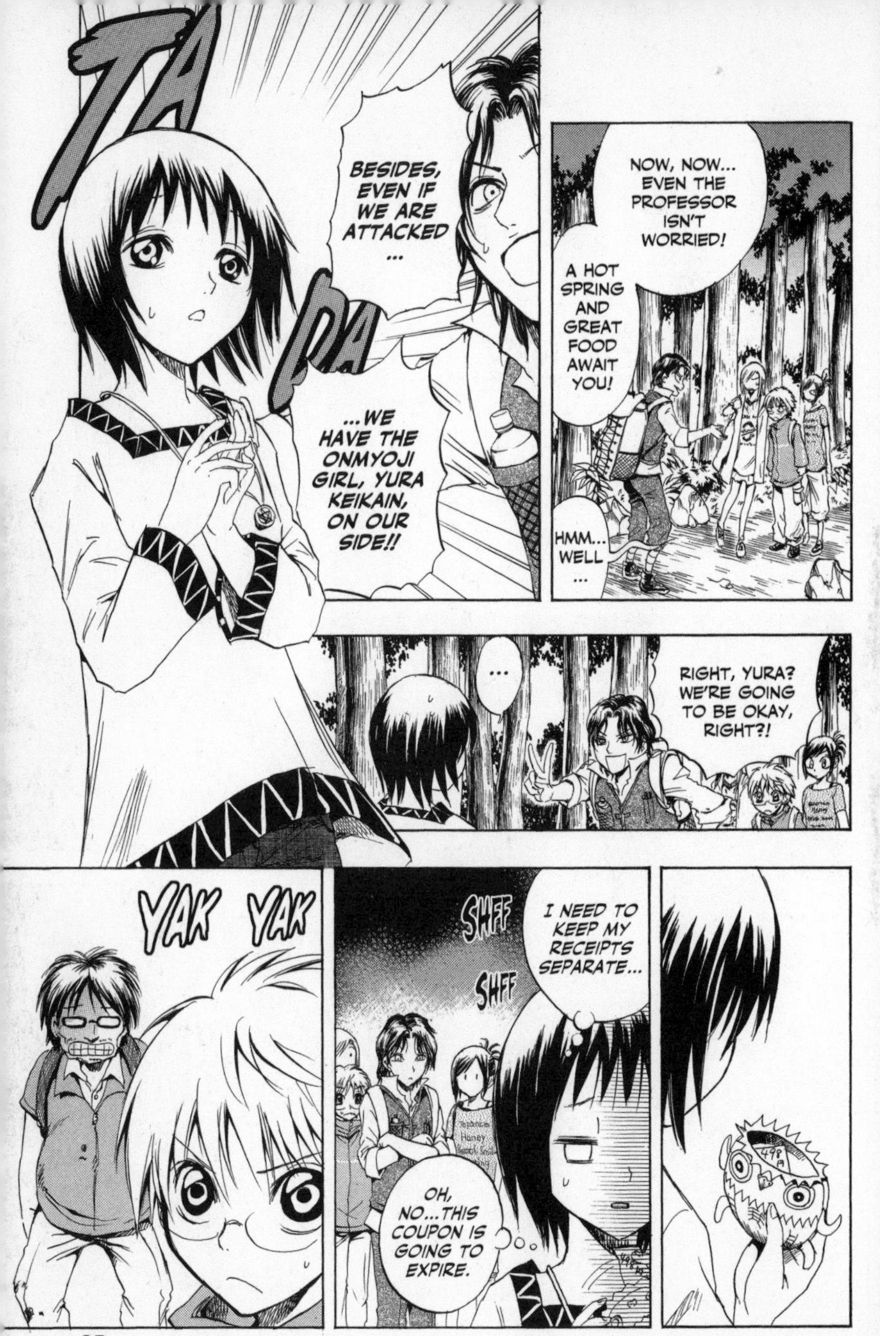
NOW, NOW... EVEN THE PROFESSOR ISN'T WORRIED!
A HOT SPRING AND GREAT FOOD AWAIT YOU!
HMM... WELL ...
BESIDES, EVEN IF WE ARE ATTACKED ...
...WE HAVE THE ONMYOJI GIRL, YURA KEIKAIN, ON OUR SIDE!!
TA DA
RIGHT, YURA? WE'RE GOING TO BE OKAY, RIGHT?!
...
SHFF
SHFF
I NEED TO KEEP MY RECEIPTS SEPARATE...
OH, NO...THIS COUPON IS GOING TO EXPIRE.
YAK YAK

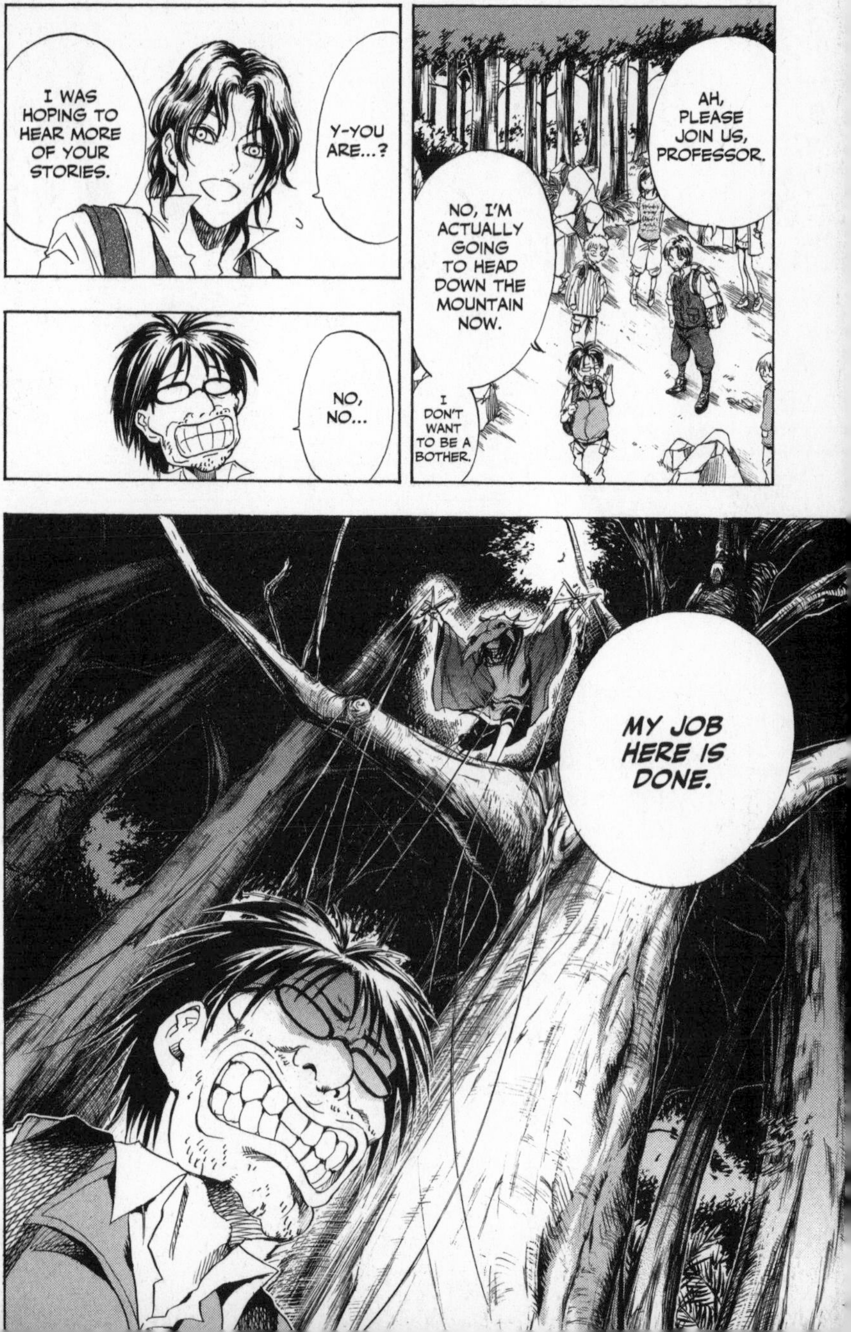
AH, PLEASE JOIN US, PROFESSOR.
NO, I'M ACTUALLY GOING TO HEAD DOWN THE MOUNTAIN NOW.
I DON'T WANT TO BE A BOTHER.
Y-YOU ARE...?
I WAS HOPING TO HEAR MORE OF YOUR STORIES.
NO, NO...
MY JOB HERE IS DONE.

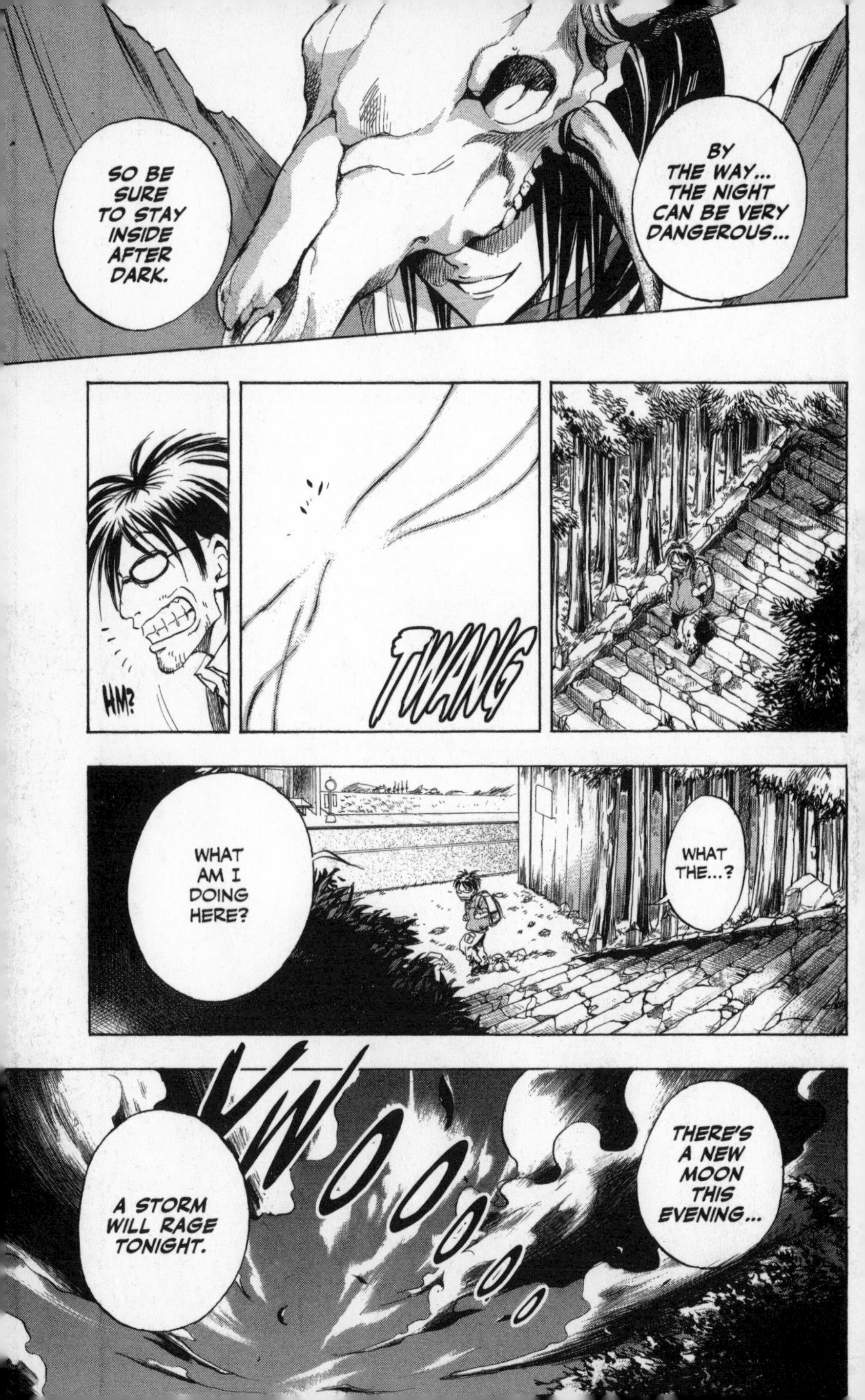
BY THE WAY... THE NIGHT CAN BE VERY DANGEROUS...
SO BE SURE TO STAY INSIDE AFTER DARK.
TWANG
HM?
WHAT THE...?
WHAT AM I DOING HERE?
THERE'S A NEW MOON THIS EVENING...
VWOOOOO
A STORM WILL RAGE TONIGHT.

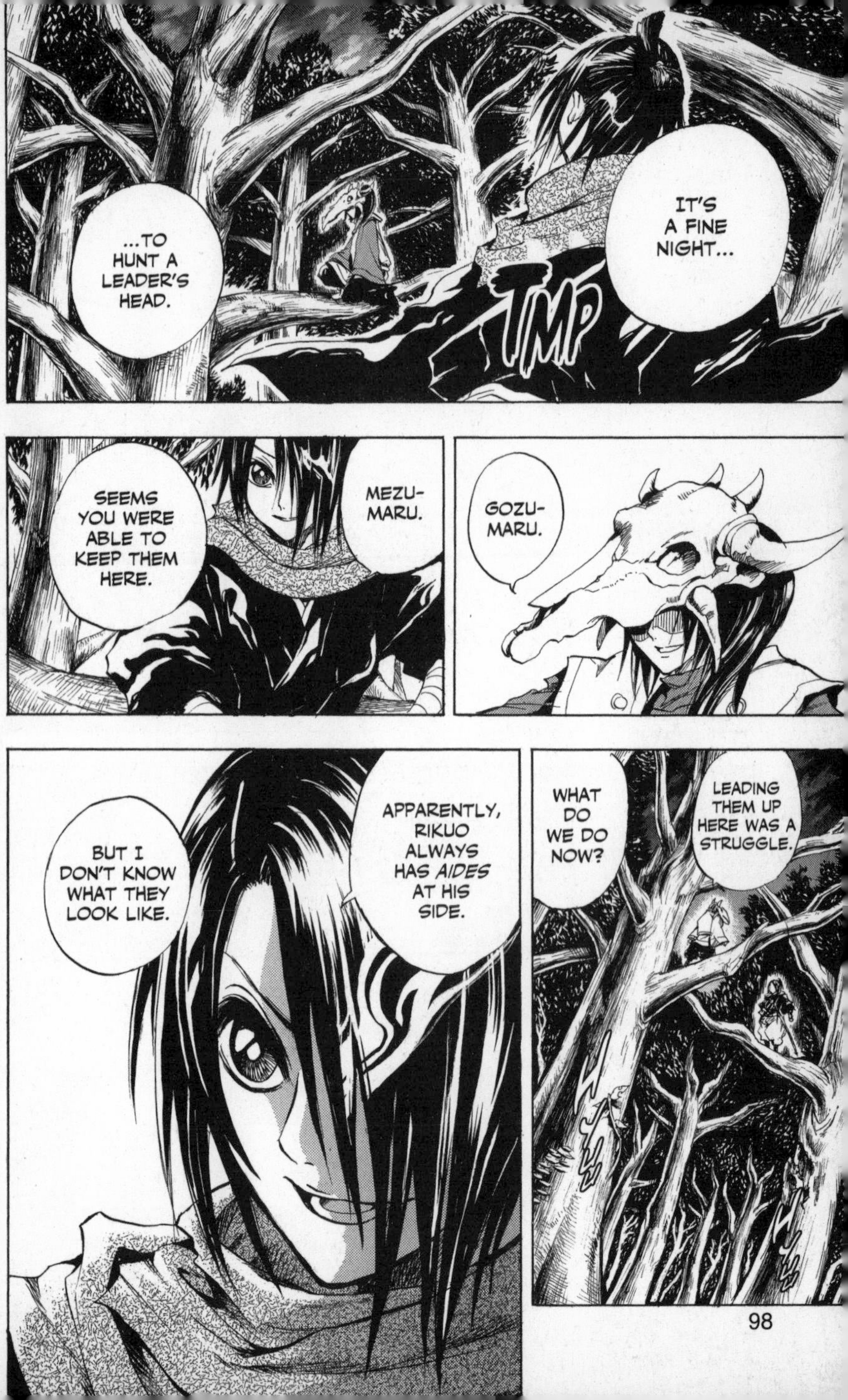
IT'S A FINE NIGHT...
TMP
...TO HUNT A LEADER'S HEAD.
GOZU-MARU.
MEZU-MARU.
SEEMS YOU WERE ABLE TO KEEP THEM HERE.
LEADING THEM UP HERE WAS A STRUGGLE.
WHAT DO WE DO NOW?
APPARENTLY, RIKUO ALWAYS HAS *AIDES* AT HIS SIDE.
BUT I DON'T KNOW WHAT THEY LOOK LIKE.

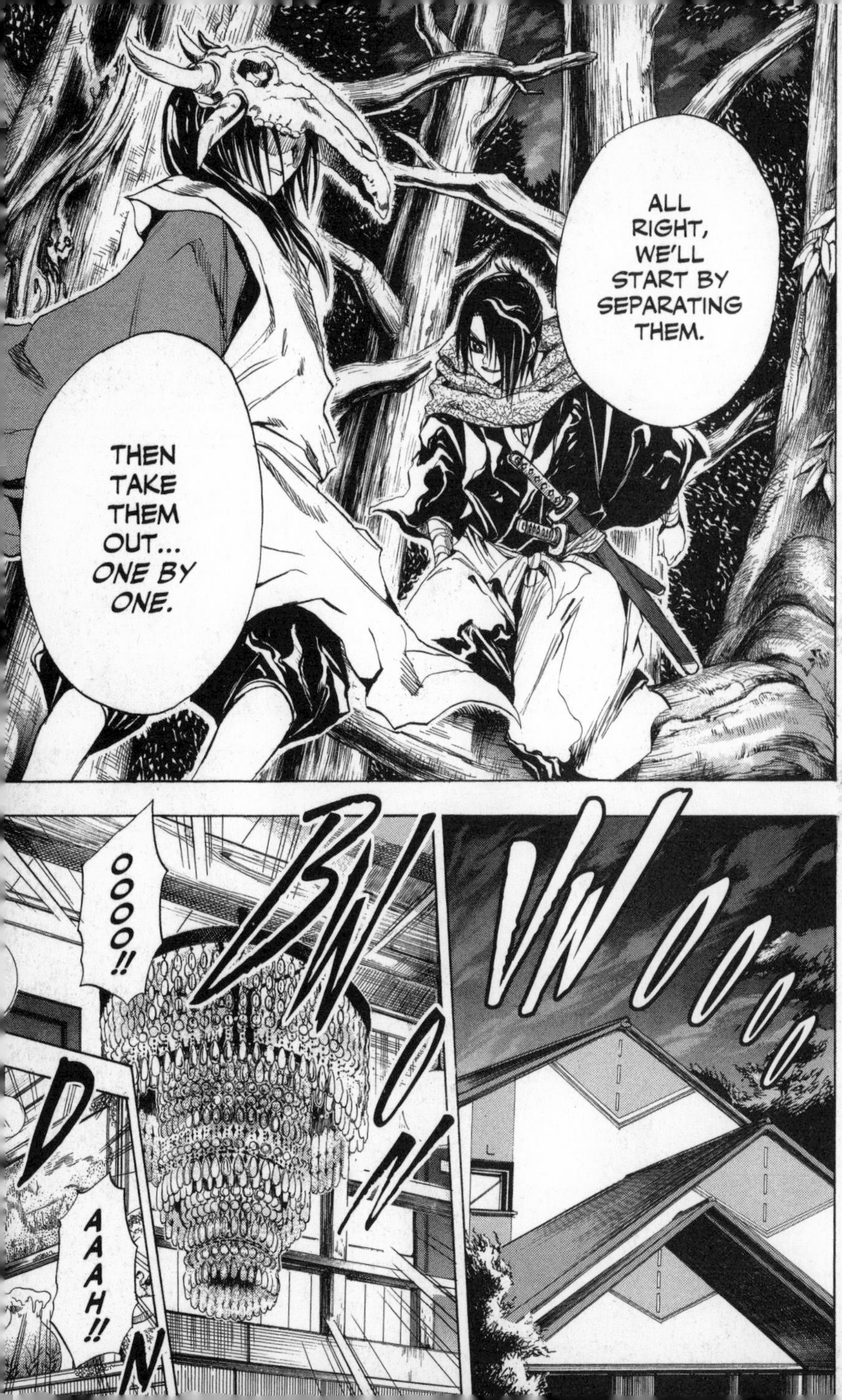
ALL RIGHT, WE'LL START BY SEPARATING THEM.
THEN TAKE THEM OUT... *ONE BY ONE.*
OOOO!!
AAAAH!!

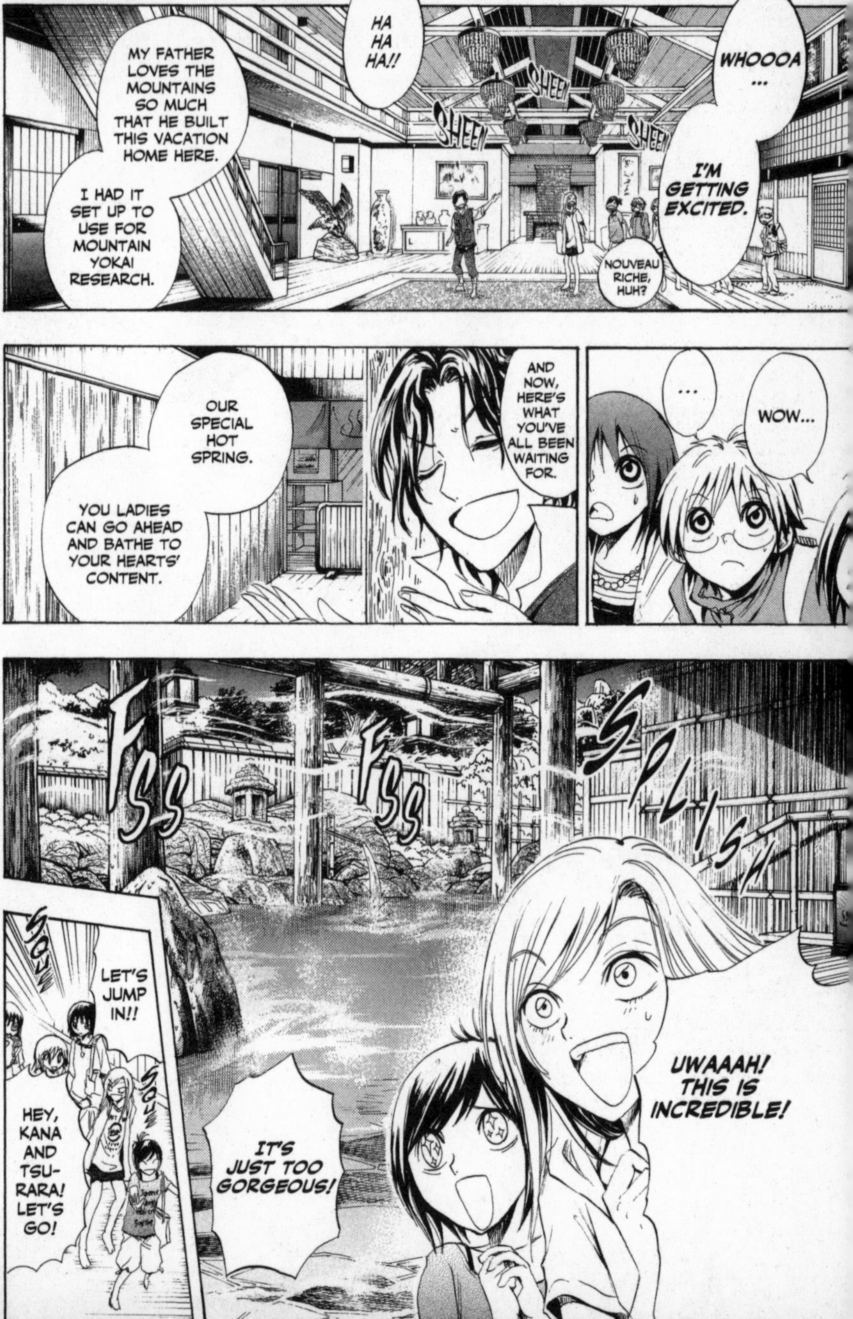
WHOOOA ...
I'M GETTING EXCITED.
NOUVEAU RICHE, HUH?
SHEEN
SHEEN
SHEEN
HA HA HA!!
MY FATHER LOVES THE MOUNTAINS SO MUCH THAT HE BUILT THIS VACATION HOME HERE.
I HAD IT SET UP TO USE FOR MOUNTAIN YOKAI RESEARCH.
WOW...
...
AND NOW, HERE'S WHAT YOU'VE ALL BEEN WAITING FOR.
OUR SPECIAL HOT SPRING.
YOU LADIES CAN GO AHEAD AND BATHE TO YOUR HEARTS' CONTENT.
SPLISH
FSS
FSS
UWAAAH! THIS IS INCREDIBLE!
IT'S JUST TOO GORGEOUS!
LET'S JUMP IN!!
HEY, KANA AND TSU-RARA! LET'S GO!

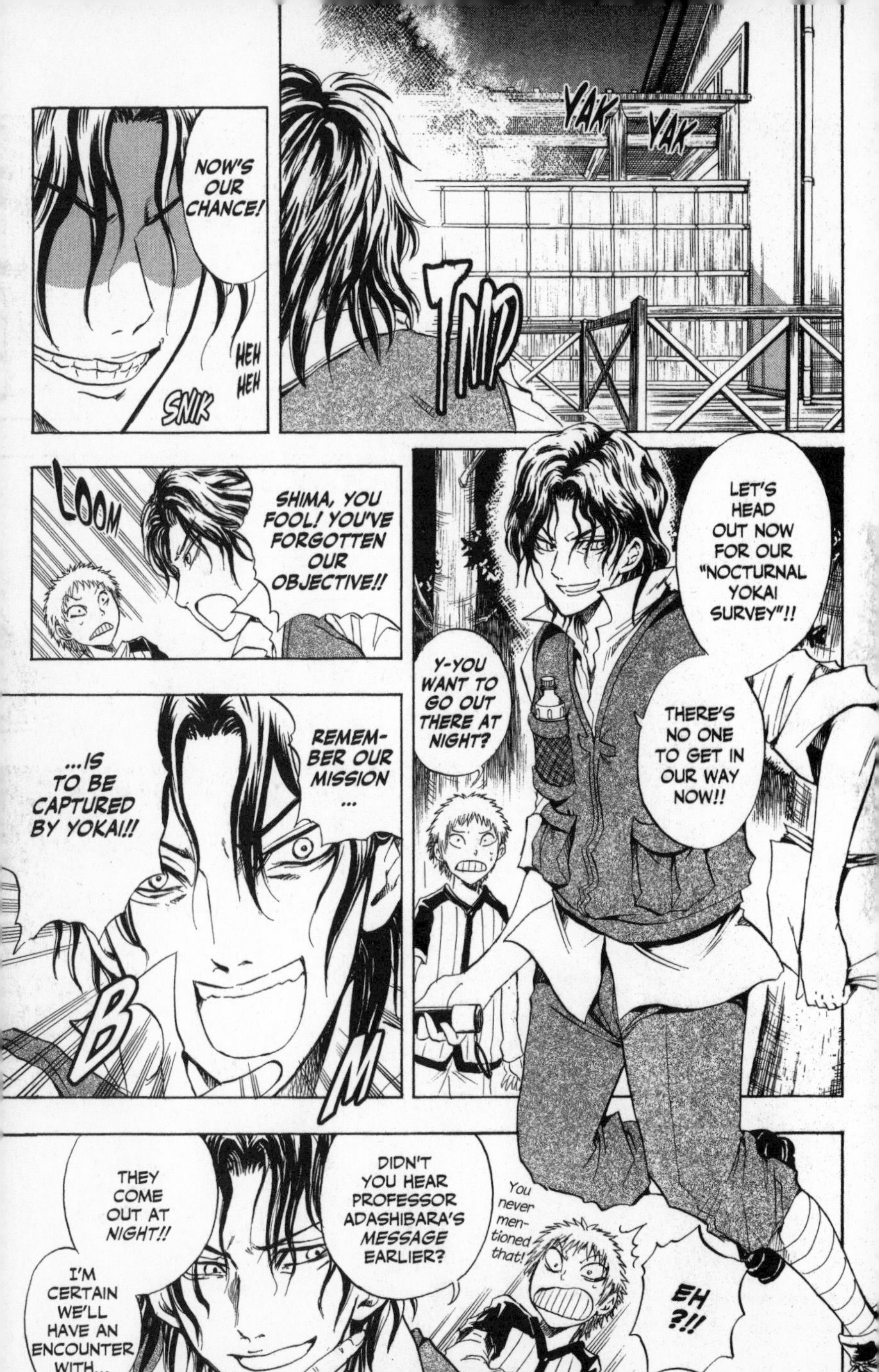
YAK YAK
TMP
NOW'S OUR CHANCE!
HEH HEH
SNIK
LET'S HEAD OUT NOW FOR OUR "NOCTURNAL YOKAI SURVEY"!!
THERE'S NO ONE TO GET IN OUR WAY NOW!!
Y-YOU WANT TO GO OUT THERE AT NIGHT?
LOOM
SHIMA, YOU FOOL! YOU'VE FORGOTTEN OUR OBJECTIVE!!
REMEMBER OUR MISSION ...
...IS TO BE CAPTURED BY YOKAI!!
BM
DIDN'T YOU HEAR PROFESSOR ADASHIBARA'S MESSAGE EARLIER?
THEY COME OUT AT NIGHT!!
I'M CERTAIN WE'LL HAVE AN ENCOUNTER WITH...
You never mentioned that!
EH ?!!

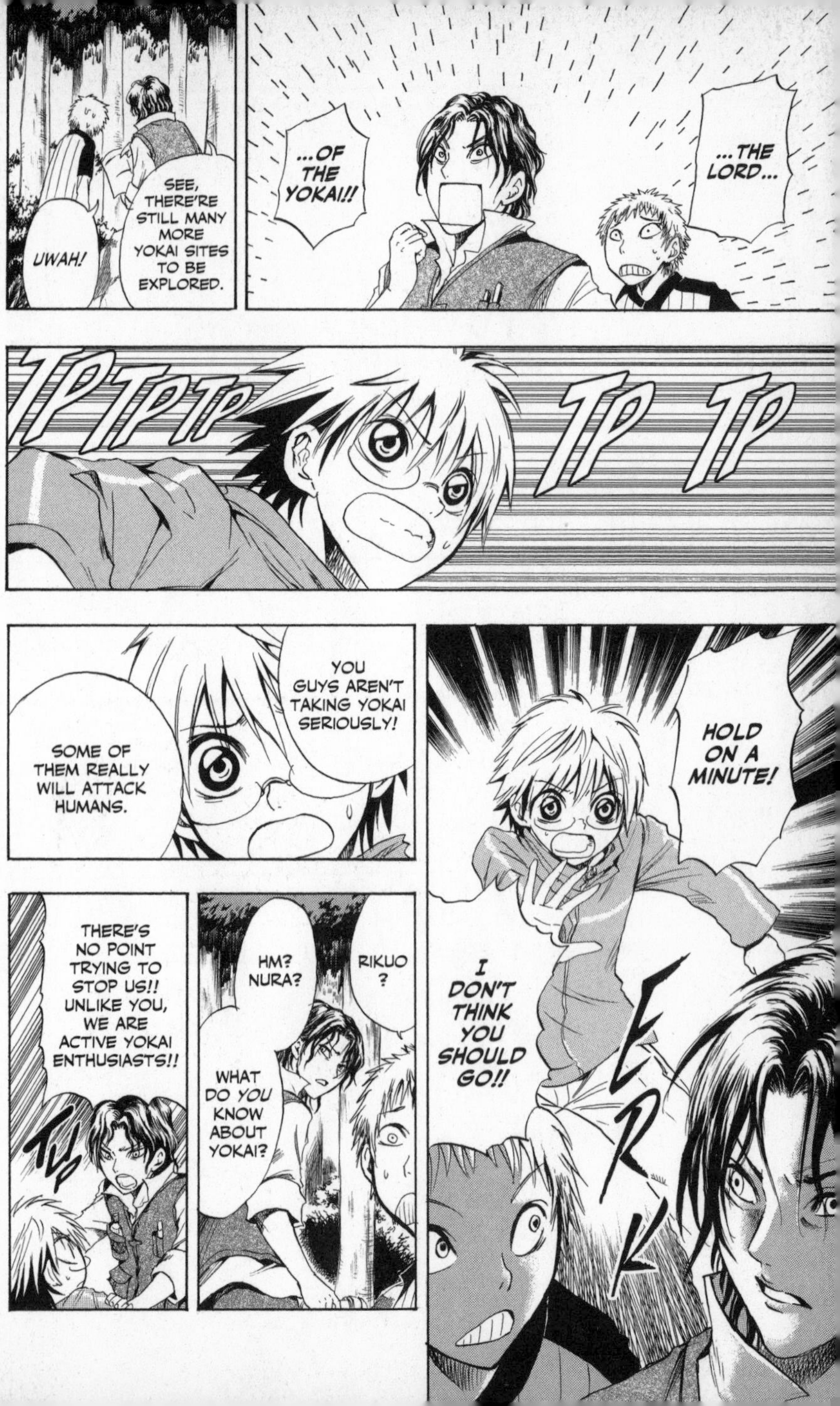
...THE LORD...
...OF THE YOKAI!!
SEE, THERE'RE STILL MANY MORE YOKAI SITES TO BE EXPLORED.
UWAH!
TP TP
TPTPTP
HOLD ON A MINUTE!
I DON'T THINK YOU SHOULD GO!!
EERK
YOU GUYS AREN'T TAKING YOKAI SERIOUSLY!
SOME OF THEM REALLY WILL ATTACK HUMANS.
RIKUO?
HM? NURA?
WHAT DO YOU KNOW ABOUT YOKAI?
THERE'S NO POINT TRYING TO STOP US!! UNLIKE YOU, WE ARE ACTIVE YOKAI ENTHUSIASTS!!
TMP

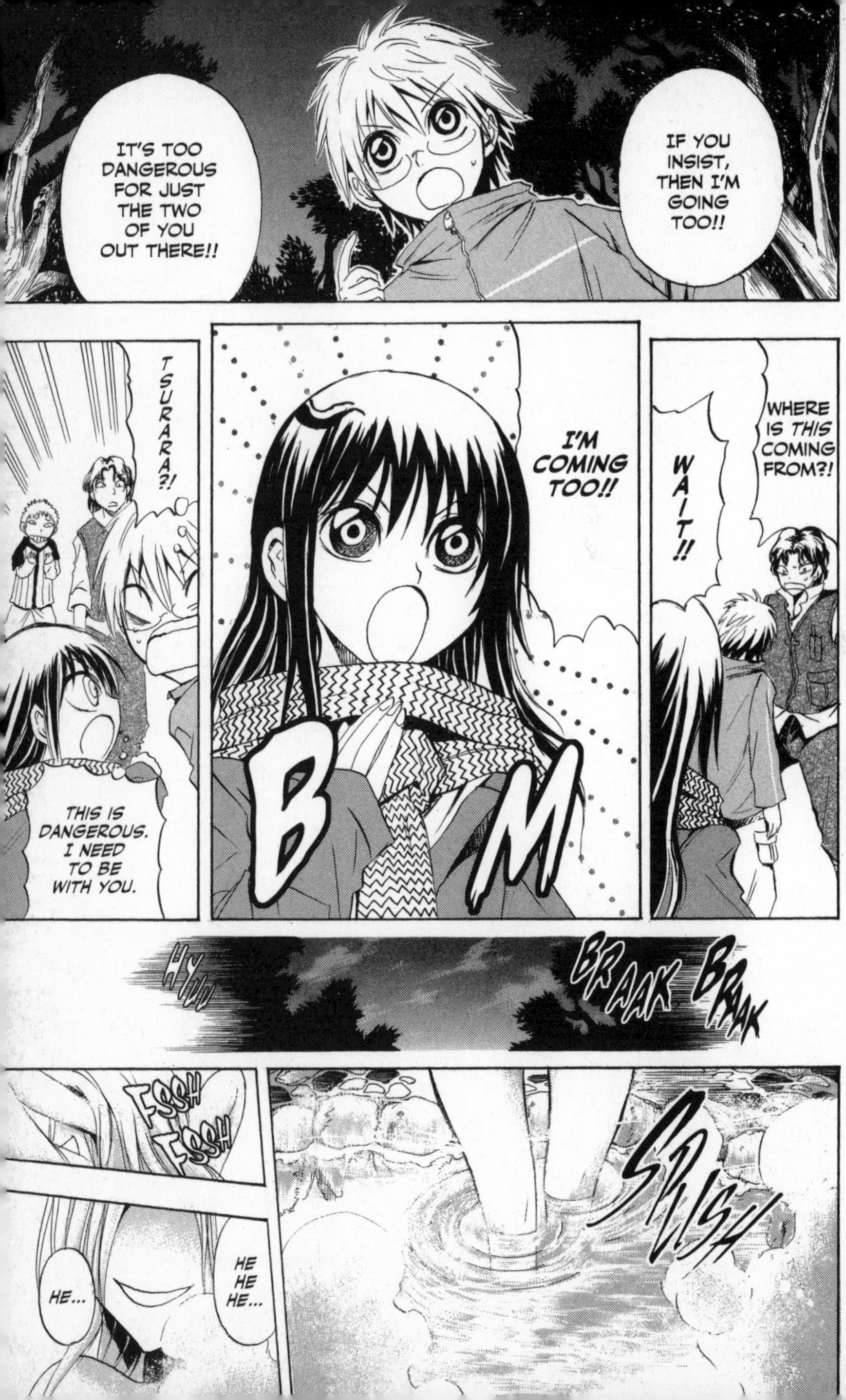
IF YOU INSIST, THEN I'M GOING TOO!!
IT'S TOO DANGEROUS FOR JUST THE TWO OF YOU OUT THERE!!
WHERE IS THIS COMING FROM?!
WAIT!!
I'M COMING TOO!!
BM
TSURARA?!
THIS IS DANGEROUS. I NEED TO BE WITH YOU.
BRAAK BRAAK
HYUU
SPLISH
FSSH FSSH
HE HE HE...
HE...

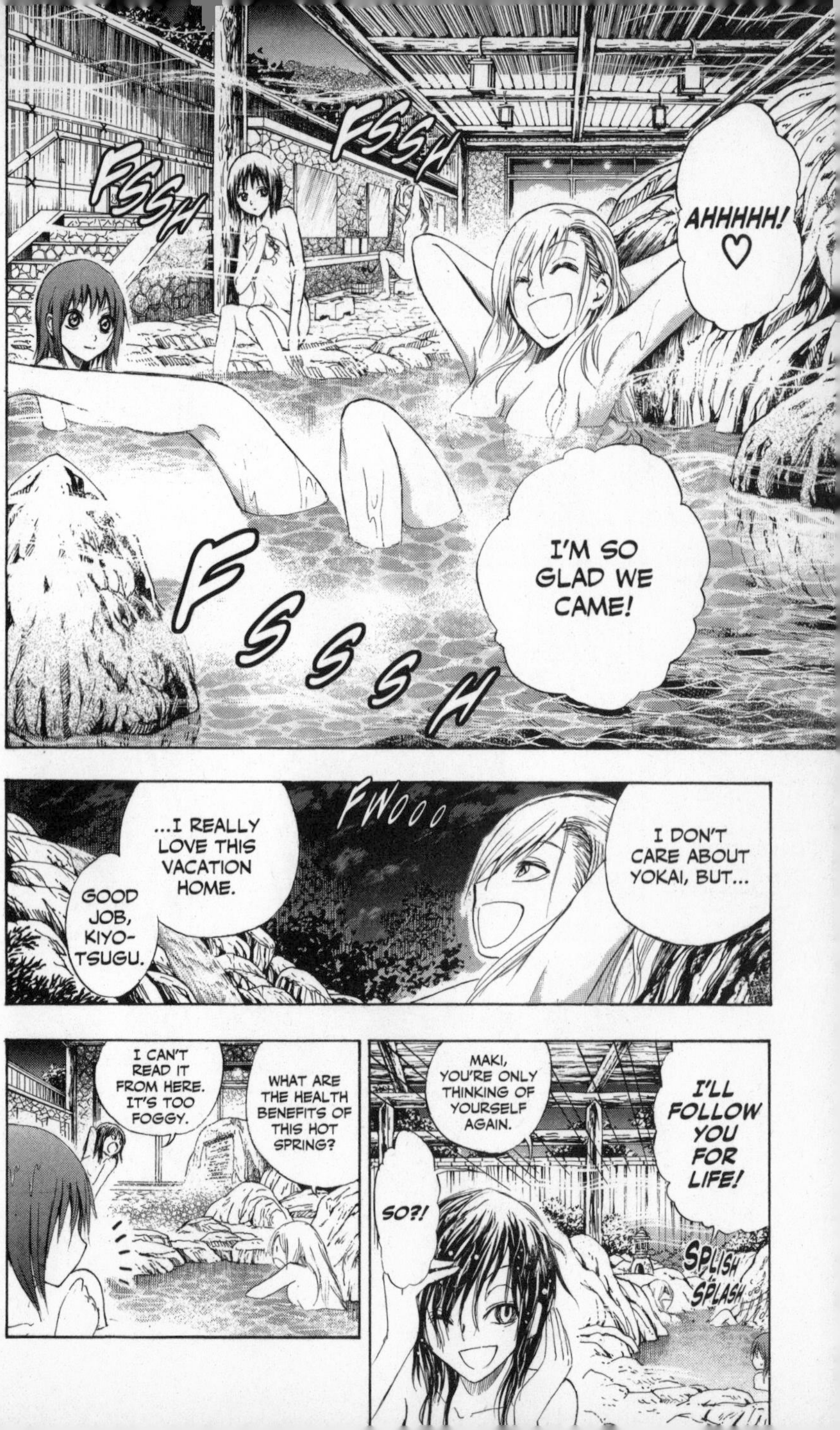
AHHHHH! ♡
FSSH
FSSH
I'M SO GLAD WE CAME!
FSSSH
I DON'T CARE ABOUT YOKAI, BUT...
FWOOO
...I REALLY LOVE THIS VACATION HOME.
GOOD JOB, KIYOTSUGU.
I'LL FOLLOW YOU FOR LIFE!
MAKI, YOU'RE ONLY THINKING OF YOURSELF AGAIN.
SO?!
SPLISH SPLASH
WHAT ARE THE HEALTH BENEFITS OF THIS HOT SPRING?
I CAN'T READ IT FROM HERE. IT'S TOO FOGGY.

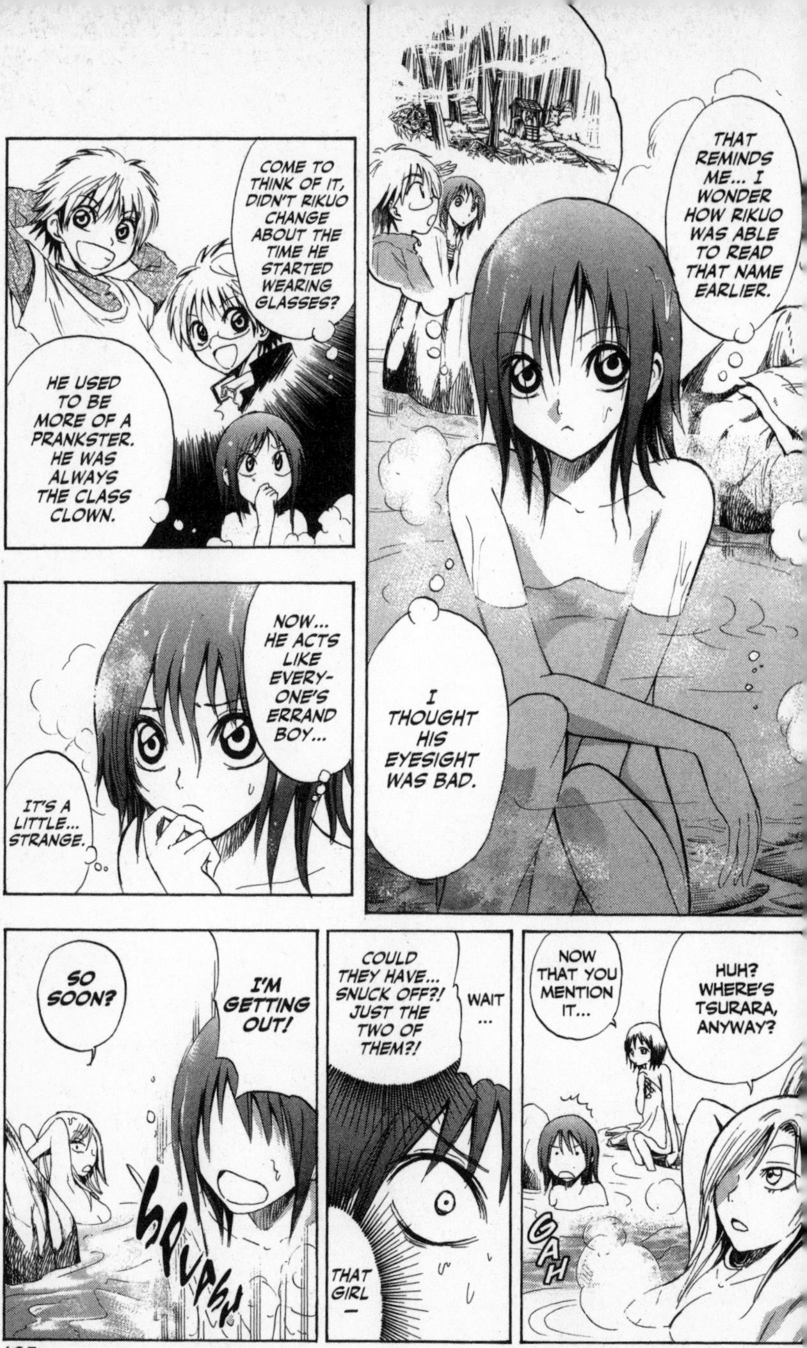
THAT REMINDS ME... I WONDER HOW RIKUO WAS ABLE TO READ THAT NAME EARLIER.
I THOUGHT HIS EYESIGHT WAS BAD.
COME TO THINK OF IT, DIDN'T RIKUO CHANGE ABOUT THE TIME HE STARTED WEARING GLASSES?
HE USED TO BE MORE OF A PRANKSTER. HE WAS ALWAYS THE CLASS CLOWN.
NOW... HE ACTS LIKE EVERY-ONE'S ERRAND BOY...
IT'S A LITTLE... STRANGE.
HUH? WHERE'S TSURARA, ANYWAY?
NOW THAT YOU MENTION IT...
GAH
WAIT ...
COULD THEY HAVE... SNUCK OFF?! JUST THE TWO OF THEM?!
THAT GIRL —
I'M GETTING OUT!
SPLASH
SO SOON?

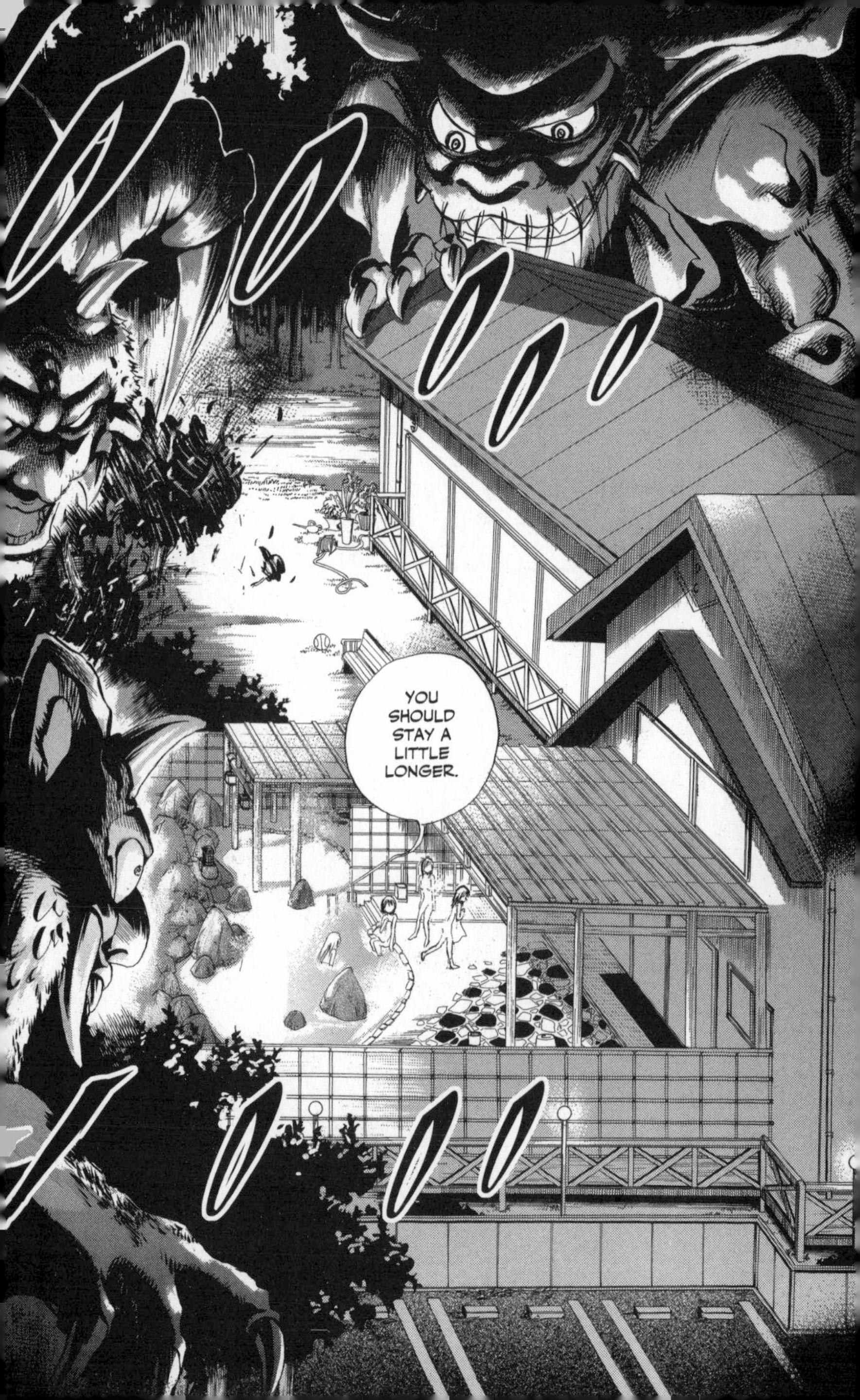
YOU SHOULD STAY A LITTLE LONGER.

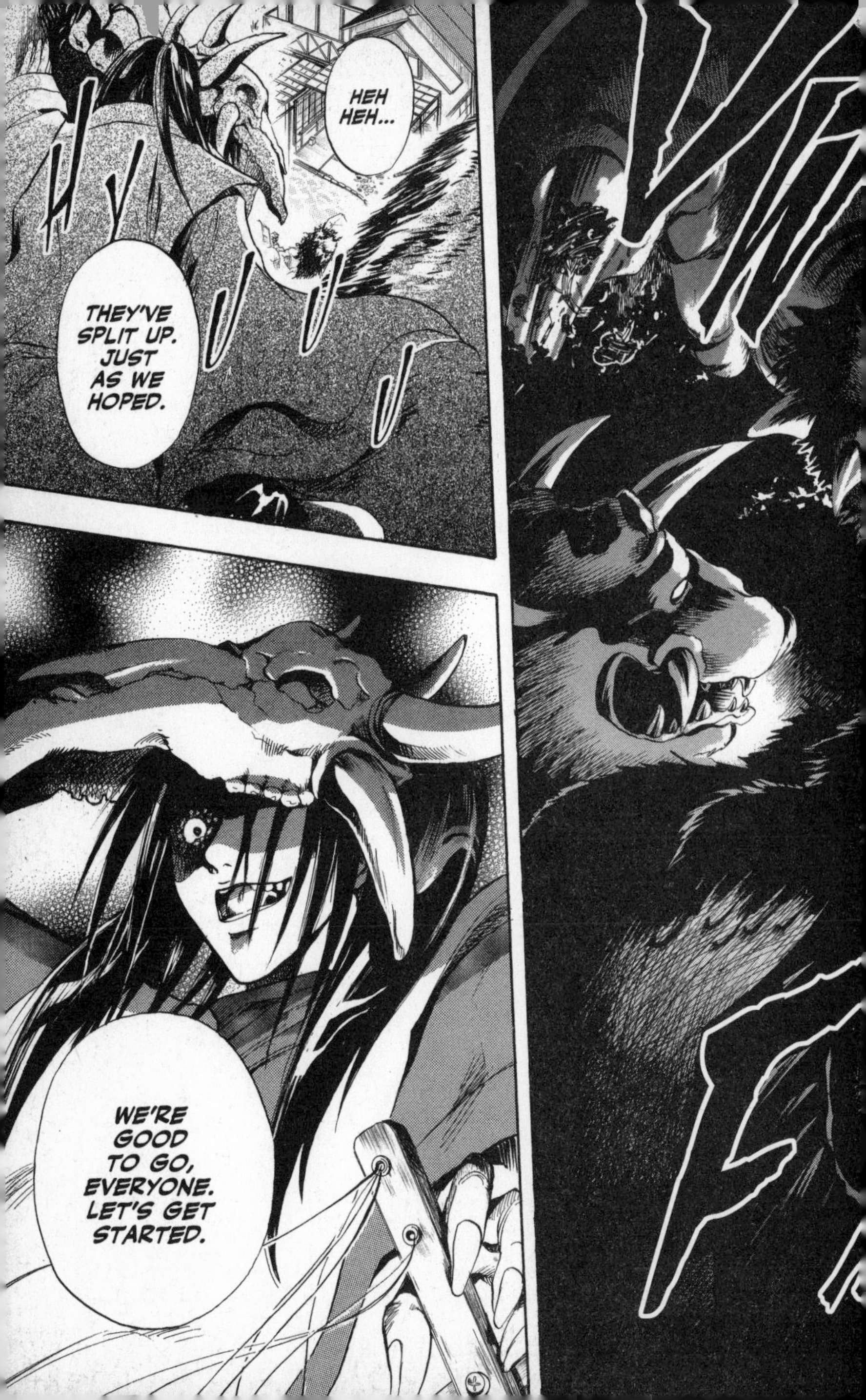
HEH HEH...
THEY'VE SPLIT UP. JUST AS WE HOPED.
WE'RE GOOD TO GO, EVERYONE. LET'S GET STARTED.

Kiyojuji Paranormal Patrol's

Melancholy Shima Part 2

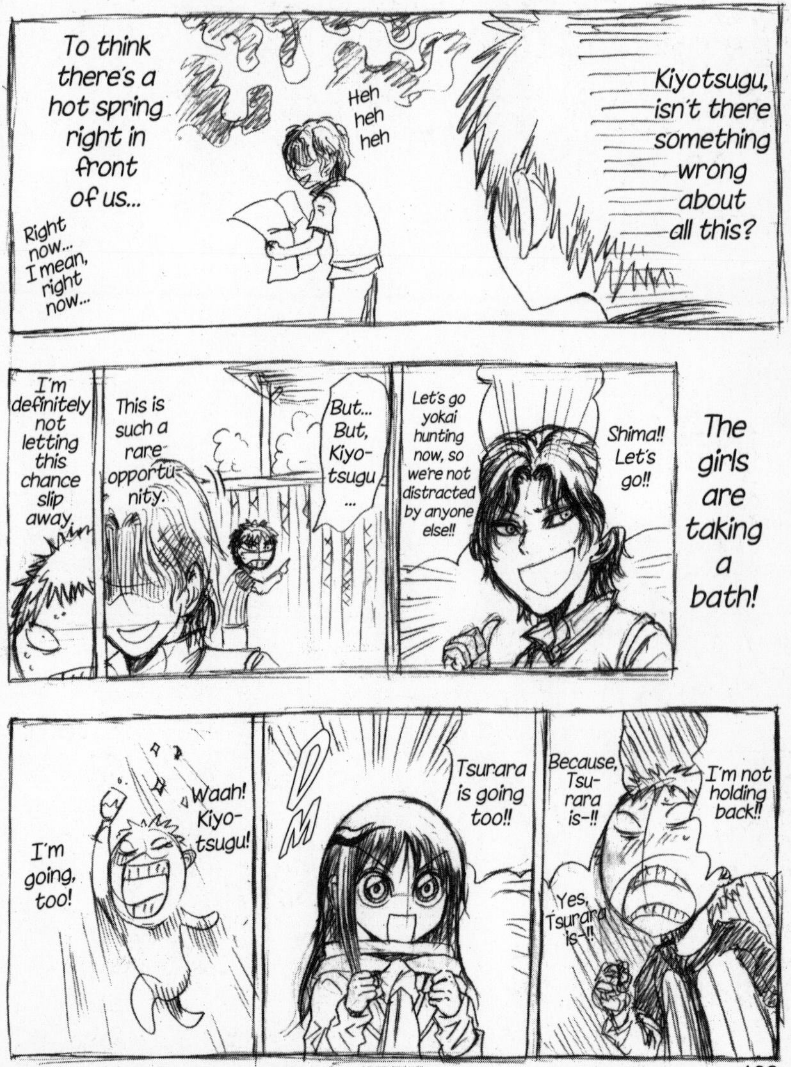
Kiyotsugu, isn't there something wrong about all this?
Heh heh heh
To think there's a hot spring right in front of us...
Right now... I mean, right now...
The girls are taking a bath!
Shima!! Let's go!!
Let's go yokai hunting now, so we're not distracted by anyone else!!
But... But, Kiyotsugu...
This is such a rare opportunity.
I'm definitely not letting this chance slip away.
I'm not holding back!!
Because, Tsurara is-!!
Yes, Tsurara is-!!
Tsurara is going too!!
Waah! Kiyotsugu!
I'm going, too!

Poor, perverted Shima. The End.

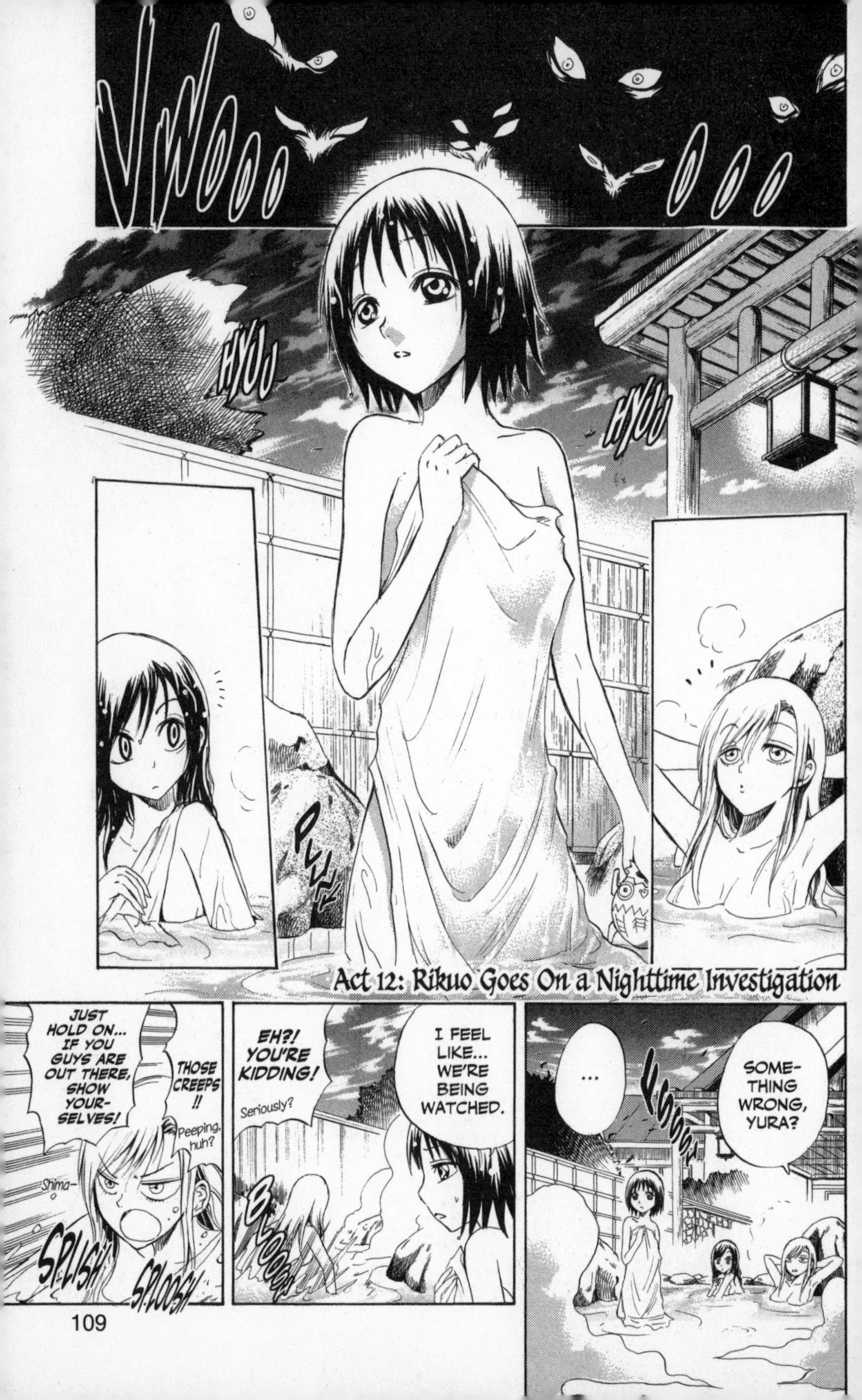
VWOOOOOOOO
HYUU
HYUU
PLUNK
Act 12: Rikuo Goes On a Nighttime Investigation
SOME-THING WRONG, YURA?
...
I FEEL LIKE... WE'RE BEING WATCHED.
EH?! YOU'RE KIDDING!
Seriously?
BLOOOP
THOSE CREEPS!!
JUST HOLD ON... IF YOU GUYS ARE OUT THERE, SHOW YOUR-SELVES!
Peeping, huh?
Shima-
SPLISH
SPLOOSH

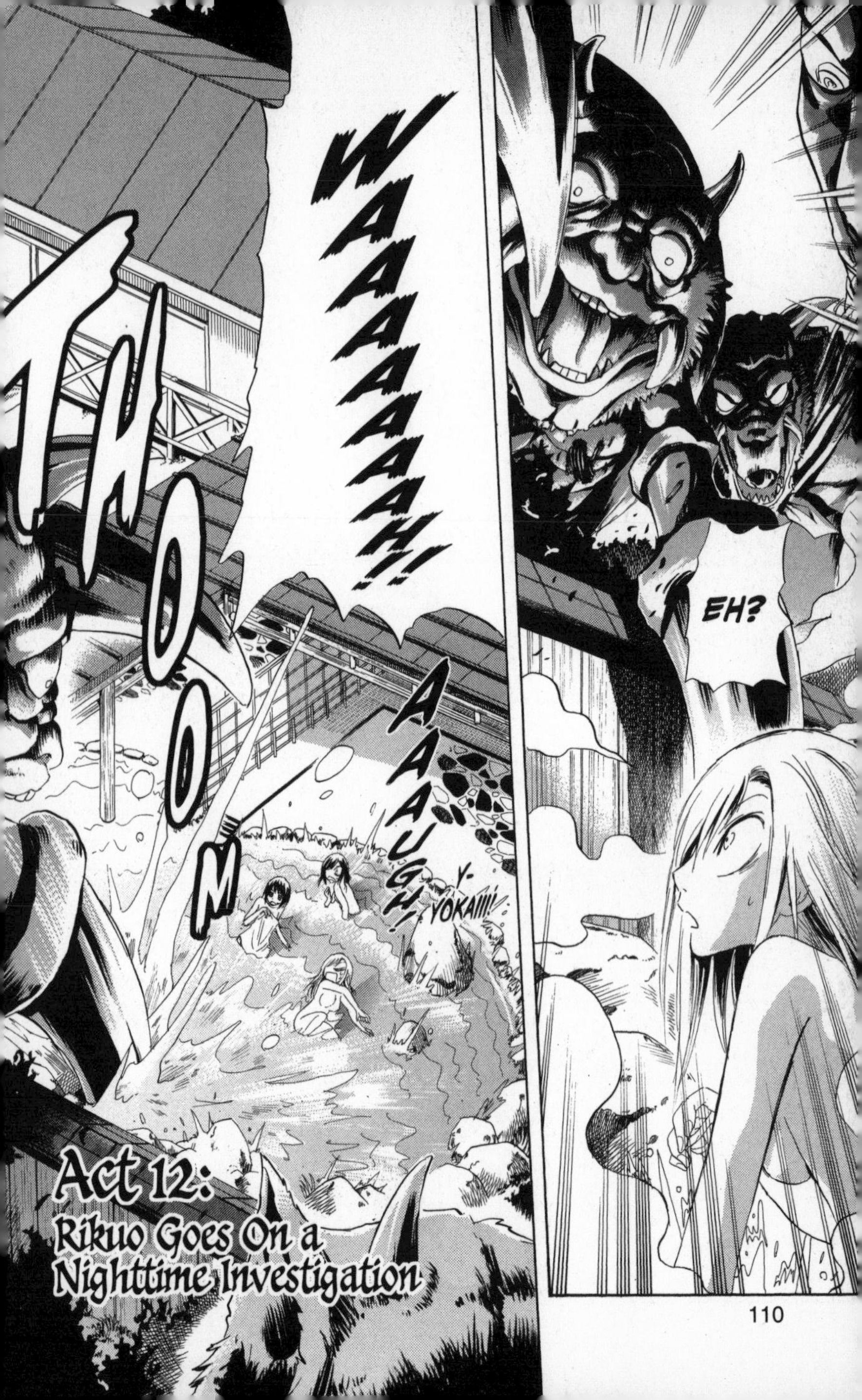
EH?
WAAAAAAAAAH!!
AAAAUGH!
Y-YOKAIII!!
THOOOM
Act 12:
Rikuo Goes On a Nighttime Investigation

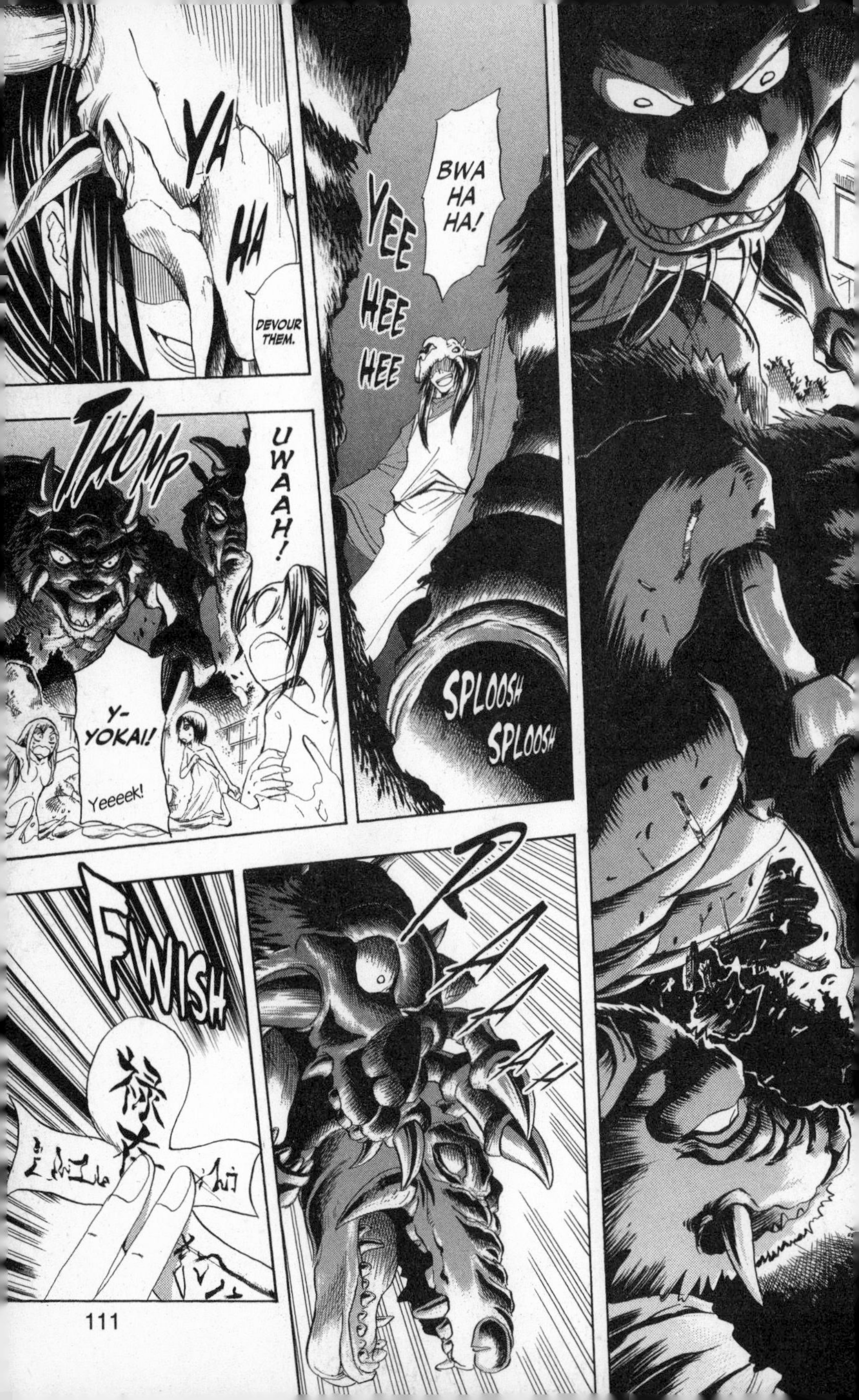
BWA HA HA!
YEE HEE HEE
SPLOOSH SPLOOSH
YA HA
DEVOUR THEM.
UWAAAH!
THOMP
Y-YOKAI!
Yeeeek!
RAAAAHH
FWISH

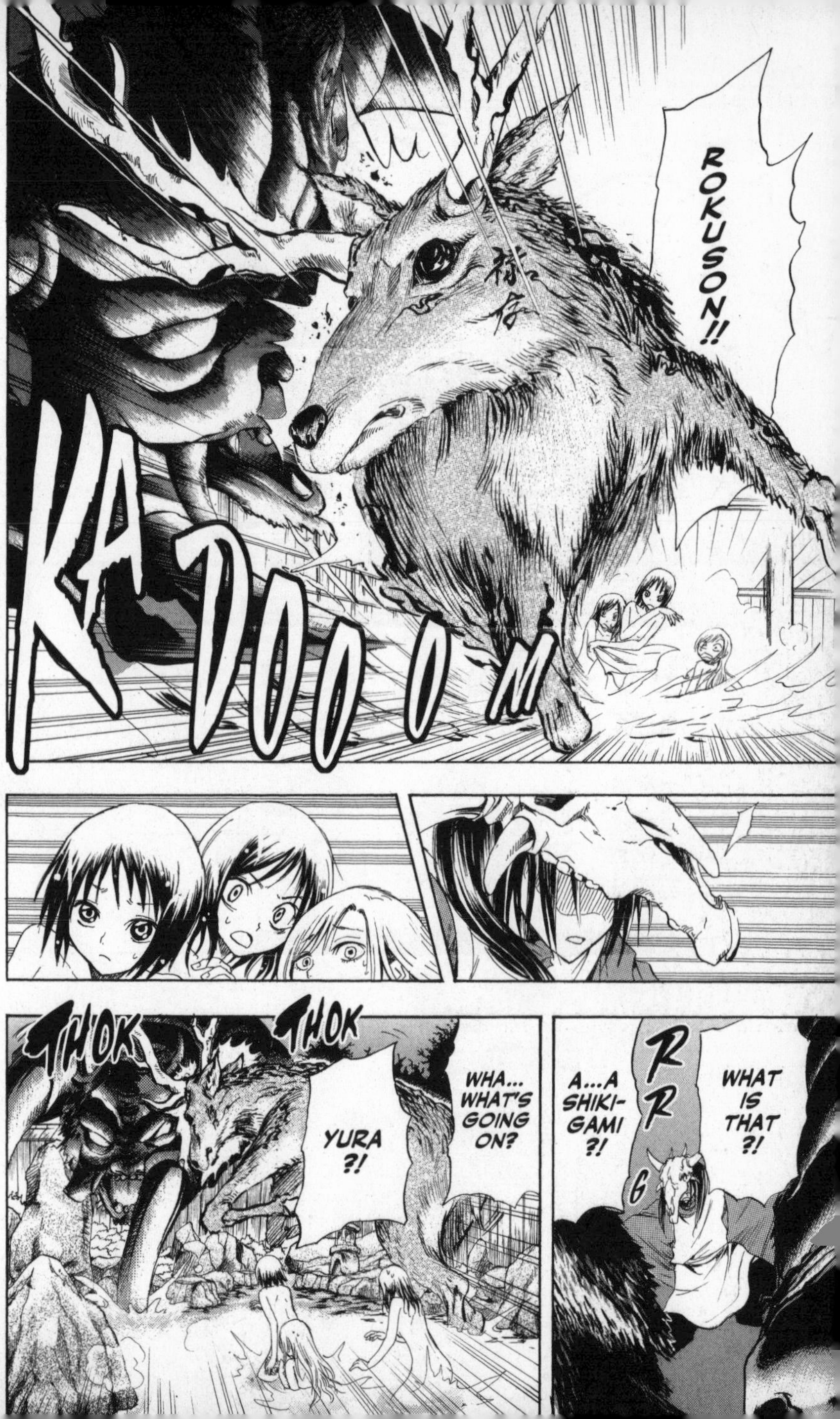
ROKUSON!!
KA DOOO M
WHAT IS THAT ?!
RRG
A...A SHIKI-GAMI ?!
WHA... WHAT'S GOING ON?
YURA ?!
THOK THOK

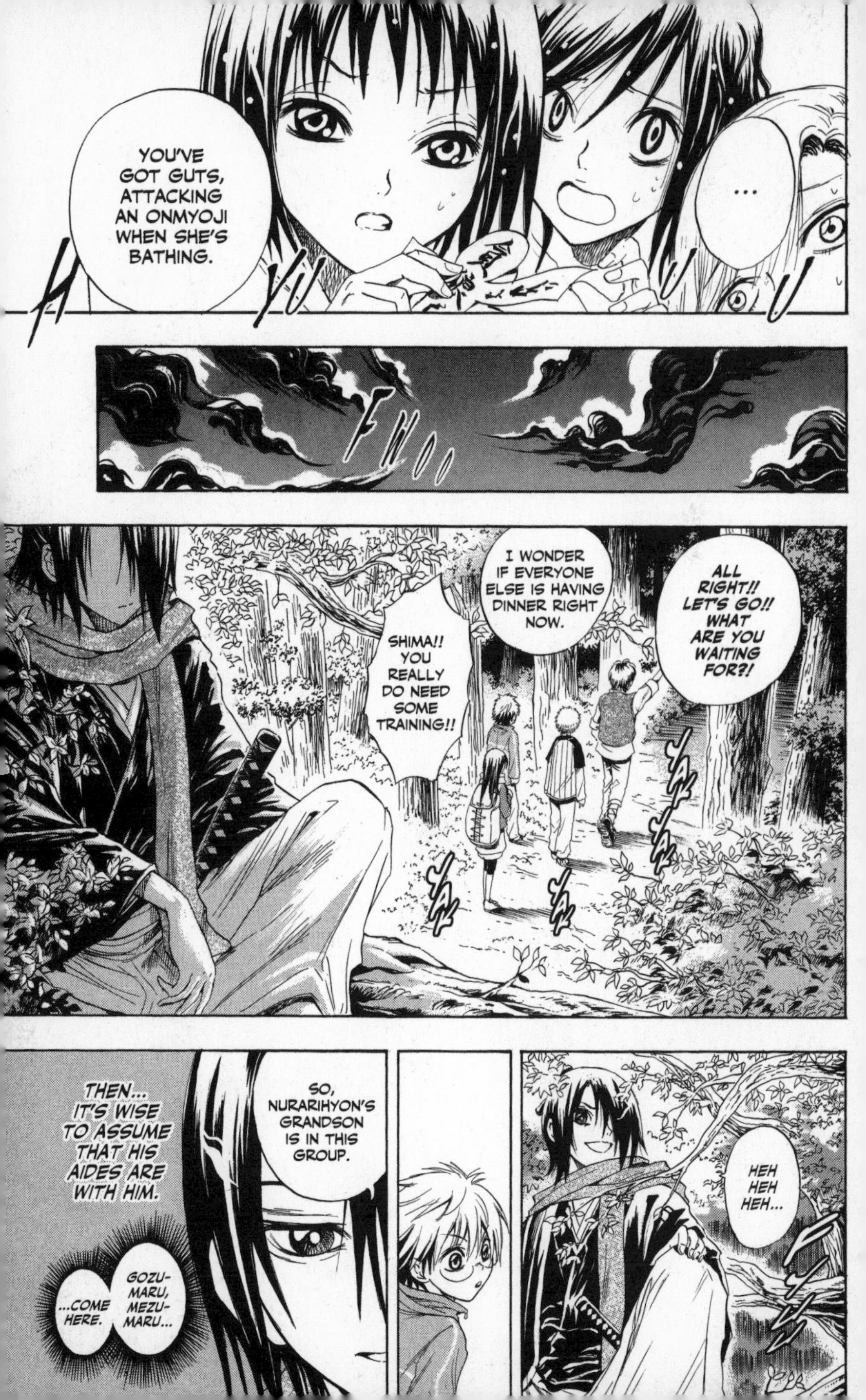
...
YOU'VE GOT GUTS, ATTACKING AN ONMYOJI WHEN SHE'S BATHING.
ALL RIGHT!! LET'S GO!! WHAT ARE YOU WAITING FOR?!
I WONDER IF EVERYONE ELSE IS HAVING DINNER RIGHT NOW.
SHIMA!! YOU REALLY DO NEED SOME TRAINING!!
HEH HEH HEH...
SO, NURARIHYON'S GRANDSON IS IN THIS GROUP.
THEN... IT'S WISE TO ASSUME THAT HIS AIDES ARE WITH HIM.
GOZU-MARU, MEZU-MARU...
...COME HERE.

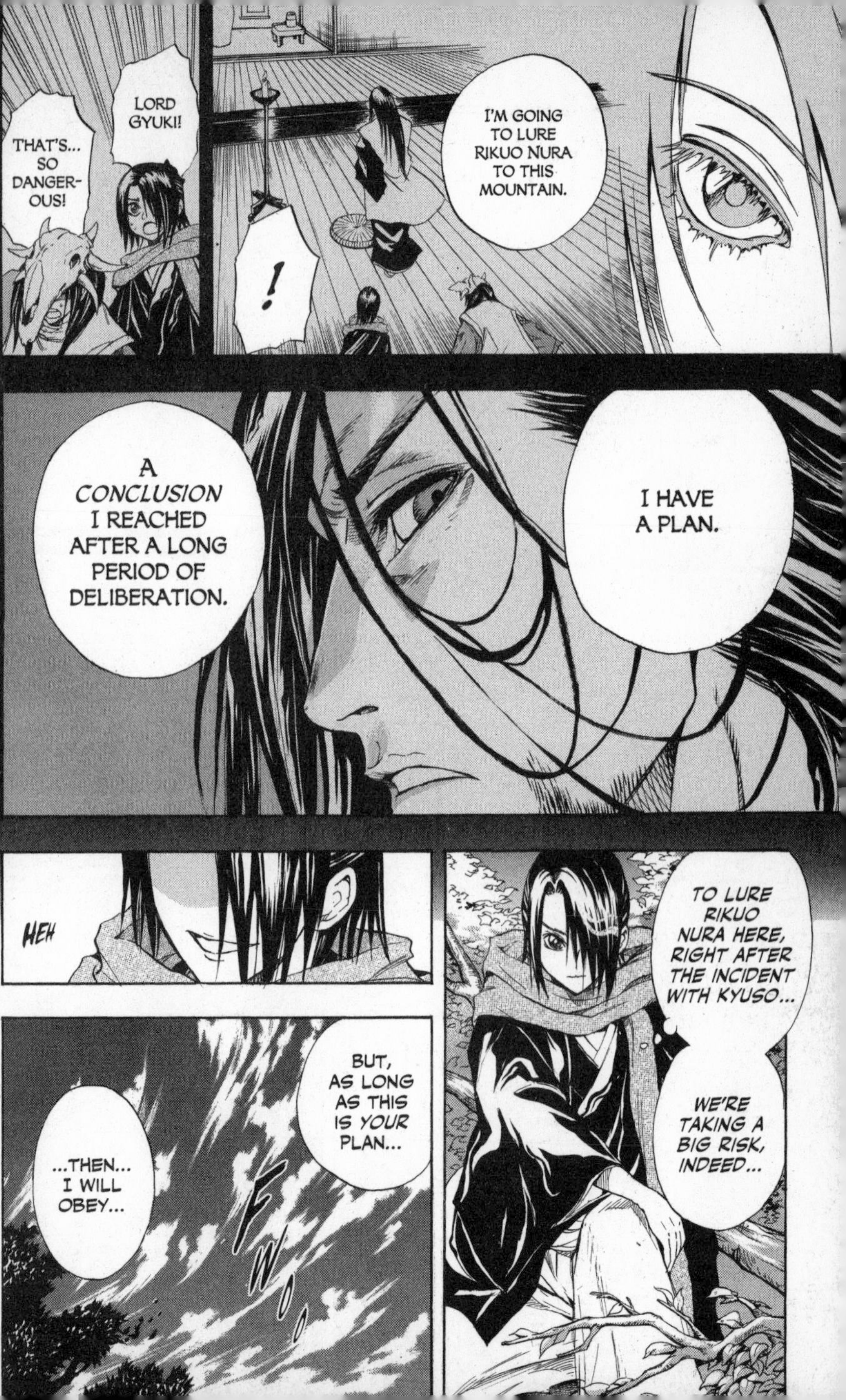
I'M GOING TO LURE RIKUO NURA TO THIS MOUNTAIN.
!
LORD GYUKI!
THAT'S... SO DANGER-OUS!
I HAVE A PLAN.
A *CONCLUSION* I REACHED AFTER A LONG PERIOD OF DELIBERATION.
TO LURE RIKUO NURA HERE, RIGHT AFTER THE INCIDENT WITH KYUSO...
WE'RE TAKING A BIG RISK, INDEED...
HEH
BUT, AS LONG AS THIS IS *YOUR* PLAN...
...THEN... I WILL OBEY...
FWOO

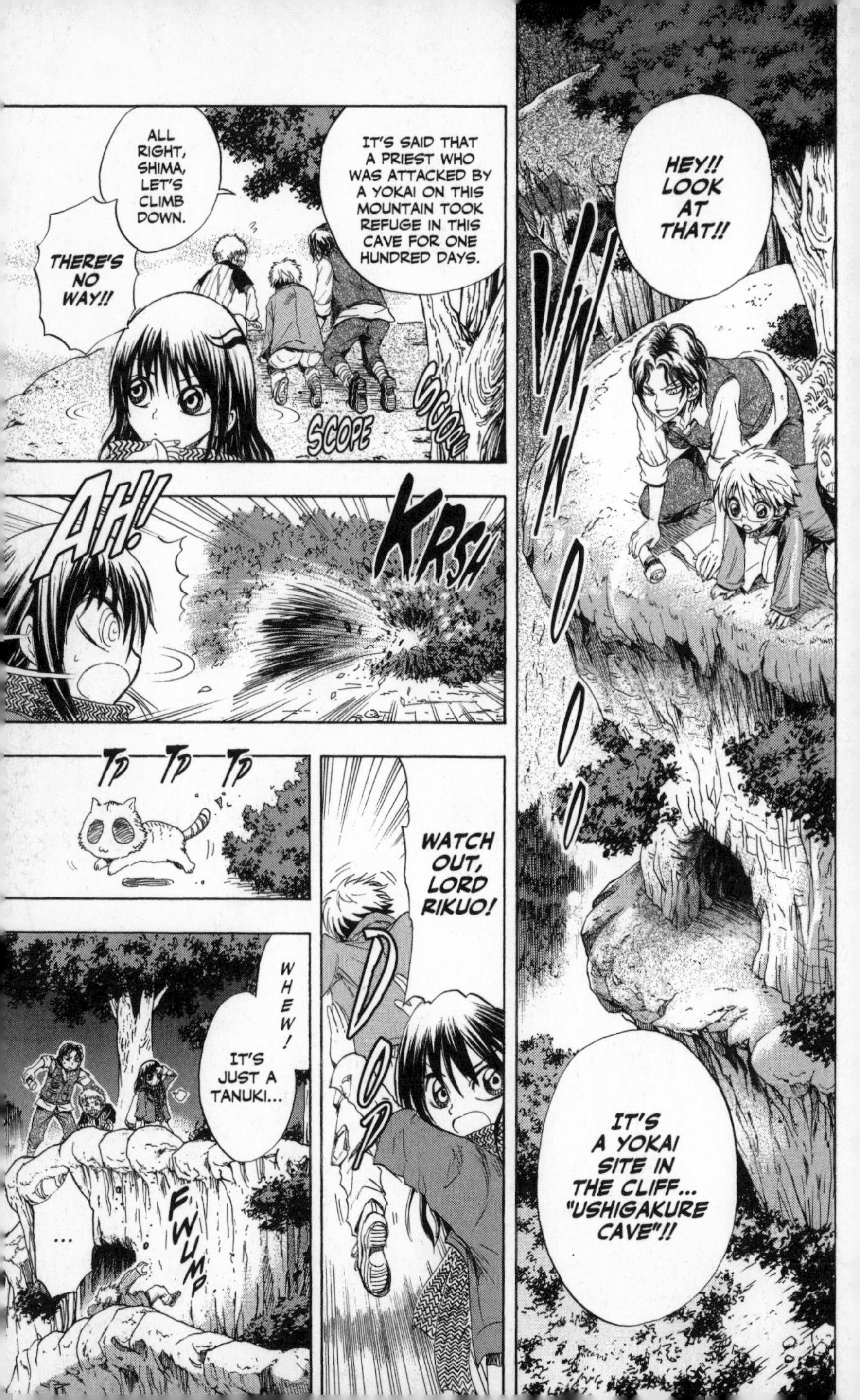
HEY!! LOOK AT THAT!!
VWOOOOO
IT'S A YOKAI SITE IN THE CLIFF... "USHIGAKURE CAVE"!!
IT'S SAID THAT A PRIEST WHO WAS ATTACKED BY A YOKAI ON THIS MOUNTAIN TOOK REFUGE IN THIS CAVE FOR ONE HUNDRED DAYS.
ALL RIGHT, SHIMA, LET'S CLIMB DOWN.
THERE'S NO WAY!!
SCOOCH
SCOPE
KRSH
AH!
WATCH OUT, LORD RIKUO!
DOOO
Tp Tp Tp
WHEW!
IT'S JUST A TANUKI...
FWUMP
...

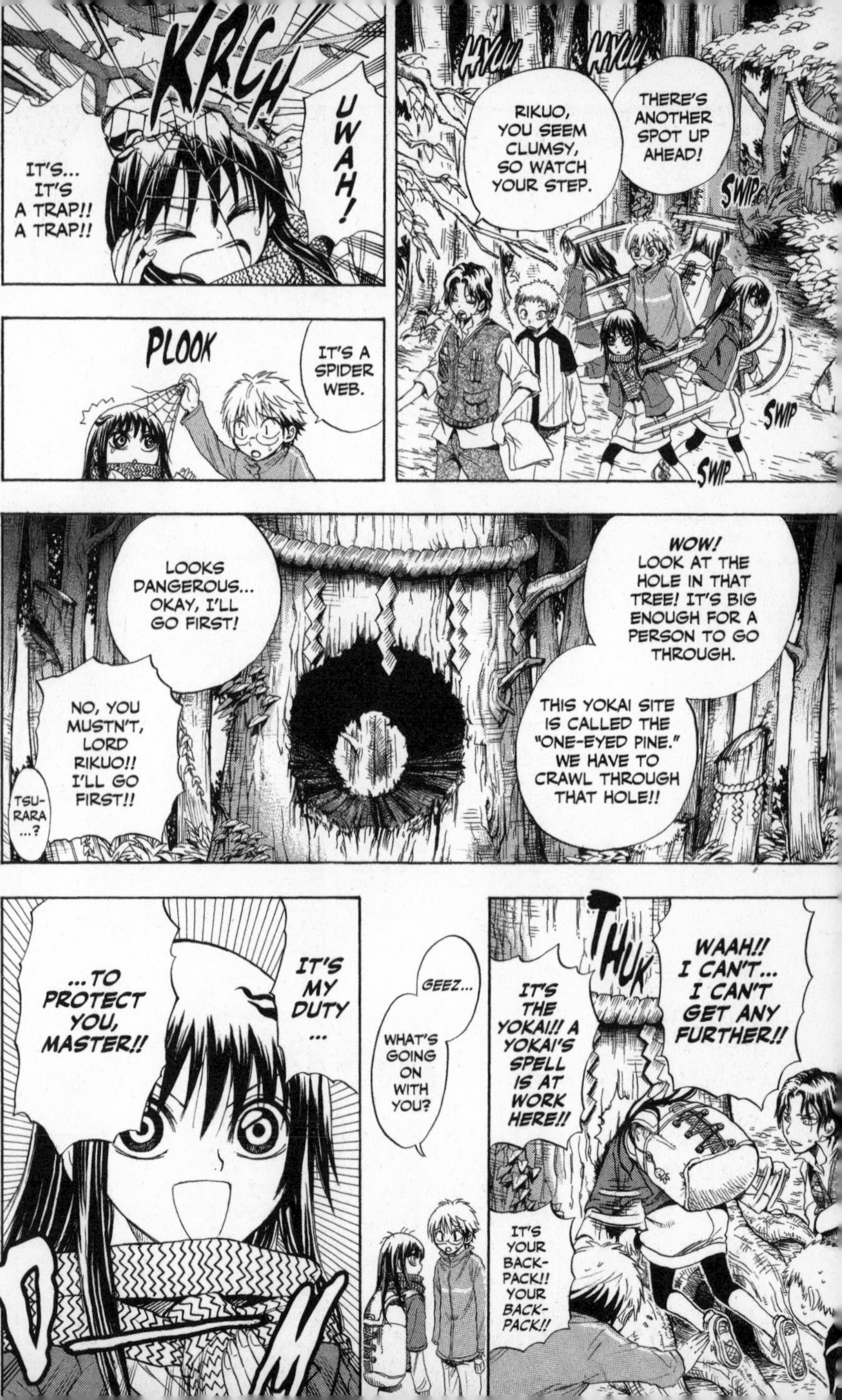
HYUU
HYUU
THERE'S ANOTHER SPOT UP AHEAD!
RIKUO, YOU SEEM CLUMSY, SO WATCH YOUR STEP.
SWIP
SWIP
SWIP
KRCH
UWAH!
IT'S... IT'S A TRAP!! A TRAP!!
PLOOK
IT'S A SPIDER WEB.
WOW! LOOK AT THE HOLE IN THAT TREE! IT'S BIG ENOUGH FOR A PERSON TO GO THROUGH.
THIS YOKAI SITE IS CALLED THE "ONE-EYED PINE." WE HAVE TO CRAWL THROUGH THAT HOLE!!
LOOKS DANGEROUS... OKAY, I'LL GO FIRST!
NO, YOU MUSTN'T, LORD RIKUO!! I'LL GO FIRST!!
TSU-RARA ...?
THUK
WAAH!! I CAN'T... I CAN'T GET ANY FURTHER!!
IT'S THE YOKAI!! A YOKAI'S SPELL IS AT WORK HERE!!
IT'S YOUR BACK-PACK!! YOUR BACK-PACK!!
GEEZ...
WHAT'S GOING ON WITH YOU?
IT'S MY DUTY...
...TO PROTECT YOU, MASTER!!

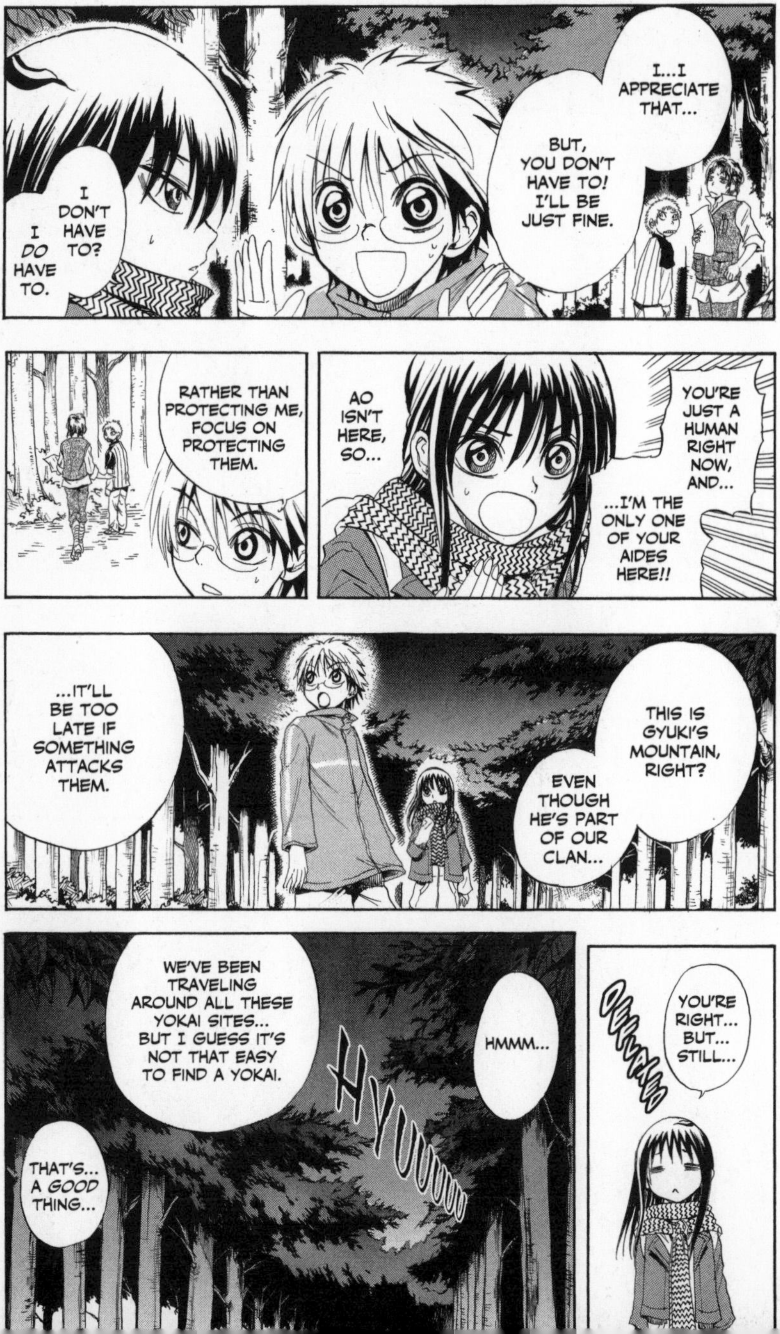
I...I APPRECIATE THAT...
BUT, YOU DON'T HAVE TO! I'LL BE JUST FINE.
I DON'T HAVE TO?
I *DO* HAVE TO.
YOU'RE JUST A HUMAN RIGHT NOW, AND...
...I'M THE ONLY ONE OF YOUR AIDES HERE!!
AO ISN'T HERE, SO...
RATHER THAN PROTECTING ME, FOCUS ON PROTECTING THEM.
THIS IS GYUKI'S MOUNTAIN, RIGHT?
EVEN THOUGH HE'S PART OF OUR CLAN...
...IT'LL BE TOO LATE IF SOMETHING ATTACKS THEM.
YOU'RE RIGHT... BUT... STILL...
HMMM...
WE'VE BEEN TRAVELING AROUND ALL THESE YOKAI SITES... BUT I GUESS IT'S NOT THAT EASY TO FIND A YOKAI.
HYUUUUU
THAT'S... A *GOOD* THING...

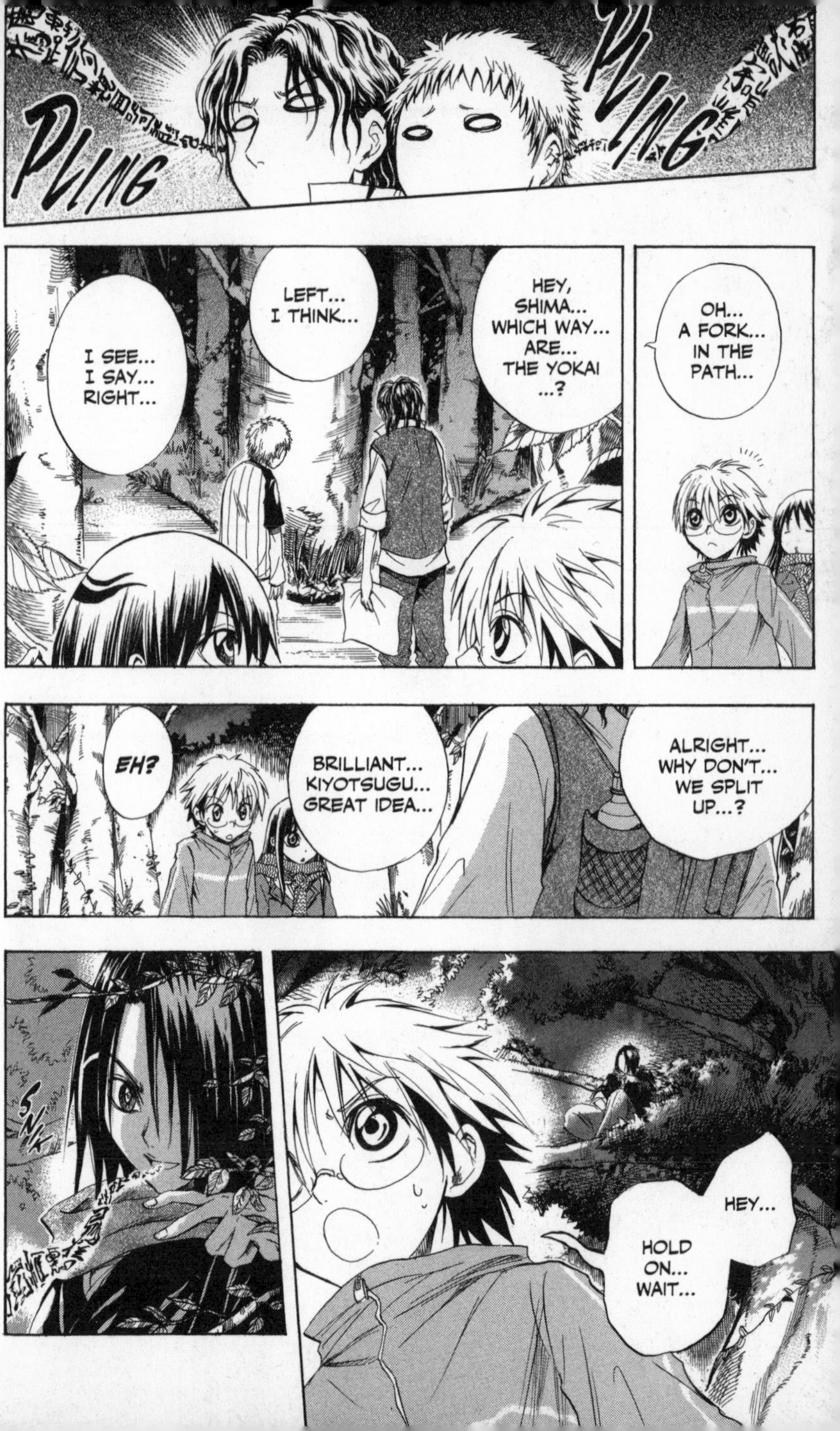
PLING
PLING
OH... A FORK... IN THE PATH...
HEY, SHIMA... WHICH WAY... ARE... THE YOKAI ...?
LEFT... I THINK...
I SEE... I SAY... RIGHT...
ALRIGHT... WHY DON'T... WE SPLIT UP...?
BRILLIANT... KIYOTSUGU... GREAT IDEA...
EH?
HEY...
HOLD ON... WAIT...
SNIK

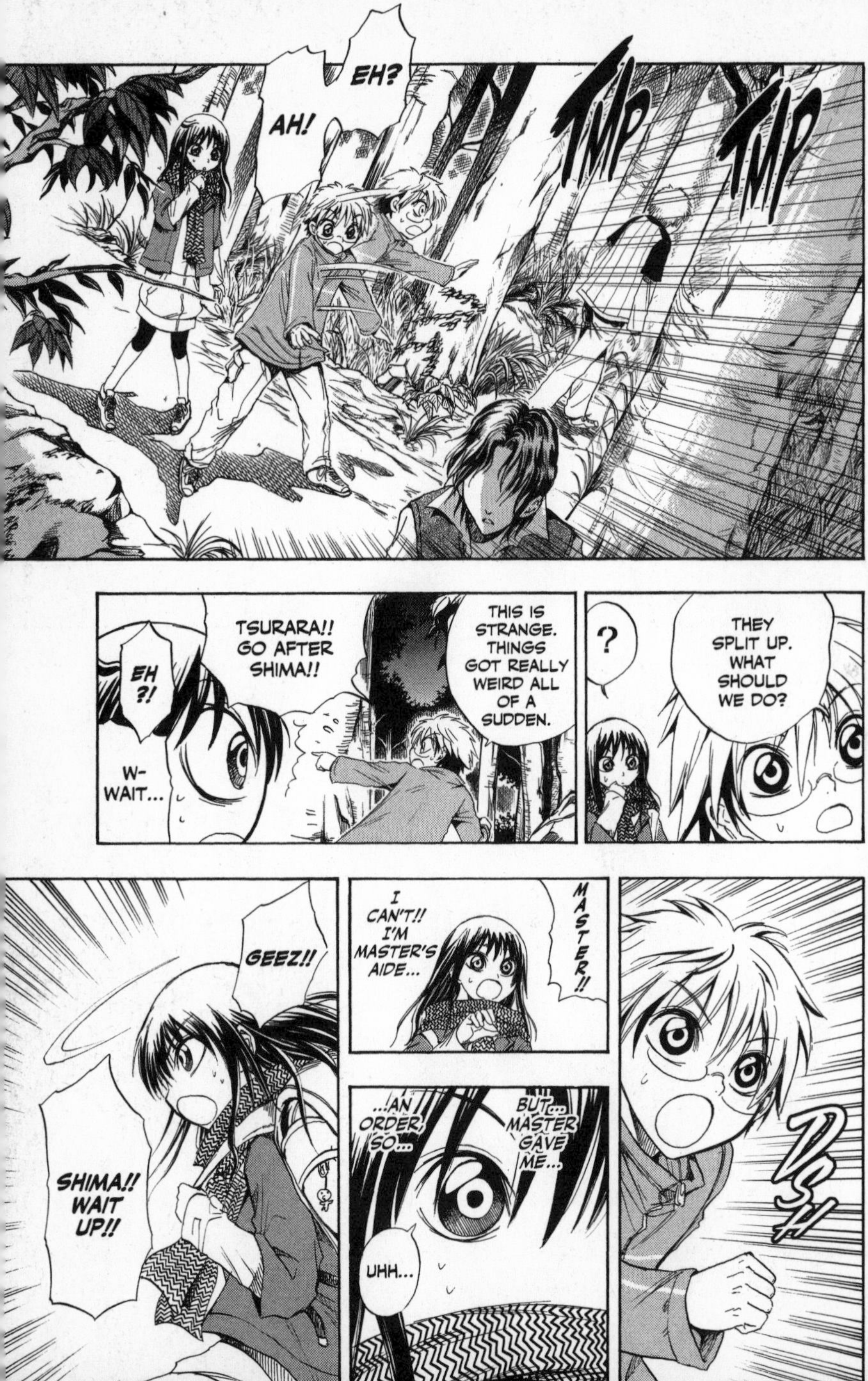
TMP
TMP
EH?
AH!
THEY SPLIT UP. WHAT SHOULD WE DO?
?
THIS IS STRANGE. THINGS GOT REALLY WEIRD ALL OF A SUDDEN.
TSURARA!! GO AFTER SHIMA!!
EH ?!
W-WAIT...
DSH
MASTER!!
I CAN'T!! I'M MASTER'S AIDE...
BUT... MASTER GAVE ME...
...AN ORDER, SO...
UHH...
GEEZ!!
SHIMA!! WAIT UP!!

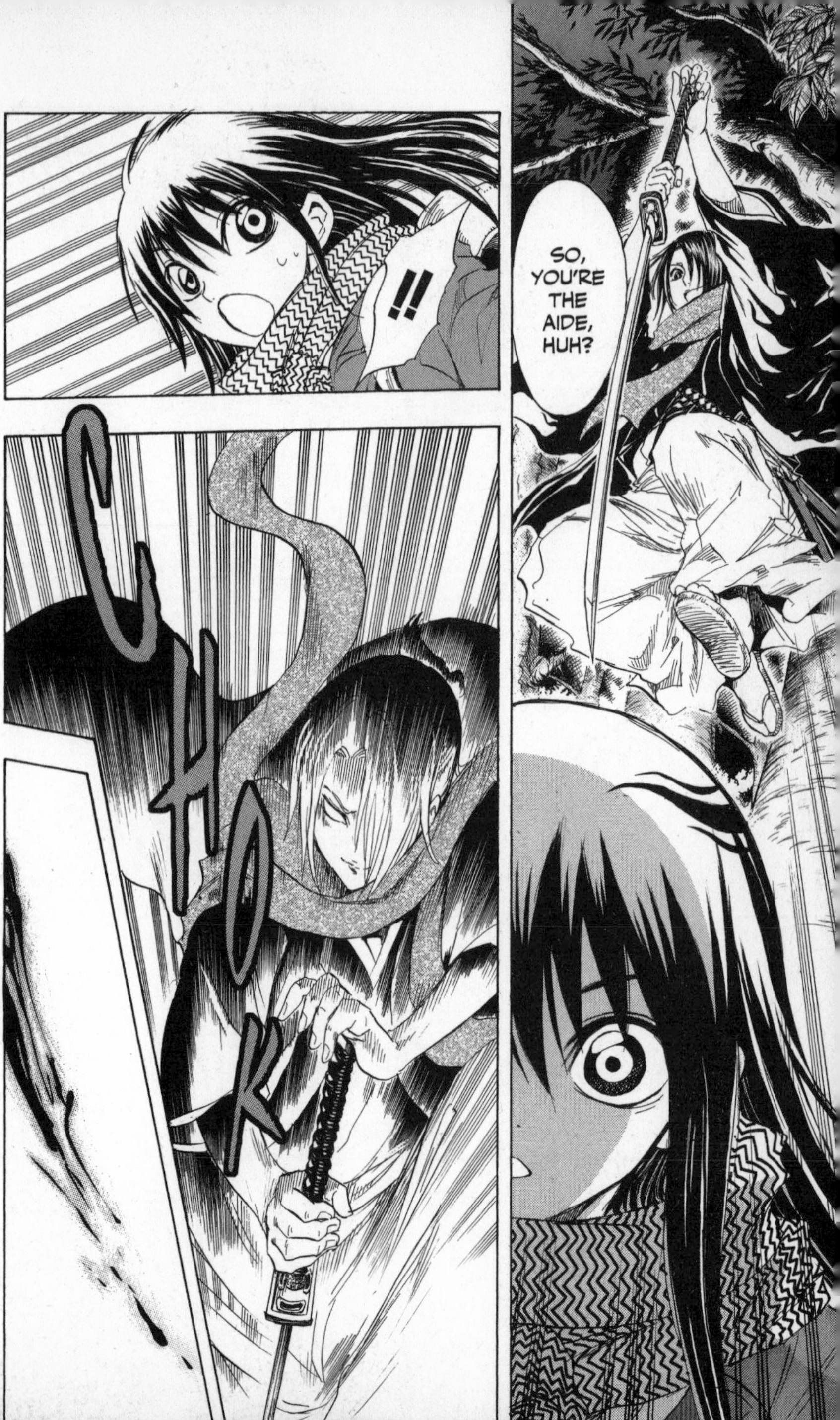
SO, YOU'RE THE AIDE, HUH?
!!
CHOOK

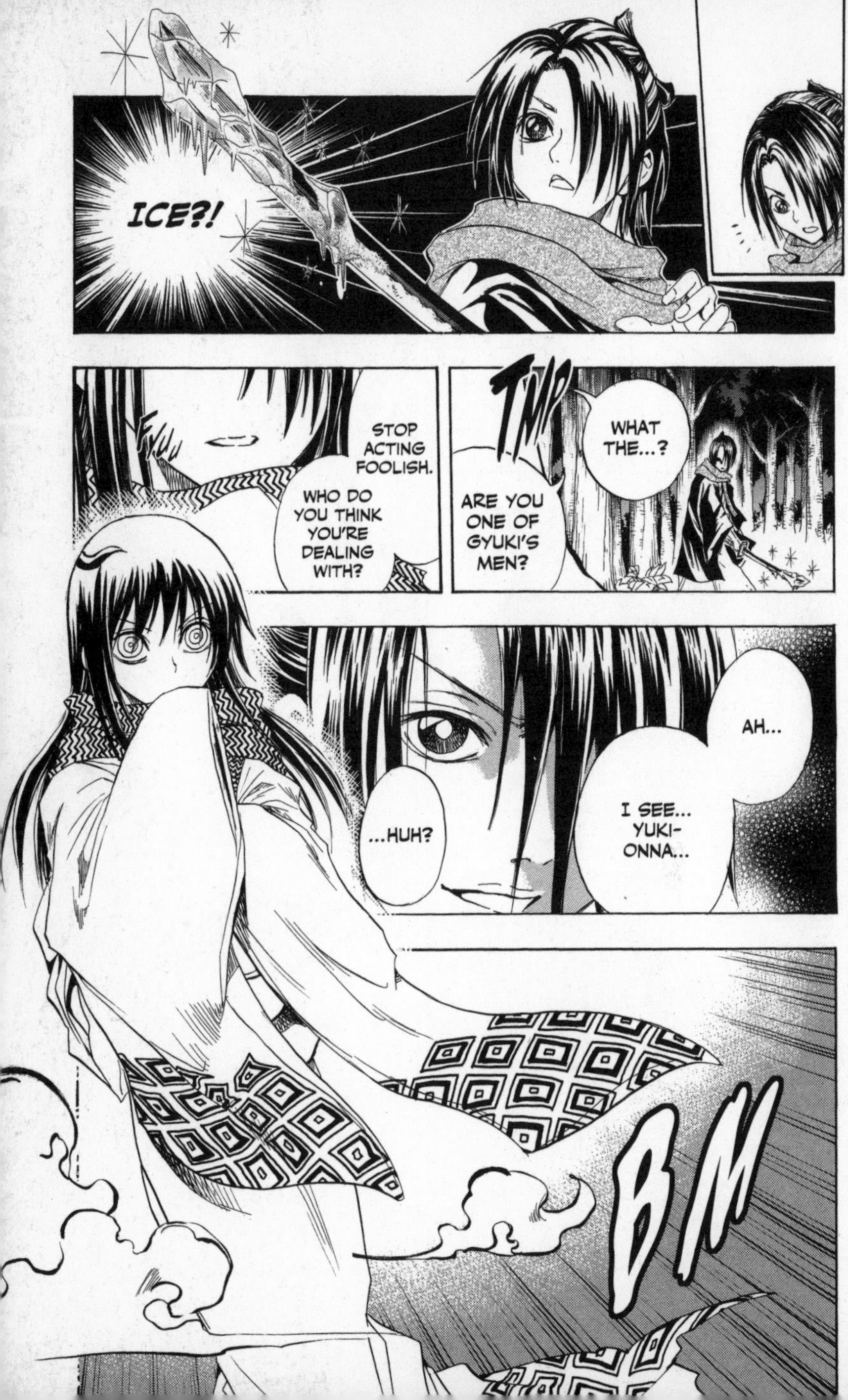
ICE?!
TMP
WHAT THE...?
ARE YOU ONE OF GYUKI'S MEN?
STOP ACTING FOOLISH.
WHO DO YOU THINK YOU'RE DEALING WITH?
AH...
I SEE... YUKI-ONNA...
...HUH?
BM

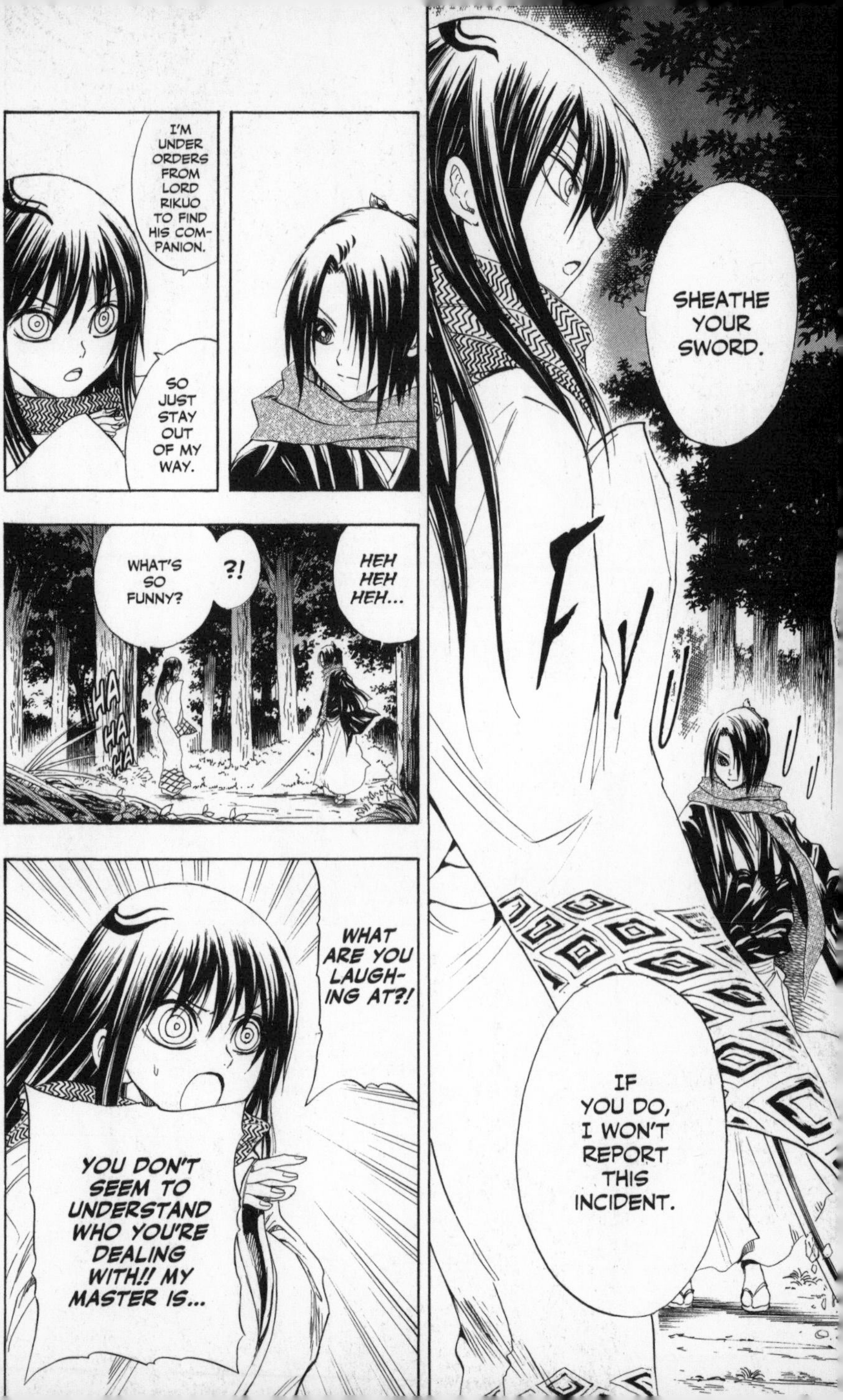
SHEATHE YOUR SWORD.
IF YOU DO, I WON'T REPORT THIS INCIDENT.
I'M UNDER ORDERS FROM LORD RIKUO TO FIND HIS COMPANION.
SO JUST STAY OUT OF MY WAY.
HEH HEH HEH...
?!
WHAT'S SO FUNNY?
HA HA HA HA
WHAT ARE YOU LAUGHING AT?!
YOU DON'T SEEM TO UNDERSTAND WHO YOU'RE DEALING WITH!! MY MASTER IS...

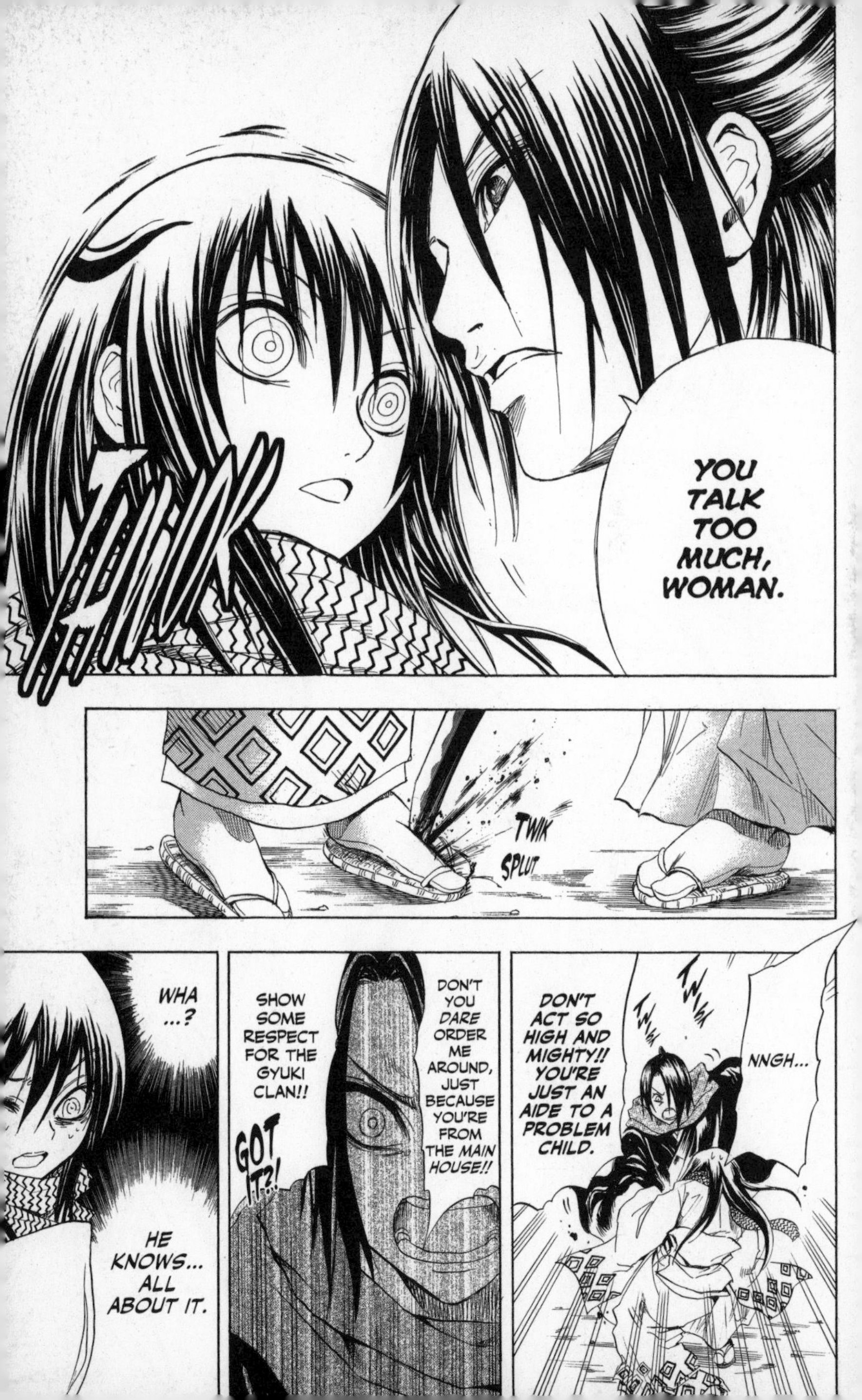
YOU TALK TOO MUCH, WOMAN.
TWIK
SPLUT
NNGH...
DON'T ACT SO HIGH AND MIGHTY!! YOU'RE JUST AN AIDE TO A PROBLEM CHILD.
DON'T YOU DARE ORDER ME AROUND, JUST BECAUSE YOU'RE FROM THE MAIN HOUSE!!
SHOW SOME RESPECT FOR THE GYUKI CLAN!!
GOT IT?!
WHA ...?
HE KNOWS... ALL ABOUT IT.

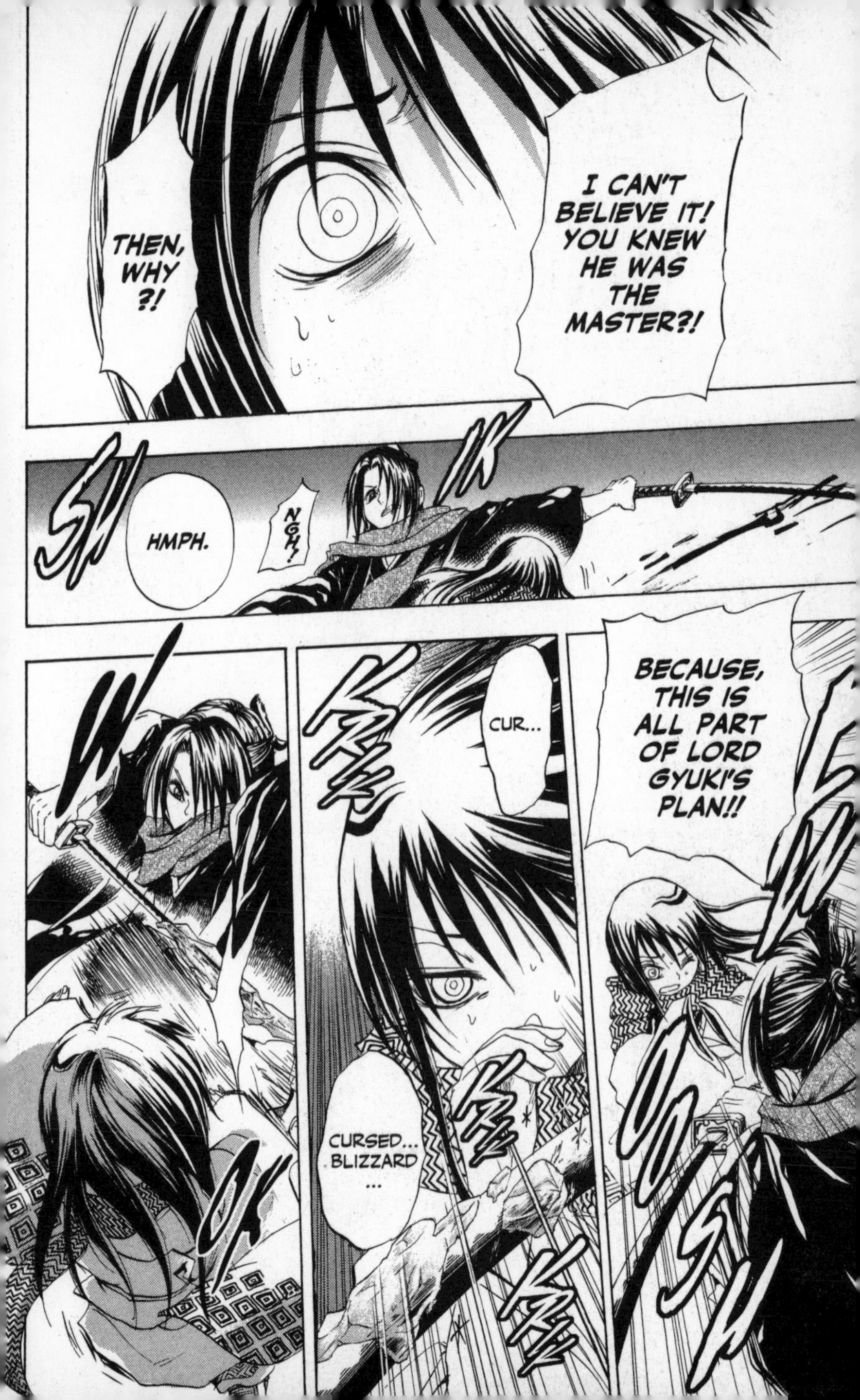
I CAN'T BELIEVE IT! YOU KNEW HE WAS THE MASTER?!
THEN, WHY ?!
NGH?!
HMPH.
BECAUSE, THIS IS ALL PART OF LORD GYUKI'S PLAN!!
CUR...
CURSED... BLIZZARD ...

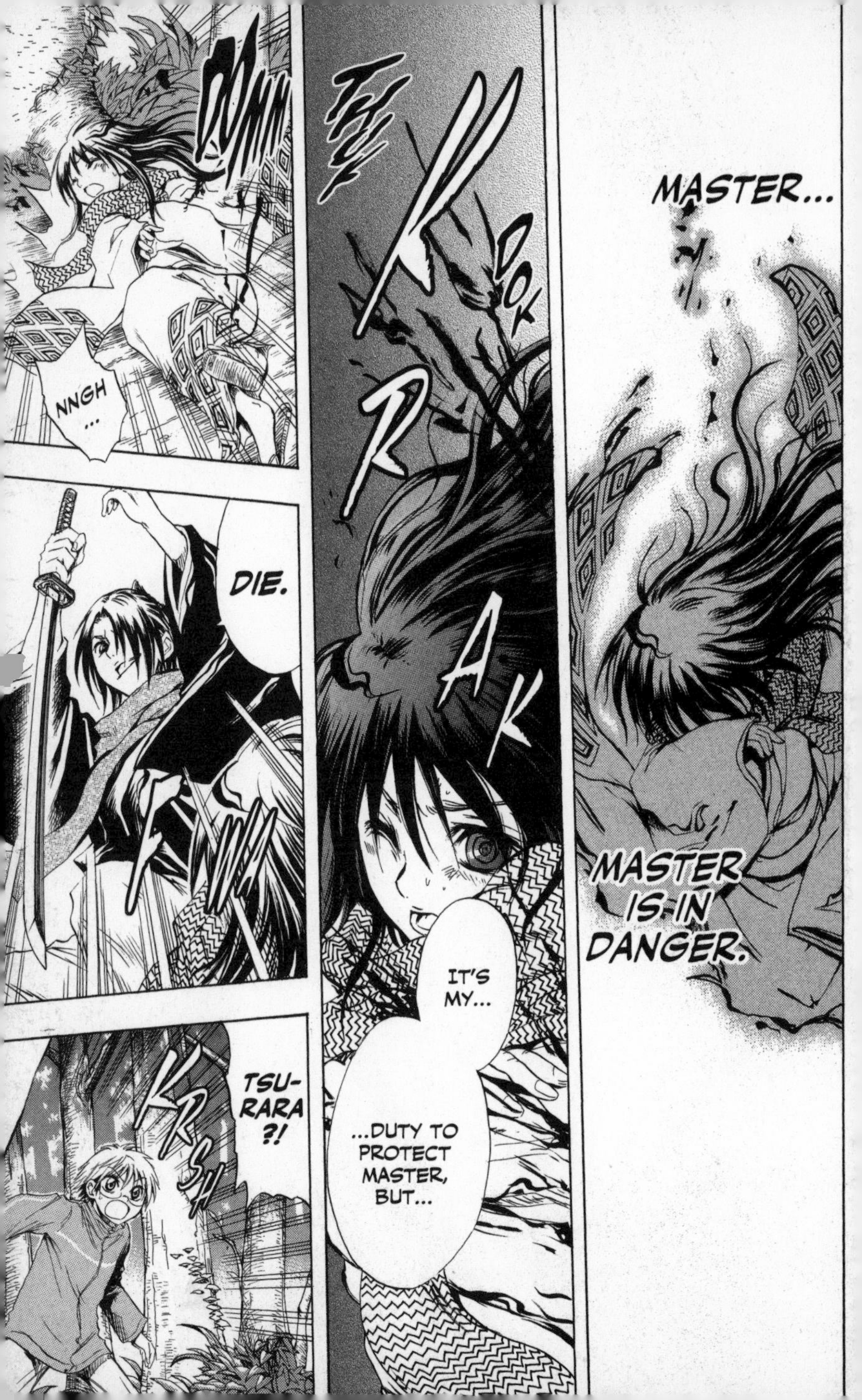
MASTER...
MASTER IS IN DANGER.
IT'S MY...
...DUTY TO PROTECT MASTER, BUT...
NNGH ...
DIE.
TSU-RARA ?!

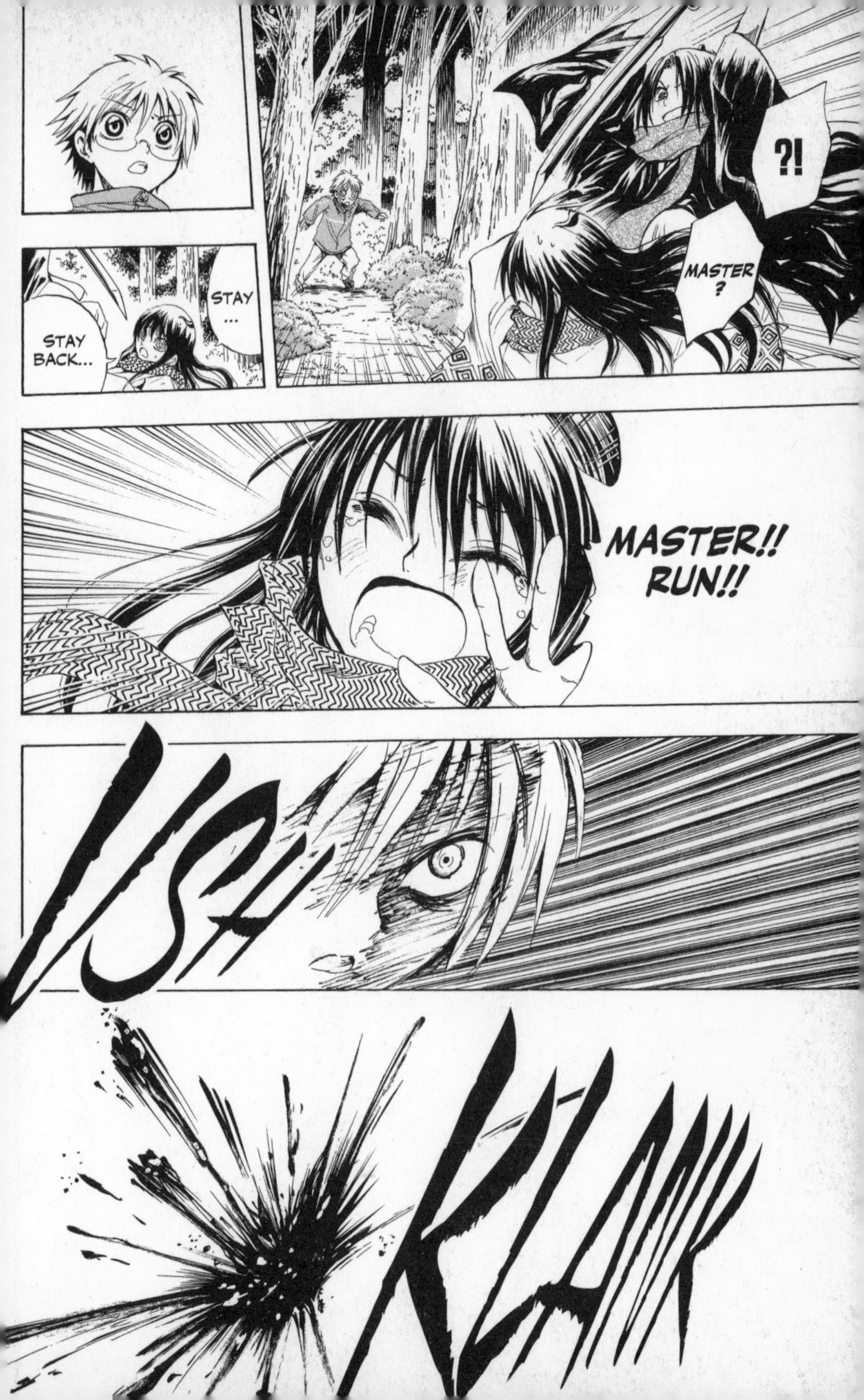
?!
MASTER ?
STAY ...
STAY BACK...
MASTER!! RUN!!

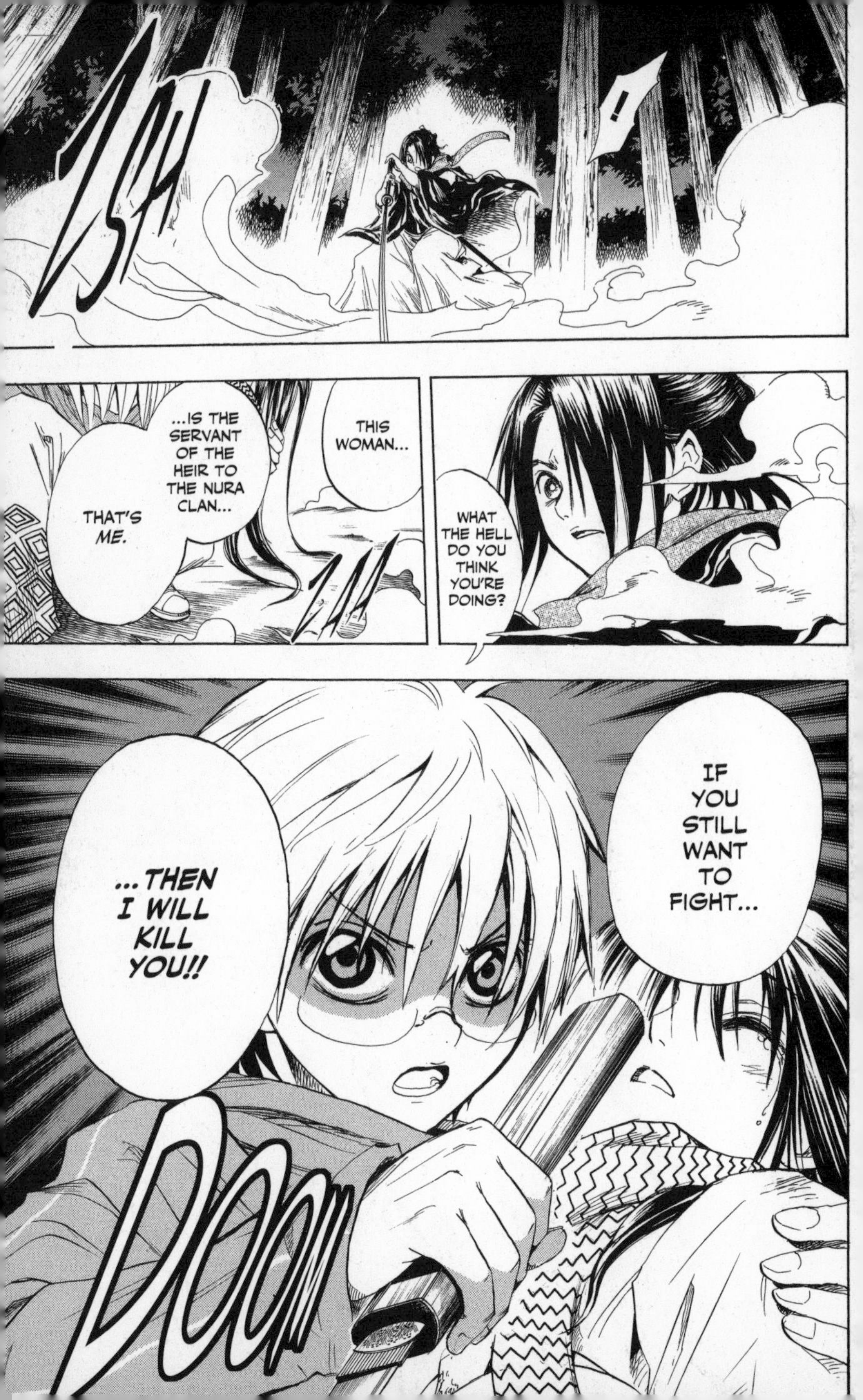
ZSPA
!
WHAT THE HELL DO YOU THINK YOU'RE DOING?
THIS WOMAN...
...IS THE SERVANT OF THE HEIR TO THE NURA CLAN...
THAT'S ME.
IF YOU STILL WANT TO FIGHT...
...THEN I WILL KILL YOU!!

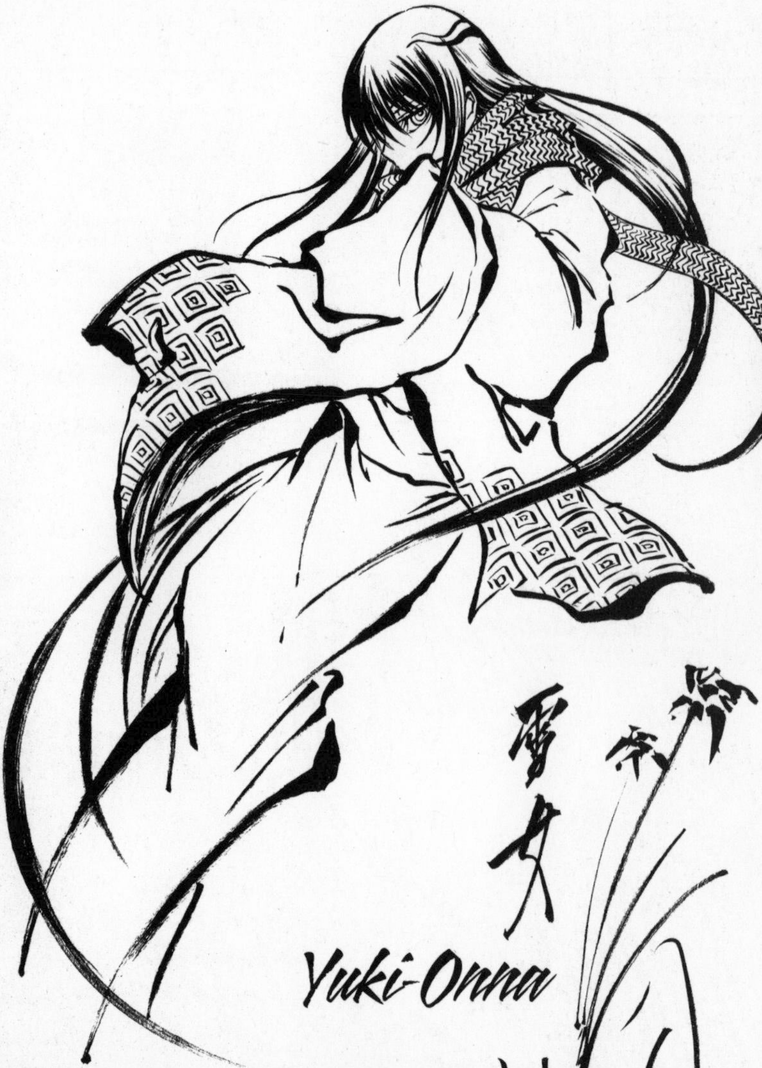
雪女
Yuki-Onna

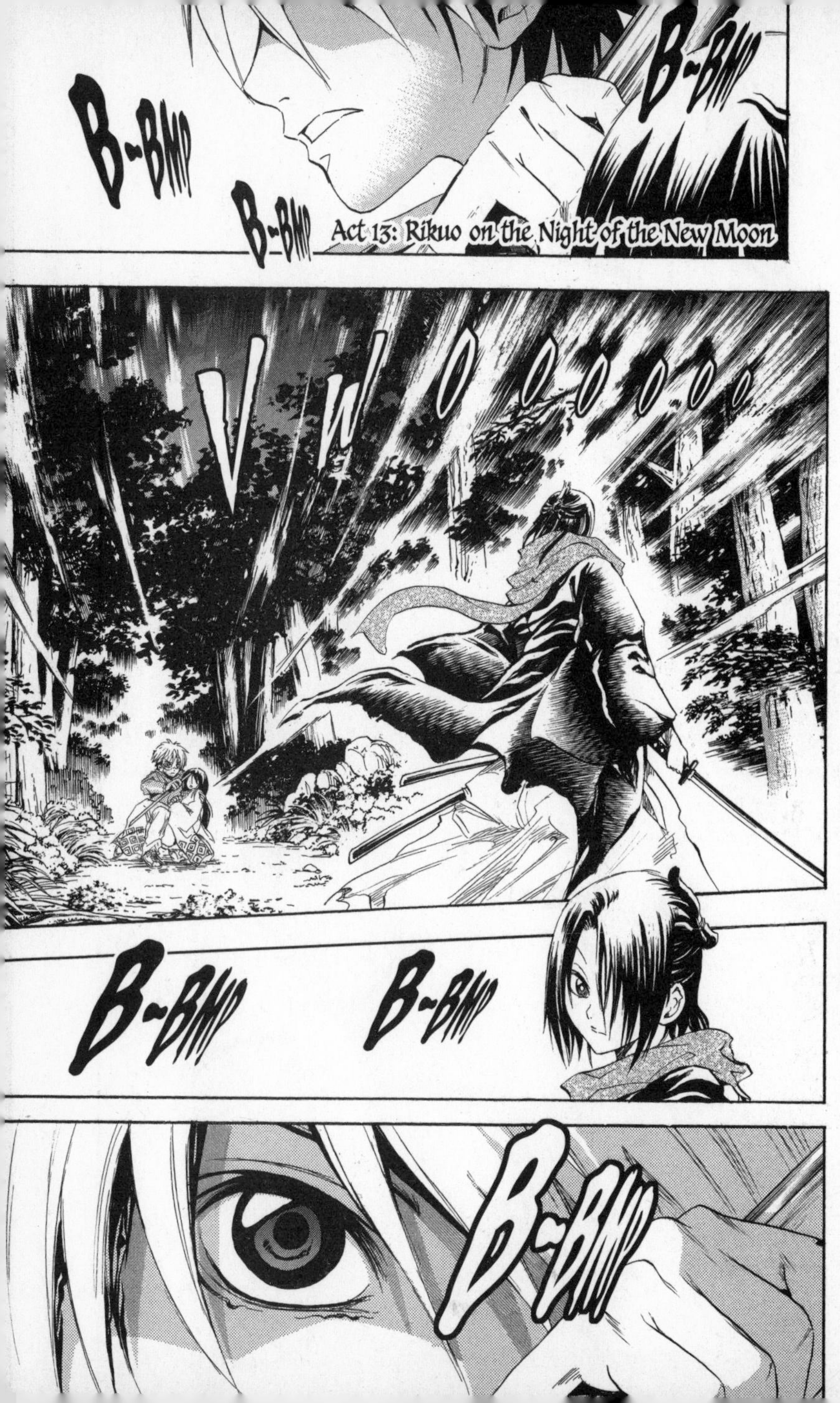
B-BMP
B-BMP
B-BMP
Act 13: Rikuo on the Night of the New Moon
VWOOOOOO
B-BMP
B-BMP
B-BMP

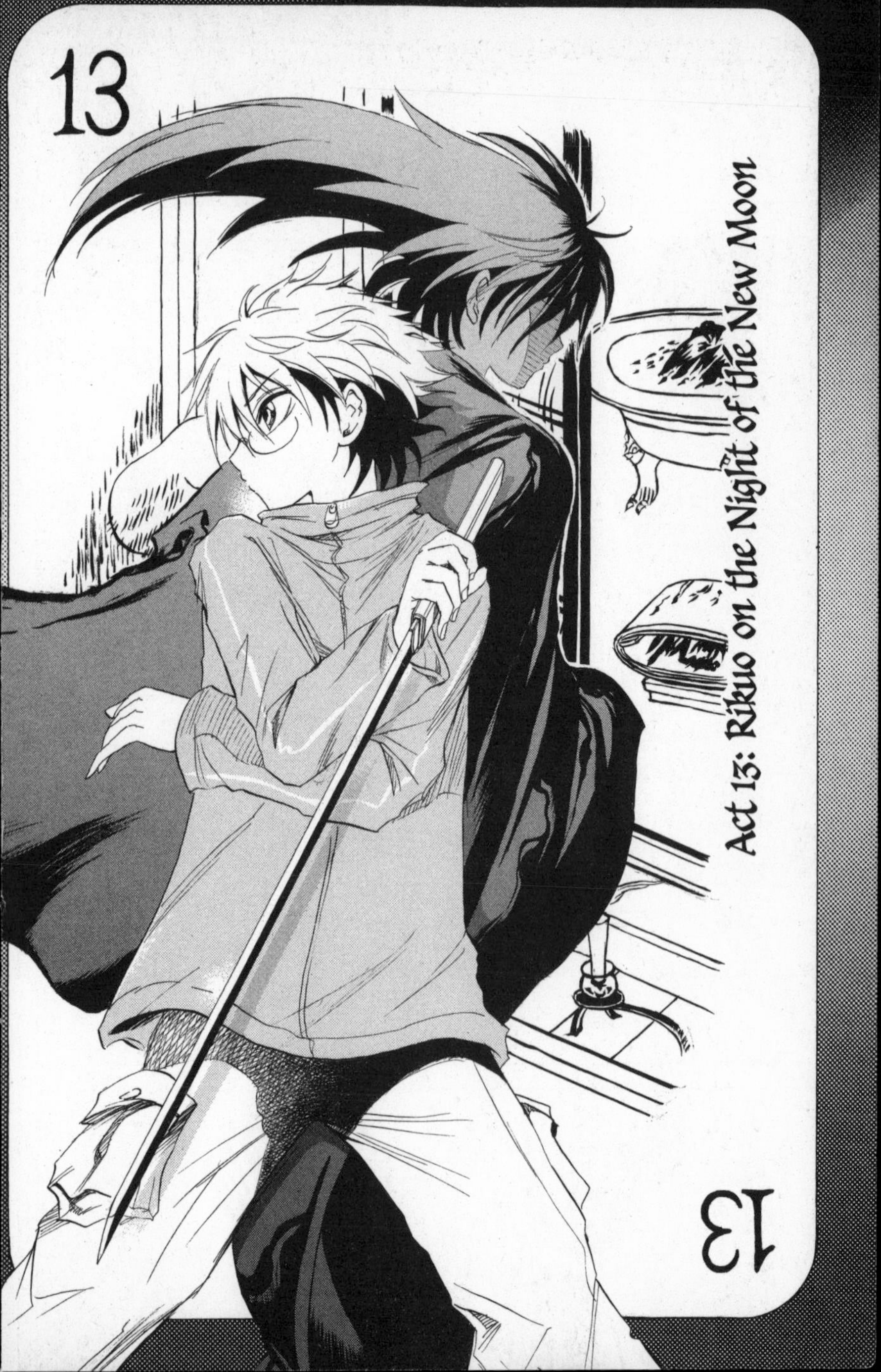
13
Act 13: Rikuo on the Night of the New Moon
13

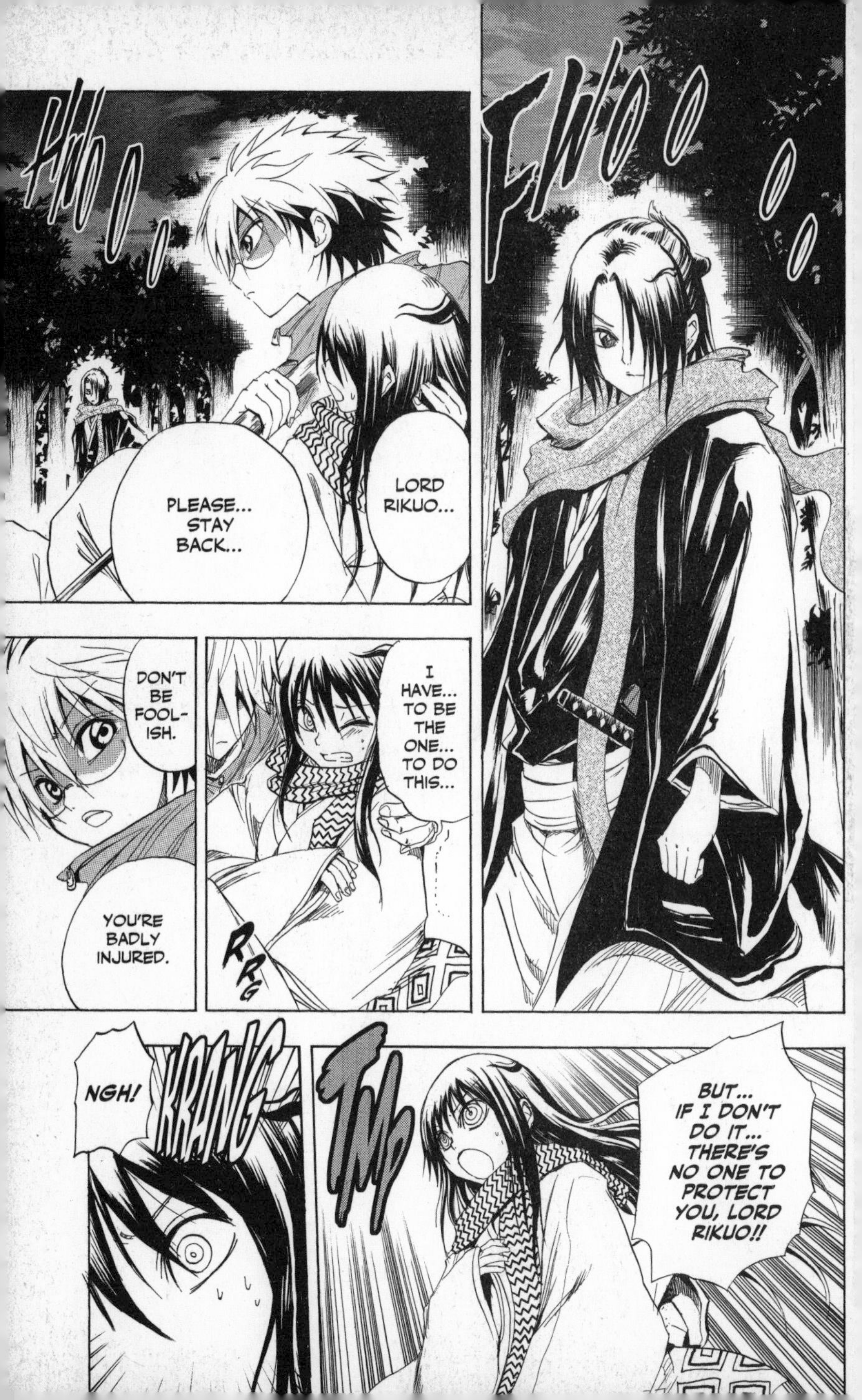
FWOOO...
FWOOO...
LORD RIKUO...
PLEASE... STAY BACK...
I HAVE... TO BE THE ONE... TO DO THIS...
RRG
DON'T BE FOOL-ISH.
YOU'RE BADLY INJURED.
BUT... IF I DON'T DO IT... THERE'S NO ONE TO PROTECT YOU, LORD RIKUO!!
TMP
KRANG
NGH!

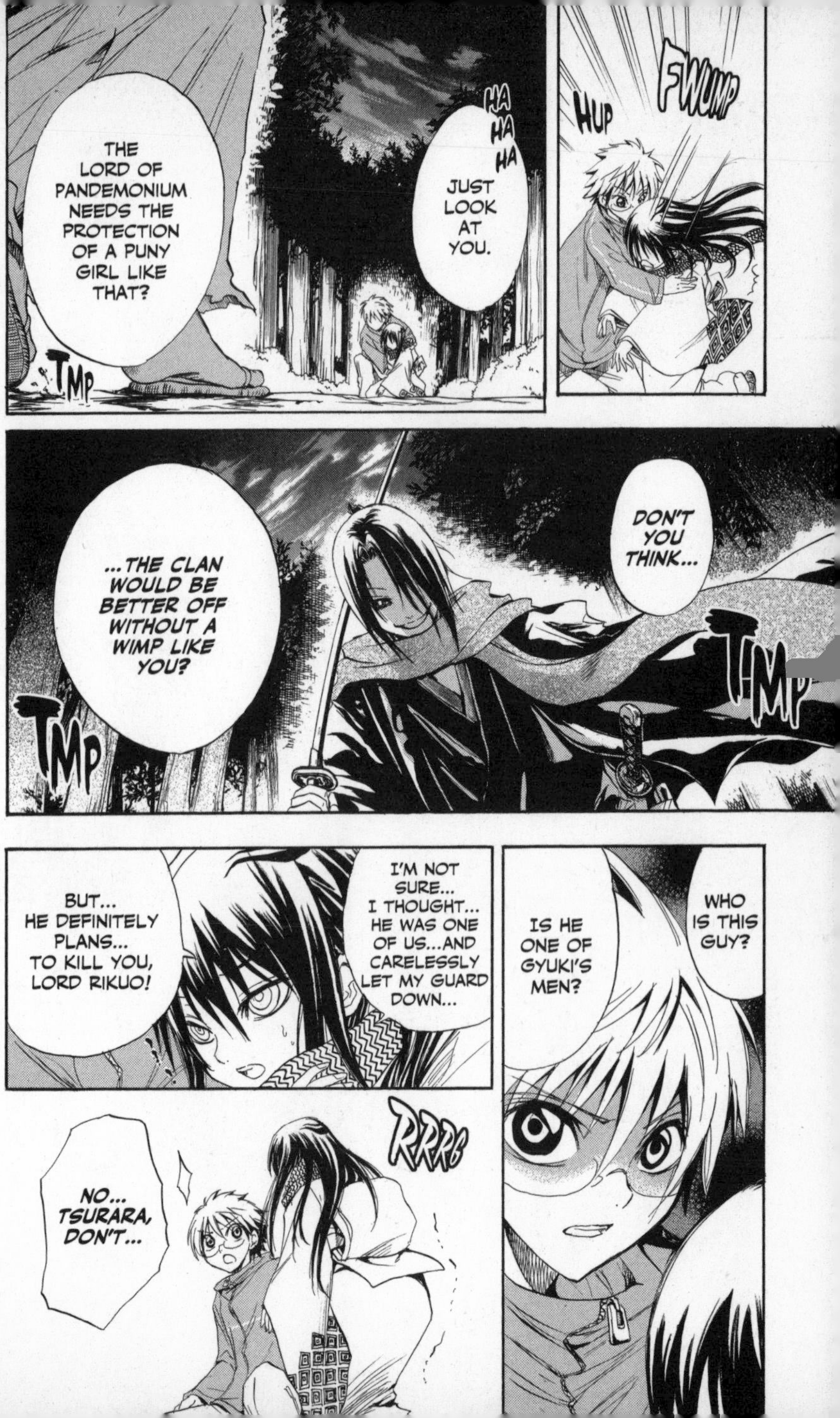
FWUMP
HUP
HA HA HA
JUST LOOK AT YOU.
THE LORD OF PANDEMONIUM NEEDS THE PROTECTION OF A PUNY GIRL LIKE THAT?
TMP
DON'T YOU THINK...
TMP
...THE CLAN WOULD BE BETTER OFF WITHOUT A WIMP LIKE YOU?
TMP
WHO IS THIS GUY?
IS HE ONE OF GYUKI'S MEN?
I'M NOT SURE... I THOUGHT... HE WAS ONE OF US...AND CARELESSLY LET MY GUARD DOWN...
BUT... HE DEFINITELY PLANS... TO KILL YOU, LORD RIKUO!
RRRG
NO... TSURARA, DON'T...

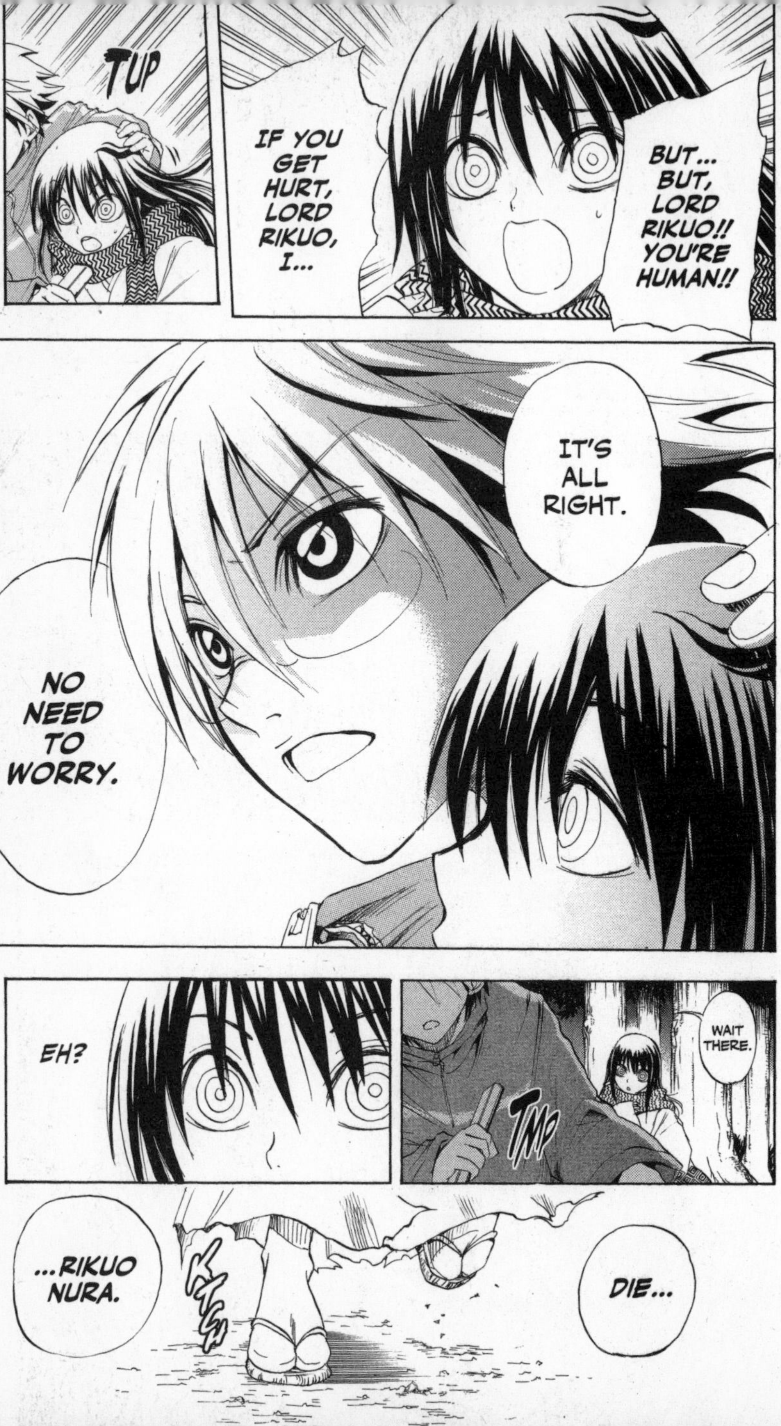
BUT... BUT, LORD RIKUO!! YOU'RE HUMAN!!
IF YOU GET HURT, LORD RIKUO, I...
TUP
IT'S ALL RIGHT.
NO NEED TO WORRY.
WAIT THERE.
TMP
EH?
DIE...
...RIKUO NURA.

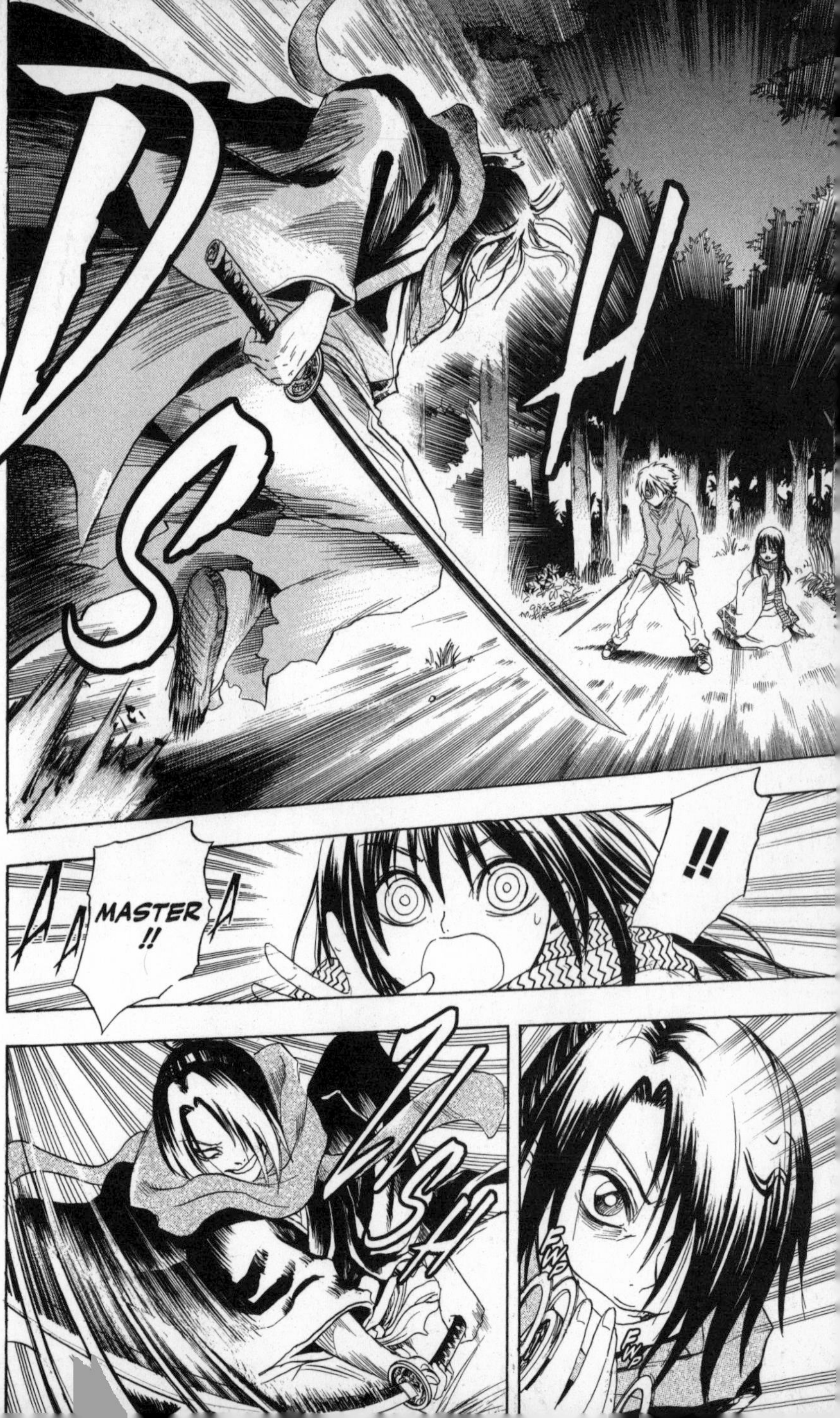
!!
MASTER!!
FWP
FWP

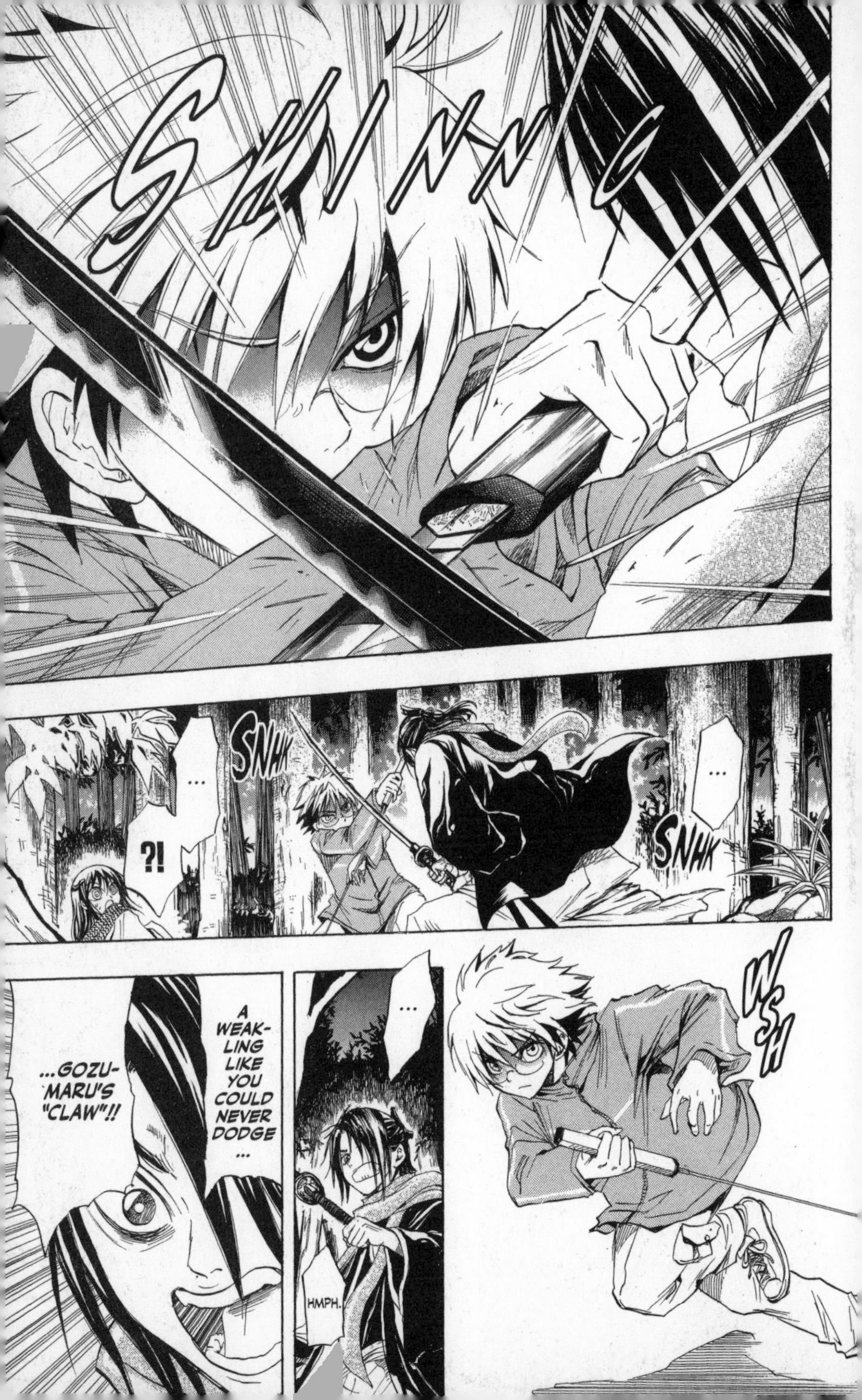

SHINNG
...
SNHK
SNHK
...
?!
WSH
...
A WEAK-LING LIKE YOU COULD NEVER DODGE ...
HMPH.
...GOZU-MARU'S "CLAW"!!

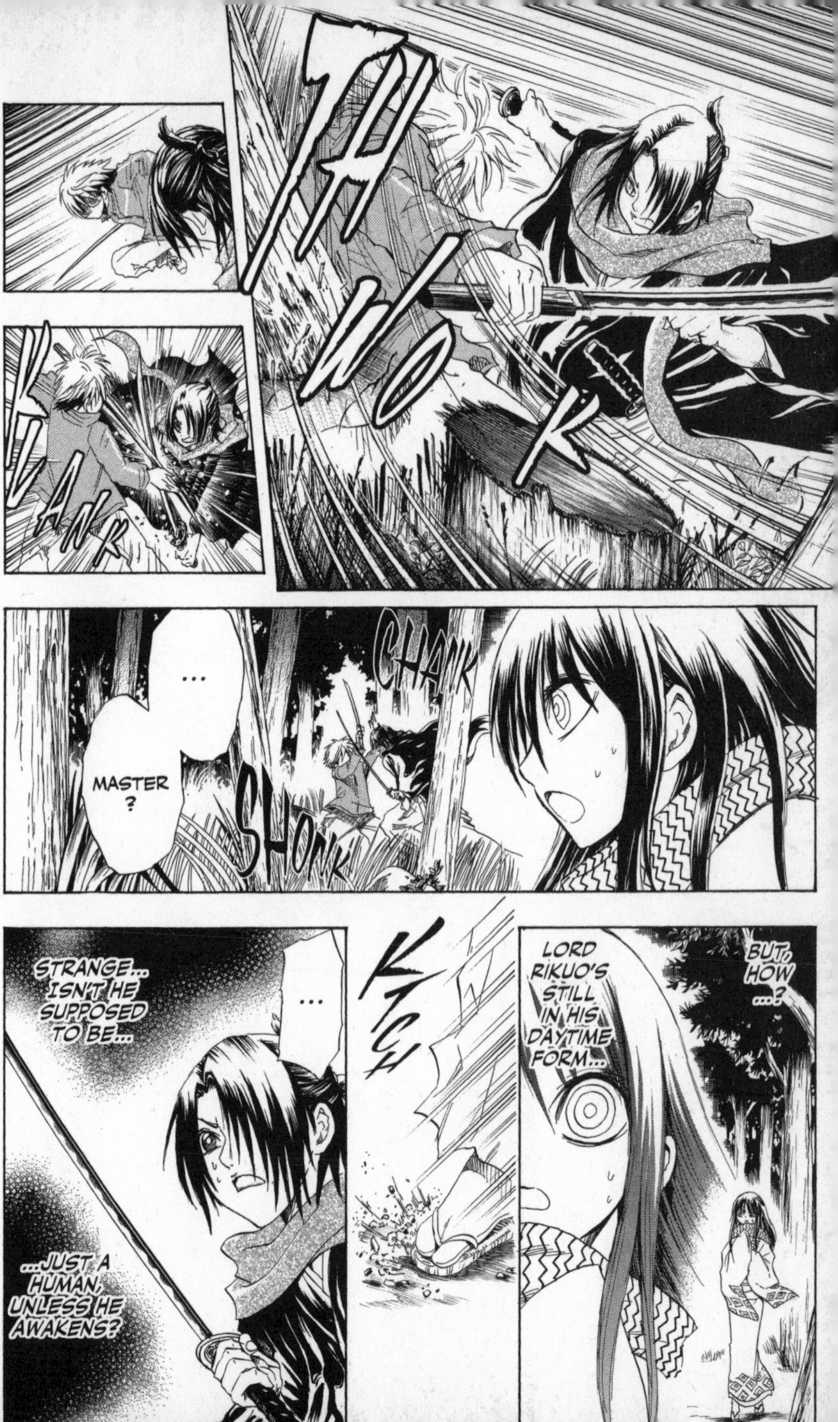
CHANK
...
MASTER ?
SHONK
BUT, HOW ...?
LORD RIKUO'S STILL IN HIS DAYTIME FORM...
...
STRANGE... ISN'T HE SUPPOSED TO BE...
...JUST A HUMAN, UNLESS HE AWAKENS?

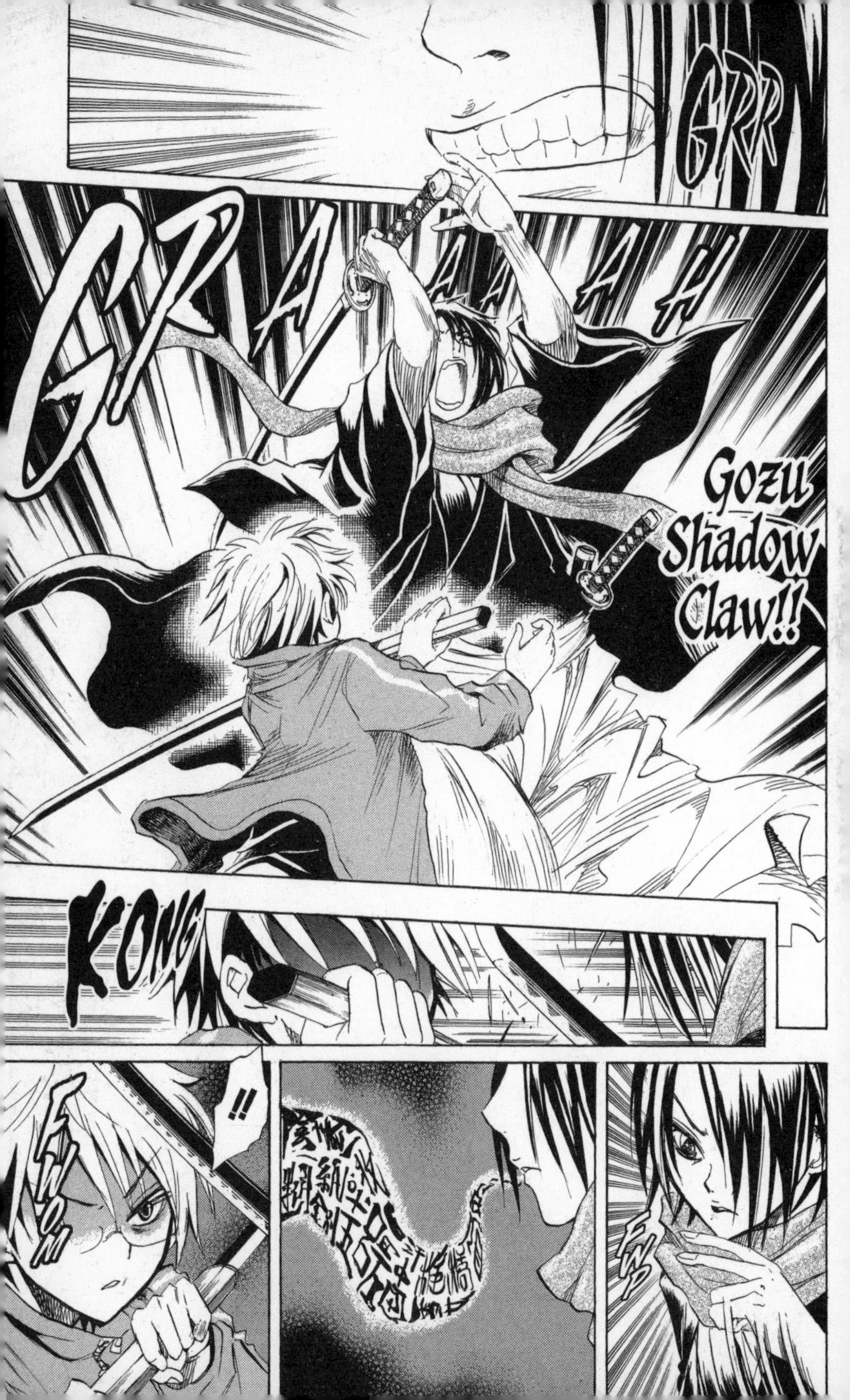
GRR
GRAAAAH
Gozu Shadow Claw!!
KONG
FWP
!!
FWOM

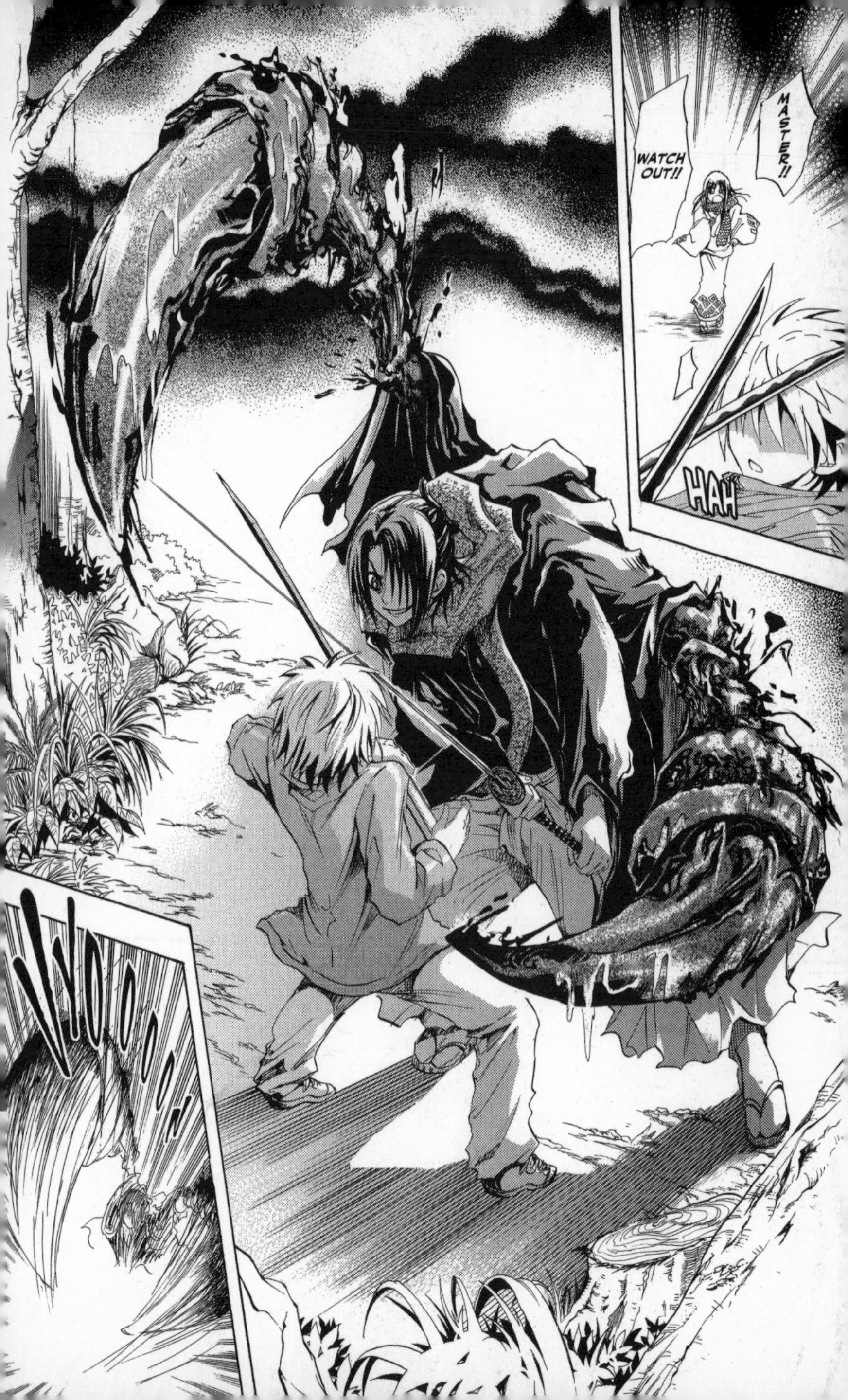
MASTER!!
WATCH OUT!!
HAH

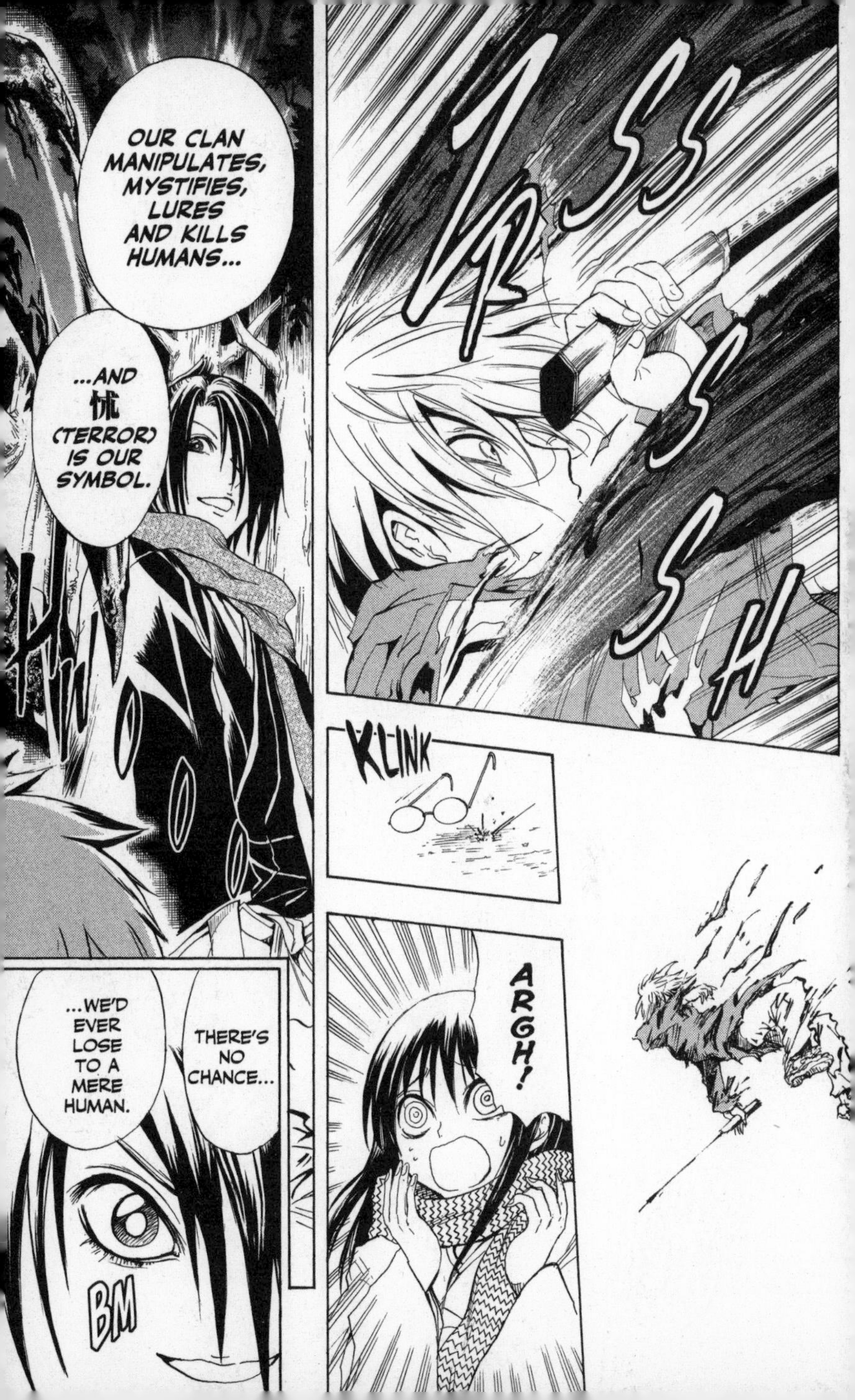
KRSSSSH
KLINK
OUR CLAN MANIPULATES, MYSTIFIES, LURES AND KILLS HUMANS...
...AND 怖 (TERROR) IS OUR SYMBOL.
ARGH!
THERE'S NO CHANCE...
...WE'D EVER LOSE TO A MERE HUMAN.
BM

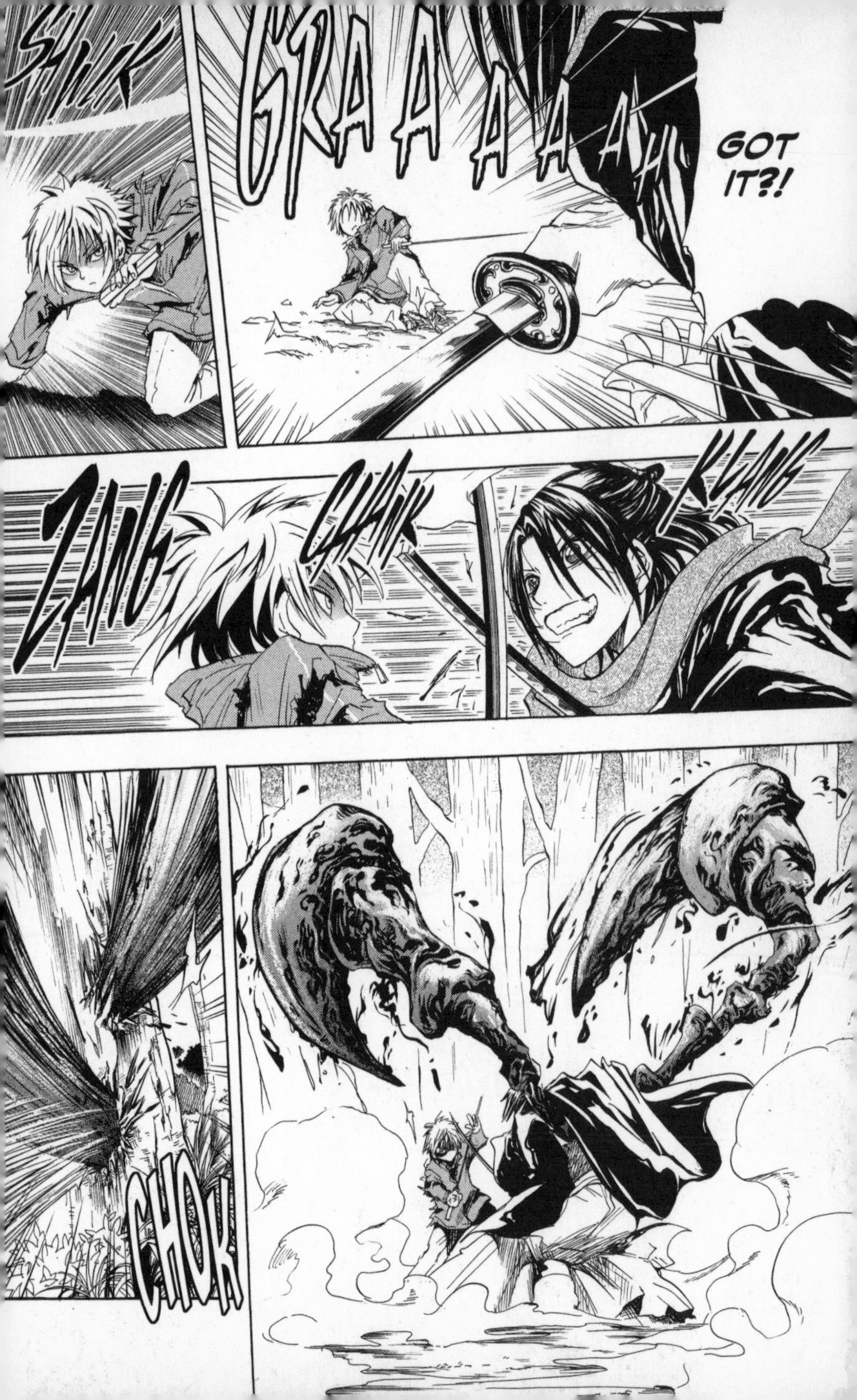
GRAAAAH
GOT IT?!
SHIK
KLANG
CHAK
ZANG
CHOK

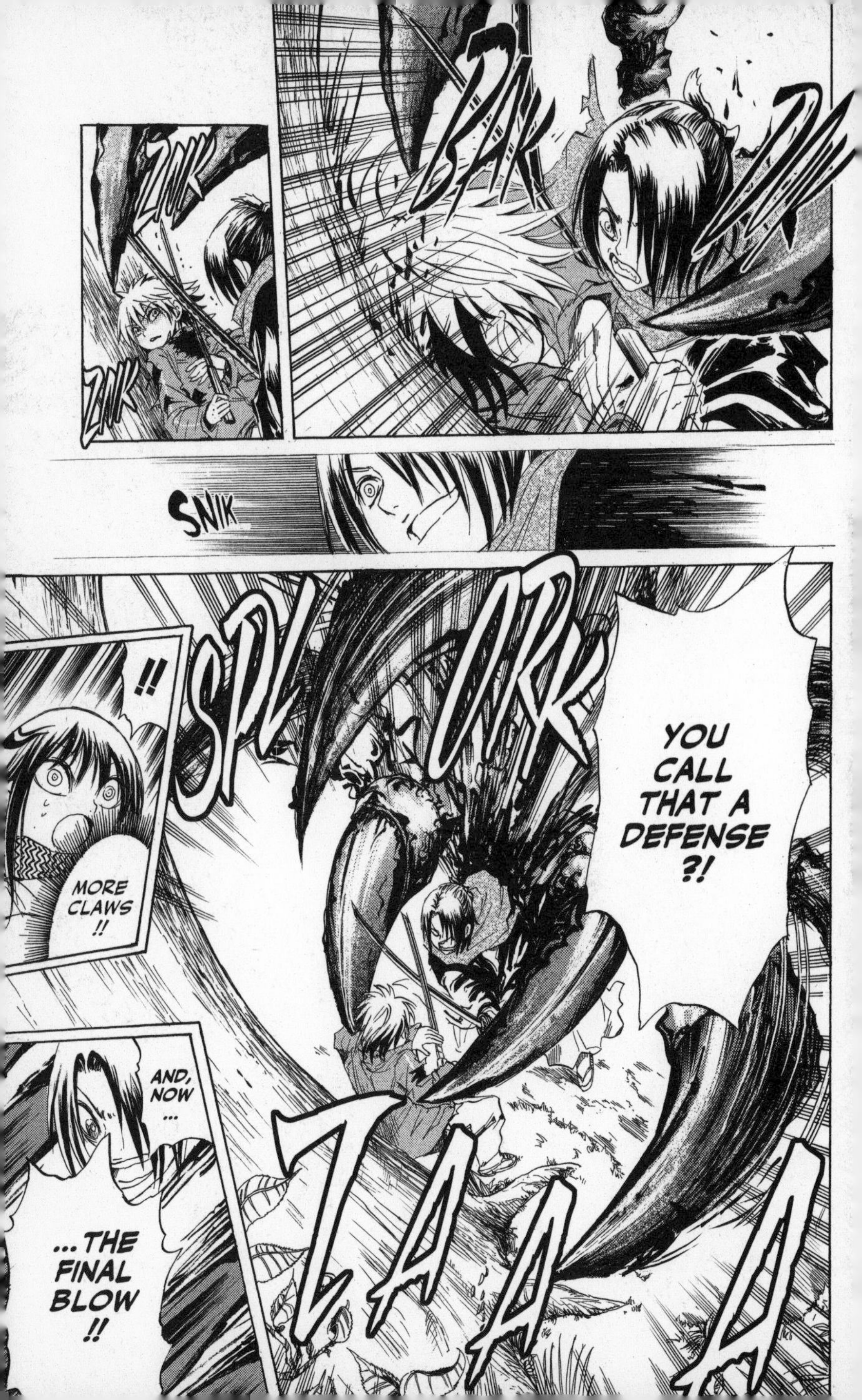
BAK
ZINK
ZINK
SNIK
YOU CALL THAT A DEFENSE ?!
!!
MORE CLAWS !!
AND, NOW ...
...THE FINAL BLOW !!

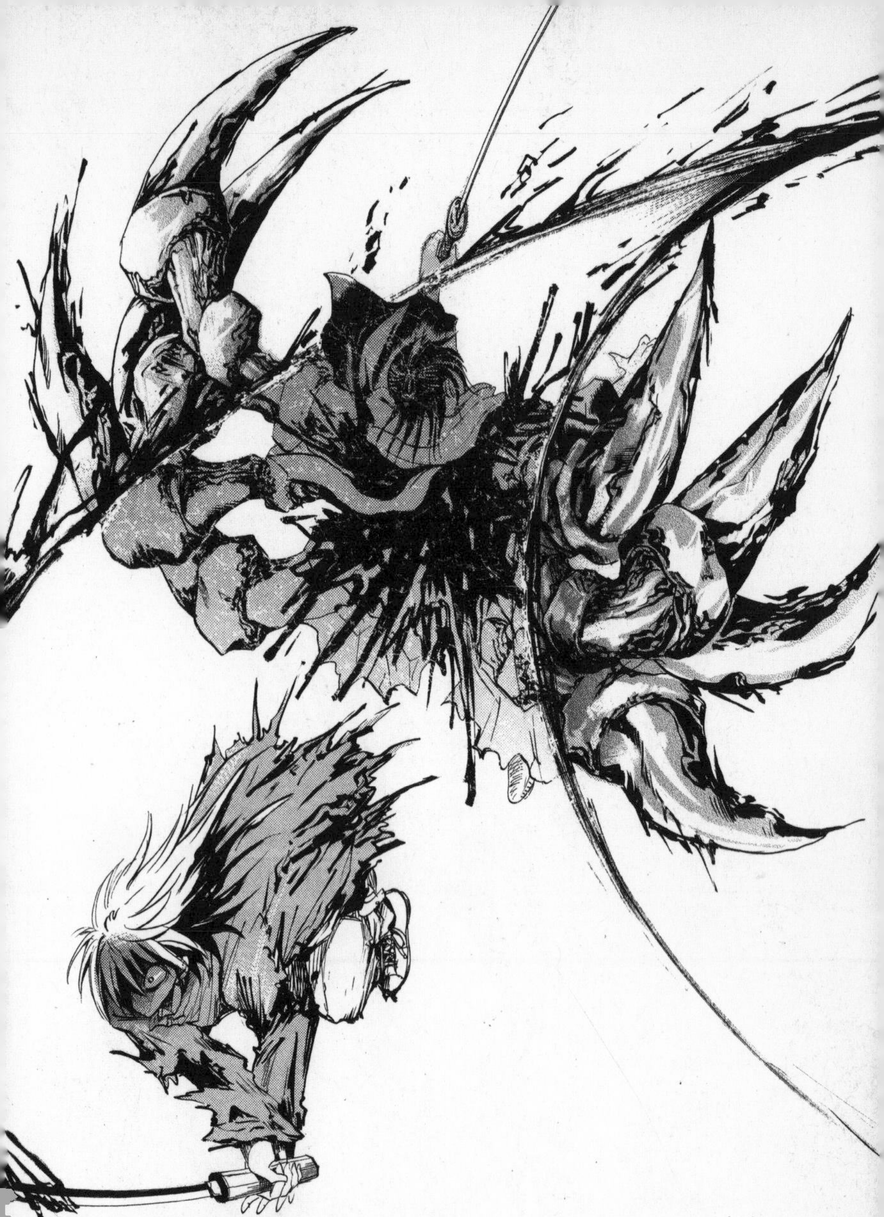

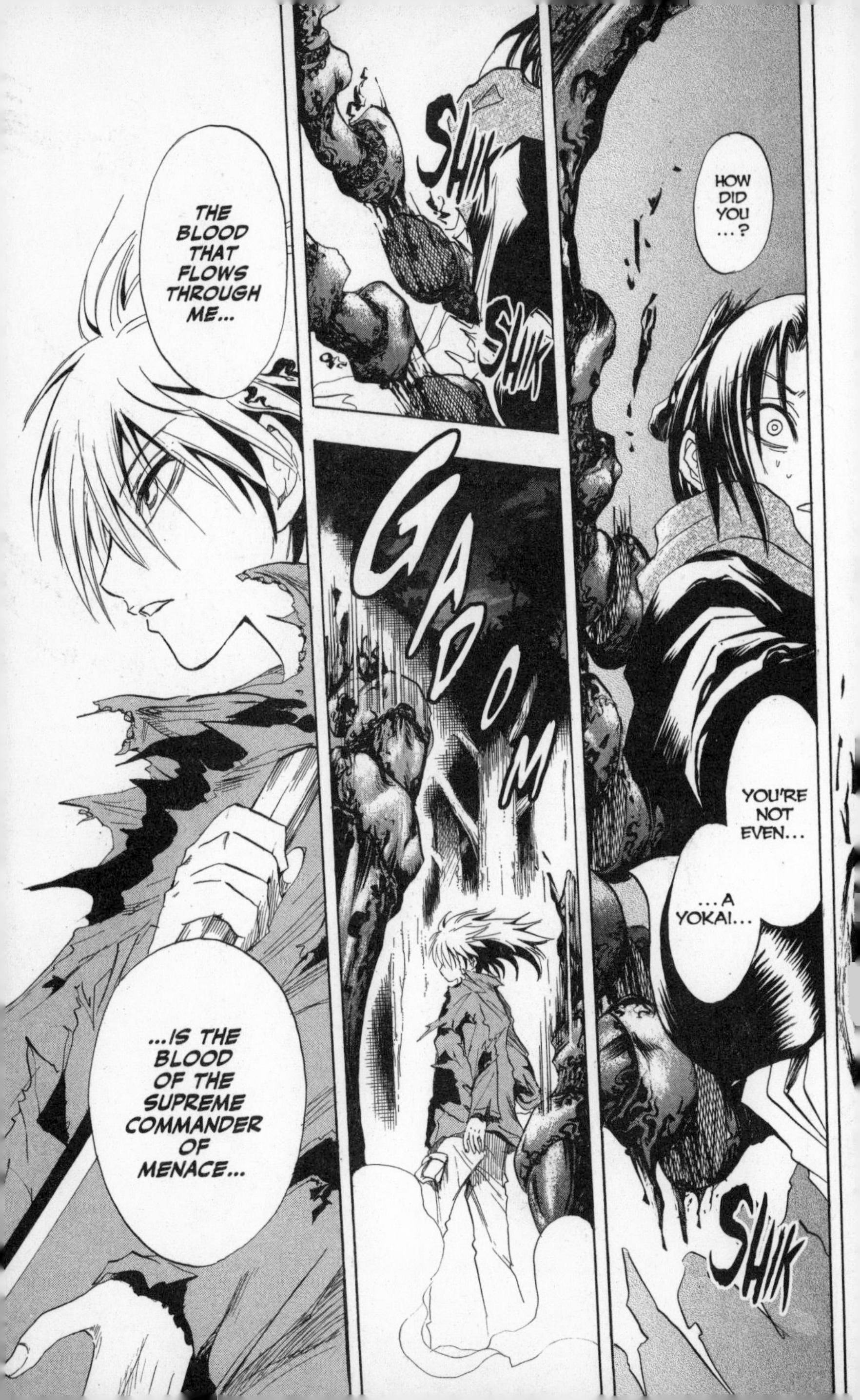
HOW DID YOU ...?
YOU'RE NOT EVEN...
...A YOKAI...
SHIK
SHIK
SHIK
GADOOM
THE BLOOD THAT FLOWS THROUGH ME...
...IS THE BLOOD OF THE SUPREME COMMANDER OF MENACE...

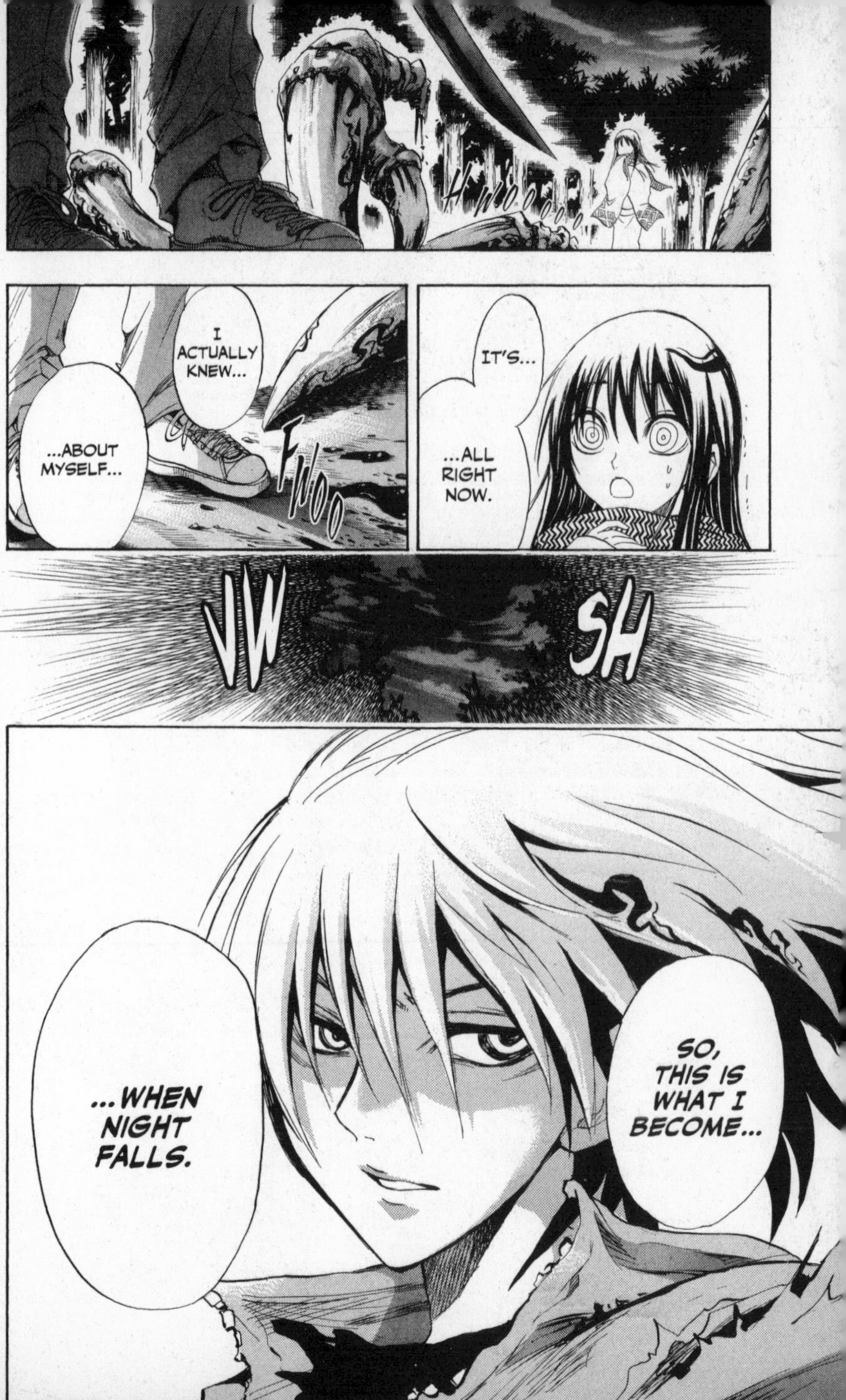
HWOOOOOO
IT'S...
...ALL RIGHT NOW.
I ACTUALLY KNEW...
...ABOUT MYSELF...
FWOO
VWSH
SO, THIS IS WHAT I BECOME...
...WHEN NIGHT FALLS.

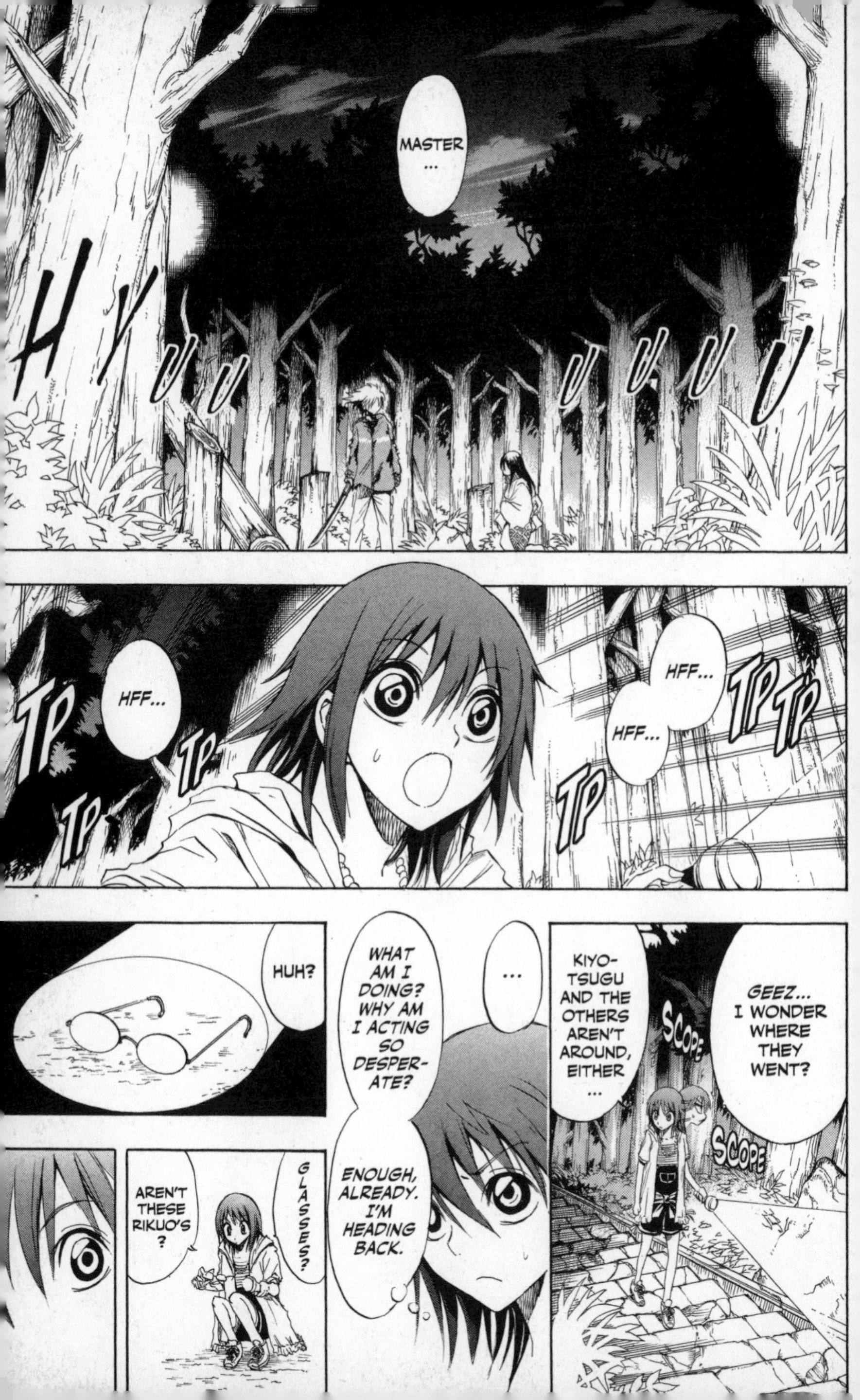
MASTER...
HYUUUUUUU
HFF...
TP TP
HFF...
TP
HFF...
TP
TP
GEEZ... I WONDER WHERE THEY WENT?
SCOPE
SCOPE
KIYO-TSUGU AND THE OTHERS AREN'T AROUND, EITHER...
...
WHAT AM I DOING? WHY AM I ACTING SO DESPERATE?
ENOUGH, ALREADY. I'M HEADING BACK.
HUH?
GLASSES?
AREN'T THESE RIKUO'S?

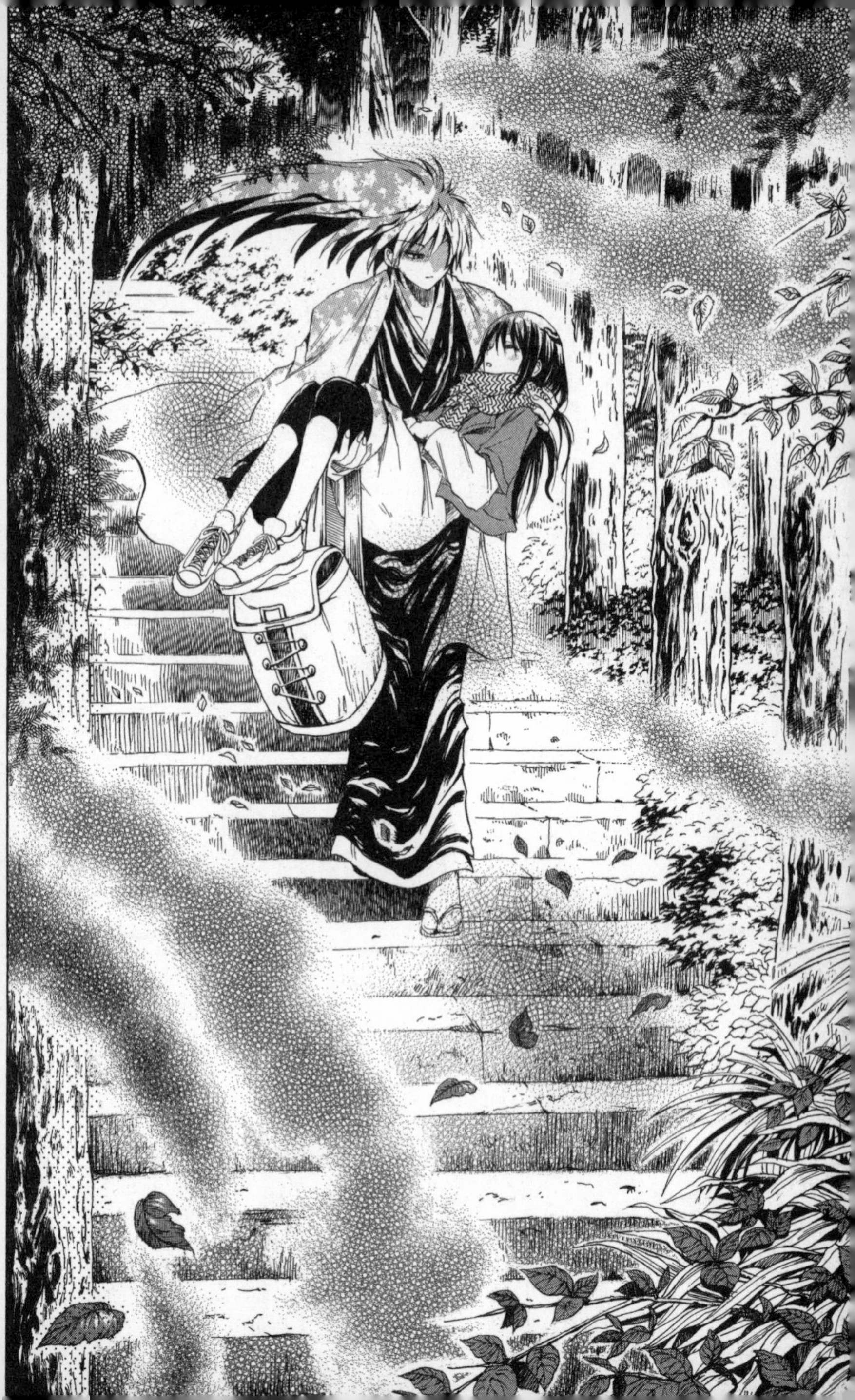

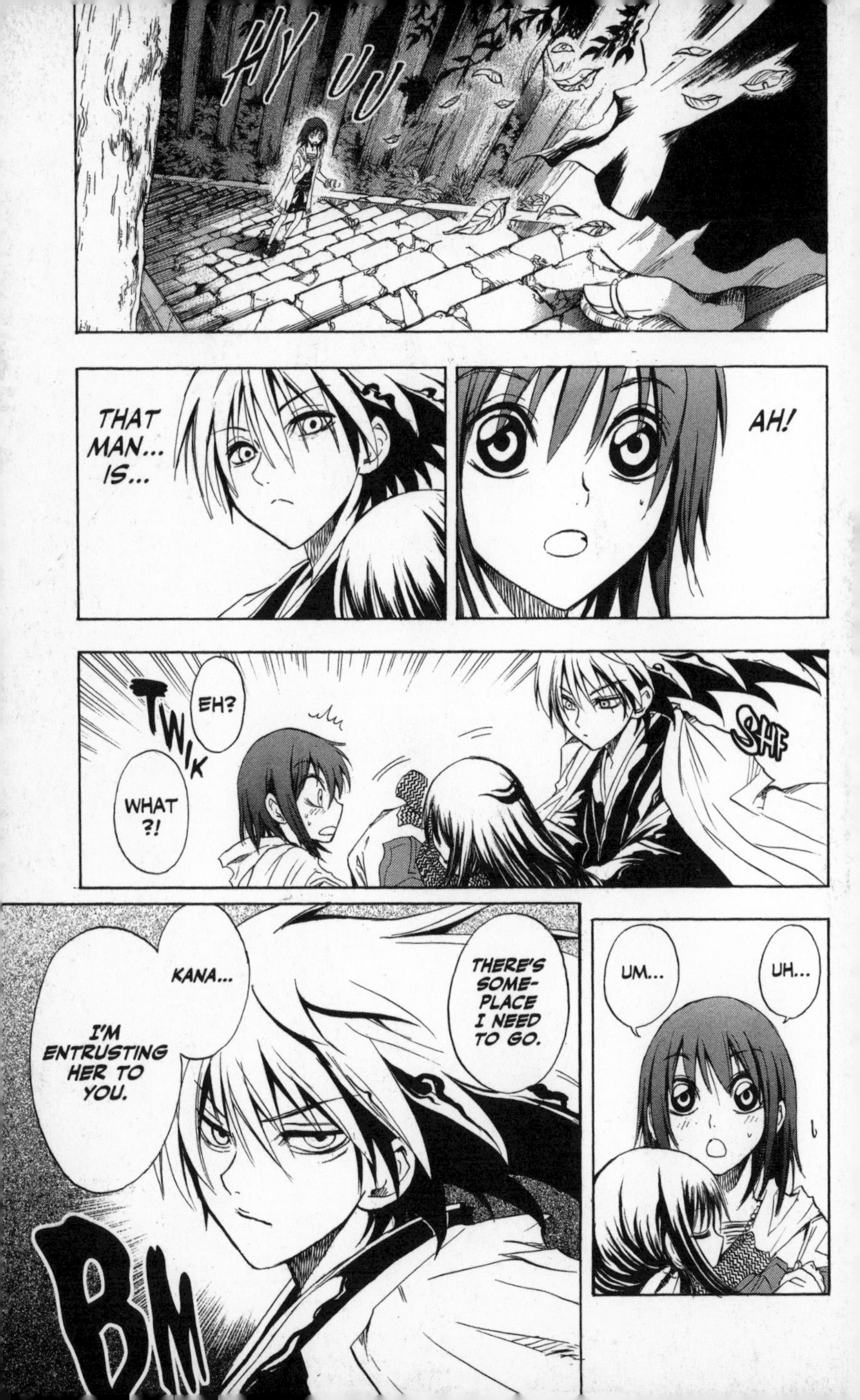
HYUU
AH!
THAT MAN... IS...
SHF
EH?
TWIK
WHAT ?!
UH...
UM...
THERE'S SOME-PLACE I NEED TO GO.
KANA...
I'M ENTRUSTING HER TO YOU.
BM

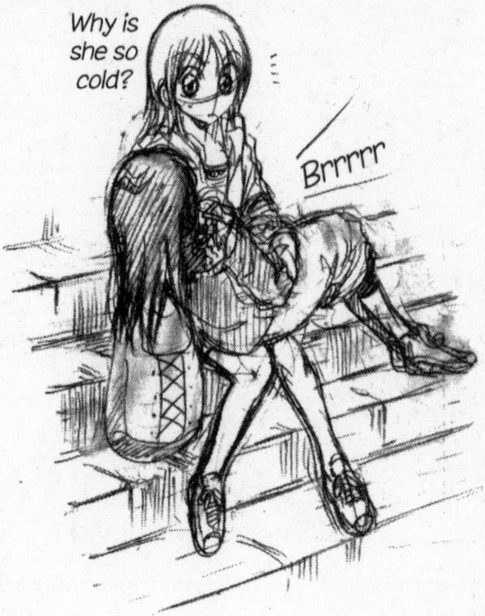
Why is she so cold?
Brrrrr

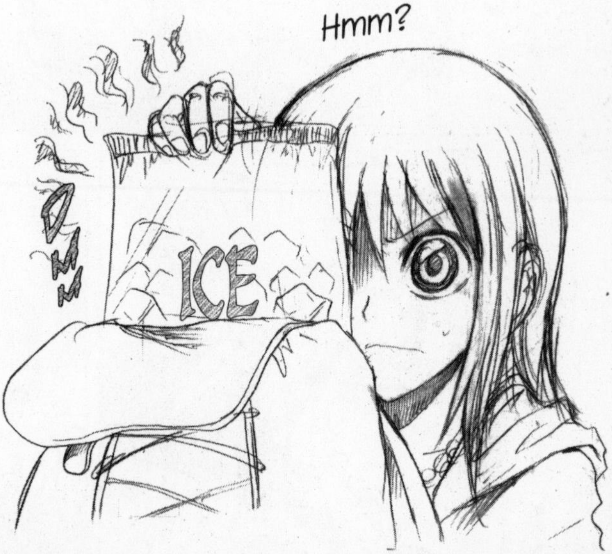
Hmm?
ICE

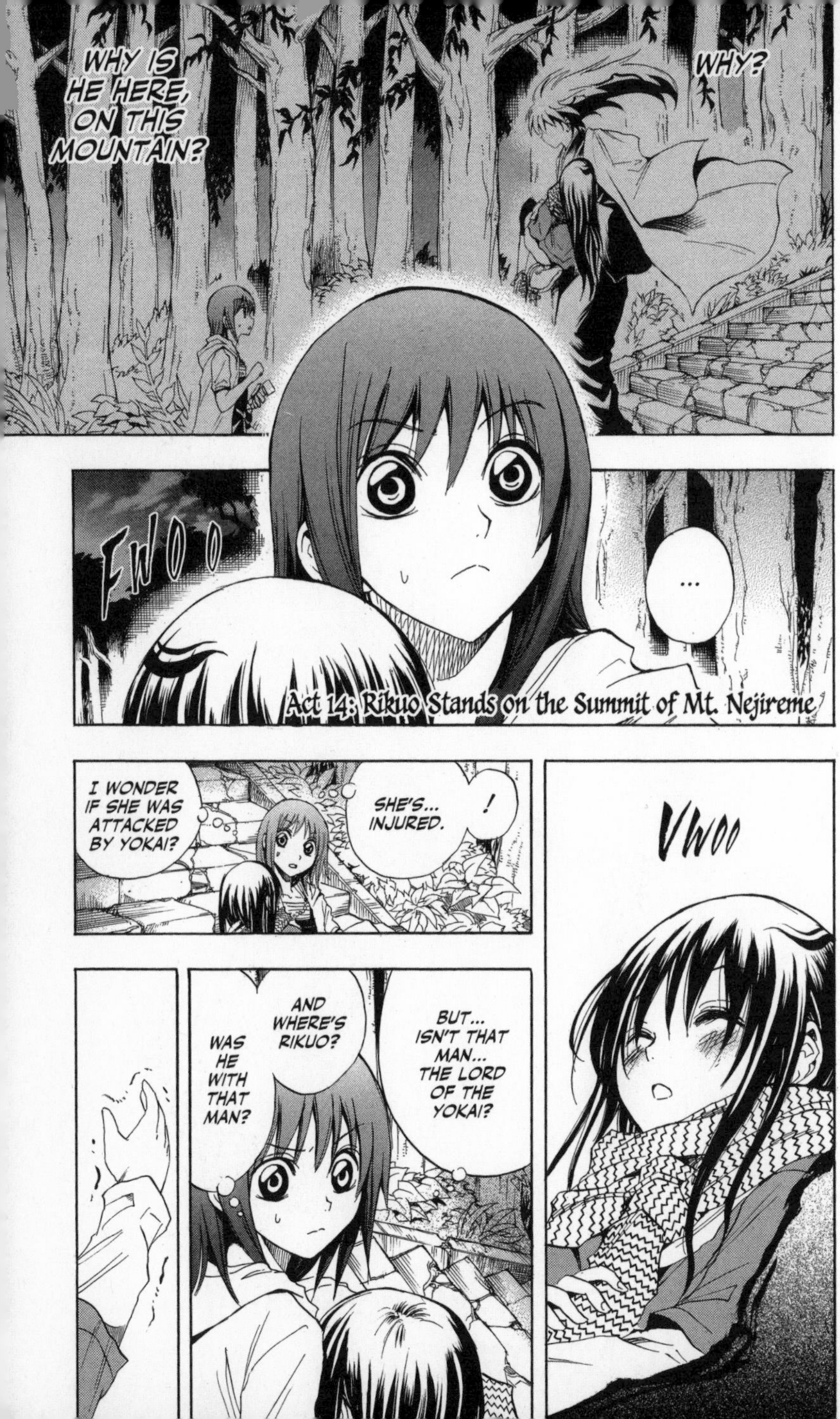
WHY?
WHY IS HE HERE, ON THIS MOUNTAIN?
...
FWOO
Act 14: Rikuo Stands on the Summit of Mt. Nejireme
VWOO
!
SHE'S... INJURED.
I WONDER IF SHE WAS ATTACKED BY YOKAI?
BUT... ISN'T THAT MAN... THE LORD OF THE YOKAI?
AND WHERE'S RIKUO?
WAS HE WITH THAT MAN?

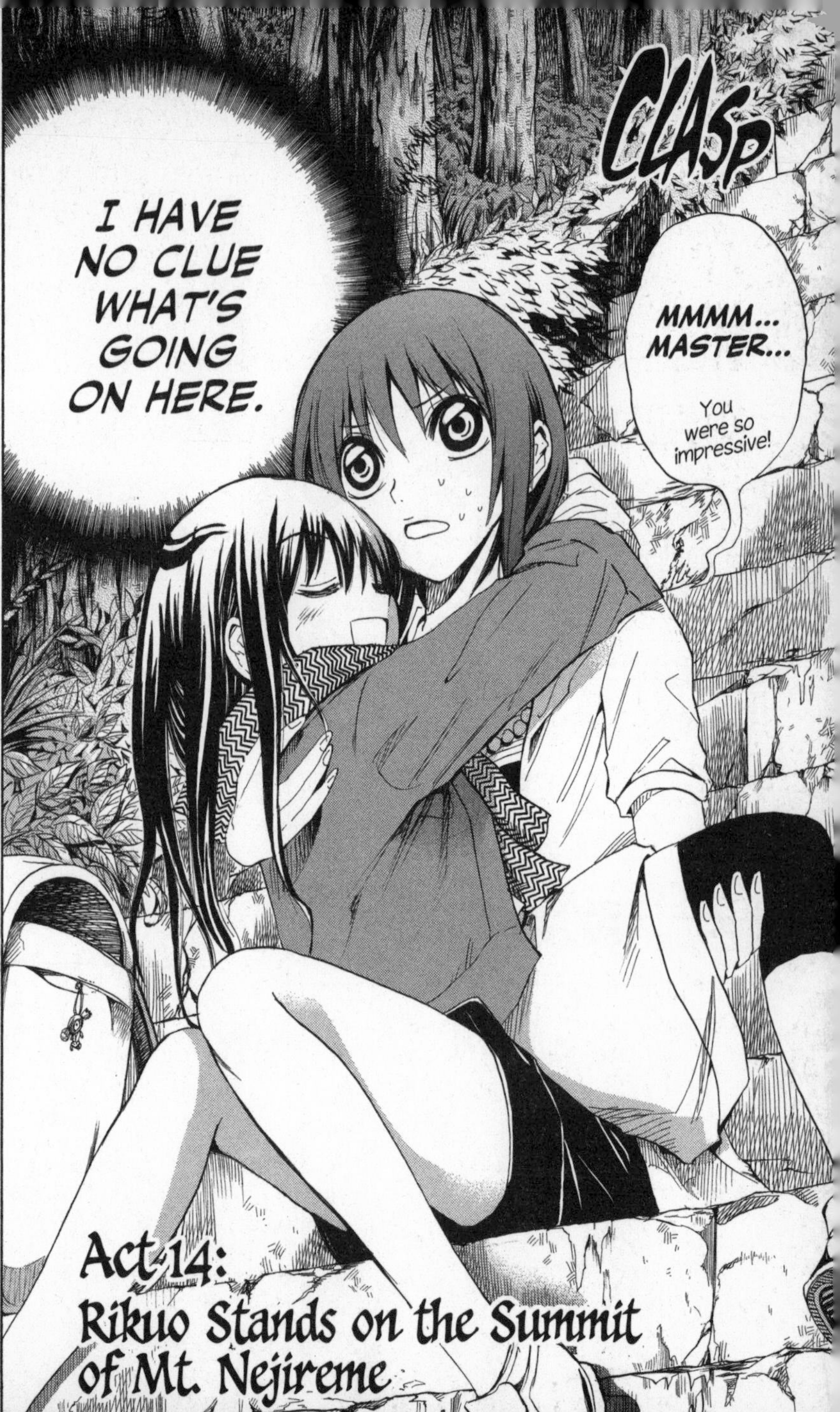
CLASP
MMMM... MASTER...
You were so impressive!
I HAVE NO CLUE WHAT'S GOING ON HERE.
Act 14:
Rikuo Stands on the Summit of Mt. Nejireme

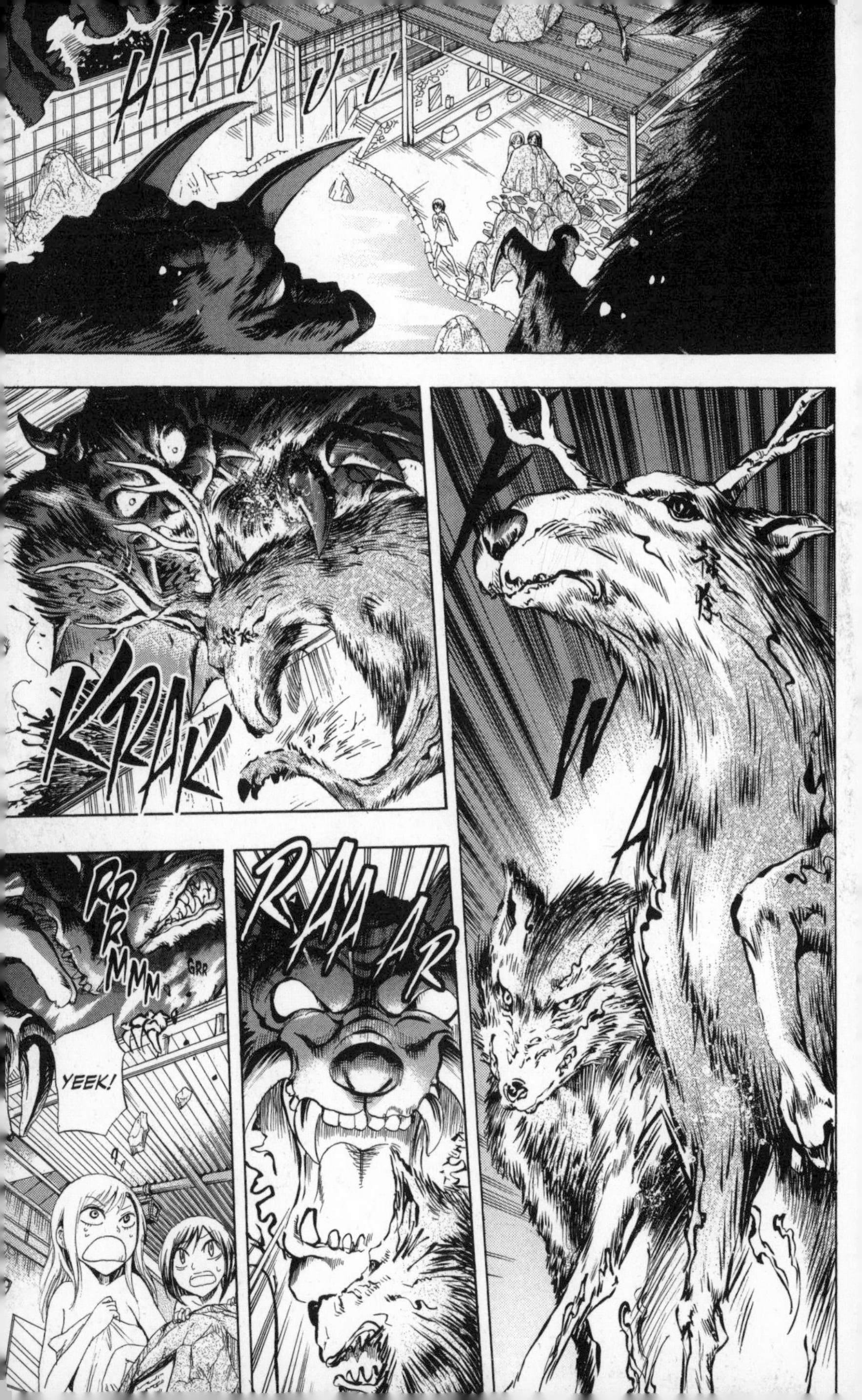
HYUUUU
KRAK
RAAAAR
PRRRMMM
GRR
YEEK!

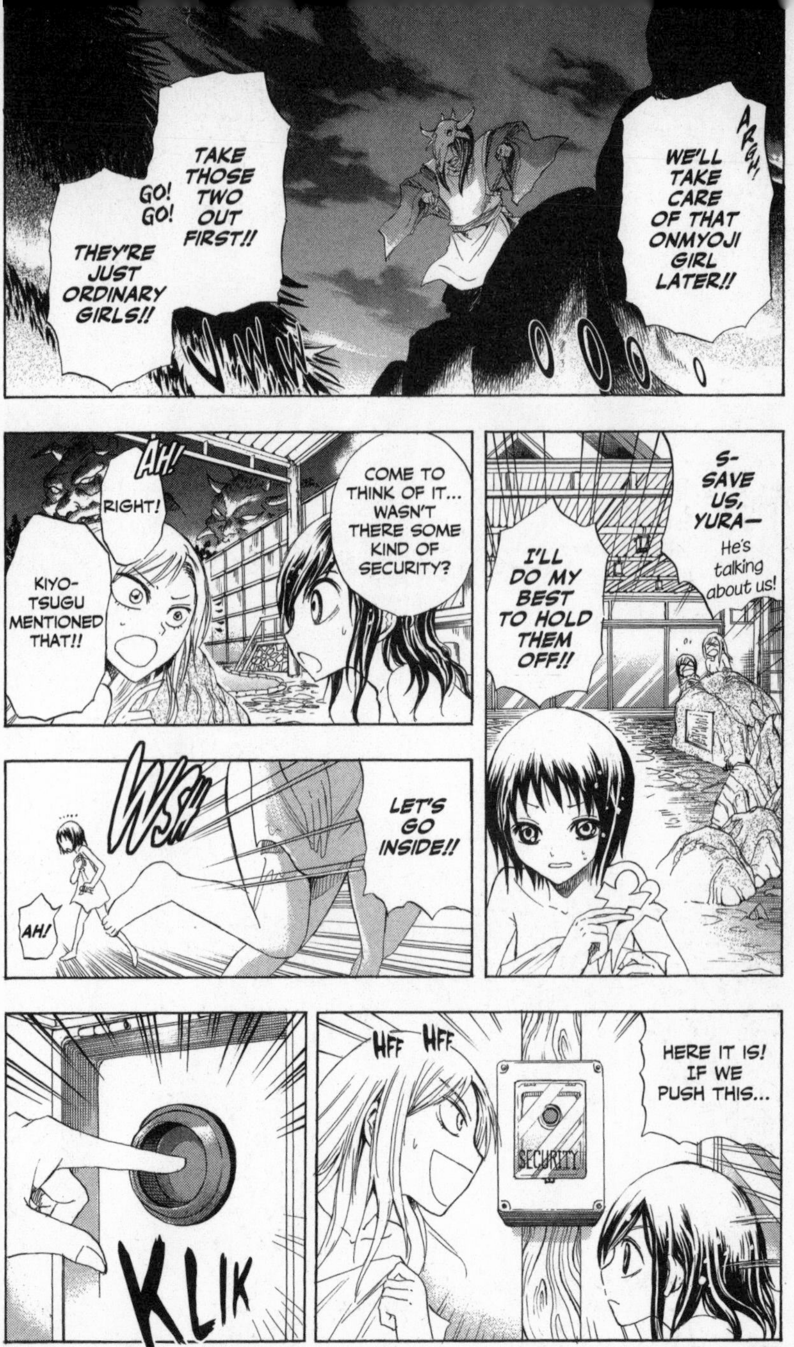
ARGH!
WE'LL TAKE CARE OF THAT ONMYOJI GIRL LATER!!
TAKE THOSE TWO OUT FIRST!!
GO! GO!
THEY'RE JUST ORDINARY GIRLS!!
S-SAVE US, YURA—
He's talking about us!
I'LL DO MY BEST TO HOLD THEM OFF!!
COME TO THINK OF IT... WASN'T THERE SOME KIND OF SECURITY?
AH!
RIGHT!
KIYO-TSUGU MENTIONED THAT!!
WSH
LET'S GO INSIDE!!
AH!
HFF HFF
HERE IT IS! IF WE PUSH THIS...
SECURITY
KLIK

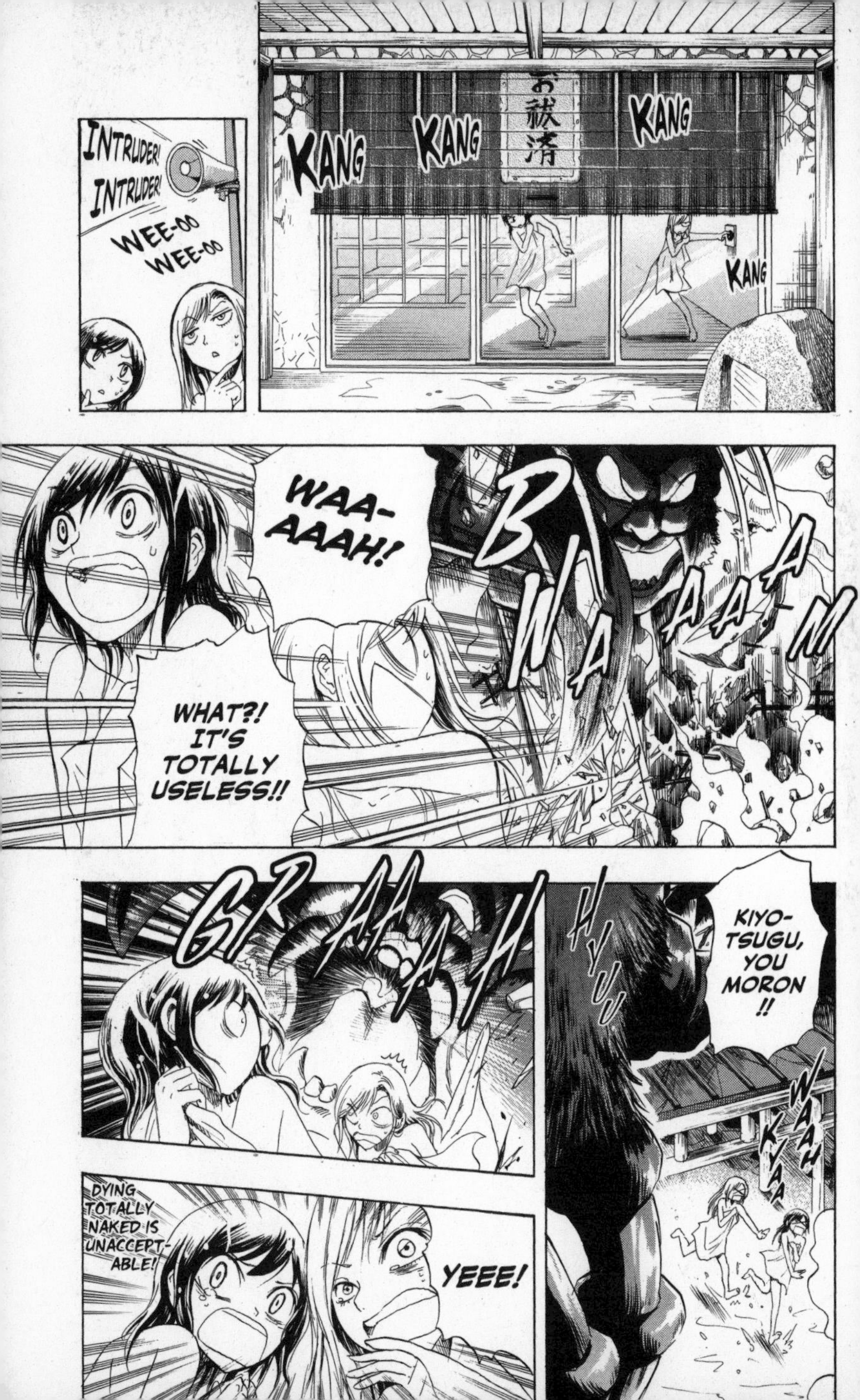
お祓済
KANG
KANG
KANG
KANG
INTRUDER!
INTRUDER!
WEE-OO
WEE-OO
BNAAAAN
WAA-AAAH!
WHAT?! IT'S TOTALLY USELESS!!
KIYO-TSUGU, YOU MORON!!
WAAAH
KYAA
GRAAAH
DYING TOTALLY NAKED IS UNACCEPT-ABLE!
YEEE!

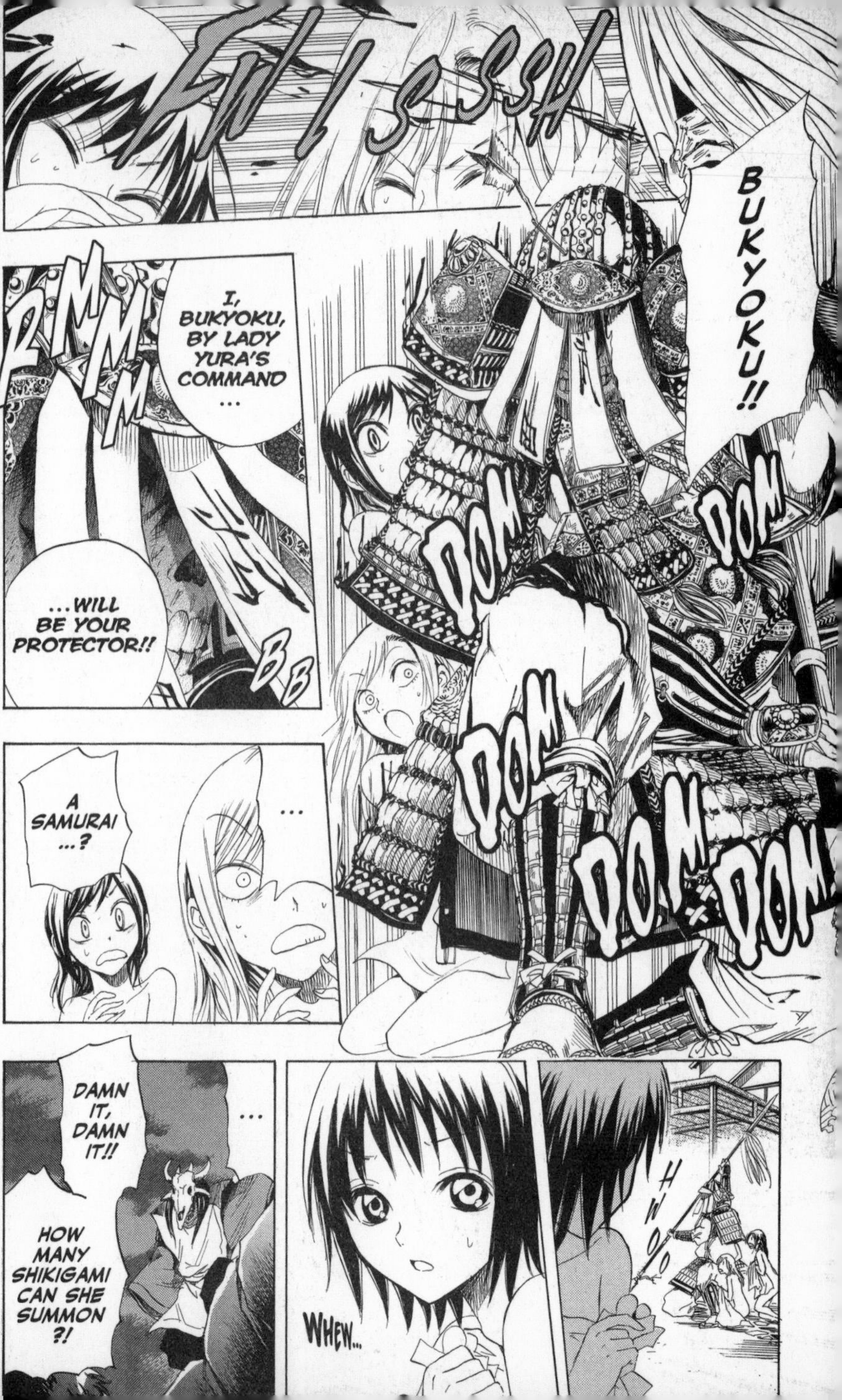
FWISSSH
BUKYOKU!!
DOM DOM
DOM
DOM DOM DOM
RMMM
I, BUKYOKU, BY LADY YURA'S COMMAND ...
...WILL BE YOUR PROTECTOR!!
BB
A SAMURAI ...?
...
HWOO
WHEW...
DAMN IT, DAMN IT!!
...
HOW MANY SHIKIGAMI CAN SHE SUMMON ?!

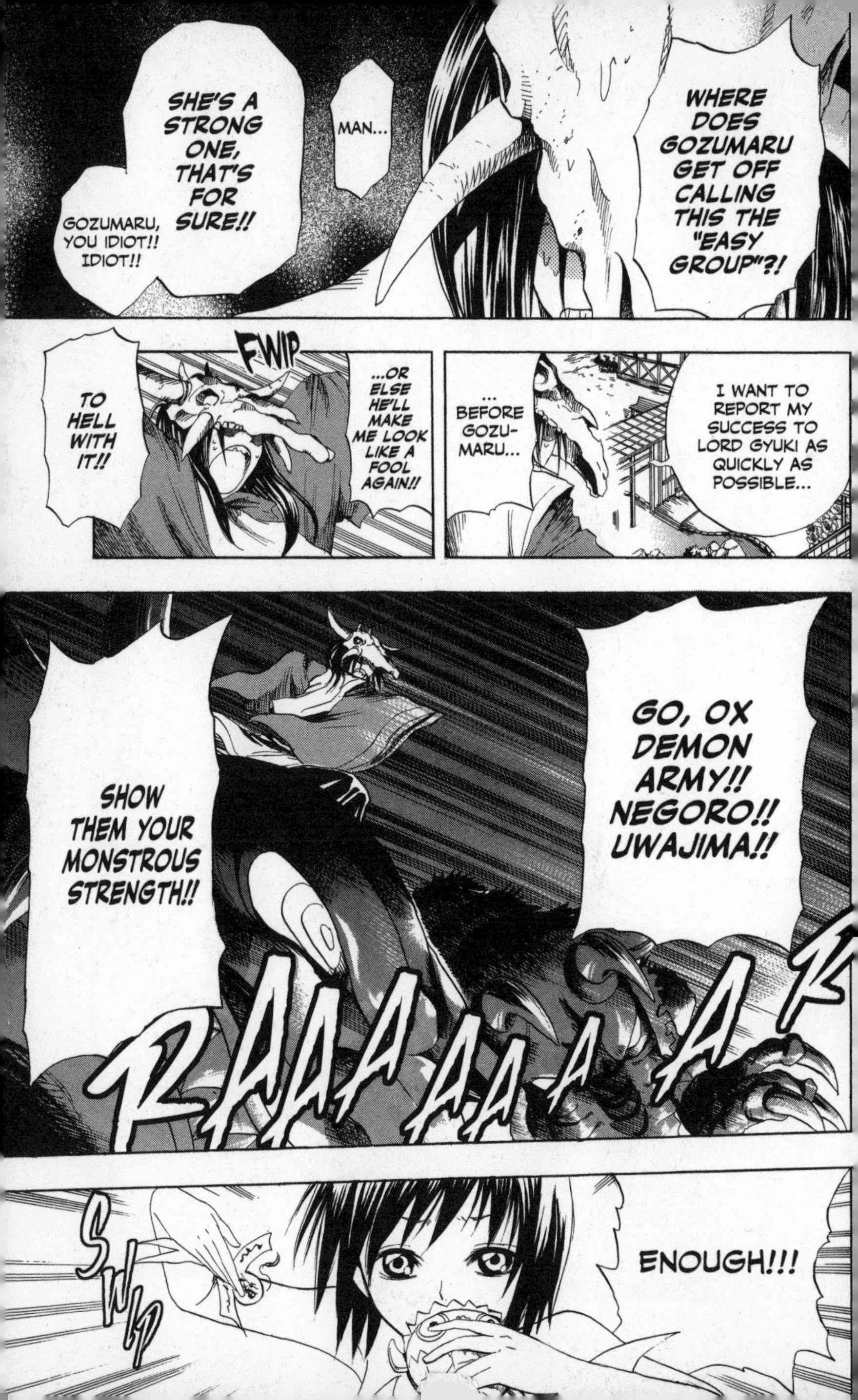

WHERE DOES GOZUMARU GET OFF CALLING THIS THE "EASY GROUP"?!
MAN...
SHE'S A STRONG ONE, THAT'S FOR SURE!!
GOZUMARU, YOU IDIOT!! IDIOT!!
I WANT TO REPORT MY SUCCESS TO LORD GYUKI AS QUICKLY AS POSSIBLE...
... BEFORE GOZUMARU...
...OR ELSE HE'LL MAKE ME LOOK LIKE A FOOL AGAIN!!
FWIP
TO HELL WITH IT!!
GO, OX DEMON ARMY!! NEGORO!! UWAJIMA!!
SHOW THEM YOUR MONSTROUS STRENGTH!!
RAAAAAAA
ENOUGH!!!
SWIP

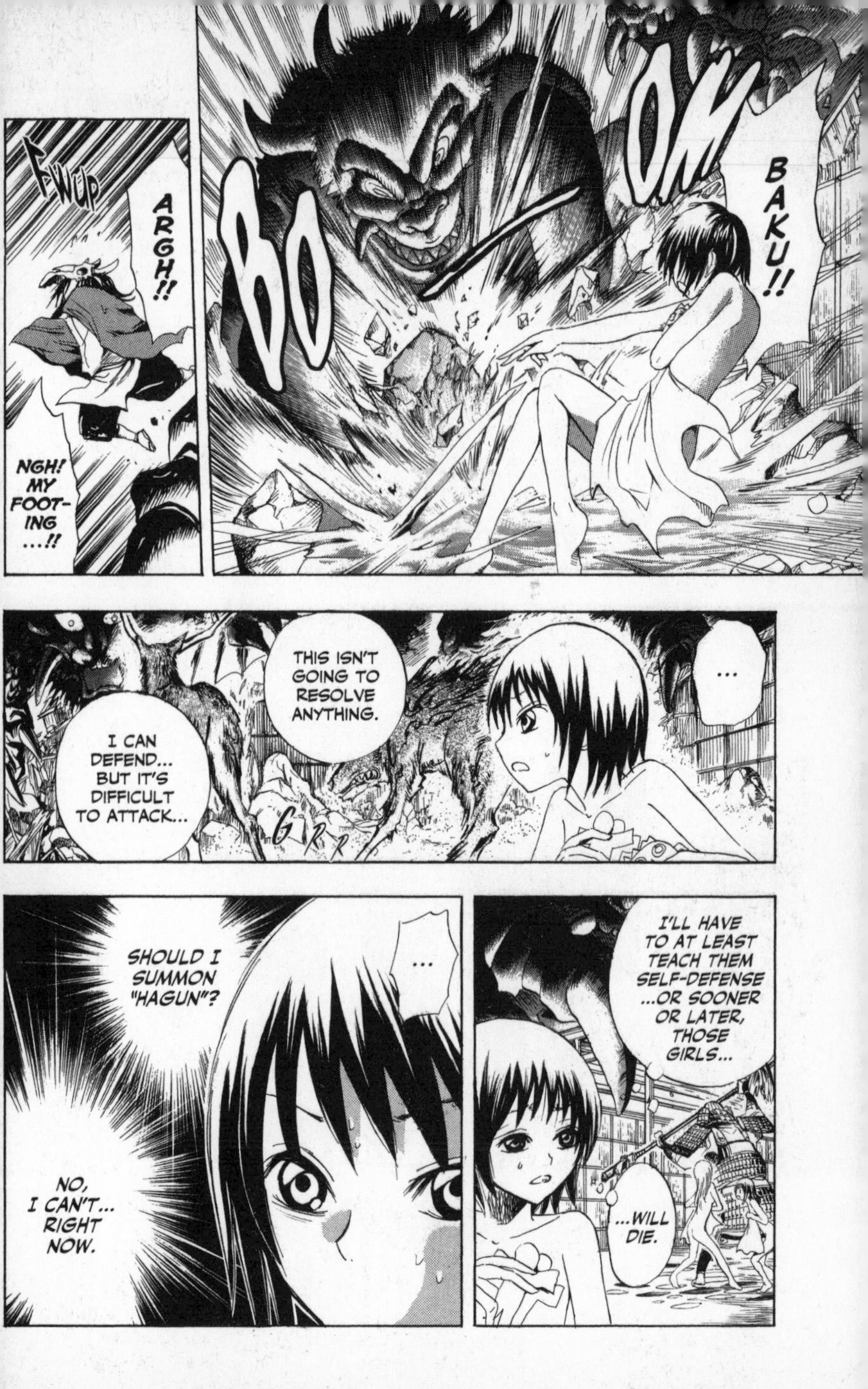
BOOM
BAKU!!
FWUP
ARGH!!
NGH! MY FOOTING...!!
...
THIS ISN'T GOING TO RESOLVE ANYTHING.
I CAN DEFEND... BUT IT'S DIFFICULT TO ATTACK...
GRRR
I'LL HAVE TO AT LEAST TEACH THEM SELF-DEFENSE ...OR SOONER OR LATER, THOSE GIRLS...
...WILL DIE.
...
SHOULD I SUMMON "HAGUN"?
NO, I CAN'T... RIGHT NOW.

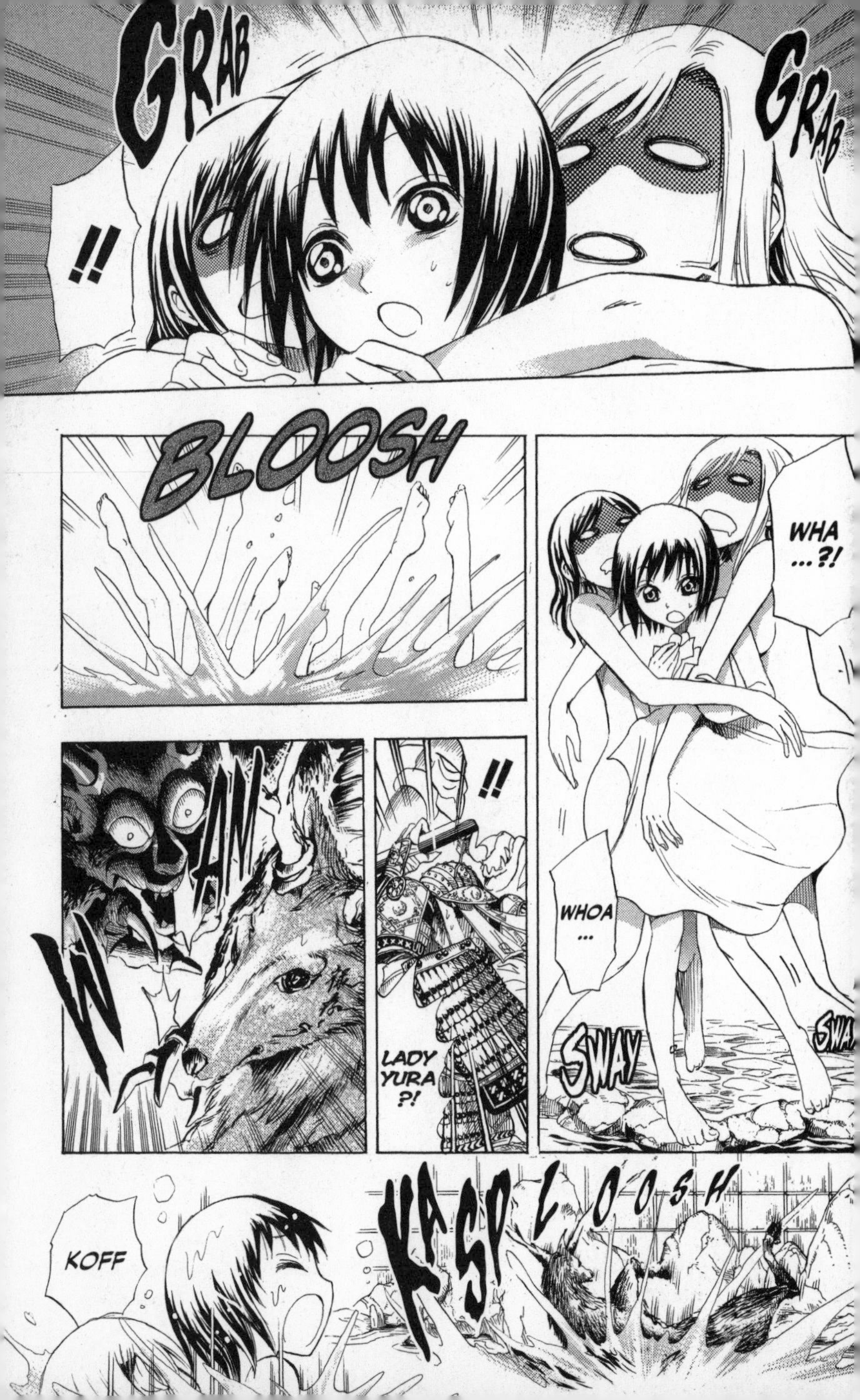
GRAB
GRAB
!!
WHA ...?!
WHOA ...
SWAY
BLOOSH
!!
LADY YURA ?!
KASPLOOSH
KOFF

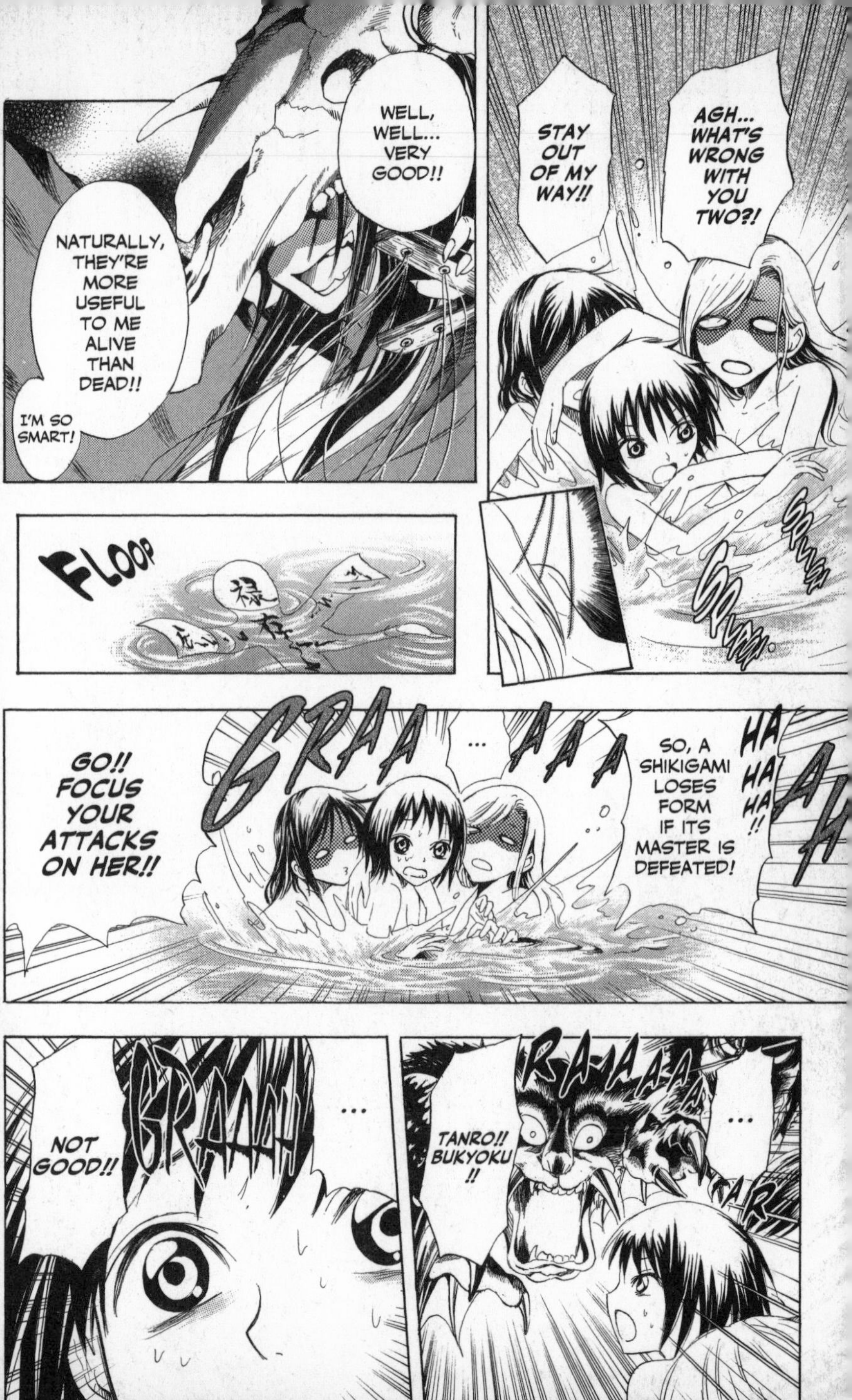
AGH... WHAT'S WRONG WITH YOU TWO?!
STAY OUT OF MY WAY!!
WELL, WELL... VERY GOOD!!
NATURALLY, THEY'RE MORE USEFUL TO ME ALIVE THAN DEAD!!
I'M SO SMART!
FLOOP
HA HA HA!!
SO, A SHIKIGAMI LOSES FORM IF ITS MASTER IS DEFEATED!
GRAA... AAA
GO!! FOCUS YOUR ATTACKS ON HER!!
RAAAAA... AR
TANRO!! BUKYOKU!!
GRAAAH...
NOT GOOD!!

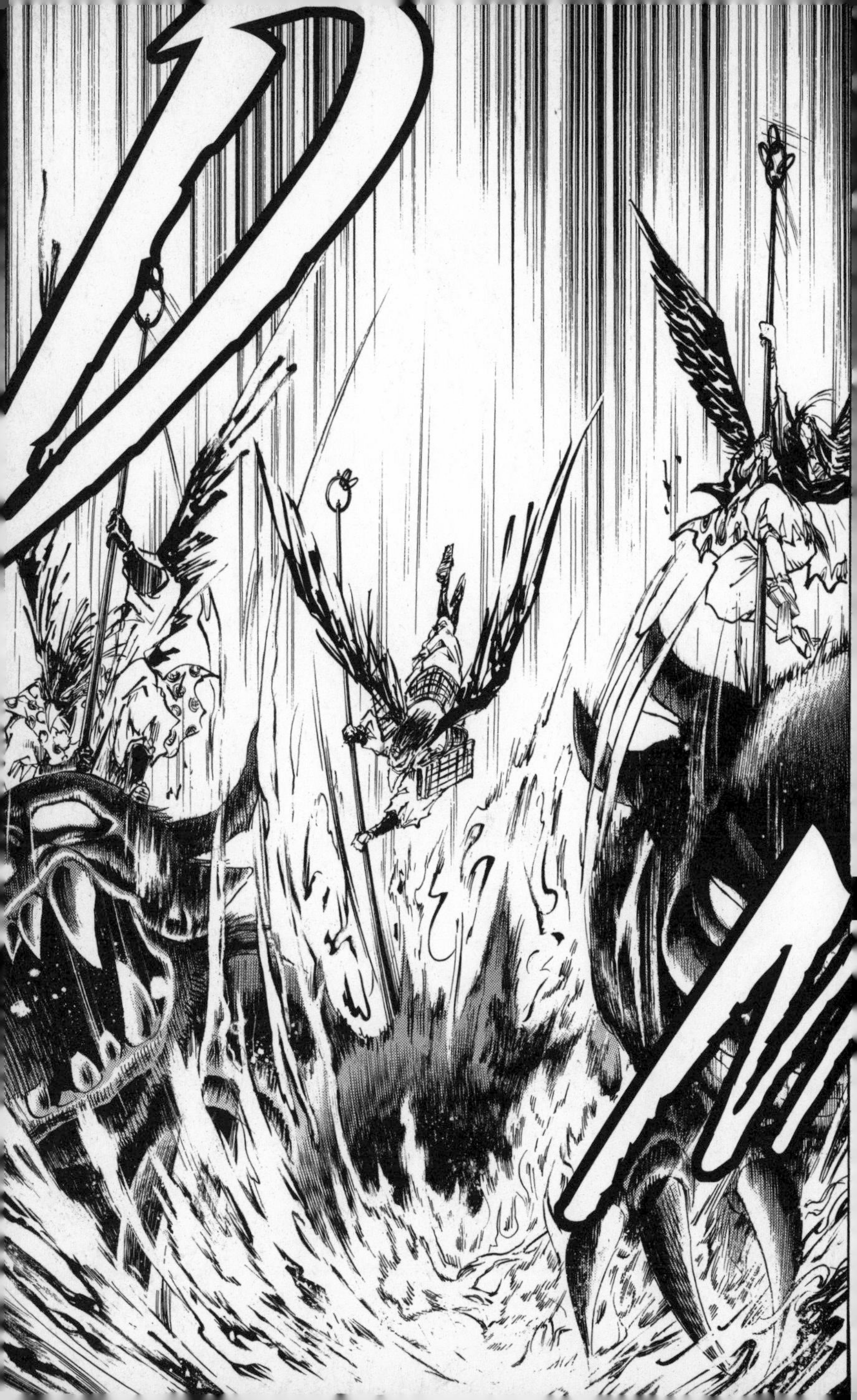

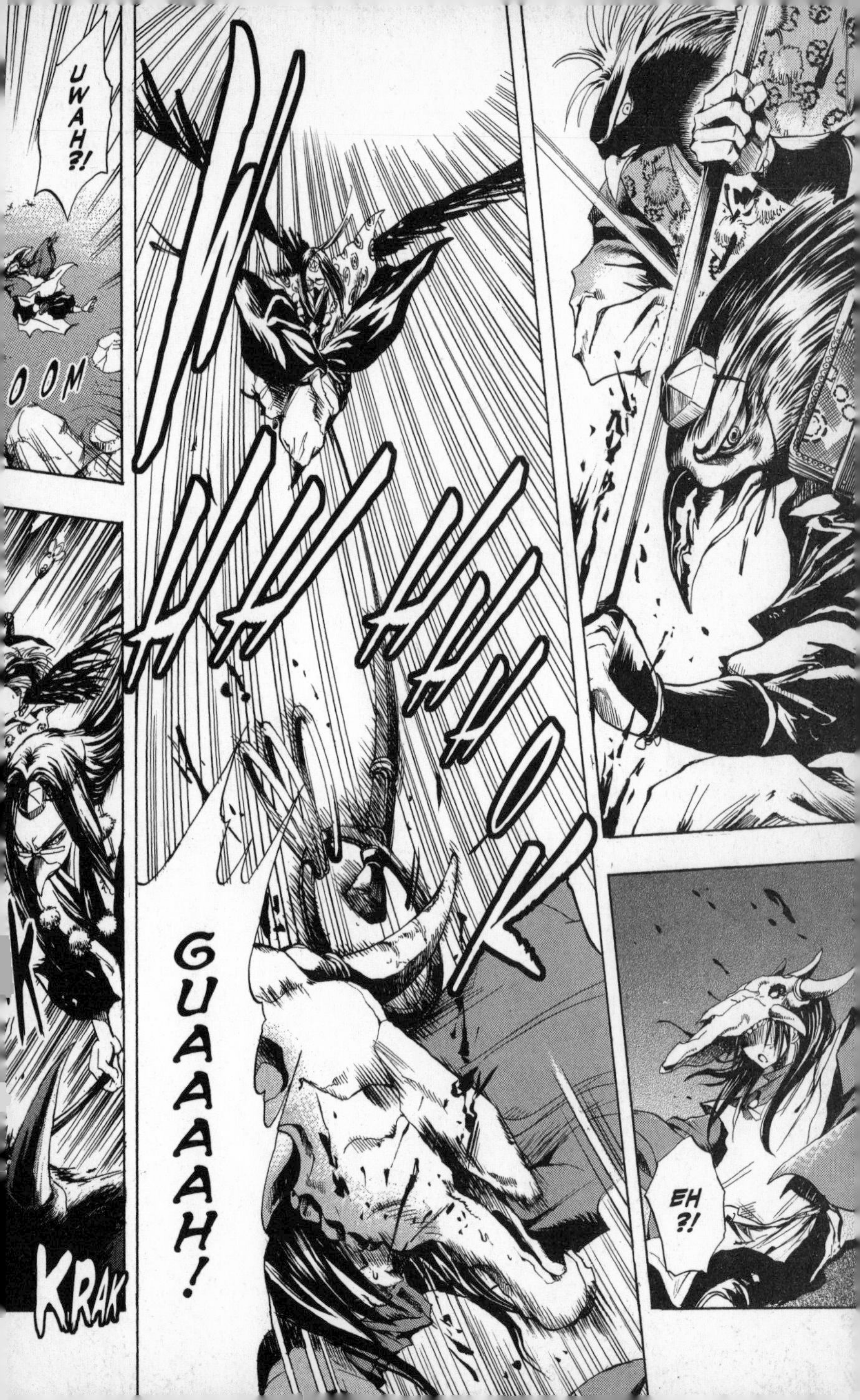
EH ?!
GUAAAAAH!
UWAH?!
KRAK

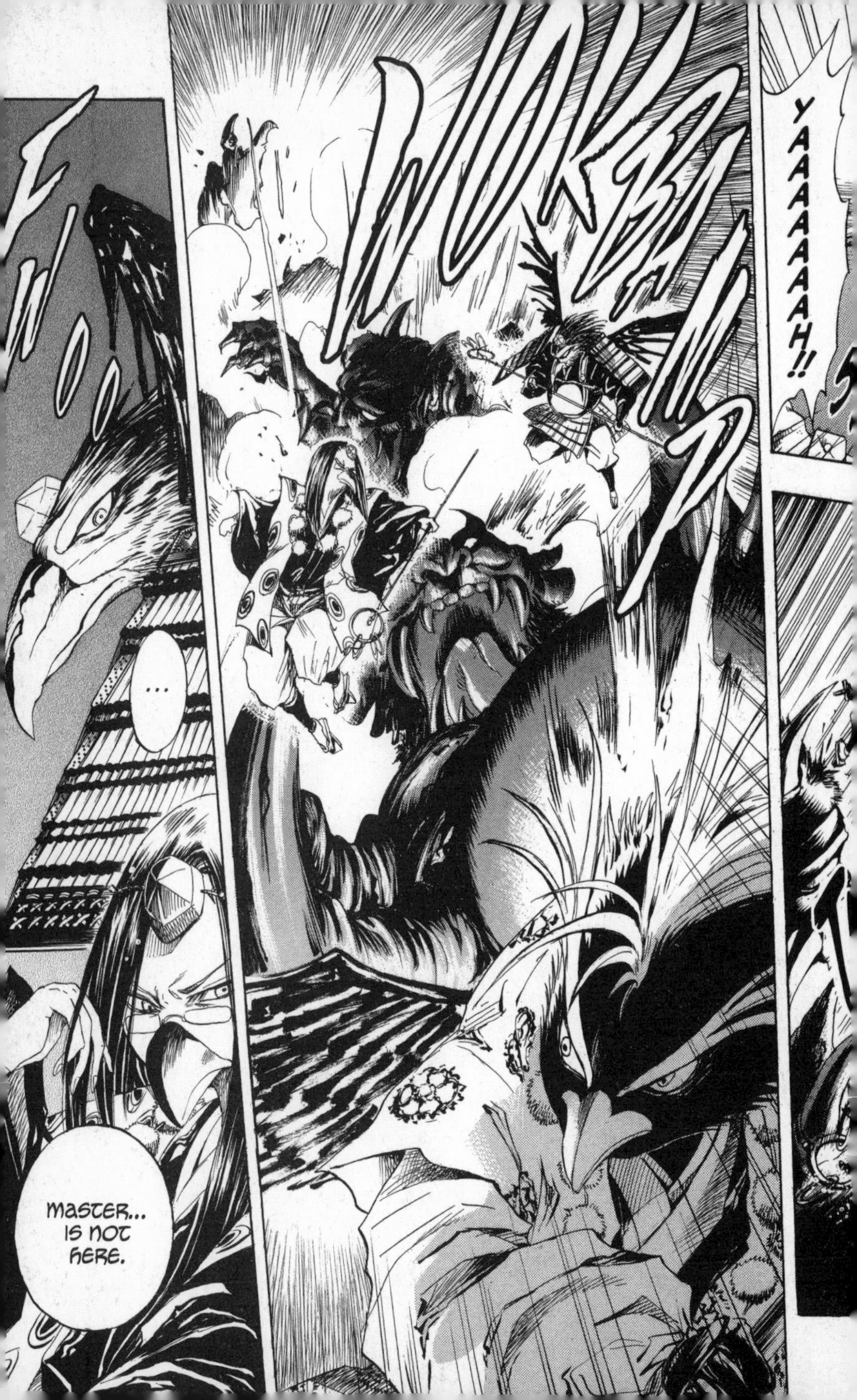
YAAAAAAAH!!
...
MASTER... IS NOT HERE.

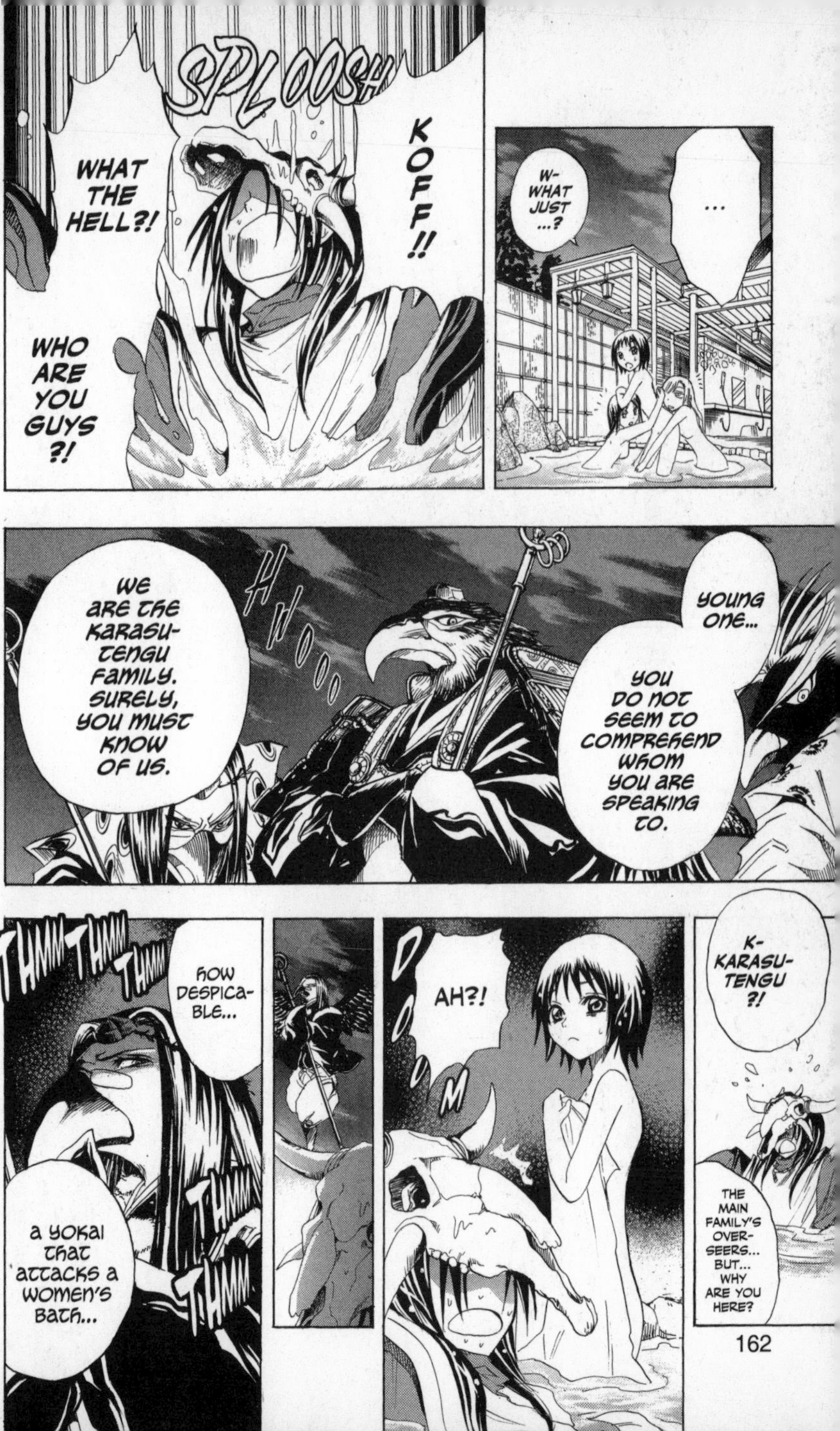
...
W-WHAT JUST ...?
SPLOOSH
KOFF!!
WHAT THE HELL?!
WHO ARE YOU GUYS?!
YOUNG ONE...
YOU DO NOT SEEM TO COMPREHEND WHOM YOU ARE SPEAKING TO.
HWOOO
WE ARE THE KARASU-TENGU FAMILY. SURELY, YOU MUST KNOW OF US.
K-KARASU-TENGU?!
THE MAIN FAMILY'S OVER-SEERS... BUT... WHY ARE YOU HERE?
DOOOM
AH?!
HOW DESPICA-BLE...
THMM THMM THMM
A YOKAI THAT ATTACKS A WOMEN'S BATH...
THMM THMM

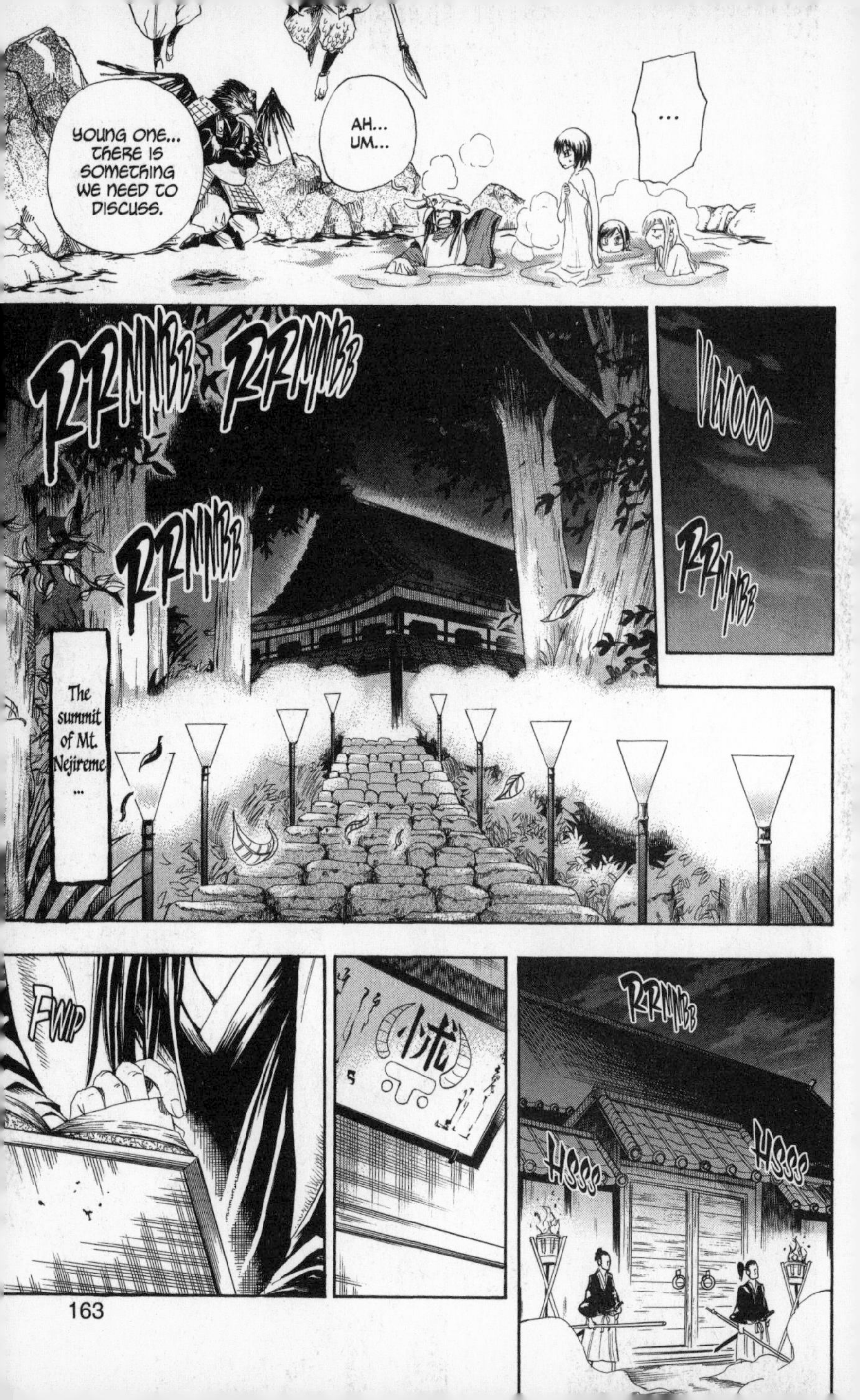
...
AH... UM...
YOUNG ONE... THERE IS SOMETHING WE NEED TO DISCUSS.
VWOOO
RRMMBB
RRMMBB RRMMBB
RRMMBB
The summit of Mt. Nejireme...
RRMMBB
HSSS
HSSS
FWIP

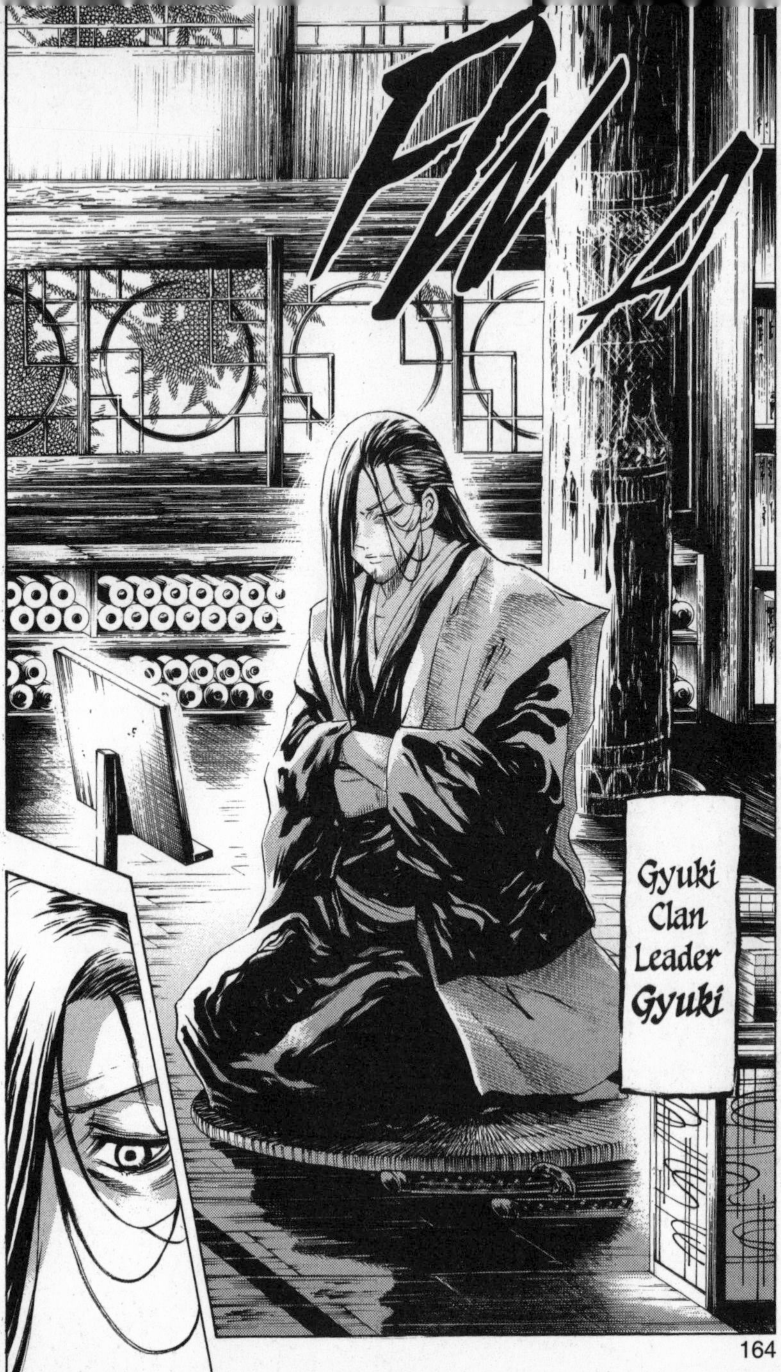
Gyuki Clan Leader Gyuki

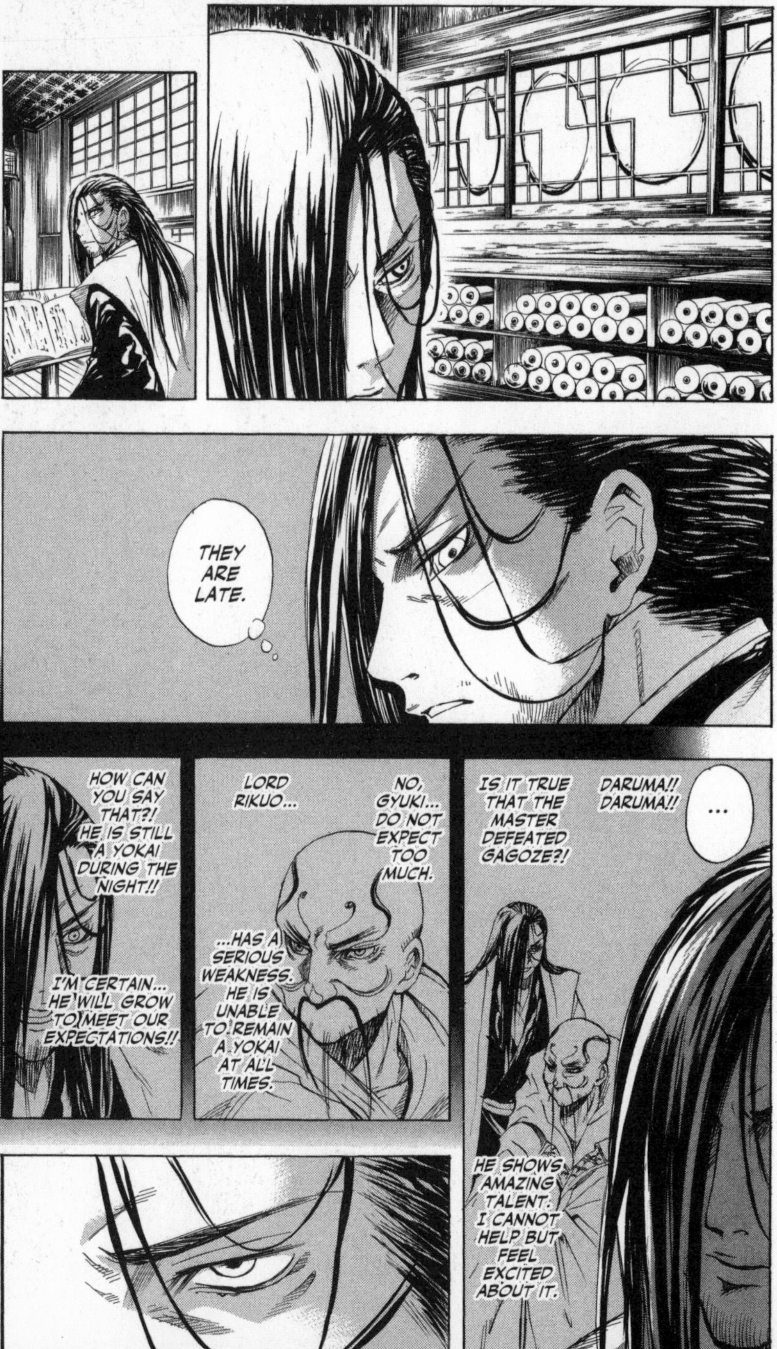
THEY ARE LATE.
...
DARUMA!! DARUMA!!
IS IT TRUE THAT THE MASTER DEFEATED GAGOZE?!
HE SHOWS AMAZING TALENT. I CANNOT HELP BUT FEEL EXCITED ABOUT IT.
NO, GYUKI... DO NOT EXPECT TOO MUCH.
LORD RIKUO...
...HAS A SERIOUS WEAKNESS. HE IS UNABLE TO REMAIN A YOKAI AT ALL TIMES.
HOW CAN YOU SAY THAT?! HE IS STILL A YOKAI DURING THE NIGHT!!
I'M CERTAIN... HE WILL GROW TO MEET OUR EXPECTATIONS!!

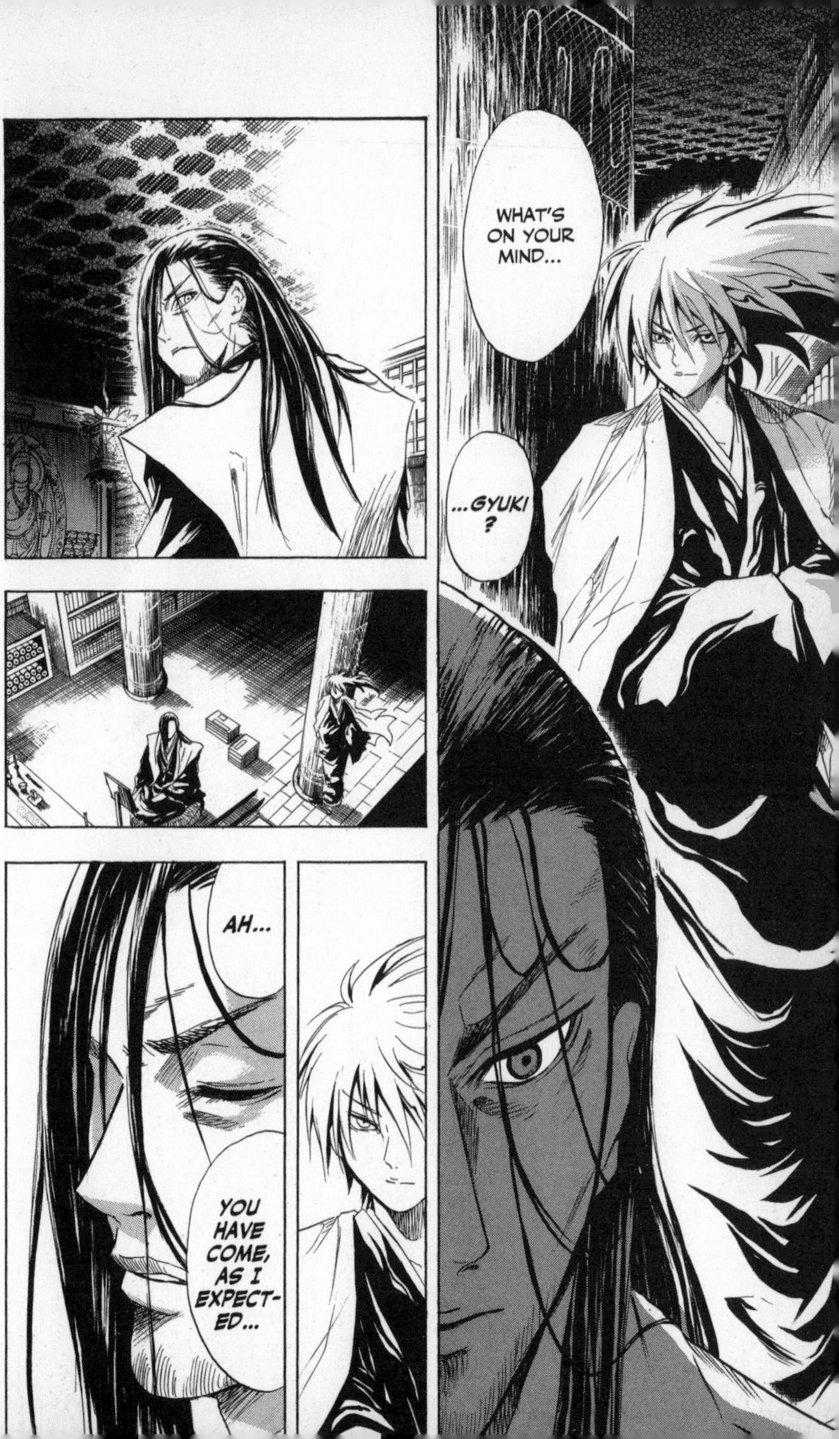
WHAT'S ON YOUR MIND...
...GYUKI?
AH...
YOU HAVE COME, AS I EXPECTED...

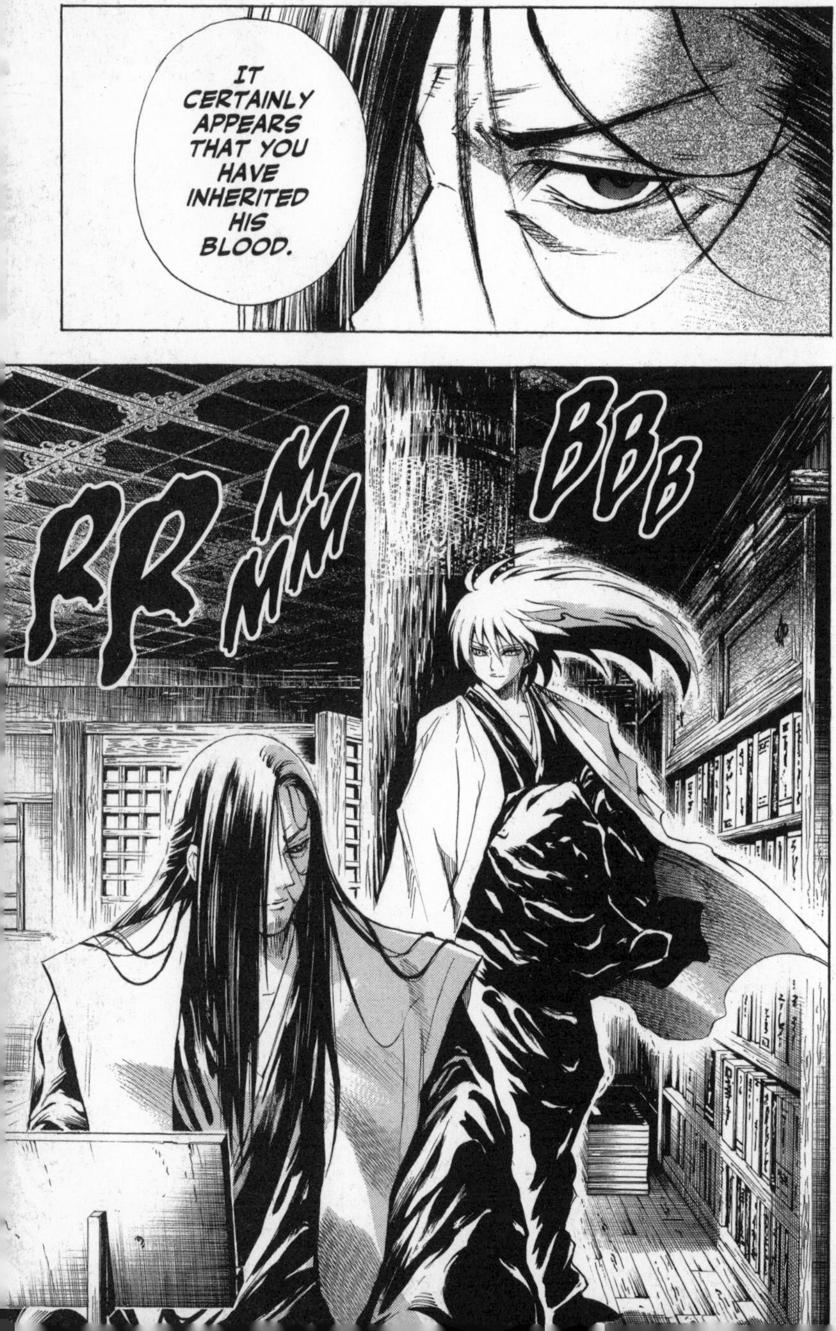
IT CERTAINLY APPEARS THAT YOU HAVE INHERITED HIS BLOOD.
RRMMMMBBB

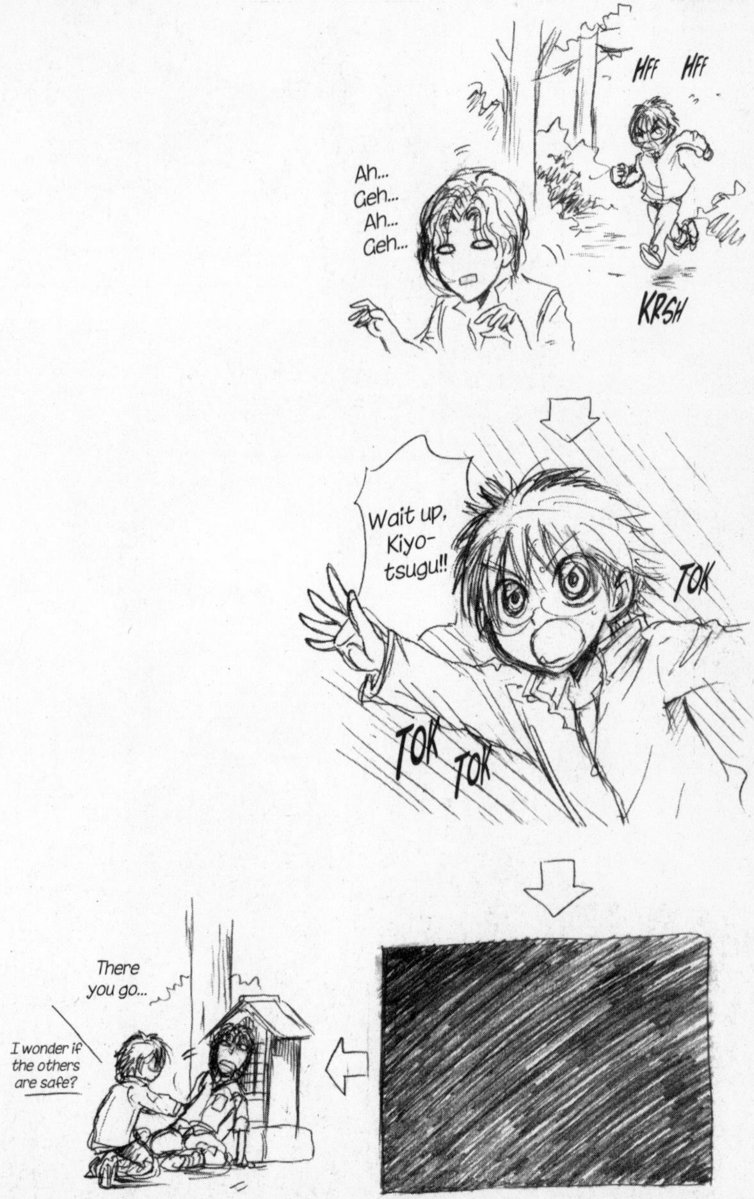
HFF HFF
KRSH
Ah... Geh... Ah... Geh...
Wait up, Kiyo-tsugu!!
TOK
TOK TOK
There you go...
I wonder if the others are safe?

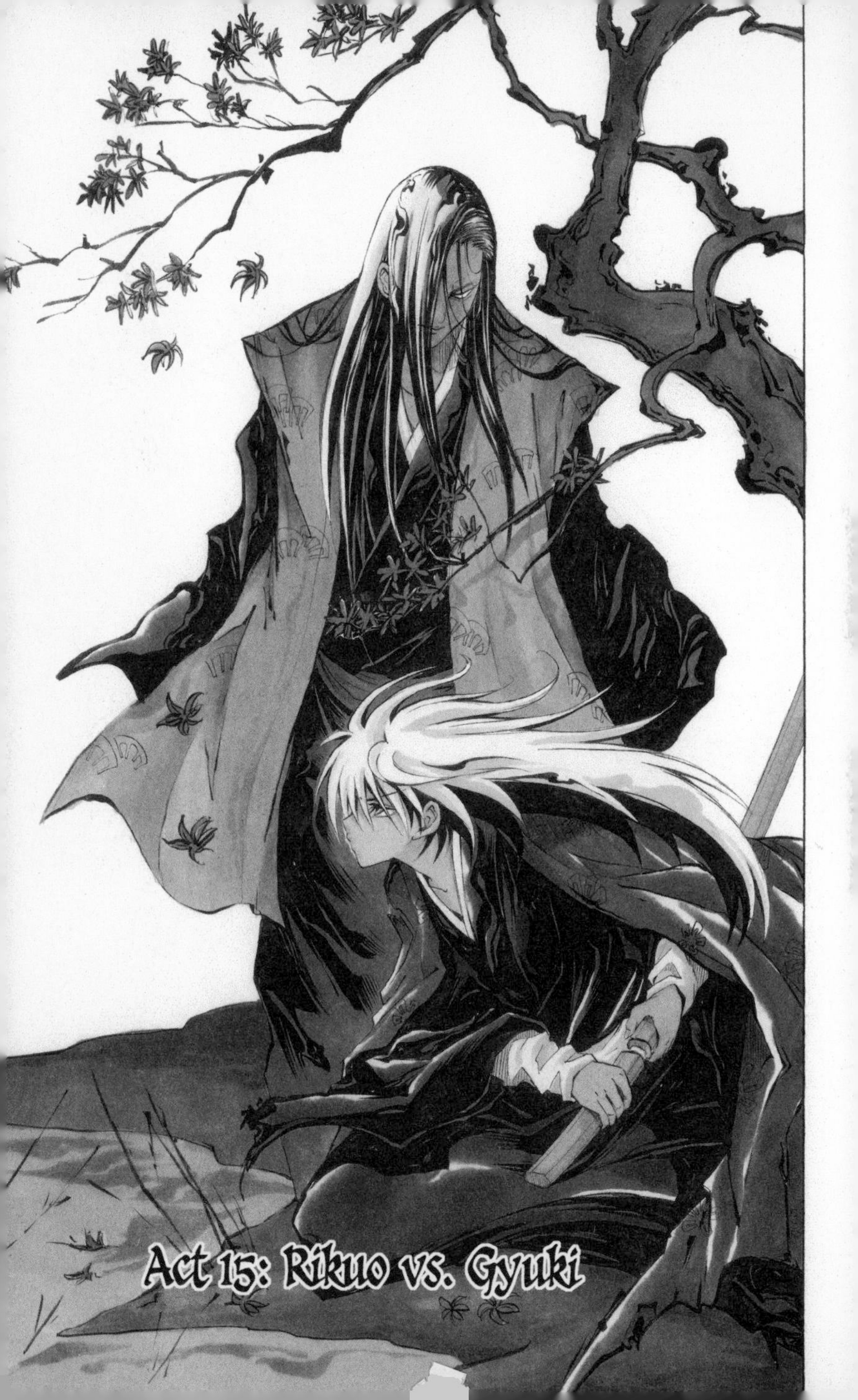
Act 15: Rikuo vs. Gyuki

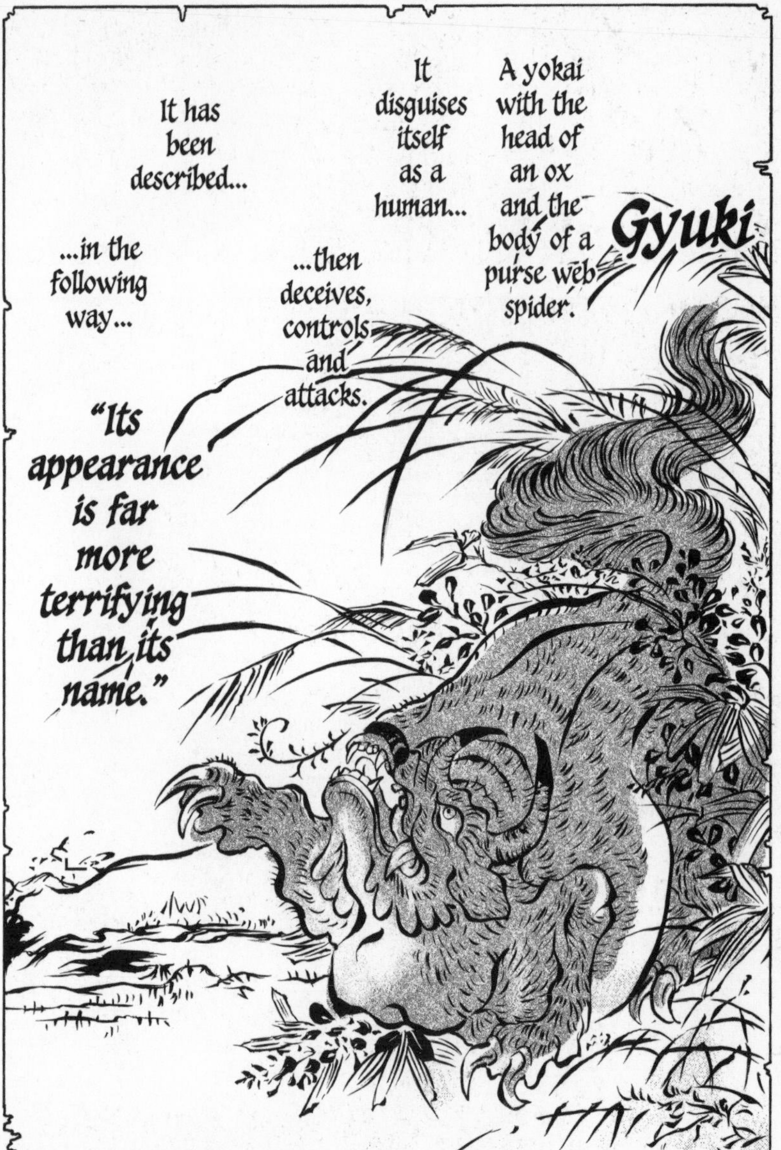
Gyuki
A yokai with the head of an ox and the body of a purse web spider.
It disguises itself as a human...
...then deceives, controls and attacks.
It has been described...
...in the following way...
"Its appearance is far more terrifying than its name."

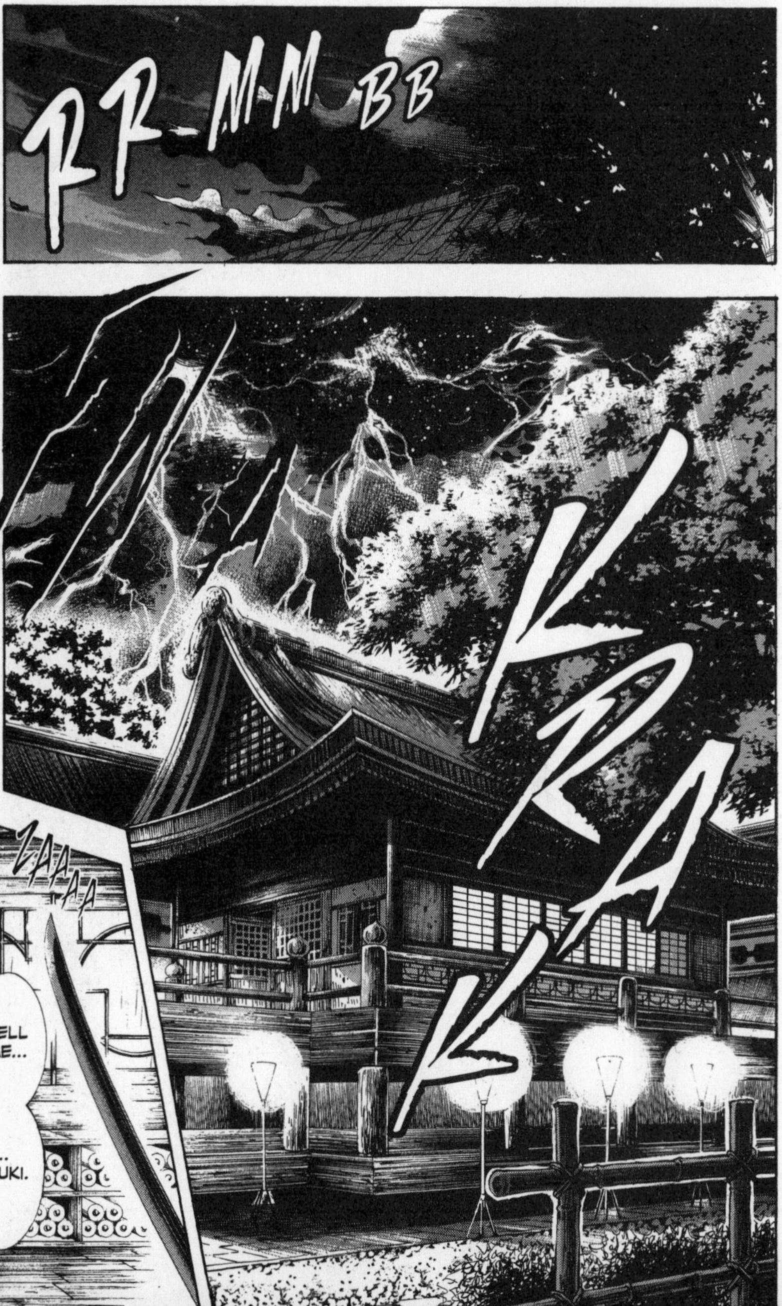
RRMMBB
KRAK
ZAAAAA
TELL ME...
...GYUKI.

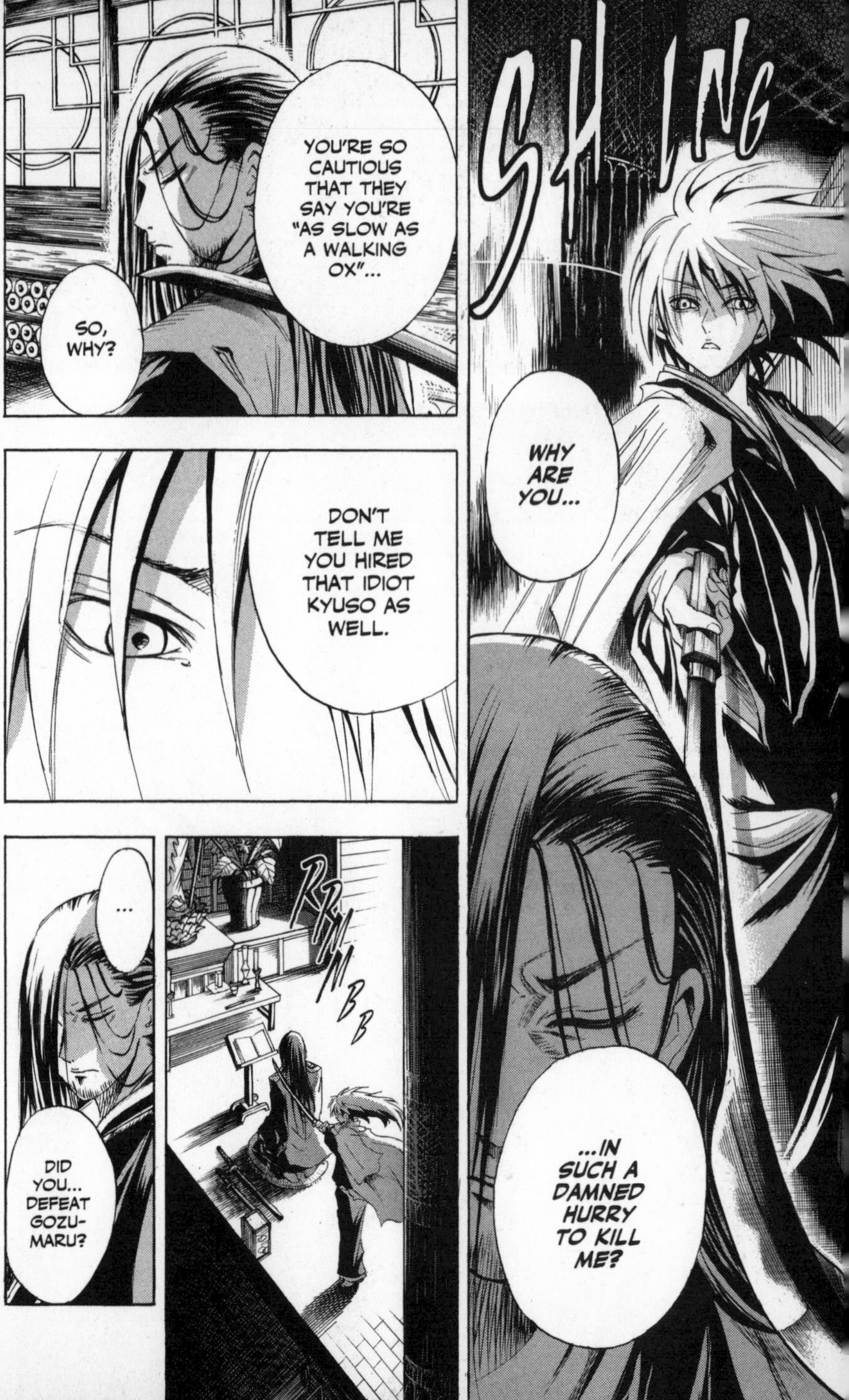
SHING
WHY ARE YOU...
...IN SUCH A DAMNED HURRY TO KILL ME?
YOU'RE SO CAUTIOUS THAT THEY SAY YOU'RE "AS SLOW AS A WALKING OX"...
SO, WHY?
DON'T TELL ME YOU HIRED THAT IDIOT KYUSO AS WELL.
RRMMBB
...
DID YOU... DEFEAT GOZU-MARU?

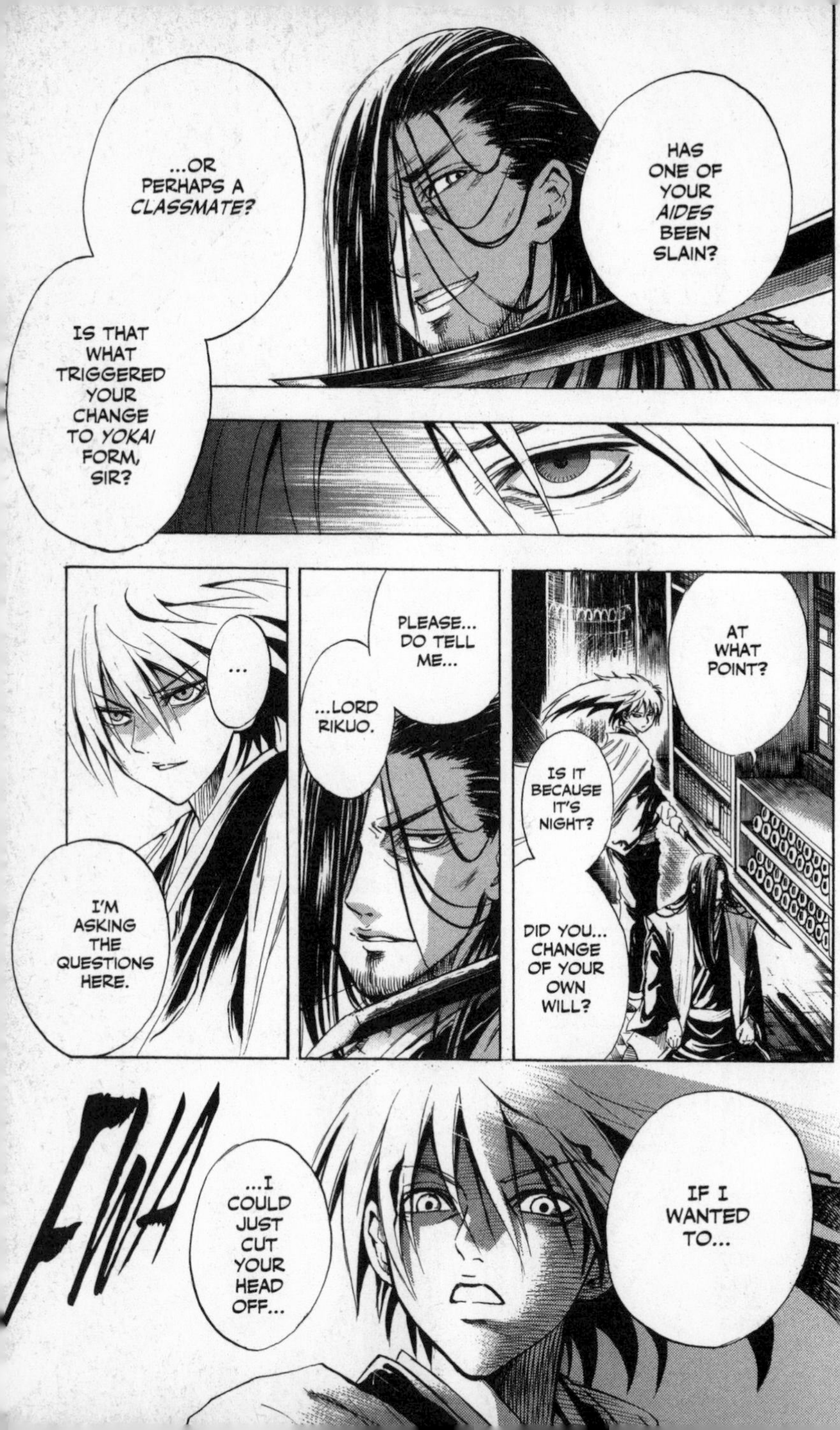
HAS ONE OF YOUR *AIDES* BEEN SLAIN?
...OR PERHAPS A *CLASSMATE?*
IS THAT WHAT TRIGGERED YOUR CHANGE TO *YOKAI* FORM, SIR?
AT WHAT POINT?
IS IT BECAUSE IT'S NIGHT?
DID YOU... CHANGE OF YOUR OWN WILL?
PLEASE... DO TELL ME...
...LORD RIKUO.
...
I'M ASKING THE QUESTIONS HERE.
IF I WANTED TO...
...I COULD JUST CUT YOUR HEAD OFF...

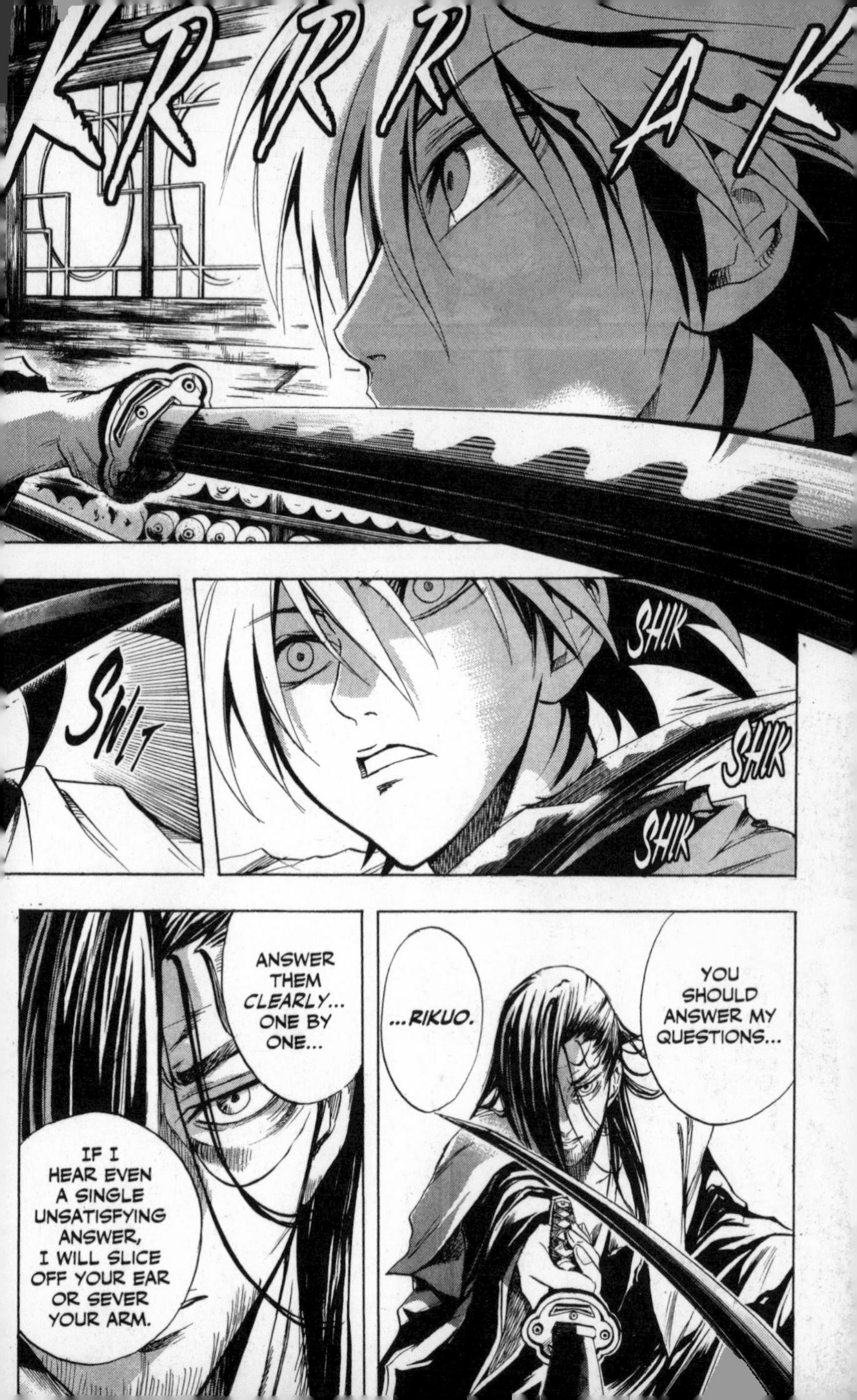
KRRRAK
SHIK
SHIK
SHIK
SWI-
YOU SHOULD ANSWER MY QUESTIONS...
...RIKUO.
ANSWER THEM *CLEARLY*... ONE BY ONE...
IF I HEAR EVEN A SINGLE UNSATISFYING ANSWER, I WILL SLICE OFF YOUR EAR OR SEVER YOUR ARM.

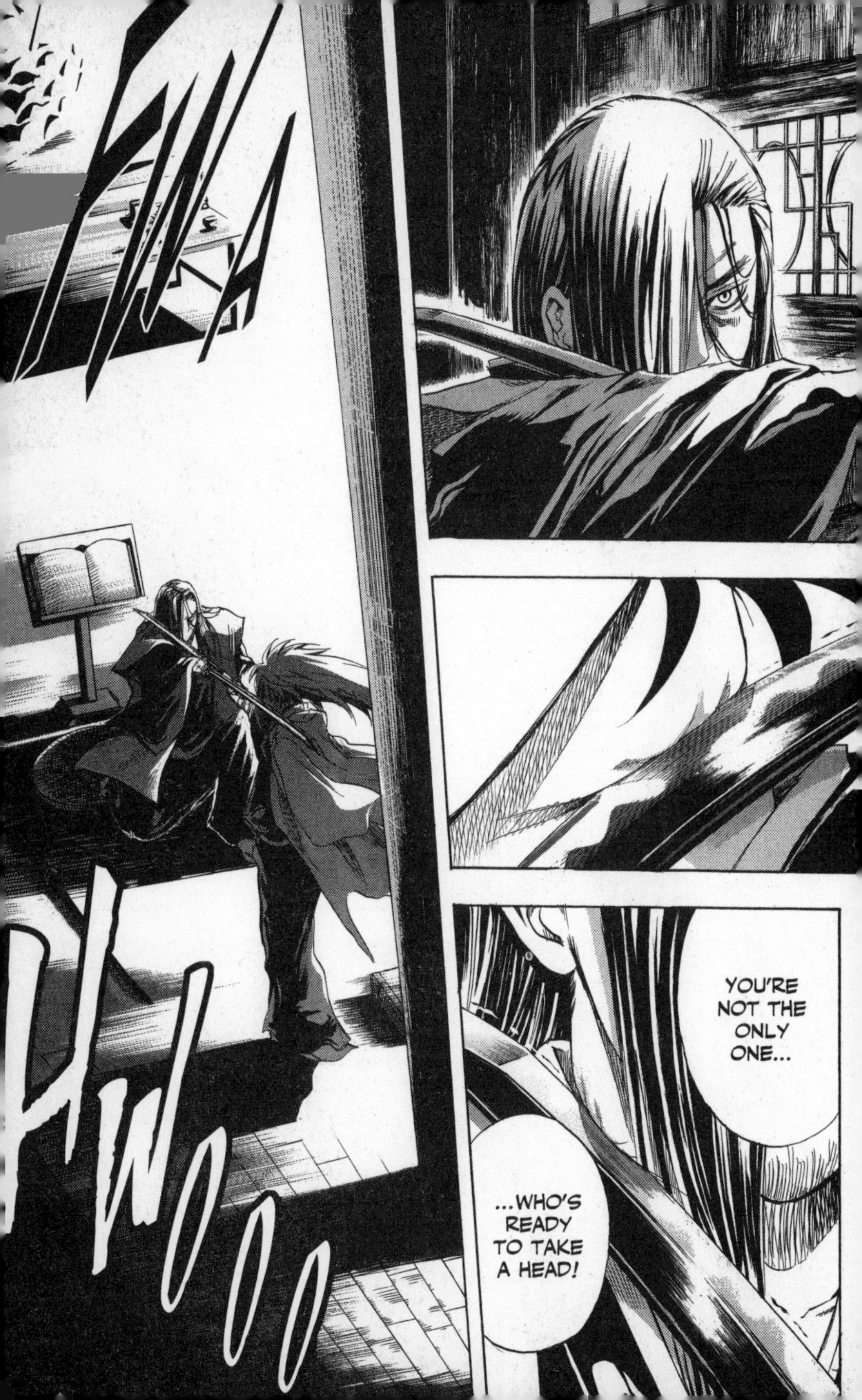
YOU'RE NOT THE ONLY ONE...
...WHO'S READY TO TAKE A HEAD!

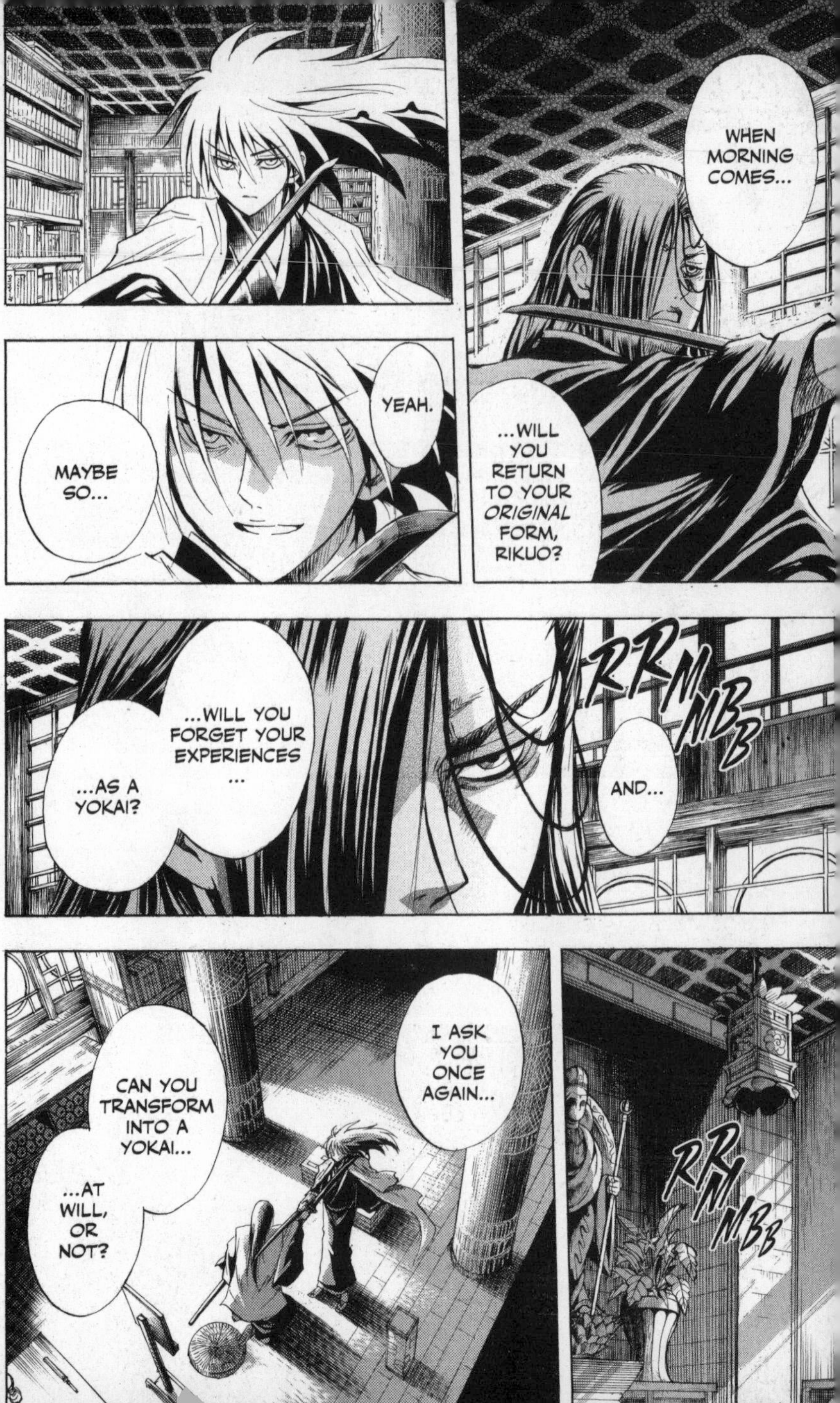
WHEN MORNING COMES...
...WILL YOU RETURN TO YOUR ORIGINAL FORM, RIKUO?
YEAH.
MAYBE SO...
RRRMMBB
AND...
...WILL YOU FORGET YOUR EXPERIENCES ...
...AS A YOKAI?
RRMMBB
I ASK YOU ONCE AGAIN...
CAN YOU TRANSFORM INTO A YOKAI...
...AT WILL, OR NOT?

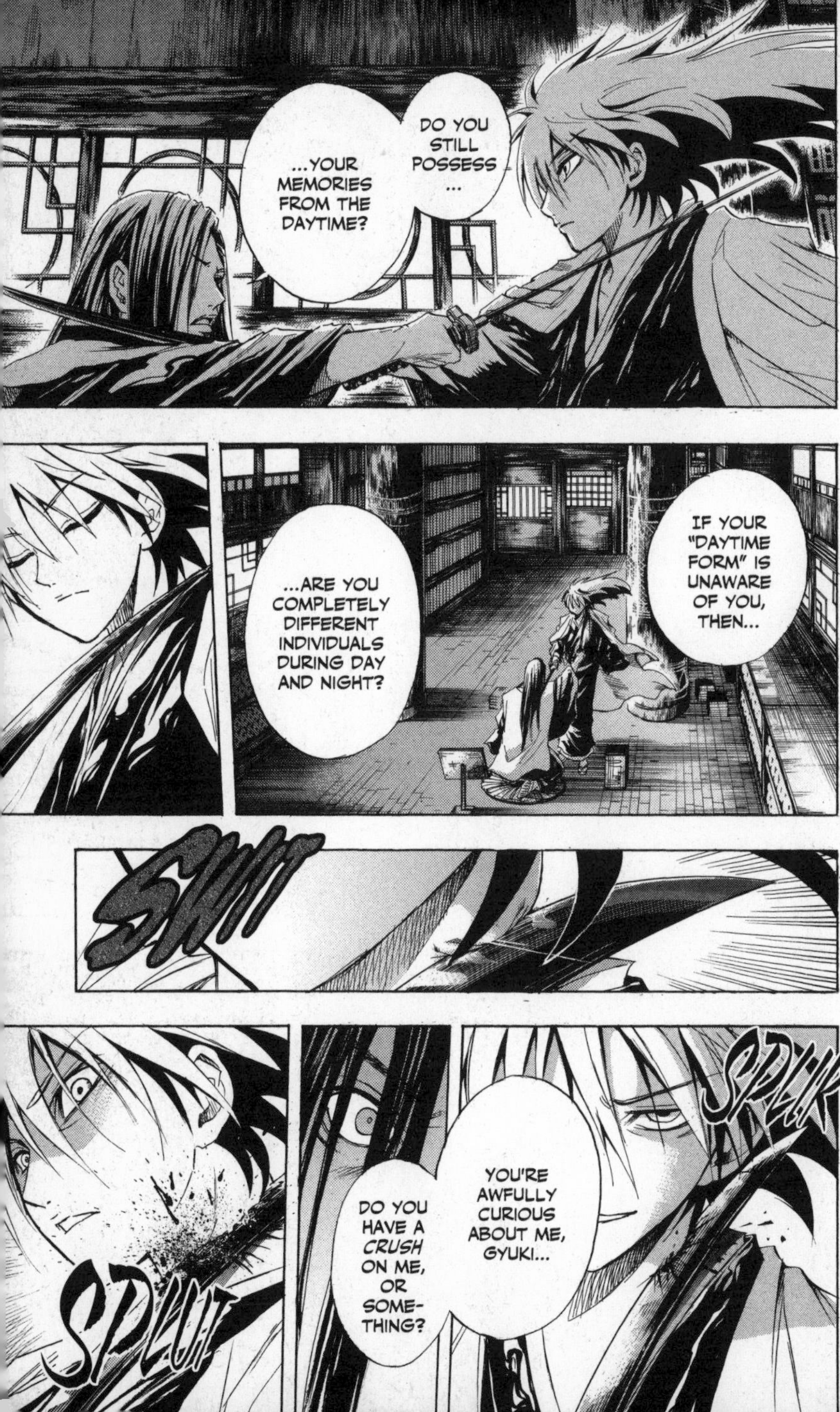
DO YOU STILL POSSESS ...
...YOUR MEMORIES FROM THE DAYTIME?
IF YOUR "DAYTIME FORM" IS UNAWARE OF YOU, THEN...
...ARE YOU COMPLETELY DIFFERENT INDIVIDUALS DURING DAY AND NIGHT?
SWIIT
SPLUK
YOU'RE AWFULLY CURIOUS ABOUT ME, GYUKI...
DO YOU HAVE A *CRUSH* ON ME, OR SOME-THING?
SPLUT

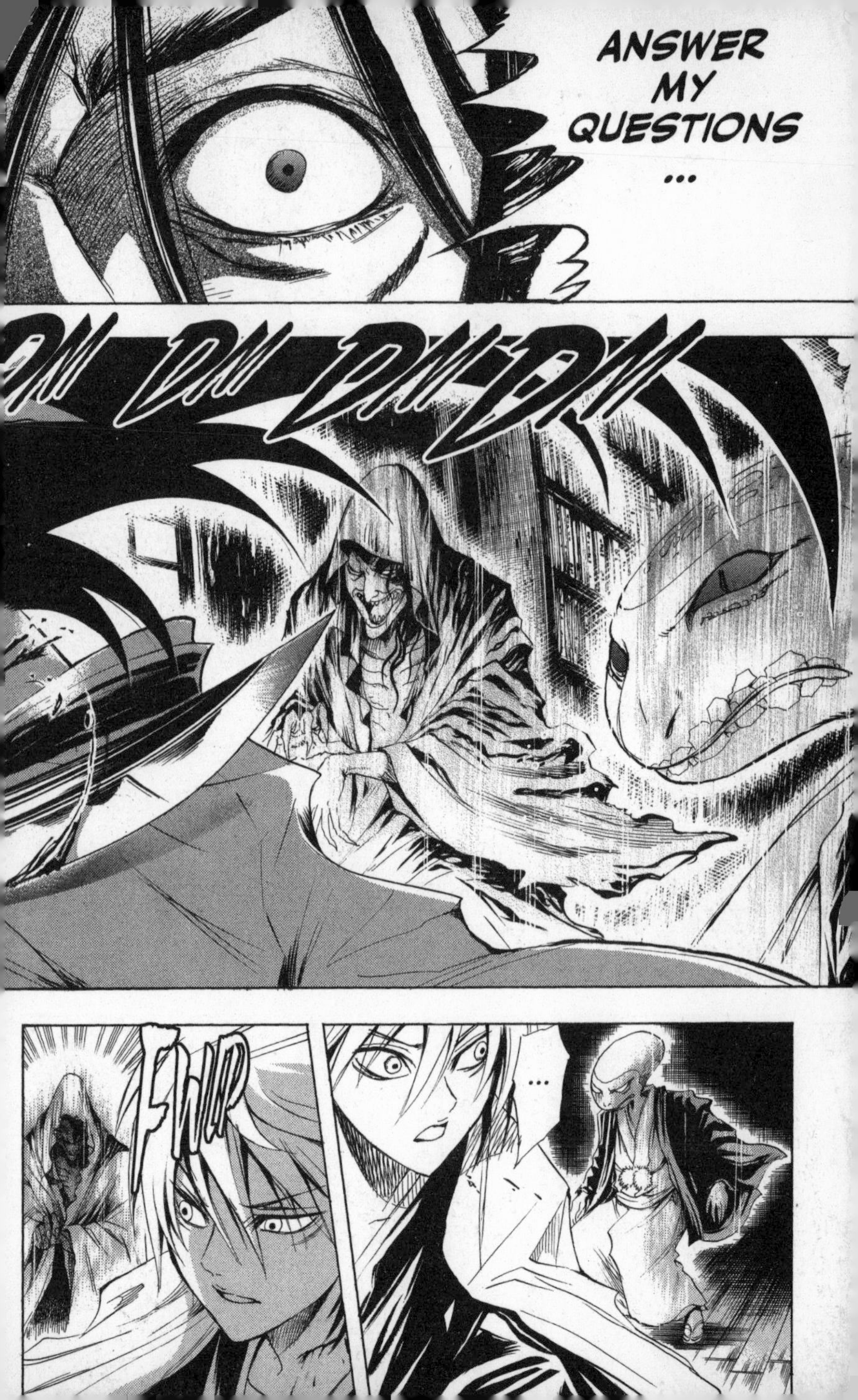
ANSWER MY QUESTIONS ...
N DN DN-DN
...
FWIP

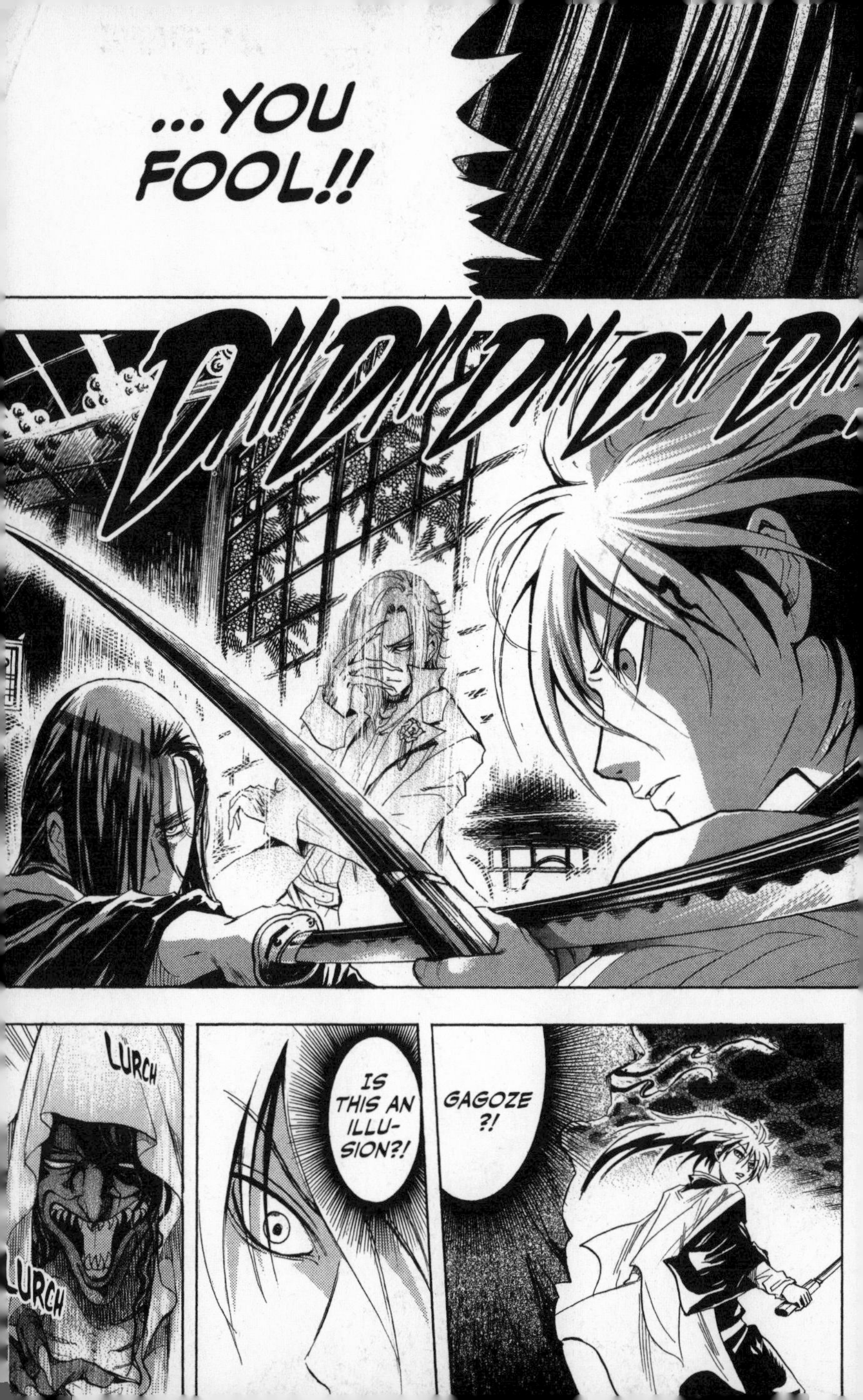
...YOU FOOL!!
GAGOZE ?!
IS THIS AN ILLU-SION?!
LURCH
LURCH
LURCH

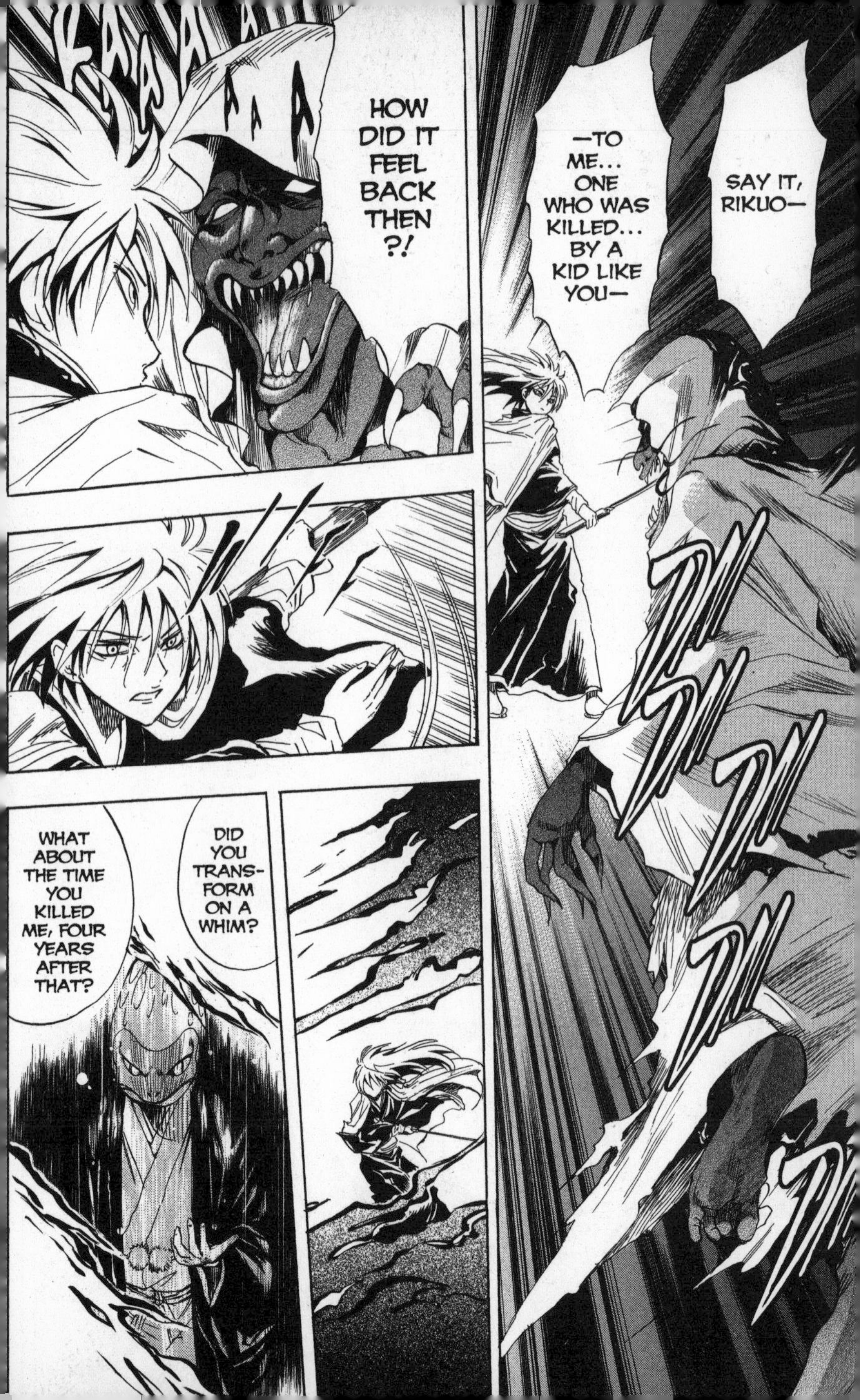
SAY IT, RIKUO—
—TO ME... ONE WHO WAS KILLED... BY A KID LIKE YOU—
HOW DID IT FEEL BACK THEN ?!
DID YOU TRANS-FORM ON A WHIM?
WHAT ABOUT THE TIME YOU KILLED ME, FOUR YEARS AFTER THAT?

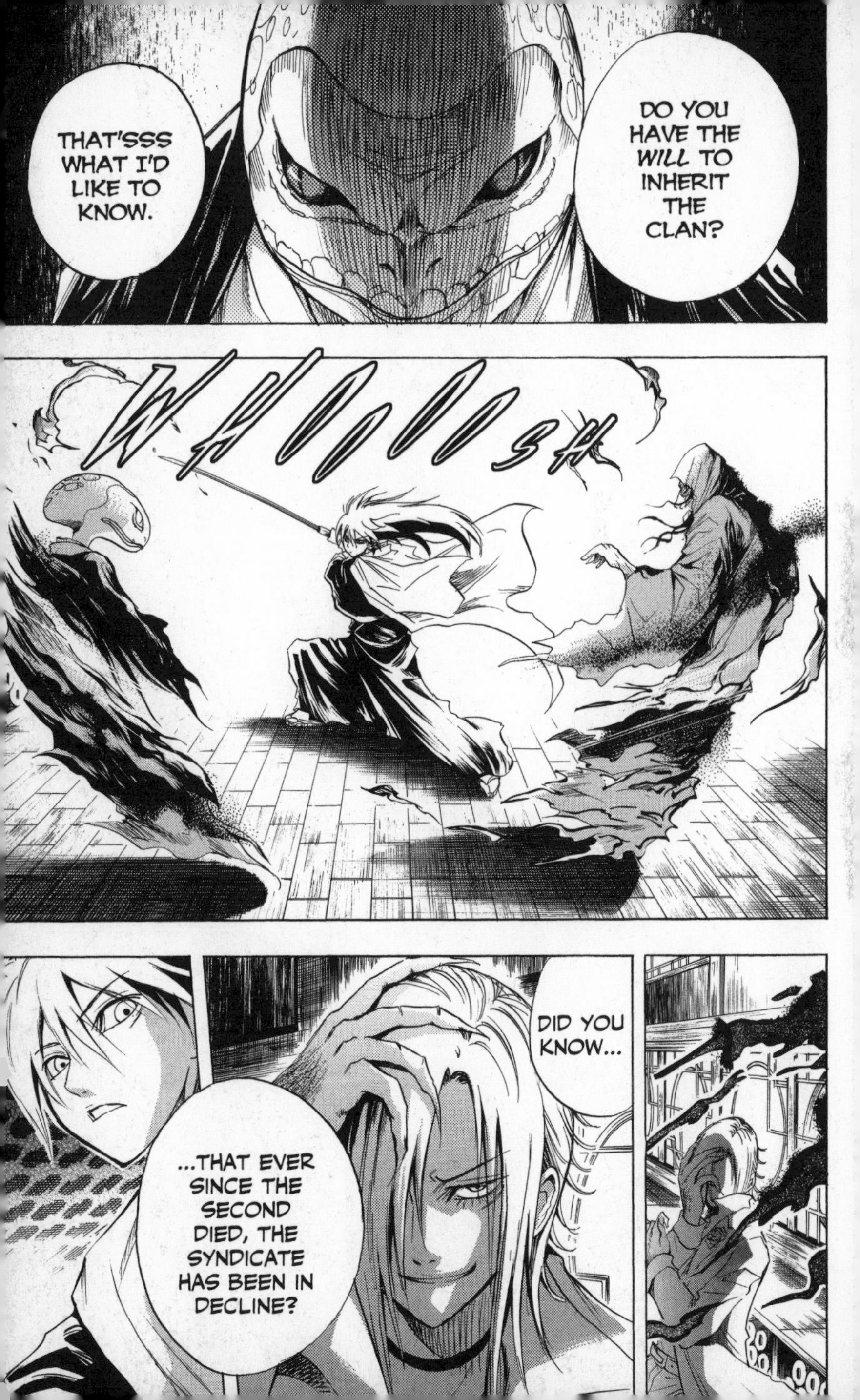

DO YOU HAVE THE *WILL* TO INHERIT THE CLAN?
THAT'SSS WHAT I'D LIKE TO KNOW.
WHOOOOSH
DID YOU KNOW...
...THAT EVER SINCE THE SECOND DIED, THE SYNDICATE HAS BEEN IN DECLINE?

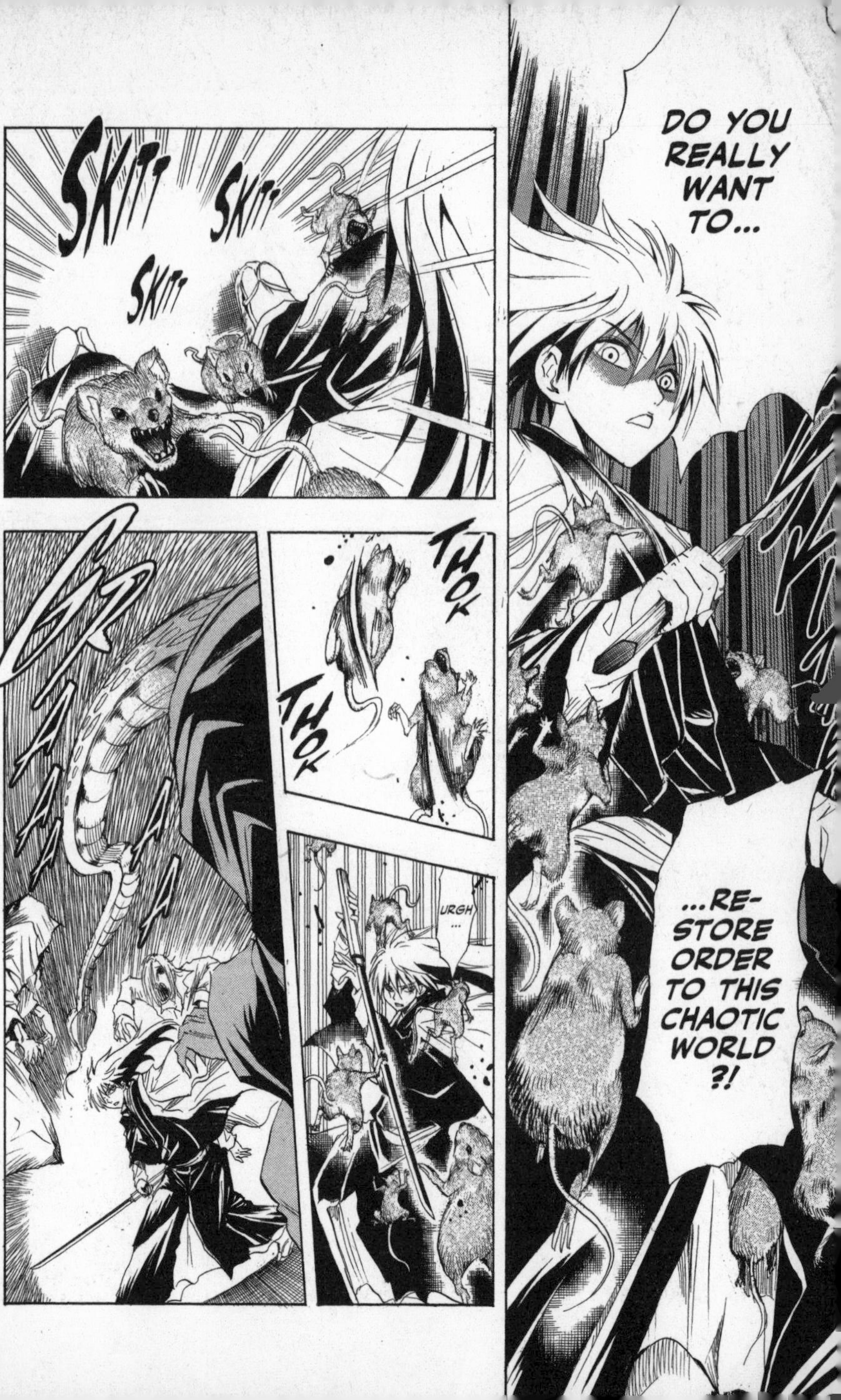

DO YOU REALLY WANT TO...
...RE-STORE ORDER TO THIS CHAOTIC WORLD?!
SKITT
SKITT
SKITT
THOK
THOK
URGH...

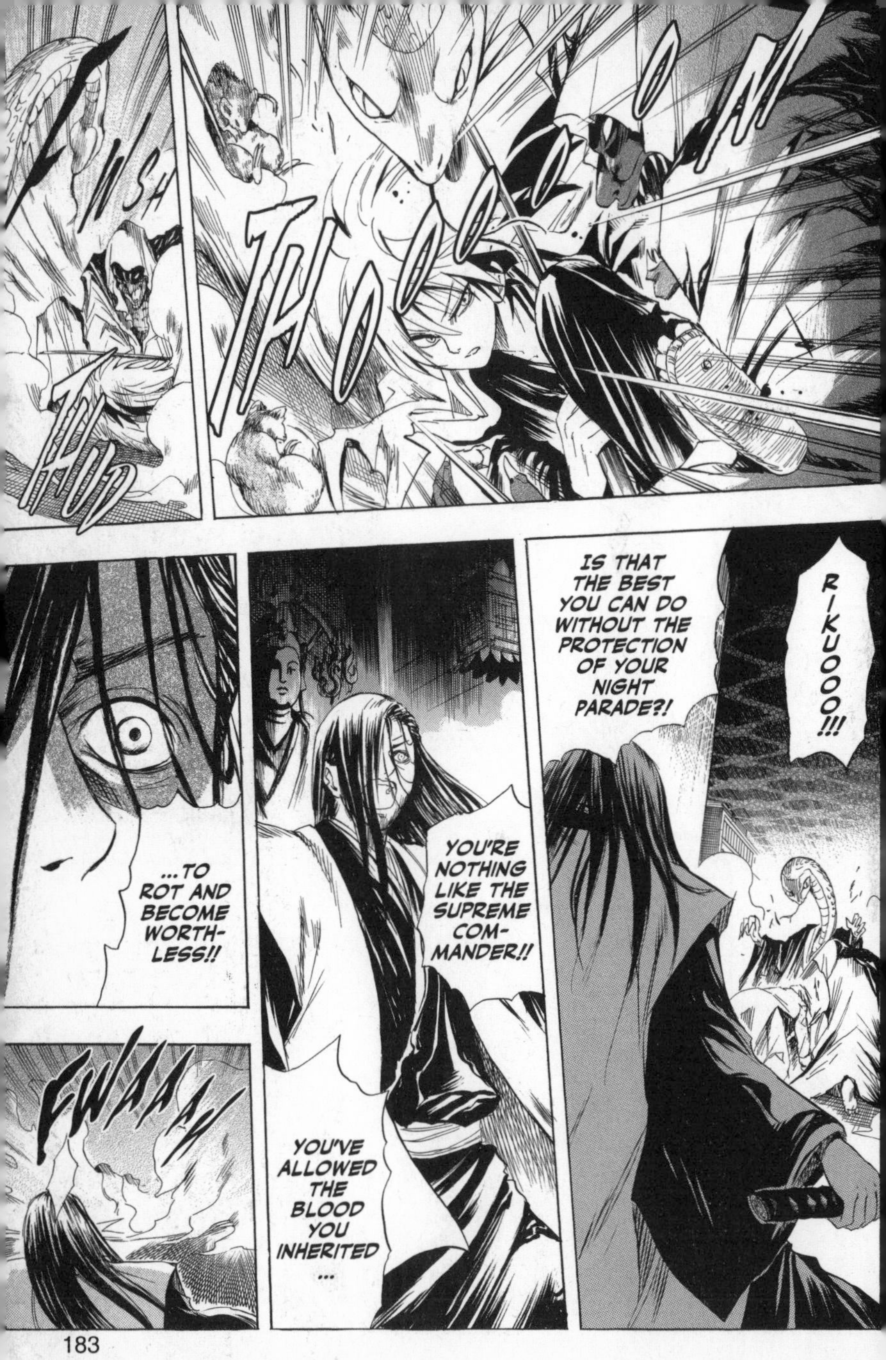
TAOOOOOON
FWISH
THUD
RIKUOOOO!!!
IS THAT THE BEST YOU CAN DO WITHOUT THE PROTECTION OF YOUR NIGHT PARADE?!
YOU'RE NOTHING LIKE THE SUPREME COM-MANDER!!
YOU'VE ALLOWED THE BLOOD YOU INHERITED ...
...TO ROT AND BECOME WORTH-LESS!!
FWAAAN

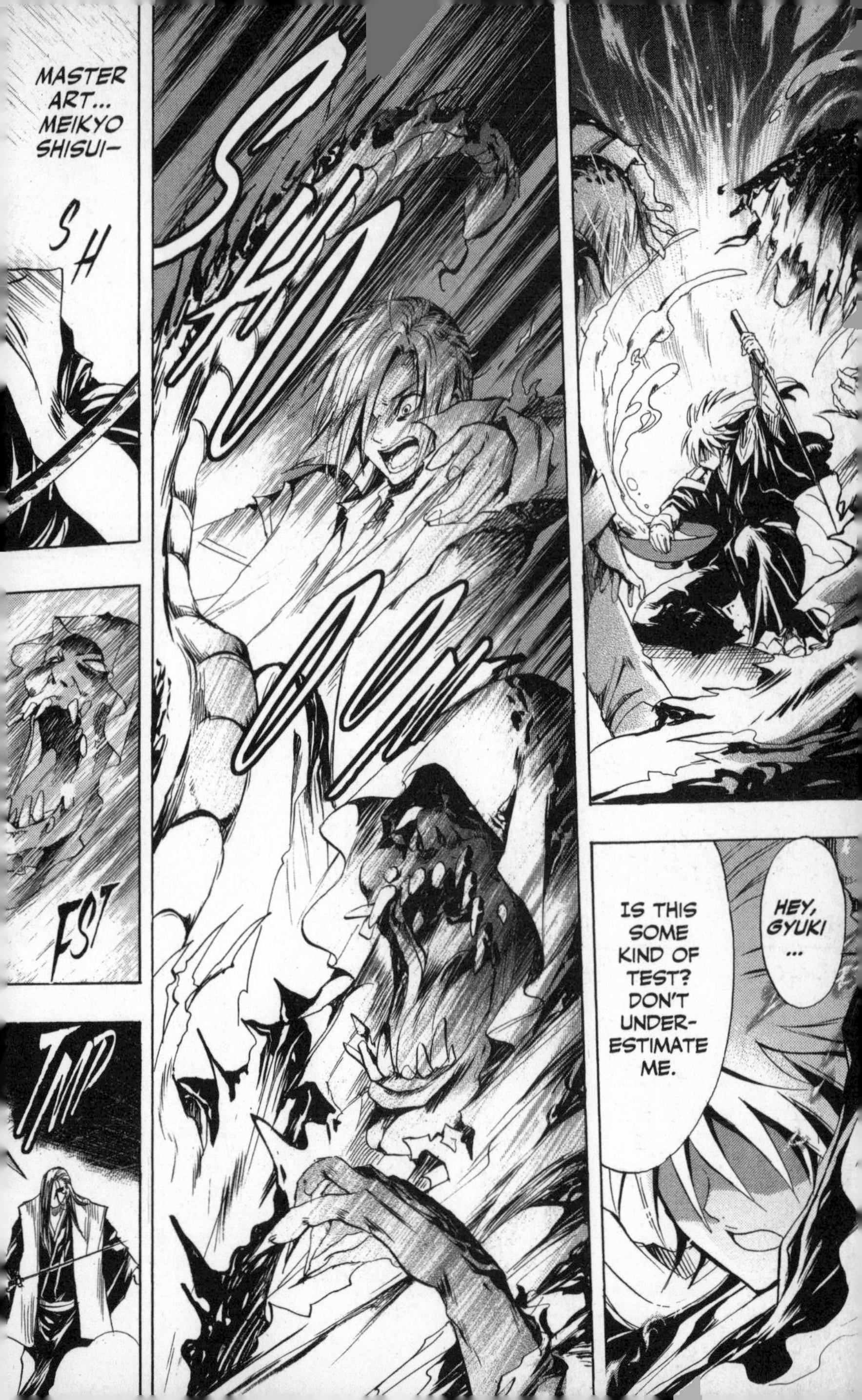
HEY, GYUKI ...
IS THIS SOME KIND OF TEST? DON'T UNDER-ESTIMATE ME.
MASTER ART... MEIKYO SHISUI—
SH
FST
TMP

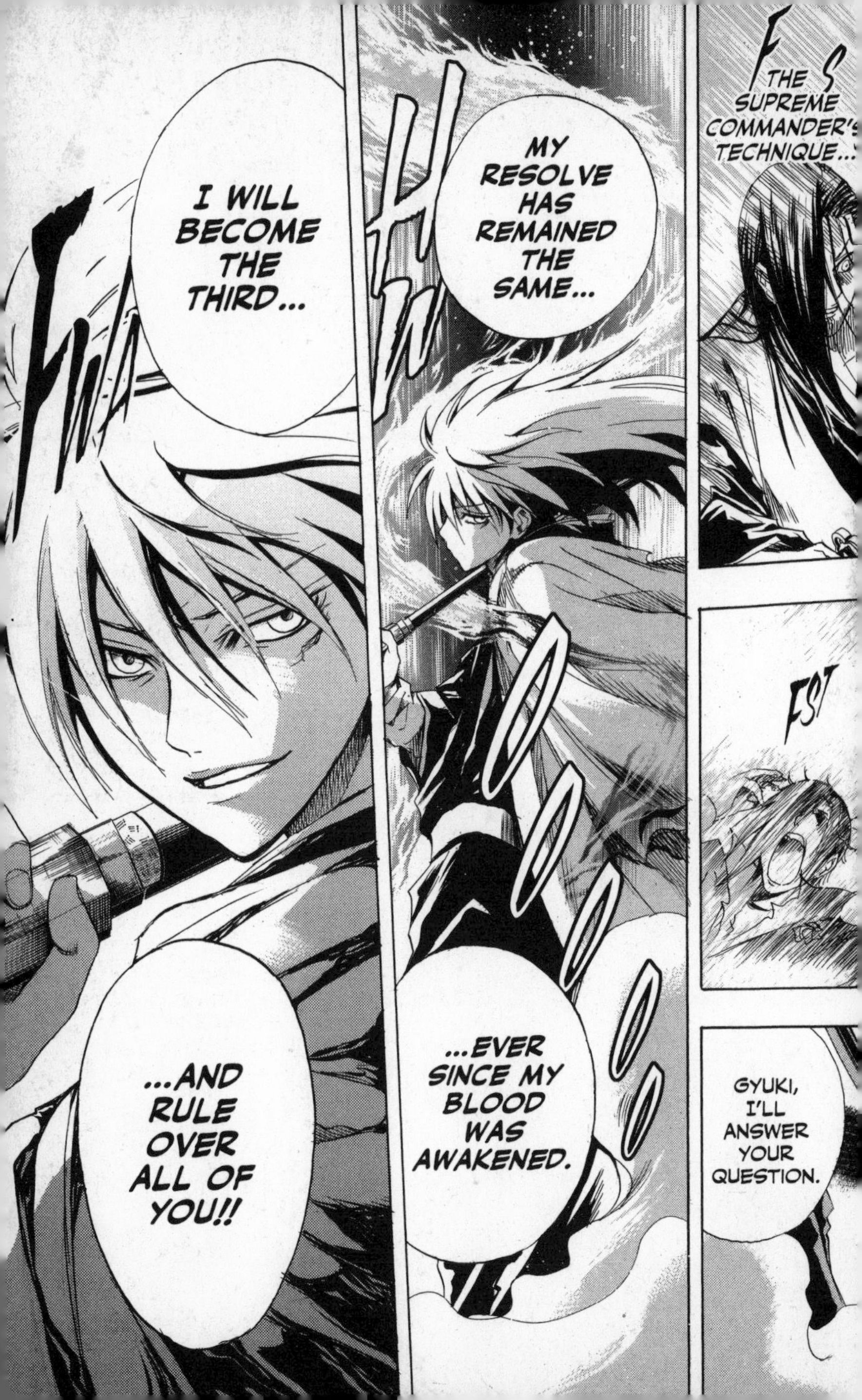
THE SUPREME COMMANDER'S TECHNIQUE...
FST
GYUKI, I'LL ANSWER YOUR QUESTION.
MY RESOLVE HAS REMAINED THE SAME...
...EVER SINCE MY BLOOD WAS AWAKENED.
I WILL BECOME THE THIRD...
...AND RULE OVER ALL OF YOU!!

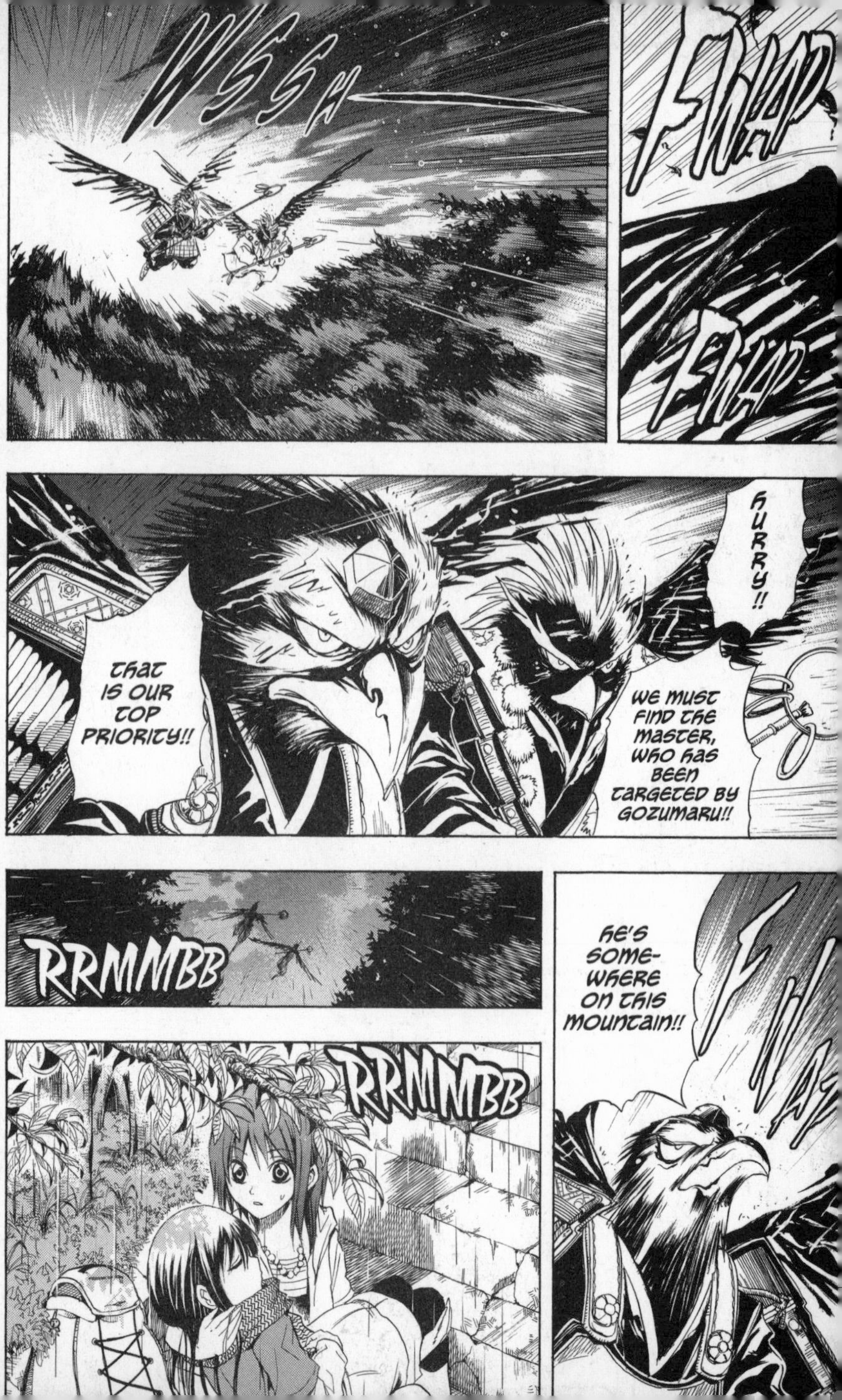
FWAP
FWAP
WSSH
HURRY!!
WE MUST FIND THE MASTER, WHO HAS BEEN TARGETED BY GOZUMARU!!
THAT IS OUR TOP PRIORITY!!
HE'S SOMEWHERE ON THIS MOUNTAIN!!
RRMMBB
RRMMBB

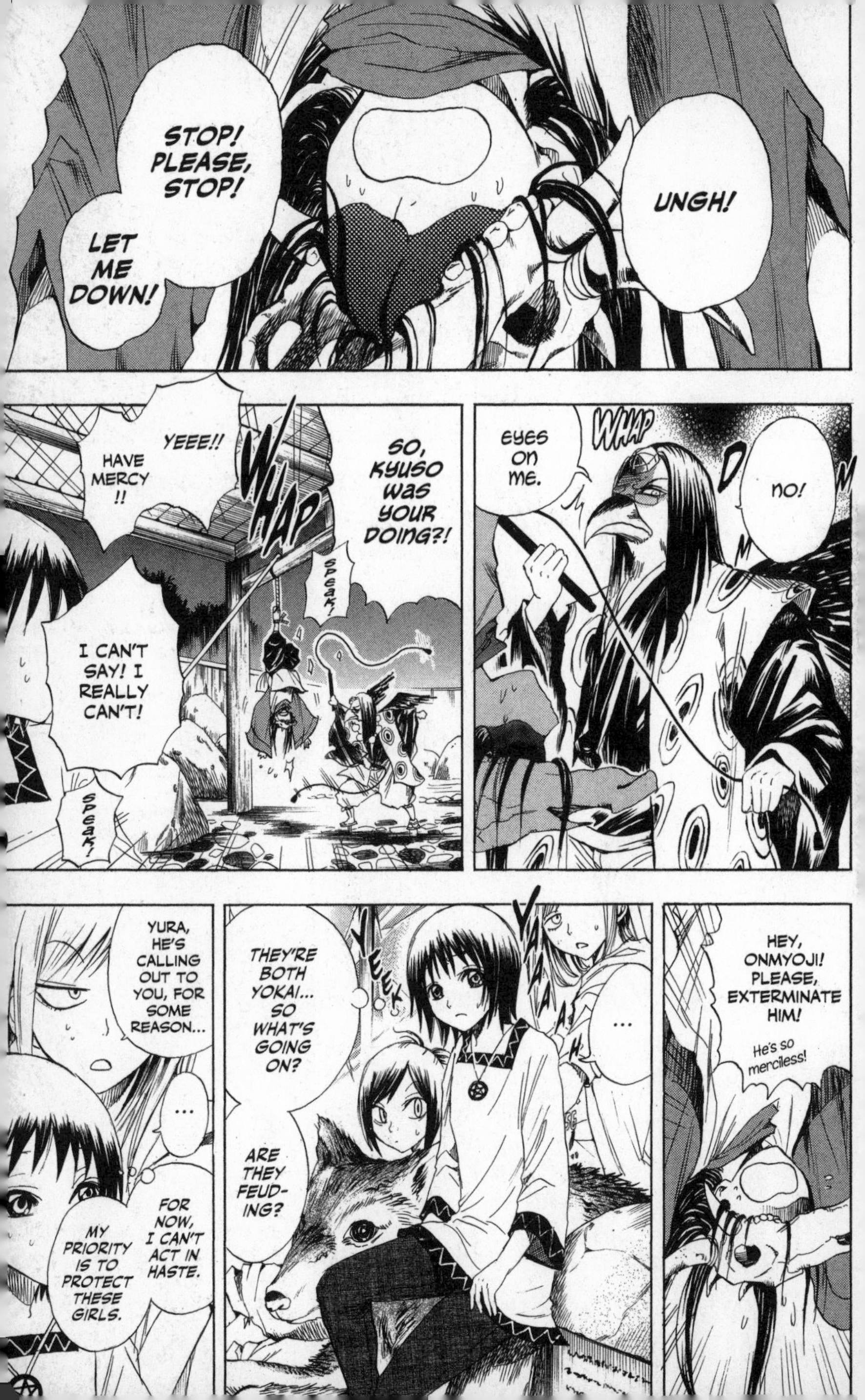
UNGH!
STOP! PLEASE, STOP!
LET ME DOWN!
WHAP
no!
Eyes on me.
SO, KYUSO WAS YOUR DOING?!
WHAP
YEEE!!
HAVE MERCY!!
SPEAK!
I CAN'T SAY! I REALLY CAN'T!
SPEAK!
HEY, ONMYOJI! PLEASE, EXTERMINATE HIM!
He's so merciless!
YEEEK
...
THEY'RE BOTH YOKAI... SO WHAT'S GOING ON?
ARE THEY FEUD-ING?
YURA, HE'S CALLING OUT TO YOU, FOR SOME REASON...
...
FOR NOW, I CAN'T ACT IN HASTE.
MY PRIORITY IS TO PROTECT THESE GIRLS.

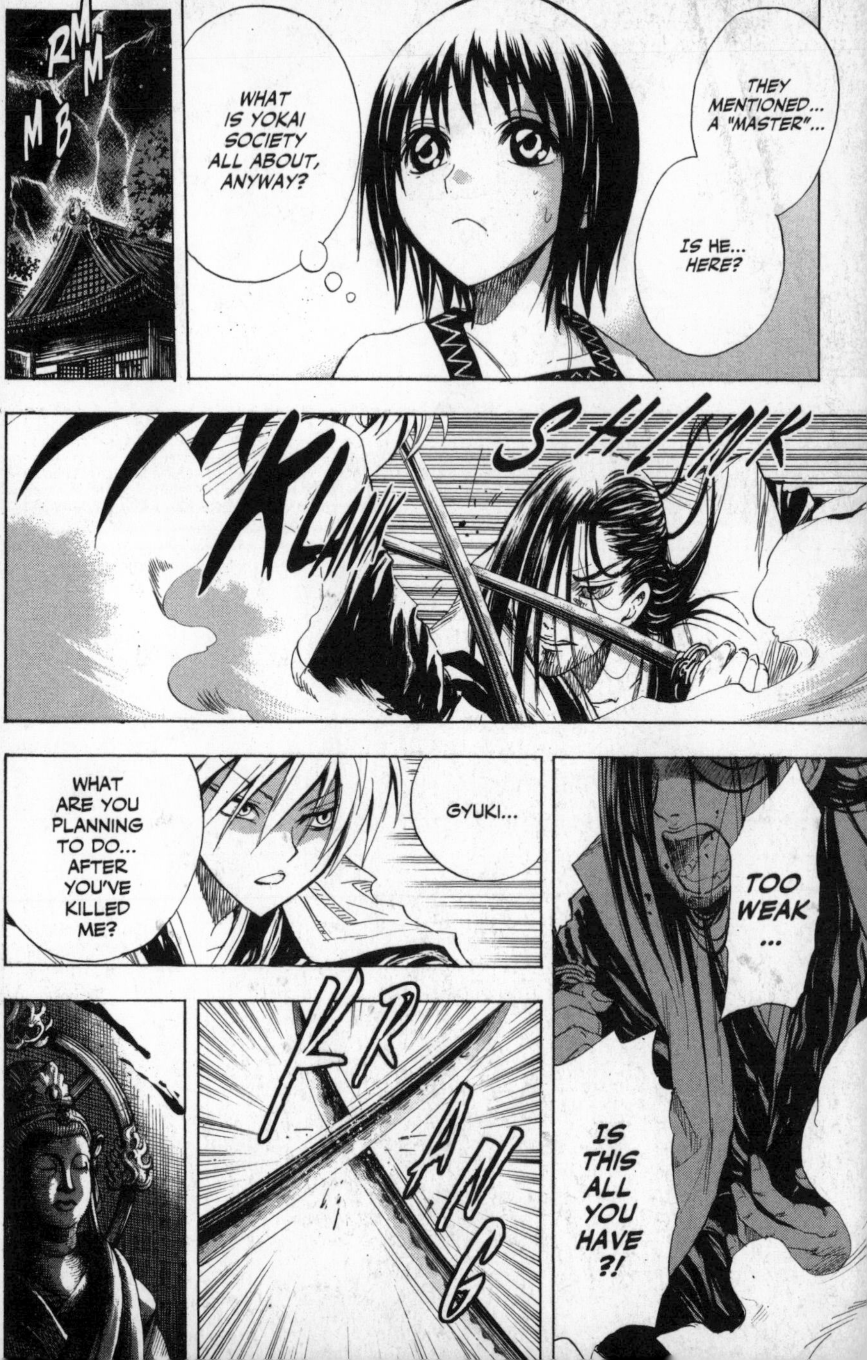
THEY MENTIONED... A "MASTER"...
IS HE... HERE?
WHAT IS YOKAI SOCIETY ALL ABOUT, ANYWAY?
RMMMMB
SHINK
KLANK
TOO WEAK...
IS THIS ALL YOU HAVE?!
GYUKI...
WHAT ARE YOU PLANNING TO DO... AFTER YOU'VE KILLED ME?
KRANG

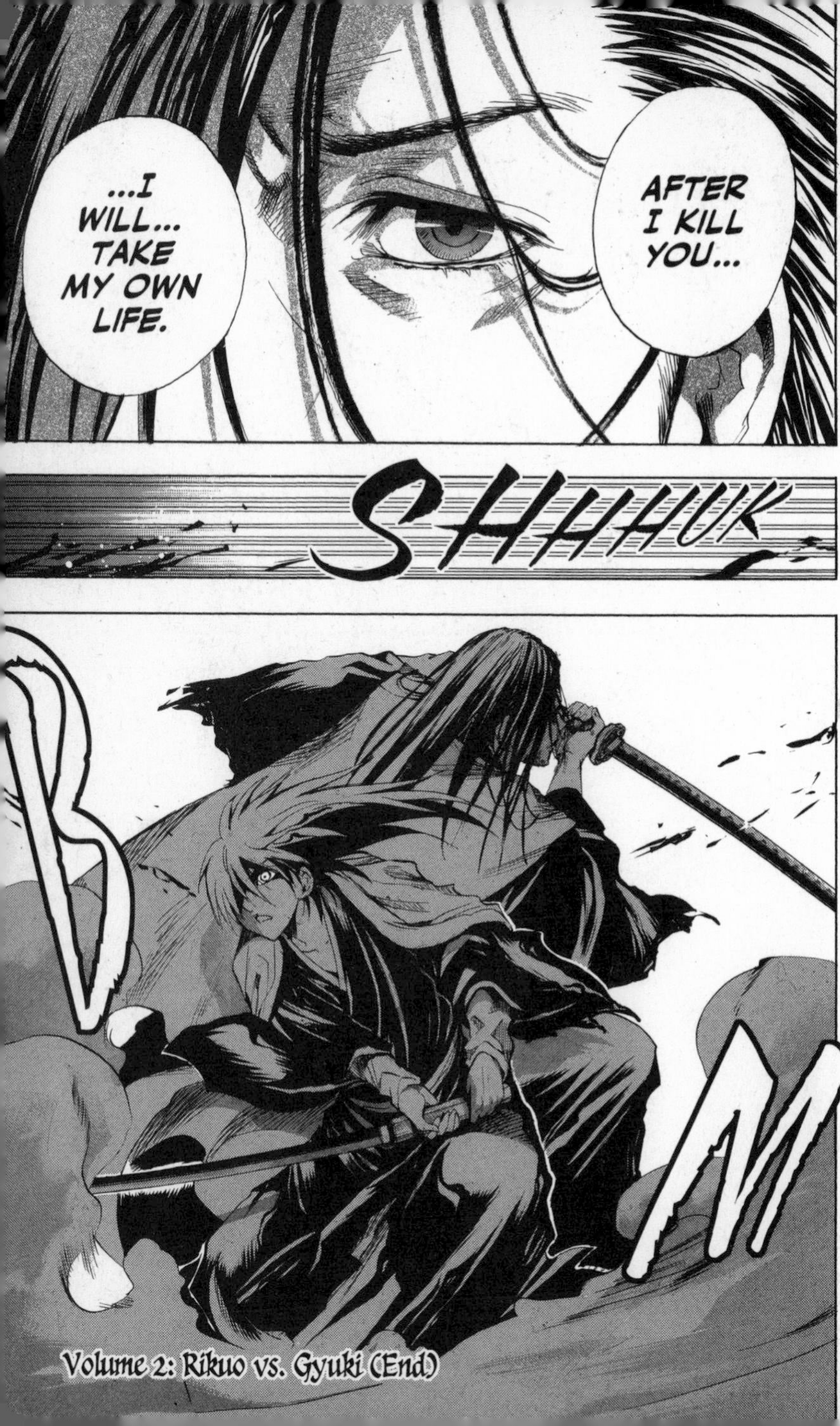
AFTER I KILL YOU...
...I WILL... TAKE MY OWN LIFE.
SHHHUK
B
M
Volume 2: Rikuo vs. Gyuki (End)

A Summer Day with the Gyuki Clan

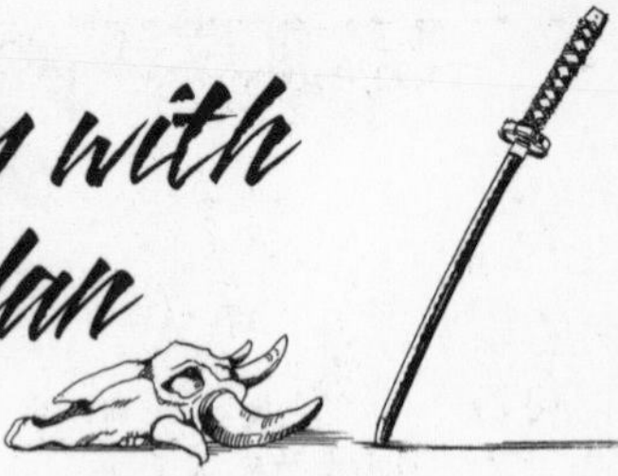

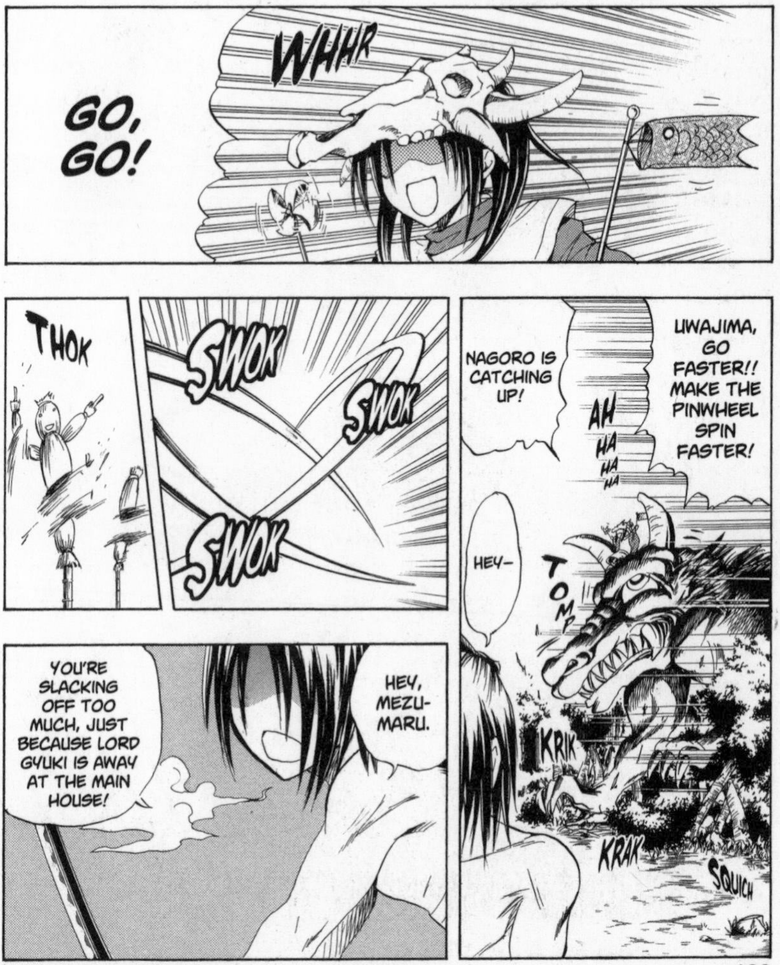
WHHR
GO, GO!
UWAJIMA, GO FASTER!! MAKE THE PINWHEEL SPIN FASTER!
NAGORO IS CATCHING UP!
AH HA HA HA
HEY–
TOMP
KRIK
KRAK
SQUICH
SWOK
SWOK
SWOK
THOK
HEY, MEZU-MARU.
YOU'RE SLACKING OFF TOO MUCH, JUST BECAUSE LORD GYUKI IS AWAY AT THE MAIN HOUSE!

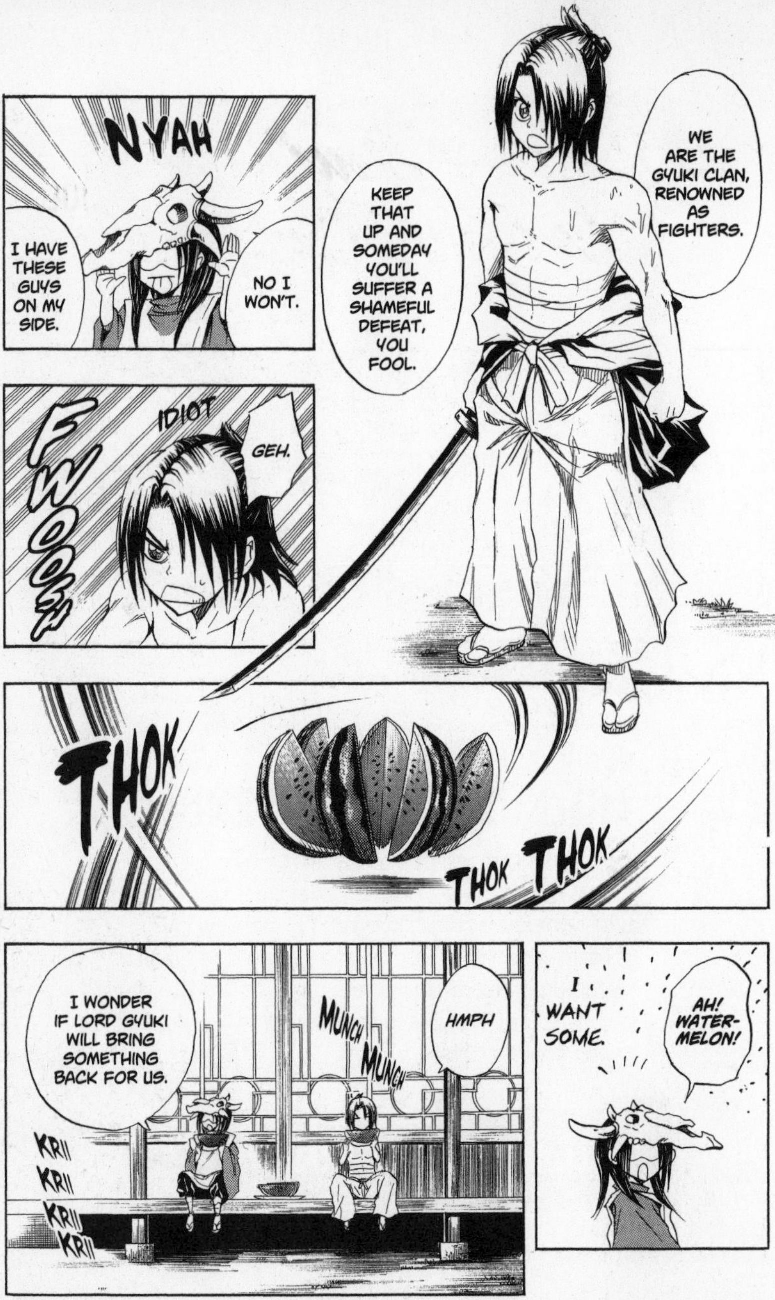
WE ARE THE GYUKI CLAN, RENOWNED AS FIGHTERS.
KEEP THAT UP AND SOMEDAY YOU'LL SUFFER A SHAMEFUL DEFEAT, YOU FOOL.
NYAH
NO I WON'T.
I HAVE THESE GUYS ON MY SIDE.
GEH.
IDIOT
FWOOOSH
THOK
THOK THOK
AH! WATER-MELON!
I WANT SOME.
HMPH
MUNCH MUNCH
I WONDER IF LORD GYUKI WILL BRING SOMETHING BACK FOR US.
KRII KRII KRII KRII

The End

IN THE NEXT VOLUME...
THE NURA CLAN ASSEMBLY

Rikuo's confrontation with Gyuki reveals a schism within the Nura clan. Nurarihyon convenes an assembly to formally name Rikuo as the next leader. But Rikuo's willingness to pardon Gyuki for his crimes causes friction within the group. Some officers doubt that this thirteen-year-old can restore the weakening Nura clan to its former glory. Meanwhile, surprise attacks from increasingly powerful rival yokai continue.

AVAILABLE JUNE 2011!